PUBLICATIONS OF

THE COLONIAL SOCIETY OF MASSACHUSETTS

VOLUME LXXVII

PORTRAIT OF A PATRIOT

THE MAJOR POLITICAL AND LEGAL PAPERS OF JOSIAH QUINCY JUNIOR

PORTRAIT OF A PATRIOT

The Major Political and Legal Papers of Josiah Quincy Junior

EDITORS

DANIEL R. COQUILLETTE

J. Donald Monan, S.J. University Professor, Boston College
Charles Warren Visiting Professor of American
Legal History, Harvard Law School

NEIL LONGLEY YORK

Karl G. Maeser Professor of General Education
Chair, History Department, Brigham Young University

VOLUME FOUR

The Law Reports, Part One (1761–1765)

BOSTON · 2009
The Colonial Society of Massachusetts
Distributed by the University of Virginia Press

ACKNOWLEDGMENTS FOR THE QUINCY PAPERS

This series of volumes represents the tireless and invaluable work of our research and administrative assistants: Brandon Bigelow, Kevin Cox, James Dimas, Jane Downing, Natalia Fekula, Eric Fox, Michael Hayden, Elizabeth Kamali, Michael Morales, Ryan Morrison, Thomas J. Murphy, Christina Nolan, Nicole Scimone, Brian Sheppard, Susannah Tobin, Elisa Underwood, and Mark A. Walsh, with special recognition to the Editorial Assistants to the Boston College Monan Chair, Brendan Farmer, Charles Riordan, and Patricia Tarabelsi, and to Inge Burgess and Thompson Potter at Harvard. Their intelligence and enthusiasm are visible on every page. Of course, we are deeply in debt to John W. Tyler, Editor of Publications of the Colonial Society of Massachusetts, as well as to the Committee of Publications, without whose guidance and support this project would have been impossible. Finally, special thanks are also due to the guardians of the Quincy heritage: the Massachusetts Historical Society with its enormously helpful Librarian, Peter Drummey, and his staff, the Museum of Fine Arts, Boston, and the Quincy family itself.

FRONTISPIECE:

The Royal Coat of Arms facing the Hallway in the Council Chamber of the Old State House, Boston (1748), the building where many of the cases reported by Josiah Quincy Jr. were argued, including Paxton's Case of the Writ of Assistance, *Reports*, 51–57 (Case 22, 1761). The Arms are a carefully researched replica of the original, removed during the evacuation of Boston, March 17, 1776. The photograph is by Steven Vedder, 2008, and is courtesy of the Bostonian Society. See caption to *Illustration 1, infra*.

ISBN 978-0-9794662-4-3

Printed from the income of the Sarah Louise Edes Fund

JOSIAH QUINCY JR.
Political and Legal Works

VOLUME FOUR

THE FIRST LAW REPORTS OF THE SUPERIOR COURT OF JUDICATURE OF THE PROVINCE OF MASSACHUSETTS BAY 1761–1765, VOLUME ONE

CO-EDITORS:
Daniel R. Coquillette
Neil Longley York

VOLUME EDITOR:
Daniel R. Coquillette

"To relieve the Oppressed, to guard the Innocent, to preserve the Order of Society and the Dignity of Government is a noble Principle of the Mind."

CHIEF JUSTICE THOMAS HUTCHINSON (1711–1780)
Superior Court of Judicature
Charge to the Grand Jury, March Term, 1765, *Reports*, 110

"Trover for a Negro. The Administratrix of one Cockran (Father-In-Law to the Defendant,) deceased, was offered as an Evidence to prove the Sale from Allison to the Father." Quincy "Qu[rie]: if this Action is well brought, for Trover lies not for a Negro."

Allison v. *Cockran*, August Term, 1764
Reports, 94–95

To My Father

CONTENTS

VOLUME 4

ILLUSTRATION 1: Purported to be Jeremiah Gridley (1701/1702–1767), one of the greatest of all colonial advocates and Attorney General, Justice of the Peace and of the Quorum, possibly by John Smibert (1688–1751). Dated 1731. See Henry Wilder Foote, *John Smibert, Painter, with a Descriptive Catalogue of Portraits* (Cambridge, 1950), pp. 240–241. The portrait is signed and dated by "John Smibert," and some experts believe that it is an authentic Smibert, while others believe the signature to be a forgery. There is also a view that the sitter is too old to be Gridley in 1731 (twenty-six), but I disagree and believe the portrait genuine. Compare portrait of Chief Justice Benjamin Lynde (1711–1780) of about 1738. *Illustration 22*, p. 263, *infra*. The painting is currently in the editor's office. Many thanks to Charles Riordan. Courtesy, Harvard Law School Art Collection.

ACKNOWLEDGMENTS

VOLUMES FOUR AND FIVE

In my editor's foreword I pay tribute to Samuel Miller Quincy, Josiah's great-grandson, who painstakingly prepared the first transcript in 1864. To prepare the next and only modern edition, nearly a century and a half later, I have been loyally and ably assisted by a team of outstanding research assistants, at both Boston College Law School and Harvard Law School. For these two volumes of Quincy's *Reports* I am particularly indebted to Brandon Bigelow, Kevin Cox, James Dimas, Elizabeth Kamali, Michael Morales, Thomas J. Murphy, Christina Nolan, Nicole Scimone, Brian Sheppard, Susannah Tobin, Elisa Underwood, and Mark Walsh. Every page has benefitted from their hard work and intelligence. I should particularly thank Mark Walsh, who was there at the very beginning of this project and was essential in creating the valuable appendices at the end of Volume Five; Brandon Bigelow and Brian Sheppard, who worked so hard to check the judicial records; and Kevin Cox, who tirelessly polished and double-checked the annotations, and contributed so much to the final result. Then there are the reference librarians, particularly Karen Beck and Mark Sullivan at the Boston College Law Library and David Warrington at the Harvard Law Libraries. Without them I would have been lost.

Page by page, illustration by illustration, the Editorial Assistants to the Monan Chair, Patricia Tarabelsi and Charles Riordan, shaped these volumes. The magnificent design work of Paul Hoffmann is also self-evident in the volumes you hold in your hand. Then there are those two great institutions, the Massachusetts Historical Society and the Colonial Society of Massachusetts. The first has safeguarded the Quincy manuscripts and generously allowed this publication. Particular thanks are due to the Massachusetts Historical Society's talented Librarian, Peter Drummey, and his expert staff. Of course, the Colonial Society of Massachusetts has generously underwritten the Quincy Project from the beginning. And the most important contributions have not been just financial, but have involved the exceptional expertise of the Committee on Publications and the wonderful Editor of Publications, John W. Tyler, who has reviewed every word and to whom we all owe a great debt. Finally, I must thank my academic colleagues, most especially Mary S. Bilder and Charles Donahue Jr., for their advice and support, my co-editor Neil York, a true gentleman and scholar, and my wife and family, who have made all this possible.

DANIEL R. COQUILLETTE
Volume Editor
Volumes Four and Five

JOSIAH QUINCY JR.'S
The Reports
(Part One, 1761–1765)

Volume Editor
DANIEL R. COQUILLETTE
J. Donald Monan, S.J. University Professor,
Boston College Law School
Charles Warren Visiting Professor
of American Legal History,
Harvard Law School

With special thanks to Brandon Bigelow, Kevin Cox, James Dimas, Elizabeth Kamali, Michael Morales, Thomas J. Murphy, Christina Nolan, Nicole Scimone, Brian Sheppard, Susannah Tobin, Elisa Underwood, and Mark Walsh, exceptional research assistants and colleagues, and Charles Riordan and Patricia Tarabelsi, the invaluable Editorial Assistants to the Monan Chair.

ILLUSTRATION 2: Council Chamber of the Old State House, Boston (1748), with the Royal Coat of Arms, see Frontispiece. From a photograph of George M. Cushing, taken in 1966. (The Arms were removed during the evacuation of Boston of March 17, 1776, and later replaced by a carefully researched replica.) Courtesy of the Bostonian Society. Many of the cases reported by Quincy were argued in this building particularly before 1769. One of the most famous, *Paxton's Case of the Writ of Assistance*, *Reports*, *infra*, pp. 51–57 (Case 22, 1761), was certainly argued here, with Quincy regrettably absent during most of James Otis's famous argument. John Adams described the scene in a letter to William Tudor of March 29, 1817, as follows:

> In this chamber, round a great fire, were seated five Judges, with Lieutenant-Governor Hutchinson at their head, as Chief Justice, all arrayed in their new, fresh, rich robes of scarlet English broadcloth; in their large cambric bands, and immense judicial wigs. In this chamber were seated at a long table all the barristers at law of Boston, and of the neighboring county of Middlesex, in gowns, bands, and tie wigs. They were not seated on ivory chairs, but their dress was more solemn and more pompous than that of the Roman Senate, when the Gauls broke in upon them.
>
> In a corner of the room must be placed as a spectator and an auditor, wit, sense, imagination, genius, pathos, reason, prudence, eloquence, learning, and immense reading, hanging by the shoulders on two crutches, covered with a great cloth coat, in the person of Mr. Pratt, who had been solicited on both sides, but would engage

> on neither, being, as Chief Justice of New York, about to leave Boston forever. Two portraits, at more than full length, of King Charles the Second and of King James the Second, in splendid golden frames, were hung up on the most conspicuous sides of the apartment.
>
> *The Works of John Adams, Second President of the United States* . . . (ed. Charles Francis Adams, Boston, 1850–1856), vol. 2, p. 124. See also Charles Warren, *History of the Harvard Law School* . . . (New York, 1908), vol. 1, p. 58.

There were even more extraordinary connections between this room and *Quincy's Reports*. Josiah Quincy's great-grandson, Samuel Miller Quincy (1833–1887), who edited the first edition of the *Reports*, was instrumental in saving the Old State House and founding the Bostonian Society. In an impassioned plea, in 1881, he wrote:

> Against these walls rattled the bullets of the Boston Massacre, and within the same walls the defense of the same men who fired these bullets was bravely undertaken by two of the foremost patriots and sons of liberty, John Adams and Josiah Quincy, Jr. And in this building, according to the former, the child Independence was born.
>
> *Proceedings of the Bostonian Society*, May 24, 1887, p. 21.

When Samuel Quincy died, on May 23, 1887, he was eulogized the very next day in this very room. See *id.*, pp. 3–27. With special thanks to Mark Sullivan. The room today has a different appearance, being used by the Bostonian Society to exhibit historical artifacts.

ILLUSTRATION 3: Samuel Miller Quincy (1833–1887), great-grandson of Josiah Quincy Jr. and editor of the 1865 edition of the *Reports*. Crayon portrait by Otto Grundmann, circa 1887. See *Proceedings of the Bostonian Society*, May 24, 1887 (Boston), p. 4. The resemblance to his great-grandfather and grandfather is striking. See the Gilbert Stuart portrait (1825) Josiah Quincy Junior, and Gilbert Stuart portrait (1824) of his son Josiah Quincy (1772–1864) in *Quincy Papers*, vol. 1, frontispiece and p. xxxiv, respectively.

EDITOR'S FOREWORD

Quincy's Reports

Daniel R. Coquillette

THESE ARE THE FIRST REPORTS of the Superior Court of Judicature of the Province of Massachusetts Bay, direct ancestor of the great Massachusetts Supreme Judicial Court. The preservation and transcription of these historic *Reports* is a story that is truly stranger than fiction. The terrible Civil War, so accurately feared by Josiah Quincy "the patriot" in his *Southern Journal* of 1773, found his great-grandson, Samuel Miller Quincy, in command of the Seventy-third United States Colored Troops north of New Orleans on the Mississippi at Port Hudson.[1] Samuel Quincy, then a Lieutenant Colonel, had been severely wounded twice at Cedar Ridge in 1862 and then taken prisoner, spending three months at the infamous Libby Prison in Richmond. On release, he was a broken man.[2]

Most others would have accepted a distinguished respite, but Samuel Quincy returned in March 1863 to lead the Second Massachusetts as Colonel at the terrible battle of Chancellorsville. Like his great-grandfather, he was sickly, "his constitution, never robust" (perhaps with the same hereditary proclivity to tuberculosis), and Chancellorsville was too much . . . he resigned in June 1863, "discharged for disability from wounds."[3]

1. See *Massachusetts Soldiers, Sailors, and Marines in the Civil War* (Norwood, 1931), vol. 1, pp. 69–70, 105, vol. 2, pp. 289, 308.

2. See "General S. M. Quincy, Death of a Gallant Soldier and Fine Scholar," *Boston Daily Globe* (1872–1922); March 25, 1887, p. 2; "The Last Roll-Call – Funeral Services Over the Remains of General Samuel M. Quincy," *Boston Daily Globe* (1872–1922); March 28, 1887, p. 4; Samuel Arthur Bent, "Eulogy on Samuel Miller Quincy," *Proceedings of the Bostonian Society*, May 24, 1887 (Boston), p. 3. (Hereafter, "*Proceedings*.") My gratitude for these notes to Mark Sullivan, Research Librarian beyond compare!

3. *Boston Daily Globe*, *supra*, March 25, 1887, p. 2. See also *Proceedings*, *supra*, p. 25, which refers to Samuel Quincy's "battle" against a "disease gnawing for years."

But like his great-grandfather, Samuel Quincy was also irrepressible. In November 1863, he joined up again, this time as Lieutenant Colonel of the Seventy-third United States Colored Troops, the former 1st Louisiana Native Guards, rising to be Colonel of that famous black regiment and to be Military Governor of New Orleans.[4] He later would command the Ninety-sixth United States Colored Infantry, as well. How his great-grandfather, whose hatred of racism and slavery filled the *Southern Journal*, would have been proud!

And what was Samuel Quincy doing in 1864, in the middle of this terrible Civil War, in command of his black troops, blockading the Mississippi north of New Orleans? He was transcribing his great-grandfather's manuscript *Law Reports*! These had been in the possession of Samuel's grandfather Josiah, our Josiah's son, the Mayor of Boston and President of Harvard. As Samuel noted in his brief Preface, dated February 9, 1864, reproduced *supra*, his grandfather was alive, and "in his ninety-third year."[5] Samuel now had the original documents, nearly a century old.[6]

We will never know what caused Samuel Quincy, on the military field in the midst of this national calamity, to transcribe his great-grandfather's manuscripts. But we are forever in his debt. He had originally hoped to do even

4. It is significant that Samuel Quincy, like his fellow officer for the Second Massachusetts, Col. William Gould Shaw, sought the command of black troops. *Id.*, p. 2. *Massachusetts Soldiers, Sailors, and Marines in the Civil War*, *supra*, vol. 2, pp. 289, 308. Samuel Quincy finally mustered out on November 30, 1866, with the rank Brevet Brigadier General, "for gallant and meritorious service." *Boston Daily Globe*, *supra*, March 25, 1887, p. 2. Again, much thanks to Mark Sullivan. There was one supreme irony, noted by Samuel Arthur Bent in his eloquent eulogy of Samuel Quincy. In Bent's words, "It is a strange illustration of *tempora mutantur*, that the man who was destined to command two regiments of United States colored troops in war to support the Constitution and the laws carried the flag as color-sergeant of the Cadets [Boston Corps of Cadets] during the three days that they were ordered out at the time of the capture and rendition of Anthony Burns in 1854." *Proceedings*, *supra*, pp. 9–10. Bent noted it was "doubtless a disagreeable duty," but that there "was a virtue in obedience to the Constitution and the laws" illustrated by the Civil War itself! *Id.*, p. 10.

5. See Samuel M. Quincy's "Preface," *Quincy's Reports*, *supra*, p. iii. His grandfather died shortly thereafter, on July 1, 1864, and did not see the publication of the *Reports* in 1865.

6. He may also have had important help, strangely unacknowledged, from the great Horace Gray (1828–1902), then Reporter to the Supreme Judicial Court and later to become Justice of the Supreme Judicial Court (1864–1873), then Chief Justice (1873–1882), and then a Justice of the Supreme Court of the United States (1882–1902). Gray also had access to the documents, and his role in the publication remains an intriguing mystery. See Mark A. Sullivan's masterful "Phantom References to *Quincy's Reports* in the Massachusetts Supreme Judicial Court *Reports*," set out in *Quincy Papers*, vol. 5, *Appendix 5*, *infra*.

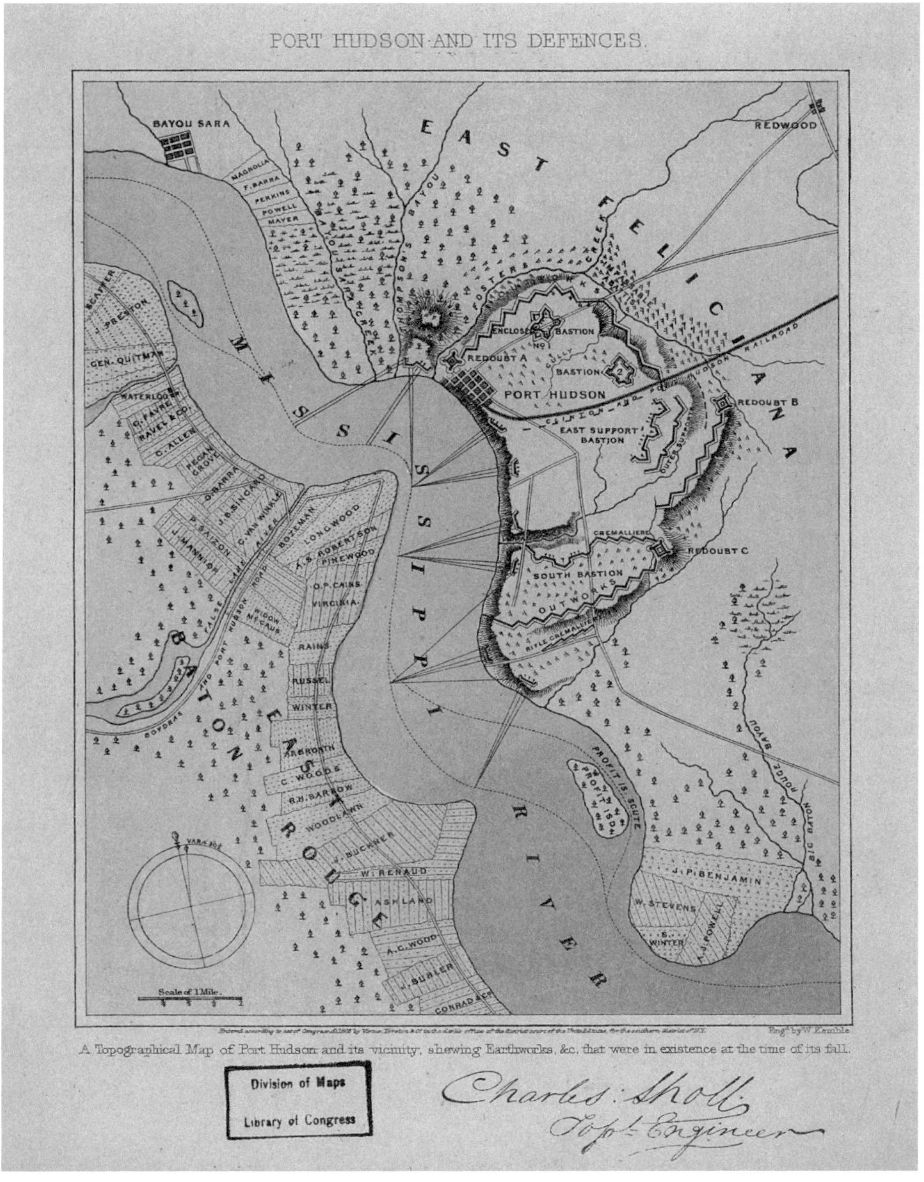

ILLUSTRATION 4: Military map of Port Hudson and Its Defences as of 1864 (Prepared by order of Major General N. P. Banks under the direction of Major D. C. Houston). Samuel M. Quincy was stationed here as Lieutenant Colonel of the Seventy-third U.S. Colored Infantry on February 9, 1864, when he wrote the "Preface" to *Quincy's Reports*, *supra*.

more. As he said, "It had been my intention to give an outline of the history of the Province during the period which it embraces, as well as some biographical sketches of the most distinguished of those whose names are mentioned, but that the breaking out of the war in which this country is still involved has suddenly called me from the profession to more engrossing duties...." *Reports*, p. iv. Under the conditions, even with the help of Horace Gray, it remains astonishing that the work was completed by February 9, 1864, and published in a single edition by Little, Brown and Company in Boston in 1865.

Samuel Quincy's transcription has been tested thoroughly against the manuscript, and has proven so accurate that, with occasional lapses marked in the notes, we have reproduced his exact pages here, with new annotations —including the biographical sketches he wished to have done. This also provides what jurists call "star pages," a text that retains the pagination of the first edition, so that citations to the *Reports* as authority will always be uniform. Few copies of the 1865 edition survive, and those few are cruelly disintegrating through the wartime use of pulp paper. But the debt this new scholarly edition owes to Samuel Quincy is great indeed.

Across these pages are spread the drama, the pathos, the greed, the cruelty, the bravery and nobility of colonial Americans, great and humble, men and women, of many races and backgrounds. As my esteemed friend and colleague, the Hon. Hiller B. Zobel, put it so well, these types of legal records are "the Pompeii of Paper." As he said, so eloquently, "No ice storms encapsulated any 18th century town; no embalming ash has brought the Revolutionary days to us intact. But we do possess pieces of that past life, preserved without change, and lying, like the wall paintings of Pompeii, beneath a layer of dust, awaiting excavation. We call them court records."[7]

Quincy was very aware that he lived in a momentous crux of American history. "Learn Wisdom from the present Times!"[8] he exhorted in his *Reports*, and, indeed, that was clearly one reason he embarked on such a novel project.

There is so much for us to learn. Let me choose just one example. On March 22, 1770, Quincy received an agonized letter from his father, the "Colonel." He had just heard that Quincy had agreed, with his cousin by marriage John

7. Hon. Hiller B. Zobel, "The Pompeii of Paper," *Boston Bar Journal* (September 1978), p. 20.

8. *Reports* (*Quincy Papers*, vol. 5), *infra*, p. 173. (Note, August 27, 1765.) This was in the context of the Stamp Act riots of August 20, 1765.

Adams, to represent the British soldiers who had fired into an unarmed Boston mob on March 5, 1770, the "Boston Massacre."[9]

> My Dear Son,
>
> I am under great affliction at hearing the bitterest reproaches uttered against you, for having become an advocate for those criminals who are charged with the murder of their fellow-citizens. Good God! Is it possible? I will not believe it.
>
> Just before I returned home from Boston, I knew, indeed, that on the day those criminals were committed to prison, a sergeant had inquired for you at your brother's house; but I had no apprehension that it was possible an application would be made to you to undertake their defence. Since then I have been told that you have actually engaged for Captain Preston; and I have heard the severest reflections made upon the occasion, by men who had just before manifested the highest esteem for you, as one destined to be a saviour of your country.
>
> I must own to you, it has filled the bosom of your aged and infirm parent with anxiety and distress, lest it should not only prove true, but destructive of your reputation and interest; and I repeat, I will not believe it, unless it be confirmed by your own mouth, or under your own hand.
>
> Your anxious and distressed parent,
> Josiah Quincy[10]

It must be remembered that the occupying Nineteenth Regiment was regarded with fear and loathing by the patriot cause.[11] Yet Quincy replied, on March 26, 1770,

> Honoured Sir,
>
> I have little leisure, and less inclination, either to know or to take notice of those ignorant slanderers who have dared to utter their "bitter reproaches" in your hearing against me, for having become an advocate for criminals charged with murder."
>
> Let such be told, Sir, that these criminals, charged with murder, are *not yet legally proved guilty*, and therefore, however criminal, are entitled, by the laws of

9. See the excellent accounts of Hiller B. Zobel, *The Boston Massacre* (New York, 1970) and Neil L. York, "A Life Cut Short," *Quincy Papers*, vol. 1, pp. 22–27.

10. Josiah Quincy, *Memoir of the Life of Josiah Quincy, Junior, of Massachusetts 1744–1775* (2d ed., Boston, 1874), pp. 26–27. (Hereafter, "*Memoir.*")

11. Quincy himself, at the outset of representing Captain Preston, made to his client "the most explicit declaration of my real opinion on the contests (as I expressed it to him) of the times, and that my heart and hand were indissolubly attached to the cause of my country." *Memoir*, *supra*, p. 28.

> God and man, to all legal counsel and aid; that my duty as a man obliged me to undertake; that my duty as a lawyer strengthened the obligation;
>
> I never harboured the expectation, nor any great desire, that all men should speak well of me. To inquire my duty, and to do it, is my aim.[12]

It took both a brilliant and courageous mind to understand that the patriot cause would be best advanced by an adherence to the rule of law, applied equally to friends and enemies.[13] "Learn Wisdom from the present Times!"[14] exhorted Quincy, as he wrote these, the first *Reports* of the now Supreme Judicial Court of Massachusetts. So, in our own "present times" we can draw again on the inspiration of Josiah Quincy Junior and the legal heritage he so powerfully records in the following pages. For here, in the words of Martin Luther King Junior, are "those great wells of democracy which were dug deep by the founding fathers. . . ."[15] Here, in these *Reports*, is something worth more than arms and money. Fortunate we are in this great inheritance. "Learn Wisdom!"

12. *Id.*, p. 27.

13. As my co-editor, Neil L. York, observed: "Instead of concluding, as the most detailed study of the massacre trials did, that 'the radicals failed to consider the possibility of an acquittal,' we should see that acquittal served their purposes even better than conviction . . . and they probably knew it." Neil L. York, "A Life Cut Short," *Quincy Papers*, vol. 1, p. 26. In all events, "[i]n his own mind, Josiah had taken the high road: he had put principle above politics." *Id.*, p. 27.

14. *Reports* (*Quincy Papers*, vol. 5), *infra*, p. 173. (Note, August 27, 1765.) See Daniel R. Coquillette, "Patriots in Defense of the 'Enemy,'" Op-Ed, *Boston Globe*, January 18, 2007.

15. Martin Luther King, Jr., "Letter from Birmingham Jail," *Christian Century* (June 12, 1963).

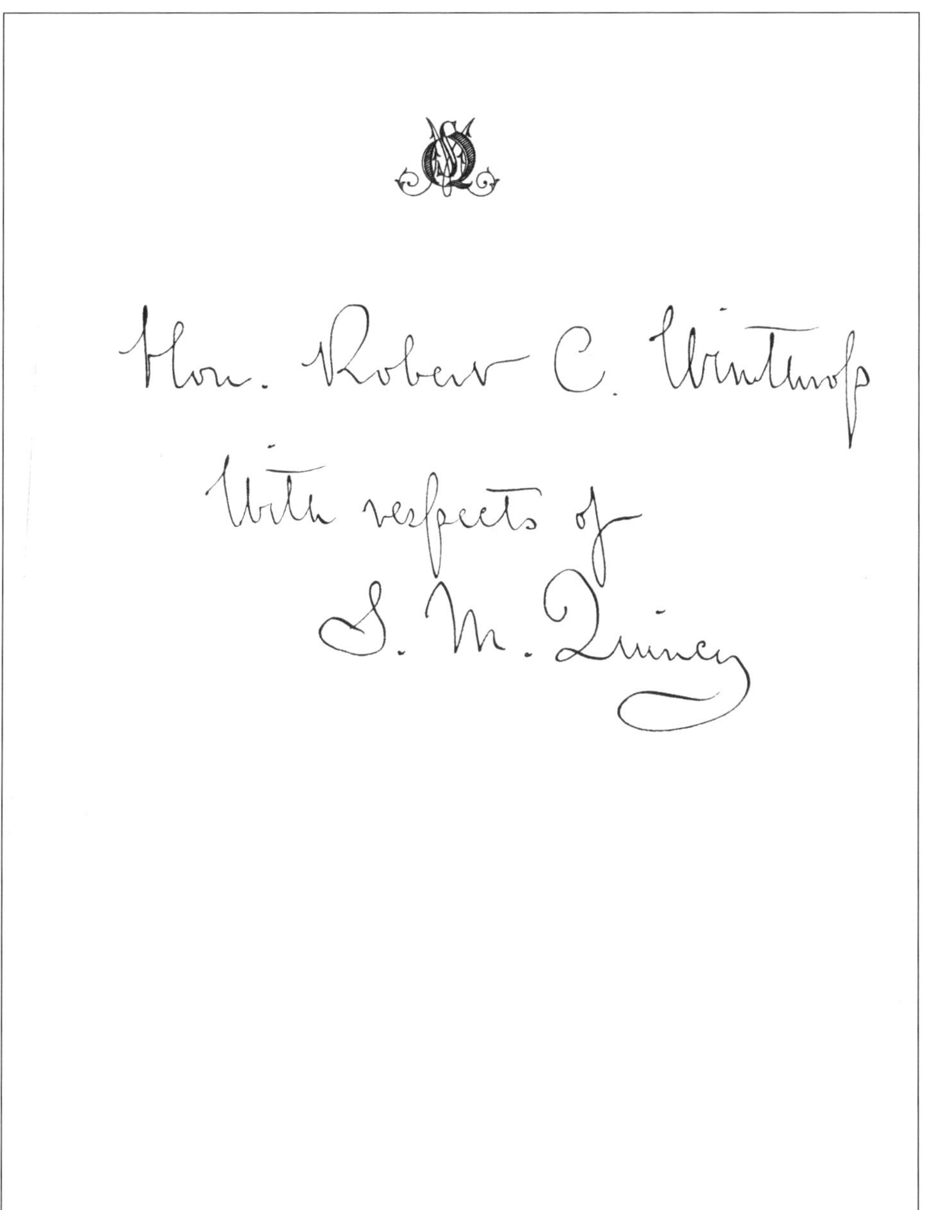

ILLUSTRATION 5: The copy of the 1865 edition of the *Reports*, reproduced photographically for this new edition, was a presentation copy by its transcriber, Josiah Quincy Junior's great-grandson, Samuel M. Quincy, to the Hon. Robert Charles Winthrop (1809–1894), Speaker of the House of Representatives in the Thirtieth Congress (1847–1849) and Senator for Massachusetts on the resignation of Daniel

Webster (1782–1852). See *Dictionary of American Biography* (ed. D. Malone, New York, 1936), vol. 20, pp. 416–417. Winthrop was defeated for the Senate in 1851 by Charles Sumner, and turned to history and scholarship. For thirty years he was President of the Massachusetts Historical Society, where he was a member from 1839 to 1894, an incredible fifty-five years. Winthrop's politics, which included opposing Lincoln's re-election in 1864 and supporting McClellan, may have differed from Samuel Quincy, who in 1865 was Colonel of a black regiment north of New Orleans. See *Editor's Foreword*, *supra*. But it is certain that they shared a profound interest in the history of their nation. Given the exceptional support of the Massachusetts Historical Society and the Colonial Society of this publication, it is most fitting to use this presentation copy for this new scholarly edition.

PREFACE

Samuel M. Quincy

Port Hudson, Louisiana, February 9, 1864

The Preface to the original printing of *Quincy's Reports*, Boston, 1865, by the Riverside Press of O. H. Houghton and Company for Little, Brown and Company. The Preface was written during the Civil War "in which the country is still involved." See *Editor's Foreword*, *infra*.

ILLUSTRATION 6: Horace Gray Jr. (1828–1902), Justice, Supreme Judicial Court of Massachusetts (1864–1873), Chief Justice of Massachusetts (1873–1881), Justice, Supreme Court of the United States (1882–1902). Horace Gray was instrumental in preparing *Quincy's Reports*. See Mark G. Sullivan, "Phantom References to *Quincy's Reports* in the Massachusetts Supreme Judicial Court *Reports*," *Quincy Papers*, vol. 5, *Appendix 5*, *infra*. Photograph c. 1884. Courtesy, Collection of the Supreme Court of the United States.

REPORTS OF CASES

ARGUED AND ADJUDGED IN THE

SUPERIOR COURT OF JUDICATURE

OF THE

PROVINCE OF MASSACHUSETTS BAY,

BETWEEN 1761 AND 1772.

By JOSIAH QUINCY, Junior.

PRINTED FROM HIS ORIGINAL MANUSCRIPTS IN THE POSSESSION OF HIS SON, JOSIAH QUINCY, AND EDITED BY HIS GREAT-GRANDSON, SAMUEL M. QUINCY.

WITH AN APPENDIX

UPON THE WRITS OF ASSISTANCE.

" Many records have in long procefs of time been loft, and poffibly the things themfelves forgotten at this day; which yet, in or near the times wherein they were made, might caufe many of thofe authoritative alterations in fome things touching the proceedings and decifions in law; the original caufe of which change being otherwife at this day hid and unknown to us." — Hale's History of the Common Law.

BOSTON:
LITTLE, BROWN, AND COMPANY.
1865.

RIVERSIDE, CAMBRIDGE:
PRINTED BY H. O. HOUGHTON AND COMPANY.

PREFACE.

THE name of JOSIAH QUINCY, JR., as a patriot, is well known to thoſe who are familiar with the provincial hiſtory of Maſſachuſetts. But of JOSIAH QUINCY, JR., as a lawyer, of his profeſſional labors and acquirements, and his poſition at the bar, nothing can now be known except by his immediate deſcendants. He was a juriſt as well as a patriot; and his love of his profeſſion for its own ſake was only ſurpaſſed by his devotion to the cauſe of his country.

The manuſcripts here publiſhed are in the poſſeſſion of Hon. JOSIAH QUINCY, the ſon of the reporter, now in his ninety-third year. It is needleſs to ſay that they are now offered to the profeſſion merely as matters of legal and hiſtorical curioſity and intereſt; the only other ante-revolutionary reports which have ever been publiſhed in this country being 1 Harris and McHenry, Jefferſon, and 1 Dallas, pp. 1 to 29.

Theſe manuſcripts conſiſt of three volumes; one with paper covers, (from the original color of which it is referred to as "Red Reports,") and two others bound in parchment, and numbered "3" and "4." The firſt two volumes of this ſet are miſſing, and were probably deſtroyed in a fire by which the reporter's law library was loſt. The Middleſex caſes reported between pp. 318 and 340 are contained in the fragment of another volume apparently juſt commenced, but not in the

handwriting

Preface.

handwriting of JOSIAH QUINCY, JR. Whether in theſe caſes he employed an amanuenſis, or whether the volume is the work of another reporter, cannot now be known, as the firſt pages were unfortunately deſtroyed by one ignorant of their value. All the others are in QUINCY'S own hand, the reports at the firſt term having been taken while he was yet an undergraduate in college. The firſt ſet of foot-notes, to which reference is made by aſteriſks, &c., are the original notes of the reporter; thoſe referred to by numerals are by the editor, as are alſo the marginals. The "Records" referred to in the margin are thoſe of the Superior Court of Judicature, and are to be found in the Clerk's Office of the preſent Supreme Judicial Court. The notes and Appendix to the celebrated caſe of the "Writs of Aſſiſtance," and the notes relating to Slavery in Maſſachuſetts and in England, are the work of HORACE GRAY, JR., ESQ., of the Boſton Bar.

This volume is printed *verbatim et literatim* from the manuſcript, and, as the reader will ſee, in ſome places partakes more of the nature of a private journal than of that of a volume of law reports. It had been my intention to give an outline of the hiſtory of the Province during the period which it embraces, as well as ſome biographical ſketches of the moſt diſtinguiſhed of thoſe whoſe names are mentioned, but that the breaking out of the war in which the country is ſtill involved has ſuddenly called me from the profeſſion to more engroſſing duties, which allow neither time nor opportunity for the completion of the taſk propoſed. For all other omiſſions of whatever the preface ſhould explain or ſupply, I muſt aſk the reader to accept the ſame excuſe.

SAMUEL M. QUINCY.

PORT HUDSON, LA., Feb. 9th, 1864.

ALPHABETICAL TABLE OF CASES

(From the 1865 Edition)

A

TABLE

OF THE

CASES Reported in this VOLUME.

---

vi

Table of Caſes.

Table of Cafes.

SEQUENTIAL AND ALPHABETICAL TABLE OF CASES

Pages in the new edition are collated to the original *Quincy Reports* 1865 pages.

NOTE: In the new edition, cases following *Draper* v. *Bicknell* (Case No. 45), *Quincy Reports*, p. 164 (1765) are in *Quincy Papers*, vol. 5. All earlier cases are in *Quincy Papers*, vol. 4. With many thanks to Charles Riordan and Patricia Tarabelsi, Editorial Assistants to the Monan Chair.

SEQUENTIAL TABLE OF CASES

[*Quincy's Reports*, Part One, 1761–1765]

Quincy Papers, vol. 4

CASE NO.	CASE NAME	QUINCY REPORTS (1865) PAGE NO.	VOLUME 4 PAGE NO.
1	Poor *v.* Dougherty (1762)	1	78
2	Baker *v.* Frobisher (1762)	4	86
3	Ingraham *v.* Cook et al. (1762)	4	90
4	Newman *v.* Homans (1762)	5	94
5	Zuill *v.* Bradley (1762)	6	98
6	Blower *v.* Campbell (1762)	8	102
7	Jones *v.* Belcher (1762)	9	104
8	Minot *v.* Prout (1762)	9	106
9	Dudley *v.* Dudley et al. (1762)	12	110
10	Jackson *v.* Foye (1762)	26	128
11	Wiswall *v.* Hall (1762)	27	132
12	Sayer et al. *v.* Thorp et al. (1762)	28	136
13	Oliver *v.* Sale (1762)	29	140
14	Hallowell *v.* Dalton (1762)	33	150
15	Gould *v.* Stevens (1762)	34	152
n/a	Memorandum of 1762, Members of the Bar	35	156
16	Wrentham Proprietors *v.* Metcalf (1763)	36	158
17	Derumple *v.* Clark (1763)	38	164
18	Daniels *v.* Bullard (1763)	41	172
19	Barnes *v.* Greenleaf (1763)	41	174
20	Elwell *v.* Pierson (1763)	42	178
21	Russell *v.* Oakes (1763)	49	188
22	Paxton's Case of Writ of Assistance (1761)	51	194
23	Ruddock *v.* Gordon (1763)	58	208
24	Gardiner *v.* Purrington (1763)	59	212

CASE NO.	CASE NAME	QUINCY REPORTS (1865) PAGE NO.	VOLUME 4 PAGE NO.
25	Rogers *v.* Kenwrick (1763)	62	218
26	Girdley *v.* Balston et al. (1763)	65	224
27	Brown *v.* Culnan (1763)	66	228
28	Dunten *v.* Richards (1763)	67	230
29	Baker *v.* Mattocks (1763)	69	234
30	Scollay *v.* Dunn (1763)	74	246
31	Angier *v.* Jackson (1763)	84	270
32	Poor *v.* Doble (1763)	86	276
33	Lovell *v.* Doble (1763)	88	280
34	Dom. Rex *v.* Doaks (1763)	90	286
35	Dom. Rex *v.* Gay (1763)	91	290
36	Allison *v.* Cockran (1764)	94	296
37	Hanlon *v.* Thayer (1764)	99	306
38	Dom. Rex *v.* Pourksdorff (1764)	104	314
39	Ballard *v.* McLean (1764)	106	320
40	Bromfield *v.* Little (1764)	108	324
n/a	Charge to the Grand Jury by the Chief Justice (March Term, 1765) ("Charge Number 1")	110	328
41	Whitney *v.* Whitney (1765)	117	340
42	Banister *v.* Henderson (1765)	119	344
43	Rochester Proprietors *v.* Hammond (1765)	159	400
44	Dom. Rex *v.* Mangent (1765)	162	406
45	Draper *v.* Bicknell (1765)	164	412

ALPHABETICAL TABLE OF CASES

[*Quincy's Reports*, 1761–1772]

Quincy Papers, vols. 4 and 5

VOL. NO.	CASE NO.	CASE NAME	QUINCY REPORTS (1865) PAGE NO.	VOLUMES 4 & 5 PAGE NO.
4	36	Allison *v.* Cockran (1764)	94	296
4	31	Angier *v.* Jackson (1763)	84	270
5	76	Anonymous (1770) [A hypothetical Quincy case similar to Fowle *v.* Richardson, 1770, in which Quincy was counsel. See annotations to Case 76.] [Note, Chronological Break—this is a Trowbridge Manuscript reproduced by Samuel Quincy]	370	780
5	53	Apthorp et al. *v.* Eyres (1766)	229	556
5	62	Apthorp *v.* Shepard (1768)	298	660
4	2	Baker *v.* Frobisher (1762)	4	86
4	29	Baker *v.* Mattocks (1763)	69	234
4	39	Ballard *v.* McLean (1764)	106	320
4	42	Banister *v.* Henderson (1765)	119	344
4	19	Barnes *v.* Greenleaf (1763)	41	174
5	78	Bishop *v.* Brig Freemason (1763) [Note: this is an incomplete fragment by Quincy, written when he was only nineteen. See annotations to Case 78.]	387	808
4	6	Blower *v.* Campbell (1762)	8	102
5	52	Box et al. *v.* Welch et al. (1766)	227	550
4	40	Bromfield *v.* Little (1764)	108	324
5	54	Bromfield *v.* Lovejoy (1767)	237	570
4	27	Brown *v.* Culnan (1763)	66	228
5	55	Carpenter *v.* Fairservice (1767)	239	574
5	60	Curtis *v.* Nightingale (1767)	256	606
4	18	Daniels *v.* Bullard (1763)	41	172

VOL. NO.	CASE NO.	CASE NAME	QUINCY REPORTS (1865) PAGE NO.	VOLUMES 4 & 5 PAGE NO.
4	17	Derumple *v.* Clark (1763)	38	164
5	74	Dewing *v.* Train (1772)	339	742
4	34	Dom. Rex *v.* Doaks (1763)	90	286
4	35	Dom. Rex *v.* Gay (1763)	91	290
4	44	Dom. Rex *v.* Mangent (1765)	162	406
4	38	Dom. Rex *v.* Pourksdorff (1764)	104	314
4	45	Draper *v.* Bicknell (1765)	164	412
4	9	Dudley *v.* Dudley et al. (1762)	12	110
5	30[B]	Dunn *v.* Scollay (1765)	187	478
		[See Scollay *v.* Dunn]		
4	28	Dunten *v.* Richards (1763)	67	230
4	20	Elwell *v.* Pierson (1763)	42	178
5	68	Flagg *v.* Hobart (1772)	332	720
5	71	Fowle *v.* Wyman (1772)	336	730
4	24	Gardiner *v.* Purrington (1763)	59	212
5	57	Gibbs *v.* Gibbs (1767)	251	592
4	15	Gould *v.* Stevens (1762)	34	152
4	26	Gridley *v.* Balston et al. (1763)	65	224
5	58	Hall *v.* Miller (1767)	252	596
5	66	Hall *v.* Richardson	329	712
4	14	Hallowell *v.* Dalton (1762)	33	150
4	37	Hanlon *v.* Thayer (1764)	99	306
5	75	Hooton *v.* Grout (1772)	343	750
4	3	Ingraham *v.* Cook et al. (1762)	4	90
4	10	Jackson *v.* Foye (1762)	26	128
4	7	Jones *v.* Belcher (1762)	9	104
5	73	Little *v.* Holdin (1772)	338	738
4	33	Lovell *v.* Doble (1763)	88	280
5	56	Malcolm *v.* Gleason (1767)	251	590
4	8	Minot *v.* Prout (1762)	9	106
4	4	Newman *v.* Homans (1762)	5	94
5	59	Noble *v.* Smith (1767)	254	600

VOL. NO.	CASE NO.	CASE NAME	QUINCY REPORTS (1865) PAGE NO.	VOLUMES 4 & 5 PAGE NO.
5	47	Norwood *v.* Fairservice (1765)	189	482
4	13	Oliver *v.* Sale (1762)	29	140
5	65	Parker *v.* Willard	326	706
5	46	Pateshall *v.* Apthorp & Wheelwright (1765)	179	466
4	22	Paxton's Case of the Writ of Assistance (1761)	51	194
5	48	Pond *v.* Medway (1765)	193	490
4	32	Poor *v.* Doble (1763)	86	276
4	1	Poor *v.* Dougharty (1762)	1	78
5	51	Pynchon, Executor *v.* Brewster (1766)	224	544
5	67	Reed's Case (1772)	331	716
4	43	Rochester Proprietors *v.* Hammond (1765)	159	400
4	25	Rogers *v.* Kenwrick (1763)	62	218
4	23	Ruddock *v.* Gordon (1763)	58	208
4	21	Russell *v.* Oakes (1763)	48	188
4	12	Sayer et al. *v.* Thorp et al. (1762)	28	136
4	30	Scollay *v.* Dunn (1763)	74	246
5	61	Silvester Richmond, Esq., Appellant *v.* Benja: & Edward Davis, Appellees	279	634
5	63	Symes & Wife, original Plaintiffs *v.* Hill, original Defendant	318	692
5	64	The King *v.* John Johnson Grant	326	704
5	77	The Petition of the Jurors in the Trial of Captain Preston and the British Soldiers (1771) [Note: this is based on a description published by Quincy in the *Boston Gazette*, May 20, 1771.]	382	798
5	72	Thwing *v.* Dennie (1772)	338	734
5	70	Tuttle *v.* Wilmington (1772)	335	728
5	50	Tyler *v.* Richards, Administrator (1765)	195	496

VOL. NO.	CASE NO.	CASE NAME	QUINCY REPORTS (1865) PAGE NO.	VOLUMES 4 & 5 PAGE NO.
5	49	Watts *v.* Hasey (1765)	194	492
5	69	Whitney *v.* Haven (1772)	334	726
4	41	Whitney *v.* Whitney (1765)	117	340
4	11	Wiswall *v.* Hall (1762)	27	132
4	16	Wrentham Proprietors *v.* Metcalf (1763)	36	158
4	5	Zuill *v.* Bradley (1762)	6	98
4	n/a	Memorandum of 1762, Members of the Bar	35	156
4	n/a	Charge to the Grand Jury by the Chief Justice (March Term, 1765) ("Charge Number 1")	110	328
5	n/a	Memorandum of August 27, 1765 (Destruction of Chief Justice's House)	168	446
5	n/a	Charge to the Grand Jury by the Chief Justice (August Term, 1765) ("Charge Number 2")	175	458
5	n/a	Memorandum of Bar Harmony (1765)	197	502
5	n/a	Memorial of the Town of Boston (1765)	198	506
5	n/a	Charge to the Grand Jury by Justice Lynde (March Term, 1766) ("Charge Number 3")	215	530
5	n/a	Charge to the Grand Jury by the Chief Justice (August Term, 1766) ("Charge Number 4")	218	534
5	n/a	Charge to the Grand Jury by the Chief Justice (March Term, 1767) ("Charge Number 5")	232	562
5	n/a	Charge to the Grand Jury by the Chief Justice (August Term, 1767) ("Charge Number 6")	241	578

VOL. NO.	CASE NO.	CASE NAME	QUINCY REPORTS (1865) PAGE NO.	VOLUMES 4 & 5 PAGE NO.
5	n/a	Charge to the Grand Jury by the Chief Justice (March Term, 1768) ("Charge Number 7")	258	610
5	n/a	Charge to the Grand Jury by the Chief Justice (August Term, 1768) ("Charge Number 8")	301	666
5	n/a	[Quincy notes that his absence from the court prevents his taking any minutes in the subsequent August Term, 1768]	305	673
5	n/a	Charge to the Grand Jury by the Chief Justice (1769) ("Charge Number 9")	306	674
5	n/a	Memoranda (August Term, 1769). Quincy observes there is not a "Quorum of the Court, without the Chief Justice, he, though now the Commander in Chief of this Province, sat and acted, at the Opening of this Court, which very speedily adjourned to November"	316	688
5	n/a	Memorandum (1771). Quincy notes resignations of Chief Justice Lynde and Justice John Cushing, and appointment of Peter Oliver as Chief Justice and Nathaniel Ropes and William Cushing as Justices, to take their seats in February Term, 1772.	330	714

5

REPORTS of Cases
solemnly adjudged in KINGS Bench
Court of Assize & Generall Goal Delivery.—
Before
The Hon.ble
Thomas Hutchinson Esq.r Ch. Justice
Benj.a Lynde
John Cushing
Chambers Russell
Peter Oliver
} Esq.rs Justices.

It is necessary to observe the Judgments & Resolutions of the SAGES of the LAW. Co: Lit: 363.b.
Judex Jus dicit, etiam cum inique dicit:—Durum, sane; sed ita Lex scripta est. Civil Law.
The reason of the judgment is the strength of the Authority. per Holt. 1 Ld Raym.d 630

ILLUSTRATION 7: Josiah Quincy Jr.'s *Law Reports*, Massachusetts Historical Society, P347, Reel 4, QP57, p. 5. Title page of second section of *Quincy's Reports*. See Cox chart, *Appendix II, Law Commonplace, Quincy Papers*, vol. 2, p. 429. The accompanying quotations read:

> It is necessary to observe the Judgments & Resolutions | Of the SAGES of the LAW. Co: Lit: 363.b. ["Coke on Littleton," Edward Coke, *First Part of the Institutes of the Lawes of England* (London, 1628), p. 363b.]
>
> *Judex Jus dicit, etiam cum inique dicit:—Durum, sane; sed ita Lex scripta est.* Civil Law. [See "Quincy's Latin Maxims," *Law Commonplace, Appendix I*, p. 323, *Quincy Papers*, vol. 2.]
>
> The reason of the judgment is the strength of the Authority. | per Holt. 1 Ld Raym.d 630 [*Lord Raymond's Reports* (London, 1743), vol. 1, p. 630.]

The Latin reads, "A judge speaks the law, even when he speaks unjustly, though strictly and precisely; but thus has the law been written." Many thanks to Elizabeth Papp Kamali, classicist beyond compare, and Charles Donahue Jr. All Quincy manuscripts courtesy of the Massachusetts Historical Society

INTRODUCTION

FIRST FLOWER—THE EARLIEST AMERICAN LAW REPORTS AND THE EXTRAORDINARY JOSIAH QUINCY JR. (1744–1775)*

Daniel R. Coquillette

I. THE INTENT

WE CAN ALL DEBATE for generations the conflicting priorities of legal history, but one fact remains: Whether you are a "structuralist," a "contextualist," a postmodern "textualist," or a "new historicist," you will always welcome improved access to original sources.[1] In no area is this more important than in the history of our colonial legal systems, where a few major archives, such as The Adams Papers, have dominated most secondary writing.[2]

* First published in an earlier version in 30 *Suffolk Law Review* (1996), 1. My thanks to the Donahue Lecture Series at Suffolk Law School and the fine student editors of the *Suffolk University Law Review* for assistance. As always, I also owe a great debt to my research assistants Brandon Bigelow, Kevin Cox, James Dimas, Thomas J. Murphy, Brian Sheppard, and Mark Walsh. Mark Walsh, in particular, was really a collaborator in the early stages of this project, and to him and to my esteemed co-editor, Neil York, I owe a special debt.

1. William W. Fisher III has brilliantly described the importance of at least the latter three schools of intellectual history to modern legal historians in his splendid "Texts and Contexts: The Application to Legal History of the Methodologies of Intellectual History," 49 Stan. L. R. 1065, 1065–1072 (1997). Fisher observes:

> While the Textualists typically concentrate on "great" or canonical texts (read noncanonically) and while the Contextualists typically seek to identify the common themes and assumptions in the writings of the members of a discursive community (and then interpret individual texts in light of those assumptions), the New Historicists typically focus on small events or anecdotes (often ones they have discovered serendipitously) that they believe are suggestive of the "behavioral codes, logics, and motive forces controlling a whole society. . . ."

Id., p. 1071 (quoting *The New Historicism* [H. Aram Veeser ed., 1989]). As will be seen, *Quincy's Reports* provides grist for all these mills.

2. See generally Daniel R. Coquillette, "Justinian in Braintree: John Adams, Civilian Learning, and Legal Elitism, 1758–1775," in *Law in Colonial Massachusetts 1630–1800*, at 359 (Daniel R. Coquillette ed., Robert J. Brink, Catherine S. Menand, ass't eds., 1984).

Thus, with invaluable assistance from my former research assistants, most particularly, Mark A. Walsh of the Massachusetts Bar, and my co-editor, Professor Neil L. York of Brigham Young University, I have set out to prepare a new edition of one of the most important original sources about colonial American law, *Quincy's Reports. Quincy's Reports* was prepared by Josiah Quincy Jr. (1744–1775), and covered cases in the Massachusetts Superior Court of Judicature between 1761 and 1772, albeit in very irregular chunks, and with some unrelated cases thrown in. It can be fairly described as the earliest of all American law reports.[3]

---

3. See Josiah Quincy Jr., *Reports of Cases Argued and Adjudged in the Superior Court of Judicature of the Province of Massachusetts Bay Between 1761 and 1772* (Boston: Little, Brown & Co., 1865) (hereafter, "*Quincy's Reports*"). *Quincy's Reports* were not published until 1865, when they appeared in an edition prepared by his great-grandson, Samuel M. Quincy. *Id.* Arguably, the earliest American law reports were either Ephraim Kirby's *Connecticut Reports* or Francis Hopkinson's *Judgments in Admiralty in Pennsylvania*, both published in 1789. Charles Warren argued for Kirby, and John W. Wallace for Hopkinson. See John William Wallace, *The Reporters* 571 n.2 (Boston: Soule and Bugbee, 1882) (touting Hopkinson as first author of American law reports); Charles Warren, *A History of the American Bar* 328 (1980) (describing Kirby as writer and publisher of first American law reports); see also Erwin C. Surrency, "Law Reports in the United States," 25 Am. J. Legal Hist. 48, 53 (1981) (discussing unresolved debate surrounding identity of first author). Compare Alan V. Briceland, "Ephraim Kirby: Pioneer of American Law Reporting, 1789," 16 Am. J. Legal Hist. 297, 297 (1972) (crediting Kirby with publishing first reports), with Wilfred J. Ritz, "The Francis Hopkinson Law Reports," 74 L. Libr. J. 298, 299 (1981) (asserting Hopkinson wrote "first true American law report").

An excellent new study of the Reports of the Supreme Court of the United States exists as well. See Morris L. Cohen & Sharon Hamby O'Connor, *A Guide to the Early Reports of the Supreme Court of the United States 1–22* (1995) (discussing importance of and rationale for reporting). One might argue that Alexander Dallas's *Reports of Cases Ruled and Adjudged in the Several Courts of the United States and of Pennsylvania* stands as the earliest report because, while it was published a year after both Kirby and Hopkinson's Reports in 1790, it contains cases as old as 1754. See *Anonymous, 1 U.S. (1* Dallas) 1 (1754) (limiting extension of statute of frauds and perjuries in province of Pennsylvania); Cohen & O'Connor, *supra*, at 11–22 (discussing Dallas and his contributions to reporting process); Francis R. Aumann, "American Law Reports: Yesterday and Today," 4 Ohio St. L.J. 331, 339–40 (1938) (advocating Dallas as earliest reporter). On the other hand, if the date of printed publication is not the test, why not consider cases recorded in lawyer's notebooks, like those of John Randolph, or Mr. Barradall and a Mr. Hopkins, which record decisions of the General Court of Virginia as early as 1730? See W. Hamilton Bryson, "Virginia Manuscript Law Reports," 82 L. Libr. J. 305, 305 (1990) (including Randolph, Barradall and Hopkins as authors of earliest law reports); Surrency, *supra*, at 50 (discussing early notebooks of Randolph, Barradell, and Hopkins). For that matter, there are two early case collections noted by Samuel Quincy in his "Preface": there is the 1809 publication of Harris & M. Henry's so-called *Maryland Reports*, which contain collected cases back to 1658, and the "thin octavo" volume published in 1829 by Jefferson's legatees, known as "Jefferson's Reports,"

This new edition, prepared under the auspices of the Colonial Society of Massachusetts, is more than just a re-edited text. It is being published as the concluding part of a five-volume series, *Portrait of a Patriot: The Major Political and Legal Papers of Josiah Quincy Junior*, Boston, 2005–2009. (Hereafter, "*Quincy Papers*"). Two other Quincy manuscripts, never before published, are included in this series. One is Quincy's personal legal notebook, which he called his *Law Commonplace*.[4] The other is a fascinating collection of political, literary and philosophical sayings, Quincy's *Political Commonplace Book*.[5] Finally, there is a new scholarly edition of Quincy's *Southern Journal* of

---

but actually containing "reports of cases from 1730 to 1740, from manuscript Notes left by Sir John Randolph, Edward Barradall, and Mr. Hopkins, and also cases from 1768 to 1772 reported by Jefferson himself." See Charles C. Soule, *The Lawyer's Reference Manual of Law Books and Citations* (Boston, 1883), pp. 28–29, 60–61. Why *Quincy's Reports* as the first?

My answer is simple. Josiah Quincy Jr. was the first American to deliberately and self-consciously prepare a set of law reports. These were not just case notes for a law notebook. As will be seen, Quincy kept a separate law notebook, his Law Commonplace. Josiah Quincy Jr., *Law Commonplace* (1763), microformed on Massachusetts Historical Society, vol. 56, reel 4 (Law Library Microfiche Consortium) (hereafter, "Quincy, *Law Commonplace*"). Quincy's *Law Commonplace* is now published in this series as *Quincy Papers*, vol. 2. See also Surrency, *supra*, at 50 (recalling how law students and legal practitioners named their law notebooks "common place" books). Quincy titled the Reports manuscript, in his own bold hand, "Reports of Cases Solemnly adjudged in King's Bench Court of Assize and General Goal Delivery," microformed on Massachusetts Historical Society, vol. 56, reel 4 (Law Library Microfiche Consortium). Further, the Massachusetts courts have accepted *Quincy's Reports* as true, authoritative law reports and have cited them regularly. See *Stamper* v. *Stanwood, 339 Mass. 549, 553, 159 N.E.2d 865, 868 (1959)* (citing Notes on *Banister* v. *Henderson*, in *Quincy's Reports*, at 119 (1765)); see also *Appendix V*, *Quincy Papers*, vol. 5, *infra*, which lists twenty-three cases of the Supreme Judicial Court citing to *Quincy's Reports* as authority, the most recent being *O'Loin's Inc.* v. *Treasurer of Worcester County*, 362 Mass. 507, 515 (1972). *Quincy's Reports* has also been cited by numerous other state and federal courts, including seven times by the Supreme Court of the United States, most recently in dissent by Justice O'Connor in *Illinois* v. *Krull*, 480 U.S. 340, 363 (1987). See *id.*, *Appendix V*, *supra*. Incidentally, it is certain that Massachusetts was the first state to appoint an official reporter, Ephraim Williams (1760–1835), appointed in 1804. See Morris L. Cohen, Paul C. Seeman, "A Man Without Qualities: Ephraim Williams, First Reporter of the Supreme Judicial Court," 9 Massachusetts Legal History (2003), 137.

4. Quincy, *Law Commonplace*, vol. 56, reel 4, published in this series as *Quincy Papers*, vol. 2.

5. Quincy's [Political] Commonplace Book (1770–1774), vol. 59, reel 4, published in this series as *Quincy Papers*, vol. 1. The [Political] Commonplace Book has been carefully transcribed and edited by the leading authority on Quincy's life, Neil L. York. I am delighted to have his collaboration on this project. Jane G. Downing and Natalia Fekula, research assistants of most uncommon intelligence and dedication, have transcribed the *Law Commonplace*. See generally Quincy, *Law Commonplace* (1763), vol. 56, reel 4, now published in this series as *Quincy Papers*, vol. 2. Michael Hayden did the same excellent job for the *Southern Journal (1773)*, *Quincy Papers*,

1773, which was full of deeply personal observations about racism, sex, politics and impending war. These other manuscripts are now cross-referenced to *Quincy's Reports* themselves.

Together, these documents put *Quincy's Reports* into the context of Quincy's life. They permit us to understand more fully the intellectual life and jurisprudence of this brilliant young lawyer, recorded at the outset of the American Revolution, and more about the tumultuous times in which he lived and, all too soon, died.

It is certainly not my intention to repeat here the full textual and legal analysis that accompanies the annotations in this new edition. Rather, I would like to step back for a moment to contemplate the overall significance of *Quincy's Reports*, both as an historic document and as a legal authority of continuing importance. For this is a document that touches on political and juristic controversies that still command our attention, still define our hopes and fears, and still divide us. And, yes, I would like to talk a bit about the people behind these dry pages, the merchants and indentured servants, the bold sea captains and bankrupt speculators, the villains and cheats, the noble patriots and kindly philanthropists, the spies and swindlers, the whores and pimps, the exploited seamen and cruelly-used slaves who walked the streets just before the American Revolution. Let me begin with Josiah Quincy Jr., himself.

II. JOSIAH QUINCY JR. (1744–1775)

Josiah Quincy Jr. (Quincy) was born on February 23, 1744, the youngest son of a prosperous Boston merchant, also named Josiah.[6] Josiah Jr.'s son would also be called Josiah and the three were thus nicknamed "Josiah the Colonel" (father), "Josiah the Patriot" (son), and "Josiah the President" or "Mayor" (grandson).[7]

---

vol. 3. Mark Walsh patiently compared the published *Quincy's Reports* against the manuscript at the Massachusetts Historical Society. Quincy, *Reports*, vols. 54–55, 57–58, reel 4. Finally, thanks are due to Peter Drummey, Librarian of the Massachusetts Historical Society, the most helpful custodian of the manuscript.

6. 15 *Dictionary of American Biography* 307 (Dumas Malone ed., 1946).

7. See 1 "The Massachusetts Bench and Bar: A Biographical Register of John Adams Contemporaries," in *Legal Papers of John Adams* at xcv (L. Kinvin Wroth & Hiller B. Zobel eds., 1965) (hereafter, "*Register of Bench and Bar*") (describing nicknames of Quincy's family). Quincy's son became Mayor of Boston (1823–1829) and President of Harvard (1829–1845)—hence Quincy

Quincy grew up in a world of opportunity and privilege. He entered Harvard College in 1759. He was fifteen. When he graduated with a bachelor's degree in 1763, at age eighteen, he was already hard at work on his legal studies and his *Reports*.[8] Known for his sensitivity, intelligence, and extraordinary gifts as an orator, Quincy seemed like a natural leader in a time of great challenge and opportunity. Indeed, his close friends and schoolmates became signers of the Declaration of Independence (Robert Treat Paine), justices of the new United States Supreme Court (William Cushing) and even President of the United States (John Adams).[9]

Market in Boston, Quincy Street and Quincy House in Cambridge. His son "Josiah the President" published the earliest account of Quincy's life. *Josiah Quincy, Memoir of the Life of Josiah Quincy Jun. of Massachusetts* (Boston: Cummings, Hilliard & Co., 1825). The biography is adulatory, but full of original source material and detail, particularly of Quincy's trip to England. *Id.* at 216–348; see also 15 *Dictionary of American Biography, supra*, note 6, at 309 (discussing Quincy's trip to England); 6 *Lamb's Biographical Dictionary of the United States,* 385–86 (John Howard Brown ed., 1903) (hereafter, "*Lamb's*") (summarizing Quincy's trip to England); L. Edward Purcell, *Who Was Who in the American Revolution*, 395–96 (1993) (discussing Quincy). In his papers, John Adams also included a substantial amount of information about Quincy. 1 *Legal Papers of John Adams, supra*, at 34–39, 51–53, 58–60, 63–75, 157–61, 263–64; 2 *Legal Papers of John Adams, supra*, at 66 n.11, 335–50, 402–04, 409–10; 3 *Legal Papers of John Adams*, *supra*, at 5–17, 20–22, 25–29, 35–42, 226–42. Other writers have included Quincy in their work on the American Revolution. See Pauline Maier, *From Resistance to Revolution*, 125, 134, 242–43, 250–55 (1972) (discussing Quincy's contributions); Dennis A. O'Toole & Lisa W. Strick, "In the Minds and Hearts of the People," *Five American Patriots and the Road to Revolution*, 59, 59–74 (1974) (providing overview of Quincy's life); Peter Shaw, *American Patriots and the Rituals of Revolution*, 22–25, 153–74, 223–24 (1981) (recounting Quincy's life); Hiller B. Zobel, *The Boston Massacre*, 219–24, 241–43, 259–60, 277–89 (1970) (discussing Quincy's work). Perhaps the best account is Professor York's introduction to his transcription of Quincy's *Commonplace Book*, "A Life Cut Short," *Quincy Papers*, vol. 1, pp. 15–46. I am very indebted to Professor York's account throughout.

Josiah Quincy Jr. was painted by Gilbert Stuart (1755–1828). Stuart painted Quincy in 1825 "'after studying family portraits and prints, and the result was considered a good likeness.'" See Descriptive List of Illustrations, in 3 *Legal Papers of John Adams, supra*, at viii (quoting 2 Lawrence Park, Gilbert Stuart 628 [1926]). The Quincy family still owns the portrait, which now is held by the Boston Museum of Fine Arts. There is a reproduction in the *Legal Papers of John Adams, supra*, at illus. 9, facing p. 196, and in the *Quincy Papers*, vol. 1, frontispiece. See Daniel R. Coquillette, "A Note on the Gilbert Stuart Portrait of Josiah Quincy Junior," *id.*, pp. xxix–xxxvi. The portrait reveals that along with his struggle against tuberculosis, Quincy also had problems focusing one eye. It was yet another physical challenge overcome by the brilliant young lawyer.

8. See 15 *Dictionary of American Biography*, *supra*, note 6, at 307 (noting Quincy began his writings during his school years).

9. See Charles R. McKirdy, "Massachusetts Lawyers on the Eve of the American Revolution: The State of the Profession," in *Law in Colonial Massachusetts 1630–1800*, *supra*, note 2, app. IV at 339, 342–43, 348–50 (listing biographical sketches of Adams, Cushing, Paine, and Quincy).

But Quincy was cursed early in life with tuberculosis. Always sickly, he achieved everything he did in a few short years. On April 26, 1775, he died aboard a ship.[10] He was returning from a desperate secret mission to England, to try to encourage a peace—even as the shots rang out at Lexington and Concord. He died in Gloucester harbor, in sight of his beloved America. His young wife Abigail hurried to the dock. She left behind their young son, the future President of Harvard, with parents in Norwich. Two weeks before, their new daughter, Abigail, had also died, not a year old. Her sorrow was inexpressible. She would survive her husband by twenty-three years. Quincy was just thirty-one.[11]

Quincy's life would have been remarkable had he left no writing. To start, he was a brilliant practicing lawyer. His law teacher was Oxenbridge Thacher, one of the colonies' leading jurists.[12] Quincy qualified for the bar by 1765, and soon had important clients of his own.

But Quincy was also a prolific writer. His writings reveal the tortured, stressful times in which he lived, because they were divided into his public "professional" work, such as the *Reports*, and his secret writings for the Committee of Correspondence. By day, the young Quincy dutifully attended the royal courts, carefully recording the arguments and holdings of the royal justices. At night, he attended the secret meetings of the patriot rebels. Under names like "Hyperion," "An Independent," "the Mentor," or simply "An Old Man," Quincy's articles appeared regularly in the *Massachusetts Gazette*.[13] They bitterly attacked the Tory establishment.[14]

10. 15 *Dictionary of American Biography*, *supra*, note 6, at 307.

11. See Neil L. York, "A Life Cut Short," *Quincy Papers*, vol. 1, pp. 44–45.

12. McKirdy, *supra*, note 2, app. IV at 350; see also 15 *Dictionary of American Biography*, *supra*, note 6, at 307 (discussing Quincy's legal training); Richard Scott Eckert, *"The Gentlemen of the Profession": The Emergence of Lawyers in Massachusetts, 1630–1810*, at 221–316 (1991) (providing overview of professional training and literature available during Quincy's time).

13. See 6 *Lamb's*, *supra*, note 7, at 386 (citing some of Quincy's articles); see also Quincy, *supra*, note 7, at 156–58 (giving text of letter that appeared in *Gazette*).

14. 15 *Dictionary of American Biography*, *supra*, note 6, at p. 307. Quincy's most important pamphlet, "Observations on the act of Parliament, commonly called 'The Boston Port Bill,' with Thoughts on Civil Society and Standing Armies," was published in May 1774. Quincy, *supra*, note 7, at 150. Quincy openly admitted authoring this work. This forthrightness led to a veiled and anonymous threat on his life and his property. See *id.* at 150–56 (reprinting ominous letter). The chilling threat and Quincy's brave reply in the *Massachusetts Gazette* are reproduced in his son's book, *Memoir of the Life of Josiah Quincy Jun. of Massachusetts. Id.* at 150–58; see also 15 *Dictionary of American Biography*, *supra*, note 6, at 308 (citing periodical in which letter appeared).

III. QUINCY'S REPORTS (1761–1772)

Despite the courage of Quincy's patriotic writings, it is—perhaps ironically—his professional work which is, today, most important. Quincy was a blazing, brilliantly innovative young man, painfully aware of his fatal illness. In 1762, at only eighteen, he began a totally new departure in American legal writing. Massachusetts had established a university and a press by 1639, 122 years before, and had an independent legal system under both the First and Second Charters. But there were no "native" law reports before Quincy.

Of course, the Massachusetts press had long been used for legal publications, with law books exceeded in output only by books on theology.[15] These law books included jury oaths, abridgments, and a regular series of printed Provincial Laws, the statutory output of the colonies. According to Morris Cohen, fifty-five separate issues of the *Laws and Orders* of the General Court appeared between 1661 and 1691, 146 issues appeared from 1692 to 1742, and 208 issues of the *Acts and Laws* from November 1742 to 1775.[16] The *Lawes and Libertyes* of 1648 was the first codified system of law to appear in print in America, and one of the first such books to be compiled anywhere.[17] But, despite the regular sittings of the Superior Court of Judicature from at least the Second Charter (1692) on, there were no law reports. Instead, very expensive English reports were imported.[18] Why should this be? There was a clear judicial recognition, documented by Quincy himself, that the decisions of the Provincial courts were, and should be, sources of authority. These decisions also could be quite different from the royal common law of England.[19] The

15. See Morris L. Cohen, "Legal Literature in Colonial Massachusetts," in *Law in Colonial Massachusetts 1630–1800*, *supra*, note 2, at 243, 243–72 (recounting types and scope of publications available during colonial times); Erwin C. Surrency, "The Beginnings of American Legal Literature," 31 Am. J. Legal Hist. 207, 207–08, 210–11 (1987) (providing overview of Massachusetts publications).

16. Cohen, *supra*, note 15, at 253.

17. See Daniel R. Coquillette, *Radical Lawmakers in Colonial Massachusetts: The "Countenance of Authoritie" and the Lawes and Libertyes*, 67 New Eng. Q. 179, 194–201 (1994) (recounting evolution of Lawes and Libertyes).

18. Surrency, *supra*, note 3, at 49.

19. Sometimes these differences were due to the existence of colonial legislation, and sometimes simply reflected the court's recognition of different customs in the colony, particularly as to the practice of merchants. See Notes on *Bromfield* v. *Little*, in *Quincy's Reports*, at 108, 108–09 (1764) (discussing differences between custom of merchants in Massachusetts and at "Home"); Notes on *Scollay* v. *Dunn*, in *Quincy's Reports*, at 74, 80–86 (1763) (noting justices' disagreement over whether rule governing appeals controls).

judges themselves were aware of this fact. Yet about 123 years passed between 1639 and the first American law reports, almost the same time as between 1775 and the twentieth century. Why, then, no reports?

One likely explanation is the small size of the bar—only about a dozen regular practitioners and only twenty-six barristers total on the rolls in Massachusetts in 1762.[20] Colonial printers needed guaranteed markets of a certain size or their business would not be successful, and, as Quincy's own *Law Commonplace* demonstrated, English reports were readily available.[21] But Josiah Quincy

20. See Memorandum, in *Quincy's Reports*, at 35, 35 (1762) (setting out roll of "Barristers at Law"). Of course, there were many "lawyers" who were not "barristers." See McKirdy, *supra*, note 2, app. IV at 339–58 (profiling Massachusetts lawyers of 1775). Ironically, the roll of barristers never included Quincy himself. See Quincy, *supra*, note 7, at 27 (discussing how the Superior Court denied Quincy "the honours of the gown"). His son claimed that the reasons for Quincy's omission were political. *Id.* "The political course of Mr. Quincy having rendered him obnoxious to the Supreme Court of the province, he was omitted in the distribution of the honours of the gown, which was due his rank and standing at the bar." *Id.* Nevertheless, Quincy appeared before the Superior Court of Judicature! This is his own account:

> At the laft Sitting of the Superiour Court in Charleftown, I argued (for the firft Time in this Court) to the Jury, though not admitted to the Gown:—The Legality and Propriety of which fome have pretended to doubt; but as no Scruples of that Kind difturbed me, I proceeded (maugre any) at this Court to manage all my own Bufinefs (for the firft Time in this County,) though unfanctified and uninfpired by the Pomp and Magic of—the Long Robe.

Memoranda, in *Quincy's Reports*, at 317, 317 (1769).

21. See Daniel R. Coquillette, Introduction, "The Legal Education of a Patriot: Josiah Quincy Jr.'s *Law Commonplace*, *Quincy Papers*, vol. 2. See also Hugh Amory, "Under the Exchange: The Unprofitable Business of Michael Perry, a Seventeenth-Century Boston Bookseller," 103 Proc. Am. Antiquarian Soc'y 31, 31–50 (1993) (discussing plight of colonial bookseller). Erwin Surrency points out that the public underwrote the statute books; whereas law reports did not receive the same funding until more than a century later. Surrency, *supra*, note 3, at 49. He adds that the very small number of lawyers and the availability of manuscript notebooks, like Quincy's *Law Commonplace*, left little demand for printed copies. *Id.* at 49–50, 54. In addition to the economics of the printing business, Surrency mentions two other factors that might have discouraged American law reports. See *id.* at 51–52 (commenting on reasons for reports). One was the lack of written opinions, and the belief of some early lawyers that the decisions of colonial courts did not warrant publication. *Id.* at 51. A second reason, not unrelated to the first, was the higher prestige of the English reports, which provided imported competition. *Id.* at 49, 54. In Jefferson's words, colonial judges were chosen:

> without any regard to legal knowledge, their decisions could never be quoted, either as adding to, or detracting from, the weight of those of the English courts, on the same points. Whereas, on our peculiar laws, their judgments, whether formed on correct principles of law, or not, were of conclusive authority.

Thomas Jefferson, Preface to Reports of Cases Determined in the General Court of Virginia 5 (Michie 1903) (1829); see also Surrency, *supra*, note 3, at 51–52 (discussing Jefferson preface).

The judges of Quincy's Massachusetts Superior Court of Judicature, with a few exceptions

clearly envisioned a new era, and his *Reports*, covering the years 1761–1772, were clearly and self-consciously designed to be the beginning of something new.

This departure, in itself, would have been extraordinary. But *Quincy's Reports* were no ordinary law reports, and these were no ordinary times. Like many of the English reports with which Quincy was familiar,[22] his own reports covered more than just judicial decisions. Like the Year Books, *Quincy's Reports* included arguments of counsel, and almost anything else that Quincy found of interest in the courtroom, including ad hominem insults and dress.[23] When Chief Justice Hutchinson's house was burned by the Boston mob, Quincy

---

like Edmund Trowbridge, Benjamin Lynde, and William Cushing, were not trained professionals. See McKirdy, *supra*, note 2, app. IV at 330, 332 (listing judges who were also lawyers); Surrency, *supra*, note 15, at 214 (suggesting colonial judges lacked legal training). Rather many of the judges were wealthy merchants and "gentlemen." See McKirdy, *supra*, note 2, app. IV at 330, 332 (listing judges' occupations). But the exchanges and questions of the judges recorded in *Quincy's Reports* leave a clear impression of professional competence. On occasion, Quincy questioned individual arguments. See *infra*, note 28 (characterizing Quincy as critical of counsel's arguments). Nevertheless, he recorded the judicial holdings with care and respect. Further, as will be discussed in Part IV *infra*, the decisions of the judges were represented as clearly authoritative in Massachusetts, even when inconsistent with English cases—at least as a practical matter. Surrency, *supra*, note 3, at 52; see also *infra*, notes 104–105 and accompanying text (summarizing that colonial judges did not strictly adhere to English precedent). Finally, in several instances, Quincy managed to obtain possession of manuscript opinions, such as the one by Judge Trowbridge in *Hooton* v. *Grout*, although this practice was clearly no more common in the Massachusetts of Quincy's day than it was in England. Notes on *Hooton* v. *Grout*, in *Quincy's Reports*, at 343, 343–69 (1772). In both locations, oral opinions from the bench were the practice. See Surrency, *supra*, note 3, at 55 (commenting that statutes modified oral practice by requiring written judicial opinions). Only in 1785 did Connecticut first require written opinions by statute. See *id.* (noting Connecticut's statute viewed law as form of science thereby requiring written opinions).

Perhaps Quincy's pride in the growing professionalism of the Massachusetts bar and bench and a growing sense of independence from English authority led him to begin his *Reports*. See *id.* at 54 (asserting that once America became independent lawyers labored to create American jurisprudence). This would be consistent with Surrency's arguments for why such reports had not occurred before, and with some of Quincy's later assertions of professionalism. See discussion *infra*, Part IV.D; *infra*, notes 52 and 130 (discussing growing need for and value of colonial reports).

22. See Quincy, *Law Commonplace*, *supra*, note 3 (evincing knowledge of English law). His *Law Commonplace* is filled with references to English reports including *Coke's Reports* (1598–1615), *Salkeld's Reports* (1689–1712), *Modern Reports* (1669–1732), *Croke's Reports* (1582–1641), *Strange's Reports* (1716–1749), and many more.

23. See generally Notes on *Banister* v. *Henderson*, in *Quincy's Reports*, at 119, 119–48 (1765) (recording barbed exchange between lawyers). The old English Year Books, which contained similar information, were kept by law students for study purposes. See John P. Dawson, *The Oracles of the Law* 50–65 (1968) (describing reasons for the contents and the evolution of the Year books).

poignantly portrayed the Chief Justice in his borrowed clothes, appearing the next day to preside over the court, despite having lost everything he owned.[24] If counsel were asked to submit written briefs, which happened occasionally, Quincy would try to include the briefs in the *Reports*. In the unusual case where there was a written judicial opinion, he would try to include that, too. Perhaps surprisingly, given the closed society of just a dozen lawyers and five judges, there were frequent dissents, over thirty-one, and there were often closely split votes among the judges. Quincy dutifully recorded these disputes, and the oral debate among the judges.[25]

Thus, *Quincy's Reports* give a graphic and detailed view of the proceedings of the Superior Court of Judicature from 1762–1772. As a "colonial" version of an English high court, like the King's Bench, the superior court had a trial jurisdiction for serious crime, a trial de novo jurisdiction, and a review jurisdiction, both in error and in a "reservation of judgment."[26] It heard cases from both the Inferior Court of Common Pleas (Civil) and the General Sessions of the Peace (Criminal). Quincy could, and did, observe all aspects of the colonial

24. See Destruction of the House of the Chief Justice, in *Quincy's Reports*, at 168, 170–71 (1765) (highlighting description of the Chief Justice after Boston mob destroyed his house).

25. See *Appendix I*, "Judicial Dissents," *Quincy Papers*, vol. 5. See also notes on *Noble* v. *Smith*, in *Quincy's Reports*, at 254, 254 (1767) (demonstrating lack of agreement among justices); Notes on *Apthorp* v. *Eyres*, in *Quincy's Reports*, at 229, 230–31 (1766) (depicting justices' dispute over admissibility of evidence); Notes on *Norwood* v. *Fairservice*, in *Quincy's Reports*, at 189, 191 (1765) (recording disagreement among justices as to whether justices or jury should decide case at bar); Notes on *Banister* v. *Henderson*, in *Quincy's Reports*, at 119, 122–23 (1765) (describing dispute over how to prove valid marriage); Notes on *Scollay* v. *Dunn*, in *Quincy's Reports*, at 74, 77–78 (1763) (transcribing justices' dispute over admiralty law); Notes on *Baker* v. *Mattocks*, in *Quincy's Reports*, at 69, 72–74 (1763) (depicting justices' lack of consensus on freehold estate issue); Notes on *Russel* v. *Oakes*, in *Quincy's Reports*, at 48, 49–50 (1763) (recording justices' dispute over negotiability of instrument).

26. See Barbara Aronstein Black, "The Concept of a Supreme Court: Massachusetts Bay 1630–1686," in *The History of the Law in Massachusetts: The Supreme Judicial Court 1692–1992*, at 43, 43–79 (Russell K. Osgood ed., 1992) (discussing origins of Supreme Judicial Court of Massachusetts). Quincy himself called his reports, "Reports of Cases Solemnly Adjudged in King's Bench Court of Assize and Goal Delivery." See *Quincy Papers*, *supra*, note 3 (noting handwritten title); see also Catherine S. Menand, "A 'magistracy fit and necessary': A Guide to the Massachusetts Court System," in *Law in Colonial Massachusetts 1630–1800*, *supra*, note 2, at 541, 541–49 (describing creation of colonial court system and its hierarchical structure); Russell K. Osgood, "The Supreme Judicial Court, 1692–1992: An Overview," in *The History of the Law in Massachusetts: The Supreme Judicial Court 1692–1992*, *supra*, at 9, 9–16 (depicting establishment of Superior Court of Judicature).

justice system.[27] In addition, his personal intelligence resulted in insights into the cases that often escaped all the active participants. In 1762, Quincy was still a college boy of eighteen, but he already had an astonishing knowledge of the English treatises and leading cases. His marginal notes, politely correcting errors by the lawyers and the judges, are frequently brilliant, and very rarely wrong.[28] Quincy also had his two personal notebooks, his *Law Commonplace* and his collection of political and philosophical "maxims," the *Political Commonplace Book*, published in volumes 2 and 1, respectively, in this *Quincy Papers* series. Taken all together, these documents provide a remarkably complete look at the private legal reasoning and public persona of an eighteenth-century lawyer—quite important in itself, even if Quincy had not also been genuinely brilliant and a great patriotic leader.

Quincy's early death and the immediate outbreak of serious fighting in the colonies put his vision of an American law report "on hold." Although the Superior Court of Judicature was not officially abolished and technically survived the Revolution intact—Justice William Cushing never resigned and was reappointed—three of the five justices fled the country. More poignantly, six of the fourteen most active members of the bar also fled—including Josiah's dearly beloved brother, Samuel Quincy.[29]

27. Black, *supra*, note 26, at 43–79.

28. The most poignant example of Quincy's critical commentary is the annotation to the infamous *Allison* v. *Cockran* case. Notes on *Allison* v. *Cockran*, in *Quincy's Reports*, at 94, 94 (1764). The case was about whether administrators were competent witnesses in matters "affecting the Eftate of their Inteftate," but the cause of action was "Trover for a Negro." *Id.* Quincy observed: "Qu. if this Action is well brought, for Trover lies not for a Negro. 2 Salk. 666. Ld. Raym. 1274, 146. Cafes in the Time of Holt, 495." *Id.* at 94 n.*. Lord Holt had held that "(T)he common law takes no notice of negroes being different from other men. . . . (T)here is no such thing as a slave by the law of England." *Smith* v. *Gould*, 2 Ld. Raym. 1274, 1275, 92 Eng. Rep. 338, 338 (K.B. 1706); see also Notes on *Allison* v. *Cockran*, in *Quincy's Reports*, at 94, 96 n.1 (1764) (quoting and citing *Smith* v. *Gould*). Of course, this may have been a "correct" observation of the common law, but it was, shamefully, not the colonial law of Quincy's Massachusetts. See Notes on *Richmond* v. *Davis*, in *Quincy's Reports*, at 279, 298 (1768) (questioning presciently whether uninterrupted practice may change rule of law); *infra*, Section IV.C (discussing colonial law). Quincy also made many technical, and largely correct, criticisms of counsel's arguments. See generally Notes on *Banister* v. *Henderson*, in *Quincy's Reports*, at 119, 126 n.* (questioning counsel's arguments).

29. See "Editor's Foreword," *Quincy Papers*, vol. 5. See also McKirdy, *supra*, note 9, app. IV at 339–58 (listing biographies of Quincy's colleagues); *Register of Bench and Bar*, *supra*, note 7, at xcv–cxiv (summarizing fates of Quincy's contemporaries).

By the time the fighting was over, other lawyers had begun to share in Quincy's vision, such as A. J. Dallas in Pennsylvania (whose reports included the first Supreme Court Reports) (1790–1807), Francis Hopkinson in the Philadelphia Admiralty Court (1789), Ephraim Kirby in Connecticut (1789), George Wythe in Virginia (1788) and, last but not least, Thomas Jefferson himself, whose *Reports of Cases Determined in the General Court of Virginia* were published in 1829.[30] In Massachusetts itself nothing was done until 1803, when an "Act providing for the appointment of a Reporter of Decisions in the Supreme Judicial Court" was passed.[31] Pursuant to this statute, Ephraim Williams was appointed Reporter and issued the first "official" Massachusetts reports, *Williams Reports* (1804–1805), forty years after Josiah Quincy's first efforts.[32]

As to *Quincy's Reports* themselves, they languished in manuscript until the Civil War, when Quincy's great-grandson Samuel Quincy retrieved the original manuscripts and edited them for publication in 1865. They then appeared in print in an edition by Little, Brown and Company, the first, and last edition, until this new effort.[33] Remarkably, *Quincy's Reports* have been regularly cited by the Supreme Court of the United States, by the Supreme Judicial Court, and by other federal and state courts, as recently as a United States Supreme Court decision in 1987.[34] See *Illinois* v. *Krull*, 480 U.S. 340, 363 (1987), Justice O'Connor in dissent.

30. See Surrency, *supra*, note 3, at 50–53 (providing historical overview of colonial notebooks); see also Aumann, *supra*, note 3, at 337–43 (discussing colonial reporters).

31. 1803 Mass. Acts 133.

32. See Ephraim Williams, *Preface to the First Edition of Reports of Cases Argued and Determined in the Supreme Judicial Court of the Commonwealth of Massachusetts* at iii–iv (3d ed., Boston: Little, Brown & Co., 1883) (1805); Surrency, *supra*, note 3, at 56 (discussing Massachusetts' novel move in appointing court reporter to record Supreme Judicial Court decisions).

33. Because it is no longer subject to copyright, the 1865 edition has been copied and distributed by publishers who have simply reproduced the exact pages. *Quincy's Reports* (Dennis & Co. 1948) (1865); *Quincy's Reports* (Russell & Russell 1969) (1865).

34. See *Appendix 5*, "Citations to *Quincy's Reports* by the Supreme Judicial Court of Massachusetts," *Quincy Papers*, vol. 5, *infra*. See also Mark A. Sullivan's masterful "Phantom References to *Quincy's Reports* in the Massachusetts Supreme Judicial Court *Reports*," included in *Appendix 5*, *infra*.

IV. THE "POMPEII OF PAPER"— OR WILLIAMSBURG THIS WAS NOT

Visitors to "colonial" Williamsburg are asked to "step back" into the elegant world of colonial life as it was in the Virginian capital in 1765, just before the Revolution. "Servants" in costumes open the doors, and great attention is paid to details like parcel wrapping and wallpaper. The effect is delightful and escapist. Mulled colonial ale is accurately served in a tankard. All seems right with the world. As a participant in one recent legal conference in Williamsburg observed, "Here we are in a fake eighteenth-century city to worry about a real eighteenth-century legal system!"[35]

The real 1765 was very different, and the Massachusetts Court records, including *Quincy's Reports*, are hard evidence of what life was actually like before the Revolution. As the Honorable Hiller B. Zobel so aptly put it, these records are a "Pompeii of Paper."[36] They capture colonial life in exquisite and candid detail, like bugs in amber. Here are the great and petty affairs of the time, "warts and all." Here is the best and the worst of society. Prostitution and exploitation of women coexists with noble sentiments of courtesy and fairness. Exhortation of human dignity is found on pages next to the blatant trade in human beings. All in all, it is a bad time. Families are split by political tension, the mob runs free, and young men fear what the future may bring.[37]

I can only begin to demonstrate here the wealth of information in these Reports, and its importance. Let me give but a few examples, moving progressively—at least in my opinion—from the narrowest categories, cases relevant as authority for constitutional construction, to the most fundamental, cases that give insights into the nature of the rule of law.

35. Participant, Meeting of the Committee on Court Administration and Case Management, Judicial Conference of the United States, (Dec. 4, 1995).

36. "No ice storms encapsulated any 18th century town; no embalming ash has brought the Revolutionary days to us intact. But we do possess pieces of that past life, preserved without change, and lying, like the wall paintings of Pompeii, beneath a layer of dust, awaiting excavation. We call them court records." Hon. Hiller B. Zobel, "The Pompeii of Paper," Boston Bar Journal (September 1978), p. 20. See also Robert J. Brink, "'Immortality brought to Light': An Overview of Massachusetts Colonial Court Records," in *Law in Colonial Massachusetts 1630–1800, supra*, note 2, at 471, 471–97 (discussing how colonial records reveal intrinsic historical details and personal sentiments of colonial life).

37. See Quincy, *supra*, note 7, 160–62 (recording heartbreaking letter to patriot Josiah Quincy Jr. from his dearly beloved loyalist brother Samuel); see also *id.* at 31–32 (articulating tension in colonial life).

A. Constitutional Construction: Controlling Juries

Certainly one function of *Quincy's Reports* is its value in resolving continuing constitutional controversies. In 1994, I filed an amicus brief with other legal history scholars in the Supreme Court of the United States. This brief was also signed by Akhil Reed Amar, Arthur R. Miller, Arthur F. McEvoy, and Erwin Chermerinsky, among others. The case, *Gasperini* v. *Center for Humanities, Inc.*,[38] was a request for certiorari to review a Second Circuit decision which substituted a de novo "weight-of-the-evidence" review for a large jury verdict, applying a New York statute.[39] The issue was whether the decision violated the Reexamination Clause of the Seventh Amendment, which provides that "no fact tried by a jury, shall be otherwise re-examined in any Court of the United States, than according to the rules of the common law."[40] The "rules of the common law" must, as a matter of historical context, be determined as of the date of the Seventh Amendment, i.e., 1791.[41]

But there are many difficulties in determining the rules of common law as of 1791. With few relevant cases in England, and, of course, almost none reported here, it has been an area of great speculation. With new efforts to limit large civil damages, this historical game is now being played intensely.

One of the few reliable sources is *Quincy's Reports*. In three cases, the justices

38. 518 U.S. 415, *116 S. Ct. 2211 (1996)*.

39. See *id.* at 2216–17 (providing procedural history of case). The Court applied section 5501(c) of the New York Civil Practice, Law and Rules. *Id.* at 2215, 2218; see also *N.Y. C.P.L.R.* 5501(c) (McKinney 1995) (defining appellate court scope of review).

40. U.S. Const. amend VII; see also Gasperini, 518 U.S. 415, 116 S. Ct. at 2222– 2223 (discussing Seventh Amendment).

41. See David L. Shapiro & Daniel R. Coquillette, "The Fetish of Jury Trial in Civil Cases: A Comment on *Rachal* v. *Hill*," 85 Harv. L. Rev. 442, 448–55 (1971), cited with approval in *Parklane Hosiery Co.* v. *Shore*, 439 U.S. 322, 333 (1979) (arguing 1791 as appropriate date for commencement of common law under Seventh Amendment). In *Gasperini*, 518 U.S. 415, 116 S. Ct. 2211, the majority opinion, by Justice Ginsburg, observes in a footnote that "If the meaning of the Seventh Amendment were fixed at 1791, our civil juries would remain, as they unquestionably were at common law, 'twelve good men and true.'" *Id.* at 2224 n.20 This view was attacked by Justice Scalia, in dissent, joined by the Chief Justice and Justice Thomas. Justice Scalia called the "12 juror" analogy "desperate," noting that there is "of course no comparison between the specificity of the command of the Reexamination Clause and the specificity of the command that there be a 'jury.'" *Id.* at 2236 (Scalia, J., dissenting). He strongly criticized the "footnote abandonment of our traditional view of the Reexamination Clause," and observed that "the court frankly abandons any pretense at faithfulness to the common law, suggesting that 'the meaning' of the Reexamination Clause was not 'fixed at 1791,' contrary to the view of all our prior discussions. . . ." *Id.* (citation omitted).

carefully deliberated the power of an appellate court to review a jury verdict, or to substitute its judgment for a jury verdict. In *Angier* v. *Jackson*,[42] a motion was made for a new trial because "the Jury gave a Verdict for Damages in Favour of Jackſon, original Plaintiff, contrary to the Mind of the Court."[43] Trowbridge, counsel for the appellant, argued that "(w)hen the Jury give a Verdict againſt Evidence, the Court may grant a new Trial. That Jury are not abſolute Judges of Evidence and Damages, ſee Holt's Rep. 701, 702, Aſh vs. Lady Aſh. Jurys are to try Cauſes with the Affiſtance of Judges."[44] The Court disagreed, holding that there can be no new trial even when it is "not clear" whether there is evidence to support a jury verdict.[45] The Chief Justice, apparently in dissent, stated that "were it evidently againſt Law and Evidence, there the Court may grant a new Trial, but not where there is Evidence on both Sides."[46]

The issue was discussed again in *Norwood* v. *Fairservice*.[47] This was an action on an indenture, with a defense based on the defendant's section of the indenture.[48] This section of the indenture clearly had different terms from that in

42. Notes on *Angier* v. *Jackson*, in *Quincy's Reports*, at 84 (1763).

43. *Id.* at 84.

44. *Id.* Auchmuty, arguing to defend the verdict from a new trial, stated, "If ever any Caſe was excepted from new Trials, this is. . . . I confess I wish for a Power in the Court to set aside Verdicts, but not for an unlimited one. This Caſe was not against Evidence. . . . The Court is not to be Judge of the Law and Fact too absolutely; if it should be, it takes away all Verdicts but such as are agreeable to the Mind of the Court." *Id.* at 84–85. Trowbridge, arguing for a new trial, replied, "It can never be supposed that a Verdict will be given against direct Evidence, without Shadow of Evidence to support it. . . . I hold, this Court always have Right to grant new Trials when they think Injustice like to be done." *Id.* at 85. Trowbridge lost. *Id.*

45. *Id.* at 85.

46. *Id.* Quincy records that "Justices Oliver, Cushing, Russell & Lynde (were) against a new Trial, because the Court were not clear in the former Trial." *Id.* There is no record of Chief Justice Thomas Hutchinson joining the opinions, and the listing of the judges implies a divided court. *Id.* The editor of the 1865 printed version, Samuel M. Quincy, observed that the Massachusetts law had now changed, citing Chief Justice Shaw in *Miller* v. *Baker*, 37 Mass. (20 Pick.) 285, 289 (1838):

> For a long time it was conſidered that a new trial could only regularly be granted, where the verdict was without evidence or againſt the whole evidence. It has however been extended to caſes, where the verdict is clearly againſt the weight of evidence, although evidence was given on both ſides.

Notes on *Angier* v. *Jackson*, in *Quincy's Reports*, at 84, 85 n.4 (quoting Chief Justice Shaw).

47. Notes on *Norwood* v. *Fairservice*, in *Quincy's Reports*, at 189 (1765).

48. *Id.* at 189. *Jowitt's Dictionary of English Law* defines an "indenture" as "a deed made between two or more parties" written two times "on one piece of parchment or paper, and then . . . cut . . . in two in an indented or toothed line, so that each copy of the deed fitted the other and could thus be identified." *Jowitt's Dictionary of English Law* (John Burke ed., 2d ed. 1977), 960.

possession of the plaintiff. Samuel Fitch, attorney for the plaintiff, "ſuggeſted a Fraud in the Defendant," and that the Court, not the jury, should view the document.[49] Robert Auchmuty, for the defense, argued that this is a "plain Matter of Fact, of which the Jury are the ſole Judges."[50] He continued, "Neither do I think the Court have any Right to determine this Matter; for 'twill be abridging the Priviledges of the Subject, to settle a Point which wholly lies with the Jury to determine."[51] On another split vote, the justices held that they should not view the indenture itself, but it should go to the jury—both parts.[52] Justice Cushing observed, "The Jury is ſole Judge of this; they muſt give what Credit they pleaſe."[53]

Obviously, the two copies ought to match, exactly. In Norwood, they did not. One half of the document gave a sum as covenanted for one year, and the other, the same sum covenanted for a quarter of the year. Notes on *Norwood* v. *Fairservice*, in *Quincy's Reports*, at 189, 189 (1765).

49. Notes on *Norwood* v. *Fairservice*, in *Quincy's Reports*, at 189, 189 (1765). Quincy then reported, "'Twas then further urged by the Plaintiff's Council (sic), that this Practice was well founded, and the Reason of it was this, that Nothing should go to a Jury which would only tend to deceive and inveigle them; and that therefore when a Piece of Evidence was offered, on the Face of which Fraud appeared, the Court rejected the Evidence, as 'would only tend to mislead.'" *Id.* at 190.

50. *Id.* at 189. Once again, Auchmuty defended the power of the jury, as he did in *Angier* v. *Jackson*. See Notes on *Angier* v. *Jackson*, in *Quincy's Reports*, at 84, 84–85 (1763) (arguing that if courts decide verdicts only causes favorable to the justices will prevail); see also Notes on *Norwood* v. *Fairservice*, in *Quincy's Reports*, at 189, 189–90 (1765) (arguing for Jury, not Court, as decisionmaker).

51. Notes on *Norwood* v. *Fairservice*, in *Quincy's Reports*, at 189, 190 (1765).

52. *Id.* at 191. Justice Cushing agreed with Justice Oliver's statement that the matter "properly belongs to the Jury." *Id.* Justice Lynde objected that "(a)s the Practice of this Court has always been otherwise, I am for viewing it." *Id.* Chief Justice Hutchinson observed that "I know the Custom has been otherwise, but, for my Part, I think 'tis Time it was altered—am for admitting it (to the Jury)." *Id.* Justice Russell, as was sometimes the case, was not sitting. See Address of the Chief Justice, in *Quincy's Reports*, at 171, 171 (1765) (listing justices present and absence of Justice Russell). He resigned a year later, in 1766. See McKirdy, *supra*, note 9, app. IV at 329–32 (listing terms of colonial Superior Court Judges in Massachusetts). Of course, the Chief Justice's willingness to change prior custom shows a need for law reports! Quincy recounts the Chief Justice's admission in Court that he had been "silent" in other cases, although "he had always doubted" (the practice of keeping the evidence from this jury). Notes on *Norwood* v. *Fairservice*, in *Quincy's Reports*, at 189, 190 (1765).

> In Answer to which, it was urged by Messrs. Gridley & Fitch, that it had always been the Custom of this Court to determine in such Cases. To which the Court agreed; and Justice Lynde said that he knew a similar Case of one Lanson's, in Middlesex: But the Chief Juſtice answered, that he had always doubted in those Cases, but whenever they arose, the Court always affirmed the constant Practice, and so he was silent.

Id.

53. Notes on *Norwood* v. *Fairservice*, in *Quincy's Reports*, at 189, 191 (1765).

The issue was raised again in *Carpenter* v. *Fairservice*.[54] The words "in one Month" were erased in a Note of Hand "payable Upon Demand." The issue was whether the words had been erased before, or after, the signing of the note.[55] Chief Justice Hutchinson observed, "(S)urely the Court could not determine the Weight of the Evidence of the Witnefs; but that the Jury are the fole Judges of the Credibility of this Witnefs, upon whofe Teftimony alone it refts, whether this Razure was before or after figning."[56] But here, Justices Oliver and Lynde disagreed, arguing "that, as the Note did not fupport the (plaintiff's) Declaration, it fhould not go in as Evidence."[57] Chief Justice Hutchinson and Justice Cushing argued that the whole matter should go to the jury.[58] Justice Trowbridge was not sitting, the court was evenly divided, and the plaintiff lost his declaration.[59] Quincy dropped one of his insightful notes here, referring the reader to the contrary holding in *Norwood* v. *Fairservice*, just discussed.[60] He was right, of course. As his grandson, Samuel M. Quincy, aptly observed, "The queftion as to the time when an alteration of a written inftrument was made, is for the jury."[61] Could this case have been one of the those that convinced Quincy of the need for national law reports? Certainly *Quincy's Reports* is still relevant today in resolving cases which involve constitutional right to jury trial, such as *Gasperini* v. *Center for the Humanities, Inc.*[62]

54. Notes on *Carpenter* v. *Fairservice*, in *Quincy's Reports*, at 239 (1767).

55. *Id.* at 239. This time Auchmuty was arguing against the jury power, objecting "that the Note thus erased did not support the Declaration; therefore not Evidence to support it." *Id.* Samuel Quincy, Josiah's brother, "reply'd, that the Jury were Judges of this Matter, and would determine whether the Razure [erasure] was before, or after signing." *Id.*

56. *Id.* at 240.

57. *Id.* at 239. Justice Oliver clearly changed his position from that in *Norwood*. See Notes on *Norwood* v. *Fairservice*, in *Quincy's Reports*, at 189, 191 (1765) (arguing evidence properly belonged with jury). Lynde remained consistent. Compare *id.* (asserting Court should decide case), with Notes on *Carpenter* v. *Fairservice*, in *Quincy's Reports*, at 239, 239 (1767) (advocating that Court decides issue).

58. Notes on *Carpenter* v. *Fairservice*, in *Quincy's Reports*, at 239, 239 (1767).

59. *Id.* at 240.

60. *Id.* at 240 n.*.

61. *Id.* at 240 n.1.

62. On June 24, 1996, the Supreme Court decided *Gasperini.*, 518 U.S. 415, 116 S. Ct. 2211 (1996). The majority duly rejected the historical arguments of our amicus brief, and ignored *Quincy's Reports*. See *id.* at 2222–24 (finding nothing in Seventh Amendment which precludes appellate review of trial judge's decision to set aside jury verdicts); *supra*, text accompanying note 38 (discussing issues raised in *Gasperini*). The primary rationale of the Court was noted

B. Colonial Jurisprudence: Herein of Hostages and "Reasonable Custom"

Another use of *Quincy's Reports* is to test current academic theories about pre-Revolutionary American jurisprudence. Where did the colonists look for their law? How bound were they by English legal doctrines? Did they consciously make new law to solve the peculiar social and economic problems of a new land?

One instructive case is *Dunn* v. *Scollay*.[63] The Scollays were wealthy Boston merchants. John Scollay owned the Brigantine *Peggy*, which was consigned to William Sitwell of London.[64] Returning in the fall of 1756, the *Peggy* was taken at sea on October 26, 1756, by a French privateer, aptly named the *Entreprenante*.[65] The Captain of the *Peggy*, Isaac Freeman, was a clever and persuasive

---

by Justice Stevens in a dissent which also rejected our historical arguments. "(T)he Framers of the Seventh Amendment evinced no interest in subscribing to every procedural nicety of the notoriously complicated English system. . . ." 116 S. Ct. at 2229 (Stevens, J., dissenting).

Our position was adopted by Justice Scalia, in an eloquent and learned dissent joined by the Chief Justice and Justice Thomas. Id. at 2231–36 (Scalia, J., dissenting). Justice Scalia observed, "(t)he weight of the historical record strongly supports the view of the common law taken in our early cases." *Id.* at 2233. He continues, "(t)he Court, as is its wont of late, all but ignores the relevant history." *Id.* at 2234. He concludes, "(a)las, those who drew the (Seventh) Amendment, and the citizens who approved it, did not envision an age in which the Constitution means whatever this Court thinks it ought to mean—or indeed, whatever the courts of appeals have recently thought it ought to mean." *Id.* at 2240. As demonstrated, *Quincy's Reports* strongly supports Justice Scalia, at least as to the historical record.

Historical records such as *Quincy's Reports* are not just useful to strict "originalists" that just look to "determinate rules that can be mined for the purposes of constitutional interpretation." See Bernadette Meyler's excellent article, "Towards a Common Law Originalism," 59 Stanford L. Rev. 551 (2006), at pp. 551, 600. Rather, Meyler's "common law originalism" would treat "the strands of eighteenth-century common law not as providing determinate answer that fix the meaning of particular constitutional clauses but instead as supplying the terms of a debate about certain concepts, framing questions for judges but refusing to settle them definitively." *Id.*, p. 551. Much of both Quincy's *Law Commonplace*, *Quincy Papers*, *supra*, vol. 2, and *The Reports*, *infra*, vols. 4 and 5, were written by Quincy himself in this spirit.

63. Notes on *Dunn* v. *Scollay*, in *Quincy's Reports*, at 187 (1765); Notes on *Scollay* v. *Dunn*, in *Quincy's Reports*, at 74 (1763).

64. Notes on *Dunn* v. *Scollay*, in *Quincy's Reports*, at 187, 187 n. 1 (1765). Samuel Quincy's note stated that the *Peggy* was "taken at sea by the French privateer *Entreprenante*, then returning from trading in negroes on the coast of Guinea." *Id.*, p. 187 n. 1. The antecedents are confusing. Was it the *Peggy* or the privateer who was the slaver? There is evidence that the *Peggy* was carrying coal. See Kevin Cox, "*Scollay* v. *Dunn*: the Conflict and Confluence of Colonial Admiralty and Common Law Jurisdiction in 1760's Boston," p. 1, an excellent, presently unpublished paper on file with the editor.

65. *Id.*

man, and convinced the French to accept a ransom bill on Sitwell and return the ship, the ransom note clearly being more than the pirates could get in France for their prize, but less than the value of the voyage.[66] Not being fools, the French took the first mate, one Dunn, as a hostage for payment.[67]

Once the ship was returned, however, neither Scollay nor Sitwell paid the bill.[68] Dunn languished in prison at Nantes where "he remained in a fick and deftiotute condition."[69] (Sitwell, apparently, sent Dunn one shilling a day for his support in prison.)[70] Neither Scollay nor Sitwell, of course, were privy to Freeman's ransom contract, as a matter of strict contract law. Six years later, Dunn's friends and family finally raised money for his ransom. On his return to Boston, Dunn promptly sued Scollay.[71]

It might, at first appearance, seem that both the strict letter of contract law and the economic interests of the Boston mercantile establishment would make this an easy case. Scollay's act may have been blatantly immoral, but there was no legal basis to bind him to a contract he had never seen nor approved. Yet for many years the customary law of the sea, as applied in the Admiralty Courts, had held that the master of a vessel could bind the vessel itself, without the knowledge of the owner, where the question was urgent repair to a vessel.[72] The reason was obvious: a valuable voyage might otherwise be cut short, and the profits lost. This doctrine, called "bottomry" or "hypothecation," was

66. *Id.*

67. *Id.* Ransom notes were not uncommon in the latter half of the eighteenth century. See Christopher P. Rodgers, "Ransom Bills and Commercial Credit in English Law—an Early Excursus in Comparative Legal Science," in *The Growth of the Bank as Institution and the Development of Money-Business Law,* 345, 349–51 (Vito Piergiovanni ed., 1993) (discussing ransom bills and English law).

68. Notes on *Dunn* v. *Scollay*, in *Quincy's Reports*, at 187, 187 n. 1 (1765). Sitwell claimed that the underwriters should pay, "but, as they refused, he wrote to Dunn, that there was "no Way to compell them without Law, and that would be attended with great Uncertainty, as this, they say, in a Case has not been try'd'—and also that he was instructed by Scollay to settle without regard to the ransom bill." *Id.* Sitwell was right that the matter was unsettled in English law. See *infra*, note 95 (discussing issue of hostages under English law).

69. Notes on *Dunn* v. *Scollay*, in *Quincy's Reports*, at 187, 187 n. 1 (1765).

70. *Id.* at 188 n. 1.

71. Notes on *Scollay* v. *Dunn*, in *Quincy's Reports*, at 74, 75 (1763).

72. See F. L. Wiswall Jr., *The Development of Admiralty Jurisdiction and Practice Since 1800*, at 9–10 (1970) (defining "hypothecation" as pledging of vessel).

well known to Quincy and the Boston lawyers.[73] Was not Dunn's case the same?

The willingness of early American courts to depart from black letter common law, particularly English law, and apply new doctrines based on the necessities of colonial trade or social policy has been a subject of hot debate among legal historians. John Murrin has argued that Massachusetts was experiencing "rapid and pervasive Anglicization" of its legal system, a process only cut off by the Revolution.[74] Morton Horwitz takes a different view. In his prize-winning and original book, *The Transformation of American Law, 1780–1860*,[75] he describes a period of stability right up to and through the Revolution.[76] There was, to be sure, an "'inevitable and rapid reception of the body of English common law,'" but only on the terms of the Americans and almost solely by local statute, not judicial activism.[77] According to Horwitz, real legal change occurred only after the Revolution, with the breakdown of the eighteenth-century "conception of law" and the emergence of an "instrumental perspective on law."[78] Only then did the courts narrow the province of the jury and undertake "an innovative and transforming role."[79] William E. Nelson takes yet a third view. A pioneer in the use of unpublished court records—as opposed to exclusive reliance on statutes and reported decisions and treatises—Nelson has concentrated on Massachusetts. His central thesis emphasizes the roles of judges and juries in the trial of cases.[80] Nelson argues, in contrast to Murrin,

73. See Notes on *Scollay* v. *Dunn*, in *Quincy's Reports*, at 74, 77–78 (1763) (describing counsel's argument on hypothecation and its applicability to hostages); see also Coquillette, *supra*, note 2, at 382–95 (noting John Adams's vice admiralty expertise). There are also a few good sources on colonial vice admiralty jurisdiction. See generally David R. Owen & Michael C. Tolley, *Courts of Admiralty in Colonial America* (1995) (studying colonial courts of admiralty); Carl Ubbelohde, *The Vice-Admiralty Courts and the American Revolution* (1960) (discussing colonial vice admiralty courts); L. Kinvin Wroth, "The Massachusetts Vice Admiralty Court and the Federal Admiralty Jurisdiction," 6 Am. J. Legal Hist. 250 (1962) (outlining colonial vice admiralty system).

74. See John M. Murrin, "The Legal Transformation: The Bench and Bar of Eighteenth-Century Massachusetts," in *Colonial America: Essays in Politics and Social Development* 540, 546–61 (Stanley N. Katz & John M. Murrin eds., 3d ed., 1983) (describing changes in provincial Massachusetts).

75. Morton J. Horwitz, *The Transformation of American Law, 1780–1860* (1977).

76. *Id.* at 1–6.

77. *Id.* at 5.

78. *Id.* at 4.

79. *Id.* at 1.

80. See William E. Nelson, *Americanization of the Common Law: The Impact of Legal*

that the pre-Revolutionary period saw the increasing power of juries, both in fact-finding and law-finding, the de-emphasis of special pleading, a limited role for judges, and a strong sense of local indigenous justice.[81]

Cases like *Dunn* v. *Scollay*[82] are direct tests of these academic theories. The case was originally brought by Dunn's lawyers, Auchmuty and Gridley, in the Vice Admiralty Court, where they clearly hoped to use an extension of the Admiralty's "hypothecation" doctrine to bind Scollay to an agreement he never joined. Their argument was that the case involved a prize "taken upon the High Seas," and was thus within the traditional admiralty jurisdiction.[83] Scollay's lawyers sought a "prohibition," an order "to restrain an inferior court with the limits of its jurisdiction," to stop the admiralty proceeding.[84] They argued that the relationship between Dunn and Scollay was just an issue of personal liability in contract, a simple common-law matter.[85] The vessel was not involved, probably because the Scollays kept it carefully away.[86]

Auchmuty, for Dunn, appealed to both the fairness and the economic necessity of permitting masters to bind owners to contracts that save the voyage, "otherwife the Whole would be loft."[87]

> Mafters may make Contracts that bind the Owners. Molloy, B. 2, C. 1, S 10; Ch. 2, SS 14 & 16. Ib. B. 2, Ch. 2, S 2. Hardres, 183, Sparks vs. Stafford. In Salkeld the Cafe is not fo well reported as the fame in Mod. Rep. 'Tis unneceffary to fet forth Order to redeem; as the Mafter may juftify throwing over Goods in Cafe of a Storm to fave a greater Lofs, fo may he redeem, as otherwife the Whole would be loft. 2 Ld. Raym. 931, Tranter vs. Watfon. As for the Cafe of

Change on Massachusetts Society, 1760–1830, at ix–xvii (Univ. of Ga. Press, 1994) (1975) (outlining hypothesis).

81. See *id.* at 165–74 (focusing on new roles for judge and jury); see also Daniel R. Coquillette, Introduction: The "Countenance of Authoritie," in *Law in Colonial Massachusetts 1630–1800*, *supra*, note 2, at liii–lvi (discussing effects of American Revolution on colonial legal system); William E. Nelson, "The Legal Restraint of Power in Pre-Revolutionary America: Massachusetts as a Case Study, 1760–1775," 18 Am. J. Legal Hist. 1, 13–26, 32 (1974). (noting American courts' divergence from English law).

82. Notes on *Dunn* v. *Scollay*, in *Quincy's Reports*, at 187 (1765); Notes on *Scollay* v. *Dunn*, in *Quincy's Reports*, at 74 (1763).

83. Notes on *Scollay* v. *Dunn*, in *Quincy's Reports*, at 74, 76 (1763).

84. See Notes on *Scollay* v. *Dunn*, in *Quincy's Reports*, at 74, 75, 77–78 (1763) (discussing prohibition issue); see also *Jowitt's Dictionary of English Law*, *supra*, note, 48, at 1443 (reviewing admiralty issue).

85. Notes on *Scollay* v. *Dunn*, in *Quincy's Reports*, at 74, 77–79 (1763).

86. *Id.* at 74–75, 77.

87. *Id.* at 76.

> Johnſon vs. Shippin in Salkeld, that the Maſter by his Contracts cannot make the Owners liable, 6 Mod. 79 is the ſame Caſe, and not ſo reported, beſides there the Contract appeared to have been made at Land; as for the Veſſell's being loſt, 'tis of no Avail—the Owners muſt be bound inſtantly or not at all; if the Maſter has a Right to bind the Owners by his Contract, they are bound, and the Contract cannot be reſcinded but by the Parties, and not depend upon ſuch a Contingency as the Arrival of the Veſſell.[88]

Thacher replied for Scollay that admiralty doctrine is limited to the security of the vessel, and cannot be the basis for personal contract liability for owners without any privity:

> Whether the Owners muſt anſwer in their Perſons for the Act of the Maſter at Sea, of which they were utterly unknowing, is the Queſtion; I take it not the Owners perſonally, for the Thing itſelf is bound. Every Ranſom is a new Purchaſe, and if the Owners are liable in this Caſe, they would be liable if the Maſter had contracted with the Captors for another Ship, and ſent an Hoſtage as a Pawn.[89]

Gridley countered for Dunn:

> There are ſome Things though tranſacted upon the High Sea are not of a Maritime Nature, are not within the Juriſdiction of the Court of Admiralty. Things of a Maritime Nature tranſacted at Sea are undoubtably within its Juriſdiction. So there are ſome Things of a Maritime Nature, though not tranſacted upon the High Seas, that are within the Juriſdiction of the Admiralty; ſuch are Wages of Seamen. There is Nothing that Owners are not liable for, which is neceſſary for the Support of the Voyage; it is no Argument that becauſe the Veſſell is liable, the Owners are not alſo; Veſſell, Maſter, and Owners are all liable for Wages. Viner, Tit. Hypoth. 329, bot.[90]

The Court was split. Justice Oliver held that the admiralty jurisdiction was good.[91] Justice Lynde disagreed, arguing that, if the action "was on the Ship or Cargo," it would have been proper for the Admiralty, "but as it is not, I cannot but be for the Prohibition ſtanding."[92] Chief Justice Hutchinson agreed:

> Ranſom as far as it reſpects Maſter and Hoſtage maritime, ſo far as Owner and Maſter does not appear to be a Contract upon the High Seas. None of the Authorities maintain the Juriſdicition in this Caſe; and where it is doubtfull, I think 'tis a Rule that common Juriſdiction ought to be maintained, and that

88. *Id.* at 76.
89. *Id.* at 77.
90. Notes on *Scollay* v. *Dunn*, in *Quincy's Reports*, at 74, 78 (1763).
91. *Id.* at 78.
92. *Id.* at 78–79.

> the Admiralty Jurifdiction ought to be made plain and clear, which I think is not the Cafe now.[93]

Hutchinson's arguments apparently carried the day, and the prohibition was sustained.[94] Moreover, the Court denied leave to appeal to the King and Council in England, despite fervent arguments by Auchmuty and Gridley that this was a "Cafe of Importance."[95]

Undeterred, Dunn then brought a straight action at common law.[96] Although he initially won a jury verdict of £700 in the Court of Common Pleas,[97] this was apparently set aside by the Superior Court of Judicature, on strict application of common-law privity doctrine.[98]

What does this case say about the theories of Murrin, Horwitz, and Nelson? Certainly, the ultimate outcome was a strict application of English doctrine, at least as the judges understood it. On the other hand, it was a split decision, and the arguments of counsel were full of instrumentalist rationales that were carefully considered by the bench.

Other, less spectacular, cases demonstrated a willingness to adopt customary remedies into the "law," particularly where this served an economic or social end. Such a case was *Bromfield* v. *Little*.[99] The issue was simple. In a straight contract action (*indebitatus assumpsit*) for an account payable, was interest payable after a year on goods sold, because such completed sale would "raife an implied Contract to pay the fame"?[100] The plaintiff argued that although there

93. *Id.* at 79.

94. *Id.*

95. Notes on *Scollay* v. *Dunn*, in *Quincy's Reports*, at 74, 80 (1763); see also *id.* at 80–82 (setting forth counsel's argument). In fact, the hostage in English law usually had a right to proceed in the Admiralty in rem against the ship and cargo to obtain payment of his ransom. See *id.* at 79 n. 2 (observing state of English admiralty law at time of case). The first case of enforceability of ransom bills directly in the King's Bench was exactly contemporaneous with *Dunn* v. *Scollay* in *Ricord* v. *Bettenham*, 3 Burr. 1734, 97 Eng. Rep 1071 (K.B. 1765). There Lord Mansfield, relying on civilian authorities such as Grotius and Pufendorf, entered judgment for the hostage. See Rodgers, *supra*, note 67, at 350–51 (commenting on Lord Mansfield's Notebooks).

96. See Notes on *Dunn* v. *Scollay*, in *Quincy's Reports*, at 187, 187 n. 1 (1765) (listing procedural history of case).

97. *Id.*

98. *Id.* at 187–88.

99. Notes on *Bromfield* v. *Little*, in *Quincy's Reports*, at 108, 108 (1764).

100. *Id.* "*Indebitatus assumpsit*," or "being indebted, he undertook," was the standard form of action for an agreement not under a written, formal covenant. For a complete explanation of the form of action, originally based on a legal fiction to avoid proceeding in debt, see J. H. Baker, *An Introduction to English Legal History* (4th ed., London, 2002), pp. 341–45.

was no specific agreement between the parties on this point, the "Cuftom of Merchants (was) here to charge Intereft after a Year."[101] The Justices permitted "Several Merchants" to be "fworn on this Head, but they did not agree about the Time, neither whether they did or did not firft inform the Debtor."[102] Then the following colloquy occurred, which focused solely on the very practical issue of whether this was an accepted and "reasonable custom":

> In Behalf of Defendant, 'twas faid, there was no fuch Cuftom here at all; yet if it could be faid there was a Cuftom here to charge after Notice either at or after Sale, certainly not before Notice.
>
> Juft. Oliver. Whether this is a reafonable Cuftom muft firft be confidered. I think it is. I think, too, it appears to be a Cuftom.
>
> Juft. Cufhing. This Cafe is very different from what it is at Home; 'tis there the univerfal Ufage, which makes it the Suppofition of every Party at firft; and, as a Perfon purchafing Goods without any fpecial Promife is fuppofed to promife the Payment of the Cuftomary Price, fo he is fuppofed to engage to pay the cuftomary Allowance for Forbearance; but here, however reafonable it may be, it is yet otherwife, nor is it implied in the Contract.
>
> Ch. Juftice. This Cafe is of much Importance to the Community. 'Tis agreeable to natural Equity that Intereft fhould be allowed; and I am glad it is growing into a Cuftom; but the Rule is that both Parties ought at the Time of contracting to underftand it fo, and I doubt whether it is fo general as that it can be fuppofed in this Cafe.[103]

Obviously, the Scollay and Bromfield cases do not, alone, confirm or vitiate the various theses of Murrin, Horwitz or Nelson. But the "tone" in the courtroom, captured so well by Quincy in his careful notation of both the arguments and the judicial exchanges, seems very adventurous. "Instrumentalist" judging was clearly not just a product of the Revolution in Massachusetts, any more than it was in Lord Mansfield's court in London.[104] Further, both counsel and

101. *Id.*

102. *Id.*

103. *Id.* at 108–09. The jury did not allow interest, and the Court let the verdict stand. *Id.* at 109.

104. See C.H.S. Fifoot, *Lord Mansfield* 82–157 (1936) (discussing Mansfield's instrumentalism); see also Daniel R. Coquillette, *The Civilian Writers of Doctors' Commons*, London 282–96 (1988) (outlining contributions of Lord Mansfield); Morton J. Horwitz, "The Historical Foundations of Modern Contract Law," 87 Harv. L. Rev. 917, 928–31 (1974) (interpreting application of contract law in American and English courts); A.W.B. Simpson, "The Horwitz Thesis and the History of Contracts," 46 U. Chi. L. Rev. 533, 565–68 (1979) (commenting on English and American court's handling of contract law).

the bench seem willing to use English precedents loosely, to achieve what they regard as fair. *Quincy's Reports* contain dozens of *Scollay* and *Bromfield*-type cases.[105] Any general thesis about American pre-Revolutionary jurisprudence needs to accommodate this evidence.

C. Law and Society: Of Jane Austen, Bawdy Houses, Slavery, Naked Wives and Entails

Today's Williamsburg is full of costumed "attendants" play acting as the happy men, housewives, and servants of the pre-Revolutionary era.[106] The "Pompeii of Paper" has a much tougher picture of Boston from 1761 to 1772. To begin, *Quincy's Reports* graphically conveys the ugliness of Boston slavery. In *Oliver* v. *Sale*,[107] Oliver sued Sale "for selling him two free Mulattos for Slaves," producing several receipts of "Money for two Negro Boys fold & delivered."[108] There was no question that humans could be bought and sold, and to sell a free human as a slave was simply to fail to deliver on the bargain. As the Chief Justice observed:

> Ch. Juft. Is there not as palpable a Fraud, when a Man sells a Negro as a Slave whom he knows to be free, as when he fells a Bag of Feathers and assures them to be Hops? That he knew them to be free they must prove, or do not support their Declaration.[109]

Ironically, *Oliver* v. *Sale* was later cited in *Merrick* v. *Betts*[110] to establish the existence of a right of slaves to marry prior to the 1780 Constitution, referring to Samuel Quincy's notes.[111]

105. See generally Notes on *Hooton* v. *Grout*, in *Quincy's Reports*, at 343 (1772); Notes on *Apthorp* v. *Shepard*, in *Quincy's Reports*, at 298 (1768); Notes on *Curtis* v. *Nightingale*, in *Quincy's Reports*, at 256 (1767); Notes on *Noble* v. *Smith*, in *Quincy's Reports*, at 254 (1767); Notes on *Pateshall* v. *Apthorp & Wheelwright*, in *Quincy's Reports*, at 179 (1765); Notes on *Russel* v. *Oakes*, in *Quincy's Reports*, at 48 (1763); Notes on *Derumple* v. *Clark*, in *Quincy's Reports*, at 38 (1763).

106. See Michael Olmet, *Official Guide to Colonial Williamsburg* (1995), which is lavishly illustrated.

107. Notes on *Oliver* v. *Sale*, in *Quincy's Reports*, at 29 (1762).

108. *Id.*

109. *Id.* at 32.

110. 214 Mass. 223, 101 N.E. 131 (1913).

111. *Id.* at 226, 101 N.E. at 132. There is actually nothing in the case itself indicating that slaves had such a right. Samuel Quincy's note, added in the 1865 edition, observes:

> The right to marry was secured to them in 1705 by Prov. St. 4 Anne. Anc. Chart. 748. The subsequent records of Boston and other towns show that their banns were published like those of white persons. In 1745, a negro slave obtained from the Governor and Council a

There are other slave and indentured servant cases in *Quincy's Reports*. We have already seen evidence of the slave trade in *Dunn* v. *Scollay*.[112] In *Allison* v. *Cockran*,[113] straight trover is brought "for a Negro," exactly as if he were a bale of cotton.[114] Quincy added a cryptic note, referring to some of the English cases and declaring that slavery could not exist in England. "Qu. if this Action is well brought, for Trover lies not for a Negro."[115] Later, Quincy would have a discussion with a potential Whig sympathizer in England, who observed how lucky it was that Quincy had come, since more than "two thirds of this Island at that time thought the Americans were all negros!"[116] Quincy snapped back that he "did not in the least doubt it, for if I was to judge by the late acts of Parliament, I should suppose that a majority of the people of Great Britain still thought so, for I found that their representatives still treated them as such."[117] In that remark was both a clear acknowledgment of American racism, and the

---

divorce for his wife's adultery with a white man. Jethro Boston's Case, 9 Mass. Archives, 248. In 1758, it was adjudged by the Superior Court of Judicature, that a child of a female slave, "never married according to any of the forms prescribed by the laws of this land," by another slave, who "had kept her company with her master's consent," was not a bastard. Flora's Case, Rec. 1758, fol. 296. And the wife of a slave was not allowed to testify against him. MS. note by John Adams of *Coesar* v. *Taylor*, in Essex, 1772, (Rec. 1772, fol. 91,) in the possession of Hon. Charles Francis Adams; which also shows that the defendant in an action of false imprisonment was not permitted under the general issue to prove that the plaintiff was his slave.

Notes on *Oliver* v. *Sale*, in *Quincy's Reports*, at 29, 30 n. 2 (1762).

112. See note 64, *supra*. See also Notes on *Dunn* v. *Scollay*, in *Quincy's Reports*, at 187, 187 n. 1 (1765).

113. Notes on *Allison* v. *Cockran*, in *Quincy's Reports*, at 94 (1764).

114. *Id.* at 94. "Trover" had become, by the eighteenth century, the general common-law action for the recovery of goods, replacing the old action of "detinue." J. H. Baker, *An Introduction to English Legal History*, 393–394 (4th ed. 2002). "'(T)rover is merely a substitute of the old action of detinue . . . (it) is not now an action ex maleficio, though it is so in form; but it is founded on property.'" *Id.* (quoting Lord Mansfield in *Hambly* v. *Trott*, 1 Cowp. 371, 374, 48 Eng. Rep. 1136, 1137 [K.B. 1776]). The essence of trover is ownership of goods. See *Jowitt's Dictionary of English Law*, *supra*, note 48, at 1810–11 (defining term).

115. Notes on *Allison* v. *Cockran*, in *Quincy's Reports*, at 94, 94 n.* (1764).

116. Quincy, *The London Journal, 1774–1775*, *Quincy Papers*, vol. 1, at 248; Quincy, *supra*, note 7, at 290. This account comes from a "journal" kept by Quincy during his visit to England from 1774 to 1775. See *id.* at 216 (describing writings).

117. *Id.* at 248. Quincy's companion, the "celebrated Col. Barré," then dropped the subject. *Id.* at 288–90. "He smiled, and the discourse dropped." *Id.* at 290. Quincy then noted that Barré had supported the hated Boston Port Bill. *Id.*

ultimate dilemma of fighting a Revolution for human freedom, while so many were to be left slaves.[118]

The situation for women was only marginally better. Husbands who abandoned their wives and children could be held liable to the Overseers of the Poor for support payments, even though they had not "agreed" to the support and there was no privity. Ironically, this is the kind of extension of contract doctrine, based on policy grounds despite lack of privity, that the Court declined to take for the abandoned first mate in the Scollay case![119]

In the "naked wife" case, *Hanlon* v. *Thayer*,[120] the issue was whether a woman with assets who marries a bankrupt husband loses all her belongings to his creditors, including her clothes.[121] The conclusion was "yes" except for "necef-fary wearing Apparell."[122] The Chief Justice observed:

118. Quincy, *supra*, note 7, at 295 (discussing fate of America). Quincy wrote this to his wife on January 7, 1775:

> The ministry, I am well satisfied, are quite undetermined as to the course they must take with regard to America. They will put off the final resolutions to the last moment. I know not, and, any further than mere humanity dictates, I care not, what part they take. If my own countrymen deserve to be free—they will be free. If, born free, they are contented to be slaves, e'en let them bear their burdens.

Id. at 293–297.

119. See Notes on *Brown* v. *Culnon*, in *Quincy's Reports*, at 66, 66 (1763) (recording court's verdict). Samuel Quincy duly notes that the town cannot recover for supplies "suitable to the wife's condition in life, beyond her necessary support as a pauper." *Id.* at 66 n. 1.

120. Notes on *Hanlon* v. *Thayer*, in *Quincy's Reports*, at 99 (1764).

121. *Id.* at 99–100.

122. *Id.* at 100. Auchmuty, arguing for the wife, Hanlon, observed that "what was necessary for one Station in Life was not so for another, and said the Law never meant the Word 'Necessary' in its strictest sense." *Id.* Gridley, for the Sheriff, Thayer, who had seized the clothes, observed:

> Nothing is necessary in the Law but what is necessary to defend from the Inclemency of the Weather, or necessary to the Degree: But before they can talk highly of Degree they must pay their Debts. If any besides what is barely necessary is allowed for Comfort, it is not the Law, but Humanity. The Law here wisely uses the Word Necessary, for the Boundary of Necessity is determinate, but Conveniency not,—Conveniency! What is convenient? &c. (a little Rhetorick and concludes.) Mr. Gridley also said: If a Judge of Probate grant to the Wife of an Intestate whose Estate is insolvent, two Beds, where one only was necessary, the other immediately became liable to be attached, and he cited Hardistey & Barney, (Comber. 356,) where Holt says if the Party have two Gowns, Sheriff may take one.

Id. at 101 (footnote omitted).

Quincy drops a note here to Edward Coke, *The First Part of the Institutes of the Lawes of England*, 351(b) asking if it "would not have been good Authority?" *Id.* at 101 n.*. Coke distinguished

> (here Ch. Juft. makes an Apology for what follows) that this may be one of thofe Cafes where the Juftice fays a Thing obiter, or fuddenly; for one Gown can never be fuppofed fufficient—musft fhe go naked when that is wafhing? Upon the Whole I think it would be very hard upon the Wife, fhould fuch a Precendent as this take Place, that her Cloaths which fhe brought in Marriage muft go to difcharge the Hufband's Debts. I fhould think it fafer to verge towards Conveniency than to ftrain the Word Neceffary.[123]

At least one form of entrepreneurship was recognized for women, running a "Bawdy House." In *Dom. Rex* v. *Doaks*,[124] Mistress Doaks was acquitted because proven "Acts of Lafcivioufnefs" were prior to her acquiring the alleged House, and no proof of character was permitted by the prosecution unless character was made an issue by the defense.[125] Strikingly, Mistress Doaks was the only woman to appear in *Quincy's Reports* alleged to have her own business, if we except Margaret Knodle, a convicted thief.[126] Several cases had women desperately trying to prove marriage to avoid bastardy, or to avoid a charge of murder of a bastard child.[127] Despite earlier progress toward "partibility" and women's rights in property law, Jane Austen would have recognized the fierce battles over property and the importance of the male entail in *Baker* v. *Mat-*

---

between a wife's "personal goods," brought into a marriage, and other property, where there is an action for recovery. See 2 Sir Edward Coke, *The First Part of the Institutes of the Lawes of England* 218–20 (Garland Publ'g 1979) (1628) (discussing wives and feoffment). This remark is just one example of Quincy's acute knowledge of English precedents.

123. Notes on *Hanlon* v. *Thayer*, in *Quincy's Reports*, at 99, 103 (1764). "Justices Oliver & Cushing both said the Case was very hard upon the Wife, who brought all these Cloaths at Marriage, yet 'as they are personal Property, they become the Husband's on Marriage, and therefore liable.'" *Id.* at 102.

The Chief Justice added, scolding the lawyers:

> Ch. Just. I should have been extremely glad if this Cafe had been argued a little more largely by the Gentlemen of the Bar, and more Authorities cited, in Matter of so great Consequence. I always took it to have been the Custom in such Cafes as this, for the Wife to have her Cloaths; in Cases that have come before me as Judge of Probate I never knew it denied to the Wife where the Estate was insolvent.

Id. at 102 (footnote omitted).

124. Notes on *Dom. Rex* v. *Doaks*, in *Quincy's Reports*, at 90 (1763).

125. *Id.* at 90–91.

126. See Notes on *Dom. Rex* v. *Pourksdorff*, in *Quincy's Reports*, at 104, 105 n. 3 (1764) (mentioning case of Margaret Knodle).

127. See Notes on *Dom. Rex* v. *Mangent*, in *Quincy's Reports*, at 162, 163 (1765) (indicting for murder of bastard child); Notes on *Banister* v. *Henderson*, in *Quincy's Reports*, at 119, 121 (1765) (claiming valid marriage existed).

tocks[128] and *Dudley* v. *Dudley*.[129] It was not a pretty picture. Costumes aside, it was better to be white and male in either colonial Williamsburg or Boston.

D. Rule of Law: The Brethren

Quincy's Reports gives a candid and forceful view of the social realities of Massachusetts in the 1760s. It also gives a particularly good view of one little society—fourteen active lawyers and six judges of the Boston legal world, whose arguments, exchanges and even jokes are carefully described.[130] It was

128. Notes on *Baker* v. *Mattocks*, in *Quincy's Reports*, at 69 (1763).

129. Notes on *Dudley* v. *Dudley*, in *Quincy's Reports*, at 12 (1762); see Jane Austen, *Pride and Prejudice* 24 (Harcourt, Brace & World, 1962) (1813) (beginning narrative of sisters' lives on passage of estate to male cousin). There is no opportunity here to adequately describe the important entail cases in *Quincy's Reports*. See the excellent study by Kevin Cox, "Entail on the Eve of Revolution: Cases From the Reports of Josiah Quincy Jr.," 2006, presently unpublished paper on file with the editor. There is no question, however, that the conflict over the will of Governor Dudley, fought out in *Dudley* v. *Dudley*, was one of the most important cases for the Boston Bar, both for the legal principle involved and the money at issue. See Notes on *Dudley* v. *Dudley*, in *Quincy's Reports*, at 12, 12–13 (1762) (outlining issue). The ultimate issue was whether, by Province Law, estates entail are "partible," i.e., capable of being divided equally to all heirs, male and female. *Id.* at 17–18. The Court decided against partibility in *Baker* v. *Mattocks*, but with the Chief Justice doubtful about the outcome. See Notes on *Baker* v. *Mattocks*, in *Quincy's Reports*, at 69, 74 (1763) (expressing doubt regarding outcome and favoring English precedent). Where there was no express provision by will, Province Law had already abolished the English common law of primogeniture (i.e., all land to the eldest male, if one exists). *Id.* at 70 n. 2 (quoting 1692 Mass. Acts 4).

"Whereas estates in these plantations do consist chiefly of lands which have been subdued and brought to improvement by the industry and labour of the proprietors, with the assistance of their children, the younger children generally having been longest and most serviceable unto their parents in that behalf, who have not personal estate to give out unto them in portions, or otherwise to recompense their labour. Sect. I. Be it therefore enacted," &c., "that every person lawfully feifed of any lands, tenements, or hereditaments within this province, in his own proper right in fee simple, shall have power to give, dispose, and devise as well by his last will and testament in writing as otherwise by any act executed in his life, all such lands, tenements, and hereditaments to or among his children or others as he shall think fit at his pleasure, and if no such disposition, gift, or devise be made," then prescribing the rules of descent to all the children. Anc. Chart. 230. *Id.*; see also 1692 Mass. Acts 14 (outlining procedure for distribution of estates).

130. See Memorandum of 1762, included by Samuel Quincy in *Quincy's Reports*, at 35 (listing lawyers on Suffolk docket). The most prominent lawyers appearing before the Superior Court in *Quincy's Reports* were, in alphabetical order: John Adams (1735–1826), Robert Auchmuty (1723–1788), William Brattle (1706–1776), William Cushing (1732–1810), Francis Dana (1743–1811), Samuel Fitch (1724–1799), Benjamin Gridley (1732–circa 1800), his father Jeremiah Gridley (1701–1767), Major Joseph Hawley (1723–1788), James Otis Jr. (1725–1783), Josiah Quincy (1744–1775), his brother, Samuel Quincy (1734–1789), Jonathan Sewall (1729–1790), and Edmund

a very small bar, and the "players" knew each other intimately. But it was also very important. Its importance is usually described in terms of "winners" history—after all, this tiny group included a future President of the United States, John Adams; a future Justice of the new Supreme Court, William Cushing; a signer of the Declaration of Independence and future Attorney General and Justice of the Supreme Judicial Court, Robert Trent Paine; a future Chief Jus-

---

Trowbridge (1709–1793). See *id.* (recording lawyers who appeared during court's term); see also *Register of Bench and Bar*, *supra*, note 7, at xcv–cxiv (providing excellent concise biographies of practitioners). See also McKirdy's excellent study, *supra*, note 9, Appendix IV at 339–58, "Brief Biographies of Lawyers Active in Boston at the Time of *Quincy's Reports*," *Appendix 6*, *Quincy Papers*, vol. 5.

Several of the fourteen, such as Adams, Auchmuty, Cushing, Dana, Fitch, Benjamin Gridley, and Edmund Trowbridge became judges, and Cushing went from the Superior Court to the new United States Supreme Court. *Register of Bench and Bar*, *supra*, note 7, at xcv–cxiv (providing biographic information). Some of these, indeed Quincy himself, were never admitted as full barristers, but appeared in court in any event. See *id.* at cvii (suggesting that Quincy's political belief prevented him from becoming barrister though he practiced unhindered). But see Quincy, *supra*, note 7, at 352–53 (noting Quincy honored with title of "barrister" as inscribed on tombstone). Some admitted as barrister, never appear. See Memorandum, in *Quincy's Reports*, at 35, 35 (1762) (listing all Suffolk barristers); see also McKirdy, *supra*, note 2, app. IV at 339–58 (providing biographical sketches of Massachusetts lawyers); *Register of Bench and Bar*, *supra*, note 7, at xcv–cxiv (providing excellent concise biographies of practitioners). Adams, Cushing, Dana, Hawley, Otis, and Josiah Quincy took the patriot side, while Auchmuty, Brattle, Fitch, Benjamin Gridley, Samuel Quincy, and Sewall were loyalists. See McKirdy, *supra*, note 2, app. IV at 339–58 (listing political affiliations). Trowbridge desperately tried to remain neutral, and Jeremiah Gridley died before the worst of the struggle. See *id.* app. IV at 355 (describing Trowbridge).

The most active judges, in order of appointment, were Benjamin Lynde Jr., Justice from 1746–1771 and Chief Justice from 1771–1772; John Cushing Jr., Justice from 1748–1771 (his son William Cushing above); Chambers Russell, Justice from 1752–1766; Peter Oliver, Justice from 1756–1772, Chief Justice from 1772–1775; Thomas Hutchinson, Chief Justice from 1760–1771 (referred to as simply "Chief Justice" throughout *Quincy's Reports*); and Edmund Trowbridge, Justice from 1767–1775. *Id.* app. I at 329–32. Of the above, only William Cushing and Edmund Trowbridge, known as "The Oracle of the Common Law in New England," could be considered "professional lawyers." See "The Banquet of the Bar of Massachusetts on the 250th Anniversary of the Founding of the Supreme Judicial Court of Massachusetts," in *The Supreme Judicial Court of Massachusetts 1692–1942*, at 1, 36 (1942) (showing painting of Trowbridge). John Cushing, Lynde, and Russell were landed gentlemen of the old school and Oliver and Hutchinson, wealthy merchants. McKirdy, *supra*, note 2, app. I at 330–332; see also Francis S. Drake, *Dictionary of American Biography* 470, 571, 671 (Boston, James R. Osgood & Co. Supp., 1872) (describing Hutchinson, Lynde, and Oliver). There are, of course, many useful secondary sources. See generally Bernard Bailyn, *The Ordeal of Thomas Hutchinson* (1974) (setting scene of troubled times leading up to Revolution); E. Alfred Jones, *The Loyalists of Massachusetts* (1930) (setting scene for Revolution).

tice of Massachusetts, Francis Dana; and three great patriots who were struck down in their prime, James Otis Jr., Major Joseph Hawley, and Josiah Quincy Jr. himself.[131]

But this is only just "winners" history. Half of this tiny band, including some of its most talented members, were loyalists.[132] Benjamin Gridley fought with Timothy Ruggles' Loyalist Corps and went into exile.[133] So did Robert Auchmuty, an able protagonist in many of the most important cases.[134] So did Samuel Fitch and Jonathan Sewall, Josiah Quincy's close friends.[135] William Brattle also took to the Tory cause.[136] So, most poignantly, did Josiah's own brother, Samuel Quincy, who ended up as a barrister in Antigua.[137] One, the skilled and knowledgeable Edmund Trowbridge, clung to neutrality, thus losing all chances for further advancement.[138] Mercifully, the great "dean" of the Boston bar, Benjamin Gridley's father and John Adams's teacher, Jeremiah Gridley, died in 1767, before he had to see his sons and students go to war with each other.[139]

And the outcome could have been very different. As Adams fully recognized, it really was glory or the gallows for the patriots.[140] Brattle, Gridley, and Auchmuty could have been the leaders of a powerful, reunited Province. As it turned out, it was the loyalists who lost everything.

Quincy's Reports contains direct reports of some of the most traumatic events of the day, including the dramatic appearance of Chief Justice Hutchinson in

131. McKirdy, *supra*, note 2, app. IV at 339, 342–45, 348–50.

132. See *id.* (listing political affiliations); see also Jones, *supra*, note 130, at xiii (listing other loyalists of time).

133. McKirdy, *supra*, note 2, app. IV at 344.

134. *Id.* app. IV at 339–40.

135. *Id.* app. IV at 343–44, 352–54.

136. *Id.* app. IV at 341–42.

137. *Id.* app. IV at 350–51.

138. McKirdy, *supra*, note 2, app. IV at 355.

139. See *Register of Bench and Bar*, *supra*, note 7, at ci (recounting his historical significance).

140. See Coquillette, *supra*, note 2, at 405–16 (describing Adams's political viewpoint); see also John C. Miller, *Origins of the American Revolution* 425–28 (1943) (describing conditions in Great Britain and America). Adams did not view his objection to the activities of the Parliament as legally rebellious, but he certainly understood the risks. Adams observed that, if the colonialist cause was lost, patriots like himself would "'not only be slaves—but the most abject sort of slaves to the worst sort of masters!'" Miller, *supra*, at 425. Compare *id.* (listing Adams' "slavery" remarks), with *supra*, notes 114–17 and accompanying text (listing Quincy's comments).

borrowed clothes after his house had been destroyed by the mob the night before.[141] Also of great importance was the second argument of *Paxton's Case*, the famous "Writs of Assistance Case,"[142] and accounts relating to the trial of Captain Preston and the British Soldiers, the famous "Boston Massacre Trial."[143] Many other political events and trials were noted by Quincy and he carefully recorded the Chief Justice's annual charge to the Grand Jury, an excellent political barometer.[144]

But the ultimate political and professional lessons of *Quincy's Reports* are very different from what one might expect. We know that Josiah Quincy Jr. was a lawyer by day, and a member of the secret Committee of Correspondence by night.[145] We know that six of these lawyers would be expelled and rejected, and that seven would become famous "patriots" and/or great men in the new republic. But the lesson, graphically and carefully taught by those pages, is not the expected and obvious one of dissension, division, and hatred. Most surprisingly, it is one of solidarity and mutual professionalism, in the face of a crumbling political order. Patriots and loyalists alike adhered to their understanding of English legal rights, legal process, and legal professionalism, even in the face of intense political pressure. It is remarkable that the so-called "Sodalitas Club," with both patriot and loyalist lawyers as members, was founded in 1767, and met for regular, collegial dinners.[146] Or that the first bar association, the Suffolk Bar Association, was founded in 1770, with John Adams as secretary.[147]

141. See *Address of the Chief Justice*, in *Quincy's Reports*, at 171, 171–73 (1765) (recording Chief Justice's remarks).

142. See *Paxton's Case of the Writ of Assistance*, in *Quincy's Reports*, at 51 (1761).

143. See *Petition of the Jurors in the Trials of Captain Preston and the British Soldiers*, in *Quincy's Reports*, at 382, 382–86 (1771) (recording observations of trial).

144. Memoranda, in *Quincy's Reports*, at 316, 316–17 (1769); *Charge of the Chief Justice*, in *Quincy's Reports*, at 306, 306–15 (1769); *Chief Justice's Charge to the Grand Jury*, in *Quincy's Reports*, at 301, 301–05 (1768); *Charge given to the Grand Jury by the Chief Justice*, in *Quincy's Reports*, at 258, 258–71 (1768); *Charge of the Chief Justice to the Grand Jury*, in *Quincy's Reports*, at 241, 241–48 (1767); *Charge to the Grand Jury by the Chief Justice*, in *Quincy's Reports*, at 232, 232–37 (1767); *Charge to the Grand Jury by the Chief Justice*, in *Quincy's Reports*, at 218, 218–24 (1766); *Charge by the Chief Justice given on the Adjournment*, in *Quincy's Reports*, at 175, 175–79 (1765); *Charge to the Grand Jury by the Chief Justice*, in *Quincy's Reports*, at 110, 110–17 (1765).

145. *Quincy Papers*, vol. 1, *supra*, note 7, at 11 (introducing Quincy's articles under pseudonym Hyperion).

146. See *Register of Bench and Bar*, *supra*, note 7, at ci (crediting Jeremiah Gridley with establishment of legal discussion group).

147. Coquillette, *supra*, note 2, at 395–97.

There are many examples of this professionalism in *Quincy's Reports*. Let me select just three: the reaction to the looting of the Chief Justice's house in 1765, the Stamp Act arguments of 1765, and the Boston Massacre Trial of 1771. Perhaps the most dramatic event was the destruction of the Chief Justice's house, on August 27, 1765, in response to the passage of the Stamp Act.[148] Quincy's political sympathies were clearly against the Stamp Act, but the entire bar united in condemning the lawlessness of the mob. Quincy's description in the Reports leaves no question of his sincerity, and also his allegiance to legal process:

> The Deſtruction was really amazing; for it was equal to the Fury of the Onſet; but what above all is to be lamented, is the Loſs of ſome of the most valuable Records of the Country, and other antient Papers; for, as his Honour was continuing his Hiſtory, the oldeſt and moſt important Writings and Records of the Province, which he had ſelected with great Care, Pains and Expenſe, were in his Poſſeſſion. This is a Loſs greatly to be deplored, as it is abſolutely irretrievable.
>
> The Diſtreſs a Man muſt feel on ſuch an Occaſion can only be conceived by thoſe, who, the next Day, ſaw his Honour the Chief Juſtice come into Court, with a Look big with the greateſt Anxiety, cloathed in a Manner which would have excited Compaſſion from the hardeſt Heart, though his Dreſs had not been ſtrikingly contraſted by the other Judges and Bar, who appeared in their Robes.—Such a Man, in ſuch a Station, thus habited, with Tears ſtarting from his Eyes, and a Countenance which ſtrongly told the inward Anguiſh of his Soul,—what muſt an Audience have felt, whoſe Compaſſion had before been moved by what they knew he had ſuffered, when they heard him pronounce the following Words, in a Manner which the Agitations of his Mind dictated![149]

For his part, the Chief Justice was careful to point out his personal opposition to the Stamp Act, and his awareness of what provoked the violence.

> The Chief Juſtice, addreſſing the whole Court, ſaid,—
>
> Gentlemen:
>
> There not being a Quorum of the Court without me, I am obliged to appear. Some Apology is neceſſary for my Dreſs—indeed I had no other. Deſtitute of Everything—no other Shirt—no other Garment, but what I have on.—And

148. See *Destruction of the House of the Chief Justice*, in *Quincy's Reports*, at 168, 168–71 (1765) (recounting chain of events); see also *Address of the Chief Justice*, in *Quincy's Reports*, at 171, 171–74 (1765) (recording Chief Justice's reaction to events).

149. *Destruction of the House of the Chief Justice*, in *Quincy's Reports*, at 168, 170–71 (1765).

> not one in my whole Family in a better Situation than myſelf. The Diſtreſs of a whole Family around me, young and tender Infants hanging about me, are infinitely more inſupportable than what I feel for myſelf; though I am obliged to borrow Part of this Cloathing.
>
> Senſible that I am innocent, that all the Charges againſt me are falſe, I cannot help feeling:—And, though I am not obliged to give an Anſwer to all the Queſtions that may be put me by every lawleſs Perſon—yet I call GOD to witneſs,—and I would not for a thouſand Worlds call my Maker to witneſs to a Falſehood,—I ſay, I call my Maker to witneſs, that I never, in New England or Old, in Great Britain or America, neither directly nor indirectly, was aiding, aſſiſting or ſupporting, or in the leaſt promoting or incouraging what is commonly called the Stamp Act; but, on the contrary, did all in my Power, and ſtrove as much as in me lay, to prevent it.—This is not declared through Timidity, for I have Nothing to fear.—They can only take away my Life, which is of but little Value when deprived of all its Comforts, all that is dear to me, and nothing ſurrounding me, but the moſt piercing Diſtreſs.[150]

Quincy concluded his account with an uncharacteristic, but revealing, outburst:

> Who, that ſees the Fury and Inſtability of the Populace, but would ſeek Protection under the Arm of Power? Who that beholds the Tyranny and Oppreſſion of arbitrary Power, but would loſe his Life in Defence of his Liberty? Who, that marks the riotous Tumult, Confuſion and Uproar of a democratic—the Slavery and Diſtreſs of a deſpotic State, the infinite Miſeries attendant on both, but would fly for Refuge from the mad Rage of the one, and oppreſſive Power of the other, to that beſt Aſyslum, that Glorious Medium, the BRITISH CONSTITUTION! Happy People! who enjoy this bleſſed Conſtitution. Happy! thrice happy People! if ye preſerve it inviolate. May ye never loſe it through a licentious Abuſe of your invaluable Rights and Blood-purchaſed Liberties! May ye never forfeit it by a tame and infamous Submiſſion to the Yoke of Slavery and lawleſs Despotism.[151]

Equally important was the genuine distress of the entire bar at the closing of the courts by the Stamp Act. Cynics could ascribe this to loss of legal business, but these fourteen lawyers would suffer far more for their beliefs. Both sides seemed genuinely convinced that it was the legal process that bound their society, and all civilized societies, together. Arguments about the Stamp Act are among the most important records in *Quincy's Reports*. Particularly important were the arguments of Jeremiah Gridley, James Otis Jr. and John Adams,

150. *Address of the Chief Justice*, in *Quincy's Reports*, at 171, 171–72.
151. *Id.* at 173–74.

on behalf of the Town of Boston, to the Governor in Council.[152] Jeremiah Gridley, it will be remembered, was no revolutionary, and his son Benjamin fought for the Tory side, whereas both Otis and Adams were known to be of the other side. Yet all three delivered a professional, and measured legal argument for their client, urging the opening of the courts.[153] Equally significant, all three invoked British constitutional authority, citing *Coke's Reports*, the *Magna Carta*, and even the great medieval source of the British Constitution, Bracton's *De Legibus*.[154] Particularly revealing was Otis's great argument:

> Mr. Otis (opened with Tears). It is with great Grief that I appear before your Excellency and Honours on this Occaſion. A wicked and unfeeling Miniſter has cauſed a People, the moſt loyal and affectionate that ever King was bleſſed with, to groan under the moſt inſupportable Oppreſſion. But I think, Sir, that he now ſtands upon the Brink of inevitable Deſtruction; and truſt that ſoon—very ſoon, he will feel the full Weight of his injured Sovereign's righteous Indignation. I have no doubt, Sir, but that the loyal and dutiful Repreſentations of nine Provinces, the Cries and Supplications of a diſtreſſed People, the united Voice of all of his Majeſty's moſt loyal and affectionate Britiſh-American Subjects, will obtain all that ample Redreſs they have a Right to expect; and that e'er long, they will ſee their cruel and inſidious Enemies, both at Home and abroad, put to Shame and Confuſion.
>
> . . .
>
> But the Time is far ſpent—I will not tire your Patience. It was once a fundamental Maxim, that every Subject had the ſame Right to his Life, Liberty, Property and the Law, that the King had to his Crown; and 'tis yet, I venture to ſay, as much as a Crown is worth, to deny the Subject his Law, which is his Birth-right. 'Tis a firſt Principle, "that Majeſty ſhould not only ſhine in Arms, but be armed with the Laws." The Adminiſtration of Juſtice is neceſſary to the very Exiſtence of Governments. Nothing can warrant the ſtopping the Courſe of Juſtice, but the impoſſibility of holding Courts, by Reaſon of War, Invaſion, Rebellion or Inſurrections. 1 Inſt. 249, a & b. This was Law at a Time when the whole Iſland of Great Britain was divided into an infinite Number of petty Baronies and Principalities; as Germany is, at this Day. Inſurrections then, and even Invaſions, put the whole Nation into ſuch Confuſion, that Juſtice could not have her equal Courſe; eſpecially as the Kings in antient Times frequently ſat as Judges. But War has now become ſo much of a Science, and gives ſo little Diſturbance to a Nation engaged, that no War, foreign or domeſtic, is a ſufficient Reaſon for ſhutting up the Courts. But, if it were, we are not in ſuch

152. *Memorial of the Town of Boston*, in *Quincy's Reports*, at 198, 198 (1765).
153. *Id.* at 198–209.
154. *Id.*; see *infra*, note 155 (discussing Bracton).

> a State, but far otherwife; the whole People being willing and demanding the full Adminiftration of Government. Vid. Bracton, 240.[155]

This devotion to the rule of law and the legal process was also reflected in the extraordinary Trial of Captain Preston and the British Soldiers.[156] Every school child knows that John Adams and Josiah Quincy Jr. undertook the defense of the British soldiers. It has even been suggested that this was a clever political maneuver, but contemporary records, including desperately worried letters from Quincy's father, make it clear that the assignment was both dangerous and problematic.[157]

155. *Memorial of the Town of Boston*, in *Quincy's Reports*, at 198, 202–04 (1765). The citation is to the great medieval treatise, Bracton, *De Legibus et Consuetudinibus Angliae* (circa 1235). This is a compelling appeal to the wellspring of English fundamental law, for Bracton was also invoked by the great English Chief Justice, Edward Coke, in personally confronting King James I in the case of the Prohibitions Del Roy. 12 Co. Rep. 63, 77 Eng. Rep. 1342 (K.B. 1608). Quincy's *Law Commonplace* has many citations to *Coke's Reports*. See *supra*, note 22 (listing some of Quincy's English citations). Otis's actual *Bracton* page citation, apparently to the "star pages" of the printed edition of 1569, does reference a discussion of the conditions of war and peace, but is otherwise inappropriate. The same is true of the 2nd edition in 1640. No other edition was available before 1878. See *Sweet & Maxwell's Legal Bibliogrphy* (2nd ed., W. H. Maxwell, L. F. Maxwell, 1989), 51.

156. *Petition of the Jurors in the Trials of Captain Preston and the British Soldiers*, in *Quincy's Reports*, at 382, 382 n. 1 (1771).

157. See Quincy, *supra*, note 7, at 34–35 (reprinting letter of Quincy Sr.). Quincy Senior wrote to his son as follows on March 22, 1770:

> My dear Son,
>
> I am under great affliction, at hearing the bitterest reproaches uttered against you, for having become an advocate for those criminals who are charged with the murder of their fellow-citizens. Good God! Is it possible? I will not believe it.
>
> Just before I returned home from Boston, I knew, indeed, that on the day those criminals were committed to prison, a sergeant had inquired for you at your brother's house,—but I had no apprehension that it was possible an application would be made to you to undertake their defence. Since then I have been told that you have actually engaged for Captain Preston; —and I have heard the severest reflections made upon the occasion, by men who had just before manifested the highest esteem for you, as one destined to be a saviour of your country.
>
> I must own to you, it has filled the bosom of your aged and infirm parent with anxiety and distress, lest it should not only prove true, but destructive of your reputation and interest; and I repeat, I will not believe it, unless it be confirmed by your own mouth, or under your own hand.
>
> Your anxious and distressed parent,
> Josiah Quincy.
>
> *Id.*

Quincy's reply to his father of March 26, 1770, remains a classic of professionalism.

> Honoured Sir,
>
> I have little leisure, and less inclination either to know, or to take notice, of those ignorant slanderers, who have dared to utter their "bitter reproaches" in your hearing against me, for having become an advocate for criminals charged with murder. But the sting of reproach when envenomed only by envy and falsehood, will never prove mortal. Before pouring their

Less well known is the fact that the prosecution was handled by a stalwart loyalist, Josiah's brother Samuel, and Robert Treat Paine, a patriot.[158] Auchmuty, a loyalist, also assisted John Adams on the defense.[159] The lesson from the Massacre trial was not about political manipulation, but about bar solidarity in the face of the the most divisive case of their generation. The self-conscious unity of the bar, their "Sodalitas," is evident at every turn.[160] And *Quincy's Reports* contains much contemporary evidence of this unity.[161] The Chief Justice, at the end of the tortured court session of 1765 in which his own house was destroyed, could still observe:

> GENTLEMEN of the Bar: I cannot but with Pleafure obferve to you the Harmony which has fubfifted between all of you in our prefent Seffion, and that Unanimity and Order which has prevailed univerfally amongft us through this whole Term. I the rather obferve this, becaufe, in moft Parts of the Province there has been great Difturbances. I thought this Notice juftly due, and cannot but hope 'twill ferve as a future Precedent to us all, and a good Example to the Community.[162]

---

reproaches into the ear of the aged and infirm, if they had been friends, they would have surely spared a little reflection on the nature of an attorney's oath, and duty;—some trifling scrutiny into the business and discharge of his office, and some small portion of patience in viewing my past and future conduct.

Let such be told, Sir, that these criminals, charged with murder, are not yet legally proved guilty, and therefore, however criminal, are entitled, by the laws of God and man, to all legal counsel and aid; that my duty as a man obliged me to undertake; that my duty as a lawyer strengthened the obligation; that from abundant caution, I at first declined being engaged; that after the best advice, and most mature deliberation had determined my judgment, I waited on Captain Preston, and told him that I would afford him my assistance; but, prior to this, in presence of two of his friends, I made the most explicit declaration to him, of my real opinion, on the contests (as I expressed it to him) of the times, and that my heart and hand were indissolubly attached to the cause of my country; and finally, that I refused all engagement, until advised and urged to undertake it, by an Adams, a Hancock, a Molineux, a Cushing, a Henshaw, a Pemberton, a Warren, a Cooper, and a Phillips. This and much more might be told with great truth, and I dare affirm, that you, and this whole people will one day rejoice, that I became an advocate for the aforesaid "criminals," charged with the murder of our fellow-citizens.

Id. at 36–37.

158. See 3 *Legal Papers of John Adams, supra*, note 7, at 1–98; (providing detailed description of case and surrounding events); *Petition of the Jurors in the Trials of Captain Preston and the British Soldiers*, in *Quincy's Reports*, at 382, 382–86 (1771).

159. 3 *Legal Papers of John Adams, supra*, note 7, at 6, 15–16.

160. See Coquillette, *supra*, note 2, at 376–82 (describing members and purpose of Sodalitas Club).

161. See generally *Address by the Chief Justice*, in *Quincy's Reports*, at 197 (1765).

162. *Id.* at 197.

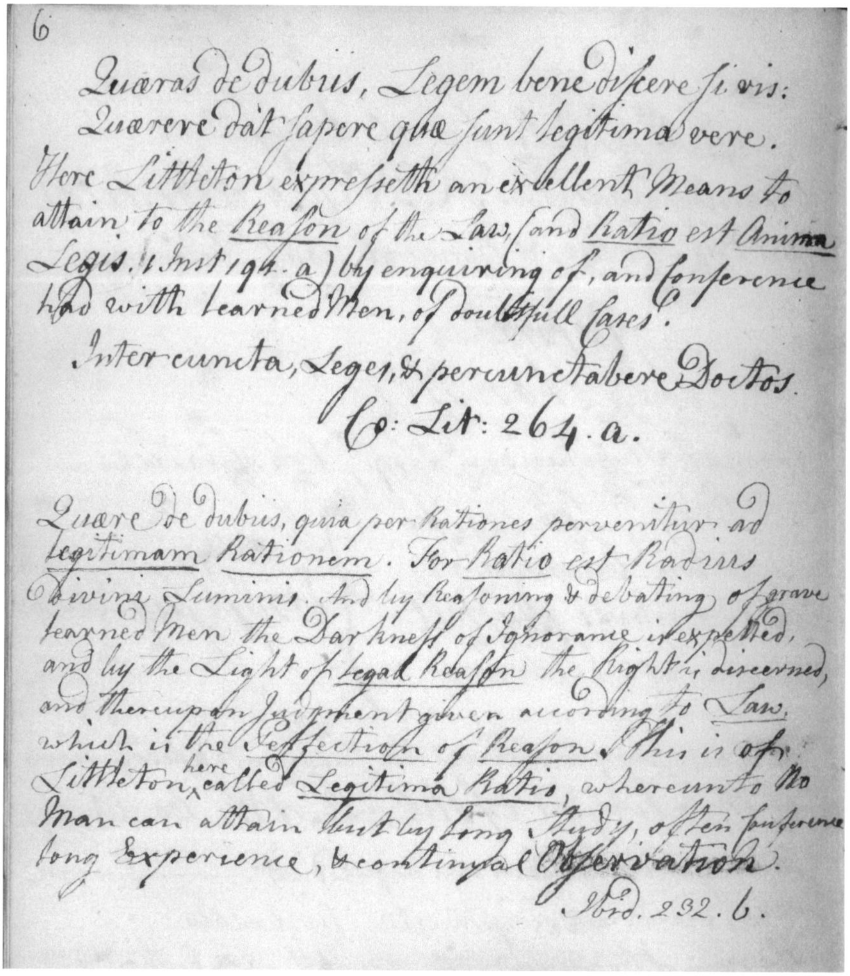

ILLUSTRATION 8: Josiah Quincy Jr.'s *Law Reports*, Massachusetts Historical Society, P347, Reel 4, QP57, pp. 6–7. Title pages of Commencement of August Term, 1764. This would precede *Quincy's Reports*, p. 94, *Allison* v. *Cockran* (Case 36, 1974). The facing quotations read as follows:

> *Quaeras de dubiis, Legem bene discere si vis:*
> *Quaerere dat sapere quae sunt legitima vere.*[1]

> Here Littleton expresseth an excellent Means to
> Attain to the *Reason* of the Law, (and *Ratio est Anima*
> *Legis.*[2] 1 Inst 191.a) by enquiring of, and Conference
> Had with Learned Men, of doubtfull Cases.

> *Inter cuncta, Leges, & percunctabere Doctos.*[3]
> Co: Lit: 264.a.

> *Quaere de dubiis, quia per Rationed pervenitur ad*
> *Legitimam Rationem.* For *Ratio est Radius*
> *Divini Luminis.*[4] And by Reasoning and debating of grave
> Learned Men the Darkness of Ignorance is expelled,
> And by the Light of Legal Reason the Right is discerned,
> And thereupon Judgment given according to Law,

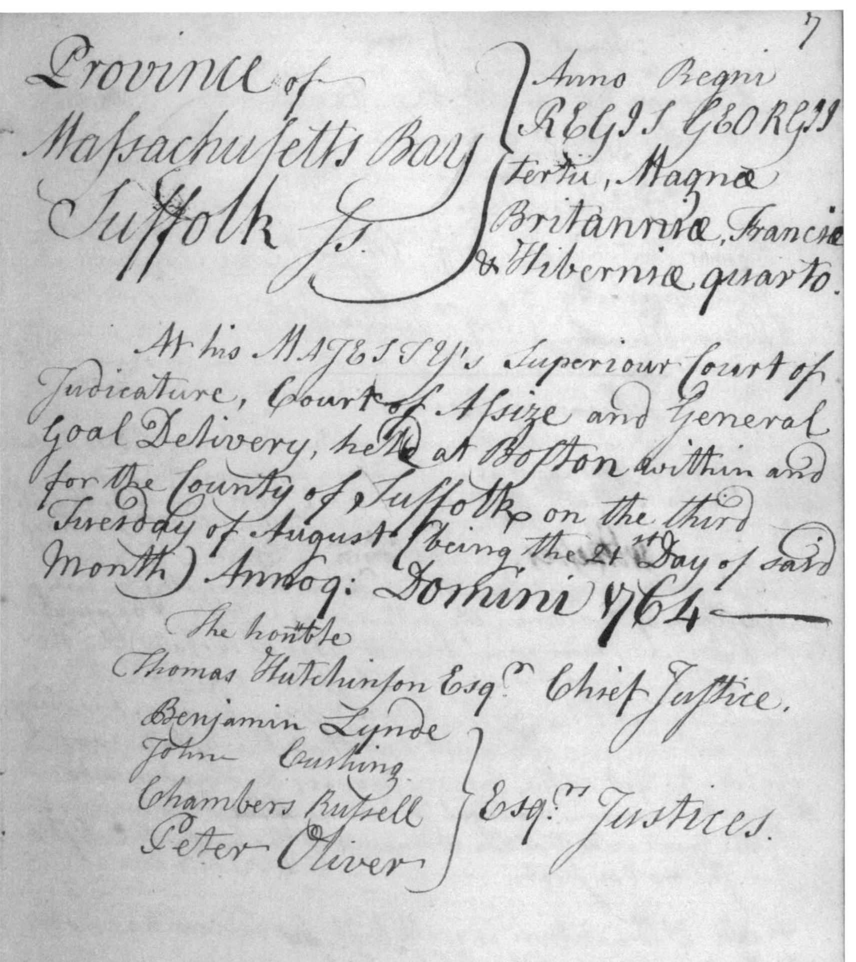
7

Province of Massachusetts Bay Suffolk ss. } Anno Regni REGIS GEORGII tertii, Magnæ Britanniæ, Franciæ & Hiberniæ quarto.

At his MAJESTY's Superiour Court of Judicature, Court of Assize and General Goal Delivery, held at Boston within and for the County of Suffolk on the third Tuesday of August (being the 21st Day of said Month) Annoq: Domini 1764—

The honble
Thomas Hutchinson Esqr. Chief Justice.
Benjamin Lynde
John Cushing
Chambers Russell
Peter Oliver } Esqrs. Justices.

> which is the Perfection of Reason. This is of Littleton here called *Legitima Ratio*,[5] whereunto No Man can attain but by Long Study, often Conference, Long Experience, & continual Observation.
>
> *Ibid. 232.b.*

Both quotations are almost exactly from "Coke on Littleton," Edward Coke, *The First Part of the Institutes of the Lawes of England*, see *Law Commonplace*, *supra*, [2], n.2. I am most grateful, as always, to my excellent student and colleague, Elizabeth Papp Kamali, for the Latin translations as follows:

1. "Inquire into doubtful matters, if you wish to learn the law well. Inquiry gives understanding as to what is truly lawful."
2. "Reason is the spirit of the law."
3. "At all times, you will read, and you will inquire of the wise." (Note that Coke has borrowed here from Horace, and the expected verb is *percontabere*.)
4. "Inquire into doubtful matters, because through reflection lawful reason is reached. For reason is the ray of divine light."
5. "Lawful reason."

Image courtesy of the Massachusetts Historical Society.

No wonder Josiah Quincy Jr. believed that, by appeal to the traditions of the English common law—that "blessed Constitution," there still might be an alternative to violent revolution.[163] No wonder that, on September 28, 1774, he secretly set sail for England, hoping that these principles, and his legal advocacy, could avert a bloody, fratricidal war.[164] It was a belief for which he died.[165]

163. See Quincy, *supra*, note 7, at 158–60 (noting Quincy's view on Revolution). Quincy's letters relating to his voyage of September 28, 1774, and his "Journal" of his visit to England from 1774–1775 are of particular importance. See *The London Journal: 1774–1775*, *Quincy Papers*, vol. 1, pp. 219–269. In one letter, Quincy observed to John Dickinson, the eminent Philadelphian lawyer and future Framer of the Constitution:

> *Sobrius esto* is our present motto. At the urgent solicitation of a great number of warm friends to my country and myself, I have agreed to relinquish business, and embark for London, and shall sail in eighteen days certainly. I am flattered by those who perhaps place too great confidence in me, that I may do some good the ensuing winter, at the court of Great Britain. Hence I have taken this unexpected resolution. My design is to be kept as long secret as possible,—I hope till I get to Europe. Should it transpire that I was going home, our public enemies here would be as indefatigable and persevering to my injury, as they have been to the cause in which I am engaged, heart and hand; perhaps more so, as personal pique would be added to public malevolence.
>
> I would solicit, earnestly, intelligence from you, sir, while in London. I shall endeavour to procure the earliest information from all parts of the continent. As I propose dedicating myself wholly to the service of my country, I shall stand in need of the aid of every friend of America; and believe me, when I say, that I esteem none more capable of affording me that aid, than those who inhabit the fertile banks of the Delaware.

Quincy, *Memoir, supra,* note 7, at 173.

164. See *id.* at 217 (describing departure for England). In England, he soon realized the immensity of his task, but his patriotism was unshaken. Thus, Quincy wrote to his loyal wife, Abigail, on January 7, 1775:

> Oh! my dear friend! my heart beats high in the cause of my country. Their safety, their honour, their all is at stake! I see America placed in that great "tide in the affairs of men, which, taken at the flood, leads on to fortune." Oh! snatch the glorious opportunity. Oh! for a "warning voice,"—or our lives are bound in vassalage and misery.
>
> The ministry, I am well satisfied, are quite undetermined as to the course they must take with regard to America. They will put off the final resolutions to the last moment. I know not, and, any further than mere humanity dictates, I care not, what part they take. If my own countrymen deserve to be free—they will be free. If, born free, they are contented to be slaves, e'en let them bear their burdens.

Id. at 295.

165. *Id.* at 348. Quincy died of his tuberculosis on the return voyage from England. Shaw, *supra*, note 7, at 155. He was in sight of Cape Ann and Gloucester Harbor, where his loyal wife, Abigail, was hurrying to meet him. See Neil L. York, "A Life Cut Short," *Quincy Papers*, vol. 1, *supra*, at 43–44. See also Quincy, *supra*, note 7, at 346–50.

V. CONCLUSION

Today we live in the democracy envisaged by Quincy and his patriot colleagues. It is still served and protected by a powerful legal profession. But our profession is torn by doubt and lack of self-respect. Effective representation has come, for some lawyers, to mean, "scorched earth tactics," disrespect for the judicial process, and disrespect for each other.[166] *Quincy's Reports* depicts a small band of lawyers struggling to keep alive a judicial system in the face of imminent civil violence and growing hatred. Patriots and loyalists alike, they saw themselves as sharing a great professional tradition and a devotion to the rule of law. It was a devotion that superceded their politics, their special interests, and even, in Josiah Quincy's case, life itself.

Quincy died carrying oral secrets about support among the "most stanch friendly to America." He observed in his shipboard notes of April 21, 1775:

> It appeared of high importance that the sentiments of such persons should be known in America. To commit their sentiments to writing, was neither practicable nor prudent at this time. To the bosom of a friend they could intrust what might be of great advantage to my country. To me that trust was committed, and I was, immediately upon my arrival, to assemble certain persons, to whom I was to communicate my trust, and had God spared my life, it seems it would have been of great service to my country.

Quincy, *supra*, note 7, at 347.

The date of Quincy's death was April 26, 1775. On April 19, 1775, the fighting began at Lexington and Concord. Quincy's son was three years old at his father's death. He would become Mayor of Boston and President of Harvard, and would eventually carry his mother's body and lay it, 23 years later, beside his father's in the family tomb on March 25, 1798. See *id.* at 353 (listing location of Quincy's and wife's remains).

166. See "'. . . In the Spirit of Public Service:' A Blueprint for the Rekindling of Lawyer Professionalism," *Report of the American Bar Association Commission on Professionalism* 1–16 (1986), reprinted in 112 F.R.D. 243 (1986). The problem is not going away. See William C. Kelly Jr., "Reflections on Lawyer Morale and Public Service in an Age of Diminishing Expectations," *The Law Firm and the Public Good* (Robert A. Katzmann ed., 1995) 90–101 (recounting problems occurring in law firms); Darlene Ricker, "Greed, Ignorance and Overbilling," A.B.A. J., Aug. 1994, at 62, 62–66 (discussing problems with profession); see also Rob Atkinson, "A Dissenter's Commentary on the Professionalism Crusade," 74 Tex. L. Rev. 259, 264–69, 343 (1995) (cautioning against over-simplifying solutions while simultaneously acknowledging that problem exists). My approach is set out in two publications. Daniel R. Coquillette, *Lawyers and Fundamental Moral Responsibility* 251–64 (1995); Daniel R. Coquillette, "Professionalism: The Deep Theory," 72 N.C. L. Rev. 1271, 1271–77 (1994).

THE REPORTS

PART ONE

1761–1765

CASE I

Auguſt Term

II Georgii Ter. in Sup. Cur.

Preſent:

The Honourable

Thomas Hutchinſon, Eſqr., Chief Juſtice.
Benja: Lynde,
John Cuſhing, } Eſqrs., Juſtices.
Peter Oliver,

1762.

POOR *v.* DOUGHARTY.

Rec. 1763. Fol. 105.

Poor *verſ.* Dougharty.

A Juſtice of the Peace cannot be admitted to teſtify to any Matter which came before him judicially, although he kept no Record of the Tranſaction.

In an Action for falſe Impriſonment, the Juſtice's Mittimus, on which the Plaintiff was committed.

THE Defendant Dougharty loſt ſome Goods, which he ſuſpected Poor had ſtolen; upon which Complaint was made to a Juſtice of the Peace, who heard their ſeveral Stories, and ordered Poor to Goal for further Examination. Poor was again examined, but Dougharty not appearing, was diſcharged, and ſuffered to go without Day. The Juſtice kept no Record of any Part of the Tranſaction. The preſent Action was commenced by Poor *vs.* Dougharty for falſe Impriſonment. *The Juſtice was offered as a Witneſs* to prove the Facts alledged, and objected to, for that whatever came before him was Matter of Record, for a Juſtice's Court is a Court of Record, and that no Parol Evidence

1

Poor v. *Dougharty* (1762)
2 George III (Aug.) in the
Superior Court of Judicature

1 · BRIEF DESCRIPTION

This was a very appropriate first case for *Quincy's Reports* (hereafter, *Reports*). It featured a hotly contested issue of evidence, and a narrowly divided court. The advocates were most distinguished, Otis and Thacher for the Plaintiff, and Gridley for the Defendant. Of particular interest was the use, on both sides, of English precedents.

The Defendant, Dougharty, "lost some goods," and accused Poor of stealing them before a Justice of the Peace. The justice ordered Poor to be examined again, but Dougharty did not appear, and Poor was dismissed. Poor then sued Dougharty in trespass for false imprisonment. But there was no record of the proceeding, as the "justice kept no Record . . . ," so Poor called the Justice as a witness.

The Court unanimously concluded that the Justice of the Peace could not give parol (oral or extrinsic) evidence of proceedings in a court of record.

The Court divided sharply, however, on the admissibility before the jury of the justice's *mittimus* (i.e., "we send," a writ used in sending a record from one court to another) ordering the Defendant to appear. The *mittimus* properly proved the fact of the arrest, but it also contained an inadmissible recitation of facts below. The members of the Court present at trial divided evenly on the question, with the effect of preventing any action, and the issue was held over for consideration by the full Court. The full Court ruled the *mittimus* admissible, by a 3–2 vote, for the limited purpose of proving the arrest. Justices Oliver and Cushing were in dissent.

2 · COURT RECORDS

Available, Rec. 1763, Fol. 105.

Indicates that "the said Poor recovered of said Dougharty four pounds lawfull money of this pro— [province?], damage and costs taxed at £20:0:6."

The records also contain:

- Affidavit of Parker, illegible, stating the substance of what Dougharty told him about the theft of nine handkerchiefs. At the top is written,

is not Evidence of the Facts therein recited.
But it may go to the Jury as a Mittimus. *Oliver & Cushing, JJ., diff.*
Whether a Paper shall go to the Jury or not when the Court is equally divided on that Question — *quære.*

dence can be given of that which is Matter of Record. For this was cited 2 Lilly, 419; Wood's Inst. Com. Law, 82.

Messrs. Otis & Thacher. It was said contrary, that though it be Matter of Record, yet, if it is not recorded, then the Justice may be called. The only Rule being that you shall produce the best Evidence you can. Now as Poor is unable to produce Record, not through any Default of his own, he may be allowed to produce Parol Evidence. That if a Record is burnt, they may swear Witnesses to prove the Fact which had been recorded, and this within the same Reason. Authorities cited: 1 Salk. 14; 1 Strange, 691; Viner, Tit. Evid. 56; 7 Mod. 169; 2 Show. 145.

Mr. Gridley. It was said further, for the Defendant, what is in Court must be proved by Record, what is *in Pais* by Witnesses; Anything which passes before a Court is not Matter of Fact, but of Record.

The Court (1) upon this Point *ruled* unanimously, that the Justice should not be sworn to Anything that came before him judicially. (2)

Then

---

(1) Under the Provincial Government, the Superior Court of Judicature consisted of five judges, and was held for all purposes by a full bench. All jury trials were conducted in the presence of the full Court, and not less than three judges were competent to preside. Anc. Chart. 330. 9 Pick. 569.

(2) S. P. *Sayles* v. *Briggs*, 4 Met. 421. There the justice was offered to prove facts of which he should have made a record. Mr. Justice Hubbard says: "It is argued that this testimony should be received from necessity,

"Mr. Parker Evidence." It appears to have been ordered by Justice Wells and both parties were present when the affidavit was written.

- Deposition of Capt. Stephen Brown—only the cover page.

3 · PROFESSIONALS INVOLVED

James Otis Jr. (1725–1783), Oxenbridge Thacher (1719–1765) for the Plaintiff; Jeremiah Gridley (1701/2–1767) for the Defendant. These were among the colony's finest. See *Appendix 6*, *infra*, for short biographies. The Judges were Chief Justice Hutchinson, Cushing, Lynde, Oliver and Russell. See *Law in Colonial Massachusetts*, *supra*, 329–332. Gridley was John Adams's tutor, and Thacher and Otis were in his exclusive *Sodalitas* club. *Id.*, 376–382. These were the best advocates of the day. Otis and Thacher frequently collaborated with each other, and with Gridley.

The case was originally tried before a full bench, as was the custom, with one judge, Russell, absent. (As Samuel Quincy observed, there was a quorum for this purpose. See S. Quincy n.1, *Reports*, 2.) This proved to be important, as the bench deadlocked, and the case had to be "adjourned for a full Court." The final vote, on the issue of admitting the justice's *mittimus* into evidence, was three to two, Hutchinson, C.J., Lynde and Russell prevailing over Oliver and Cushing. Such closely split dissents are unusual. See *Appendix 1*, *infra*, "Judicial Dissents."

4 · AUTHORITY

English sources were offered on both sides. Gridley relied on *Lilly's Abridgment* (1719) vol. 2, 419. See *Law Commonplace*, page [48], n.3. He relied further on *Wood's Institute of the Laws of England* (1720), 82. See *id.*, page [7], n.3. Otis and Thacher relied on 1 *Salkeld's Reports* (1689–1712) 14. See *id.*, page [32], n.7; 1 *Strange's Reports* (1716–1749) 691 (the case of *Chambers* v. *Robinson* (1726), which actually appears in vol. 2), see *id.*, page [21], n.12; *Viner's Abridgment* (1742–1753), under the entry "Evidence," 56, see *id.*, page [16], n.2; 7 *Modern Reports* (1669–1732) 169, see *id.*, page [35], n.2 and page [96], n.4; and 2 *Shower's Reports* (1678–1694) 145, see *id.*, page [82], n.1. None of the authorities cited seem particularly compelling on the point being argued. As the cross-references to Quincy's *Law Commonplace* demonstrate, all these sources were used by Quincy in his education, and were familiar to him. Most were in his library. See "Catalogue of Books Belonging to the Estate of Josiah Quincy, Jr.," set out at *Appendix 8*, *infra*.

Then the Juſtice's Mittimus was produced as Evidence. The Mittimus, as a Mittimus, was allowed by the Council for the Defendant. But the Recital of the Fact contained in it was excepted to, and the Exception was *ruled by the Court* to be *good.*

It was then debated whether the Mittimus was to be given to the Jury or not, as one Part of it was legal Evidence and the other not — on which *the Court* was divided. (3)

It was then debated whether it muſt go in, as *the Court* was divided upon it, or be taken out, upon which they were alſo divided, and the Caſe was adjourned for a full Court. (4) At February, A. D. 1763, the Mittimus was admitted: *Oliver & Cuſhing* against; *Ch. Juſt., Lynde, & Ruſſell* for it.

---

neceſſity, as there is no way by which the plaintiff can obtain redreſs; and that this is the beſt teſtimony which now exiſts. But it will be productive of leſs miſchief for an individual to ſuffer from the neglect or misfortune of an officer in not making a judicial record, than to eſtabliſh a precedent that the record itſelf, or a part of it, may be proved by parol. It has been argued that the record may be preſumed to be loſt. The rules which apply to the admiſſion of teſtimony to prove the contents of a loſt record, or to the introduction of minutes by which the record may be extended, have no real bearing on a caſe like the preſent, where no ſuch loſs ever took place, and no ſuch minutes were ever made." See alſo *Kendall* v. *Powers*, 4 Met. 553; *Wells* v. *Stevens*, 2 Gray, 115; *Tillotſon* v. *Warner*, 3 Gray, 574.

(3) In *Commonwealth* v. *Wingate*, 6 Gray, 485, the Court allowed a complaint in evidence to go to the jury, although the record of the conviction of the defendant was upon the ſame paper — the jury being inſtructed that ſuch conviction could not be conſidered as evidence.

(4) The effect of a diviſion is to incapacitate the Court from taking any action whatever on that point. 3 Chit. Prac. 10. 12 Co. 118. 1 Salk. 15. *Goddard* v. *Coffin*, Daveis, 381. And the burden being on the party offering the paper, it would ſeem that a divided court would have no power to admit it.

5 · LATER CITATIONS

As Samuel M. Quincy explained in his notes: "the Superior Court of Judicature consisted of five judges, and was held for all purposes by a full bench. All jury trials were conducted in the presence of the full court," with not less than three judges competent to preside. See *The Charters and General Laws of the Colony and Province of Massachusetts Bay* (1814), 330. (Hereafter, "*Anc. Chart.*") See also *Appendix IV*, 9 Pick. (26 Mass.) 566 at 569 (1830). The grandson then cross-references similar cases from the early history of the Commonwealth discussing the use of parol evidence to recreate the record of a judicial proceeding. See *Sayles* v. *Briggs*, 4 Met. (45 Mass.) 421 (1842); *Kendall* v. *Powers*, 4 Met. (44 Mass.) 553 (1842); *Wells* v. *Stevens*, 2 Gray (68 Mass.) 115 (1854); *Tillotson* v. *Warner*, 3 Gray (69 Mass.) 574 (1854).

Like the *mittimus* ultimately admitted in this case, the grandson observes that in *Commonwealth* v. *Wingate*, 6 Gray (72 Mass.) 485 (1856), the court allowed an admissible complaint in evidence to go to the jury, even though the inadmissible conviction of the Defendant appeared on the same paper. The court admonished the jury to not consider the conviction as evidence. Finally, demonstrating the difficulty of managing a trial court with between three to five judges on the same bench, the grandson explains that where the court was evenly divided on a question, the effect was to incapacitate the court from taking any action whatsoever on the point. See *Proctor's Case*, 12 *Coke's Reports* 118 (1615) ("In the King's Bench, Common Pleas, and Exchequer, where all the justices are equally divided, no judgment can be given . . ."). See also *Iveson* v. *Moore*, 1 *Salkeld's Reports* 15, 91 English Reports 16 (1699), *Goddard* v. *Coffin*, 10 F. Cas. 505 (Circuit Court, D. Maine, 1849).

6 · NOTES

This case gives a fascinating insight into the internal dynamics of the Court, and how it resolved tough issues. As the later Massachusetts cases show, the legal problem presented is capable of a simple solution: i.e., rely solely on the official record except where—through no fault of the Plaintiff—it is unavailable. Even today, judges are most reluctant to require other judges to testify under oath about things that occurred before them in their official capacity as a court of record. See *In the Matter of Cook*, 49 F.3d 263 (7th Cir., 1995), where a federal district court judge refused to be questioned under oath by the Illinois

August Term.
2 Georgii Ter. in BR &c
Present
The Honble
Thomas Hutchinson Esqr Ch Just.
Benja Lynde
John Cushing } Esqrs Justices.
Peter Oliver

Dougharty vs Poor.
The Dft Dougharty lost some Goods wch
he suspected Poor had stolen, upon which
Complaint was made to a Justice of the Pea
who heard their several Stories & order'd
Poor to Goal for further Examination
Poor was again examin'd, but Dougharty
not appearing was discharg'd & suffer'd to
without Day. The Justice keeping no Rec
of any Part of the Transactions. The pres
Action was commenced by Poor vs D. for
false Imprisonment; the Justice was
offer'd as a Witness to prove the Fa
alledg'd & objected to, for that wh

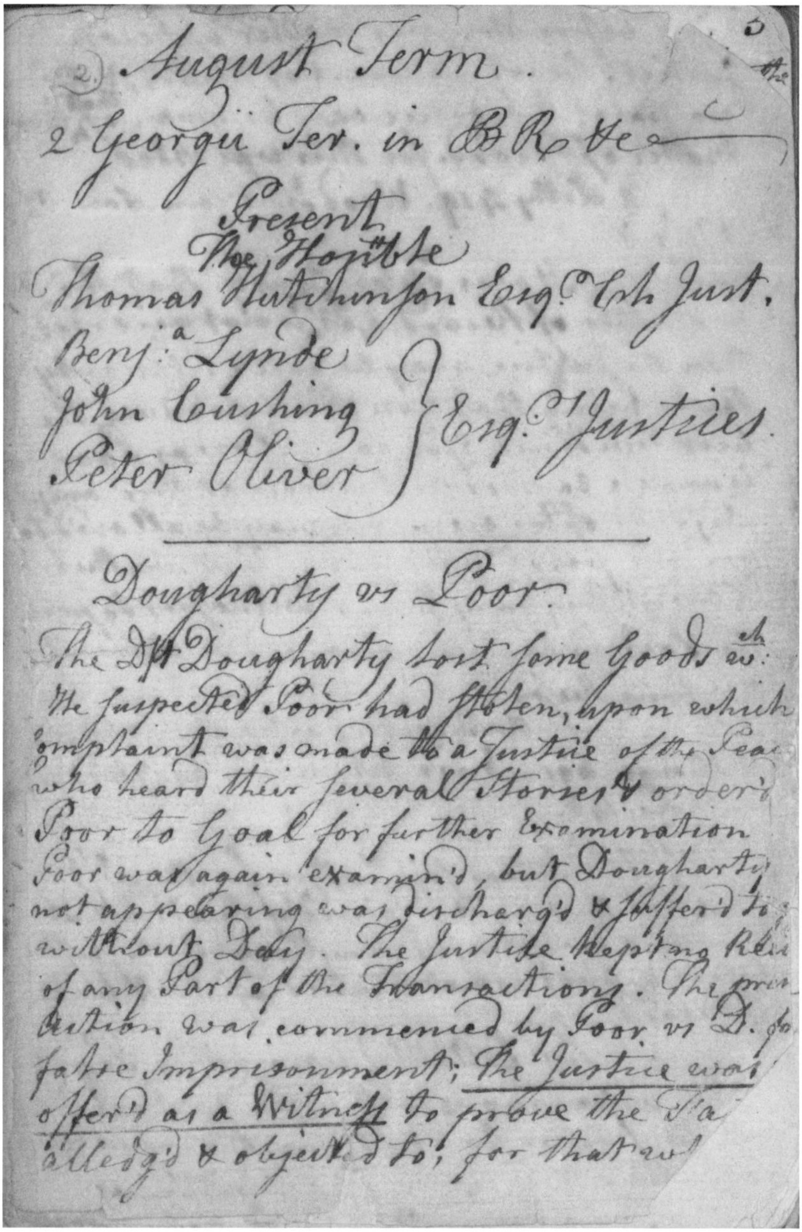

ILLUSTRATION 9: First page of *Quincy's Reports*. MHS P347, Reel 4, QP55, p. 3. *Poor* v. *Dougharty* (Case 1, 1762), *Quincy's Reports*, p. 1. Samuel Quincy lists the case "Poor v. Dougharty," rather than "Dougharty v. Poor" because, while the original case was brought by Dougharty before the Justice of the Peace for goods stolen, in this case Poor was the plaintiff for false imprisonment. See Annotations, *Poor* v. *Dougharty* (Case 1, 1762). Courtesy, Massachusetts Historical Society.

state authorities as to attorney misconduct in a matter before that judge in court. See McMorrow, Coquillette, *The Federal Law of Attorney Conduct* (2001), 806–59 – 806–60.

Here, the Court was unanimous that the "Justice should not be sworn to Anything that came before him judicially," but divided as to whether the Justice's *mittimus* ("we send"), the order compelling the Plaintiff to appear to respond to the complaint, was admissible, particularly since part of it was legal evidence. The Court resolved the issue by admitting the *mittimus*, a fair result for a Plaintiff who, through no fault of his own, was deprived of a record. But the vote was three to two, showing a stubborn formalism in the dissenters.

It is noteworthy that the majority result was apparently not based on the English authorities cited on both sides, but rather to achieve a workable result and a fair rule.

CASE 2

BAKER *v.* FROBISHER.

Baker *verſ.* Frobiſher.

Rec. 1762. Fol. 387.

On a Sale of Goods, there is an implied Warranty that they are merchantable, unleſs ſold by Sample.

FOR ſelling the Plaintiff unmerchantable Soap.(1) It was ſaid there was no expreſs Warranty at the Time of the Sale. But 2d Lord Raymond, 1120, was cited *contra.* And *the Juſtices* were of the Opinion that every Man is bound to ſee his Goods are merchantable at the Time of Sale.(2) But Evidence being brought to prove that the Plaintiff's Wife, who was the Contractor, ſaw a Sample of the Soap, the Jury were directed to find Coſts for the Defendant.

---

(1) The declaration in this caſe alleged that the defendant, a ſoap-boiler, "deceitfully contriving to defraud" the plaintiff, delivered him "unmerchantable ſoap of ſtinking material," and "falſely affirmed the ſame to be good and merchantable."

(2) The oppoſite doctrine now prevails—all ſuch caſes being held to be within the principle of *caveat emptor. Winsor* v. *Lombard*, 18 Pick. 60. *Mixer* v. *Coburn*, 11 Met. 559. But the rule intimated above ſeems once to have been aſſumed in Maſſachuſetts. See *Oliver* v. *Sale*, poſt—*Otis, arguendo:* "The rule of merchandiſe which obliges the vendor to anſwer for what he ſells without warranty, is confined to manufactures of the country, which a man muſt be ſuppoſed to know the quality of."

[P. 4]

Baker v. *Frobisher* (1762)
2 George III (Aug.) in the
Superior Court of Judicature

1 · BRIEF DESCRIPTION

This was an early "consumer protection" case, about an implied warranty of merchantability for soap. The Court relied on English authority that an express warranty at the time of sale was not required, and this is generally the law today. (If a merchant sells something for a particular purpose, i.e., soap, a customer can rely on an implied warranty that the substance will, indeed, wash your hands, and not be, as alleged here, "stinking material.") But where the Plaintiff's wife, apparently an experienced business woman, examined a sample before purchase (and the amounts purchased were in wholesale quantities), the case was dismissed, and the jury directed to find costs for the Defendant.

2 · COURT RECORDS

Available, Rec. 1762, fol. 387.

The Plaintiff first brought suit against the Defendant in a plea of trespass upon the case at the Inferior Court of Common Pleas in Boston in October 1761. The Plaintiff alleged that the Defendant agreed to sell "twenty five boxes of good merchantable soap" for shipment to Canada, but instead delivered to the northward-bound sailing vessel "corruptly unmerchantable soap, ill manufactured and made of bad and stinking materials." The Inferior Court of Common Pleas awarded costs to the Defendant. The Plaintiff appealed to the Superior Court of Assize and General Gaol Delivery, where the Defendant again was awarded costs. The Plaintiff yet again appealed to the Superior Court of Judicature, where he was represented by Robert Auchmuty. The record merely indicates that a jury was sworn, heard evidence and returned a verdict of costs for the Defendant, without substantiating or contradicting the directed verdict reported by Quincy.

The record contains the initial pleadings, as follows:

John Baker of Boston in the County of Suffolk Merchant Plaintiff & William Frobisher of said Boston Soapboiler Defendant. In the plea of Review of a plea of trespass on the case commenced and prosecuted at an Inferior Court of common pleas held at Boston in and for the County of Suffolk on the first

Tuesday of October A.D. 1761 by the said John Baker against the said William Frobisher in the words following viz. "In a plea of trespass on the case for that the plaint. on the third day of October A.D. 1760 being in want of a quantity of good merchantable soap to ship aboard a vessell and transport to Canada and there to sell the same, at Boston aforesaid applied to the deft to purchase of him the same and the deft accordingly then and there bargained and sold to the plaint. twenty five boxes of good merchantable soap containing two thousand two hundred net weight of such soap for and at eight pence each pound of said soap and one shilling apiece for said boxes and agreed with and promised the plaint. to deliver said twenty five boxes of good merchantable soap on board as [illegible]. . . . Yet the deft never delivered said quantity of good merchantable soap nor any part thereof, but deceitfully contriving to defraud the plaint. delivered on board vessell for the plaint. instead thereof twenty five boxes of bad corruptly unmerchantable soap, ill manufactured and made of bad and stinking materials [illegible]. . . .lost the benefit of the sale that he might have made of good merchantable soap together with the money paid for good soap as aforesaid all of which is to the damage of the said John as he saith the sum of two hundred pounds."

3 · PROFESSIONALS INVOLVED

Robert Auchmuty (1723–1788) represented the plaintiff, as indicated by the court records, above. See *Appendix 6*, *infra*, for a short biography.

4 · AUTHORITY

The Court relied on 2 *Lord Raymond's Reports* (1694–1732), 1120 [the case of *Lysney* v. *Selby* (1705), which begins on 1118]. See *Law Commonplace*, page [26], n.2. While accepting the basic English doctrine of implied warranty, the Court made exception for sale by examined sample. *Lord Raymond's Reports* were frequently cited in Quincy's *Law Commonplace*. See *id.*, page [26], n.2.

5 · LATER CITATIONS

As Samuel Quincy observed, the opposite doctrine of *caveat emptor* prevailed in Massachusetts, citing *Winsor* v. *Lombard*, 35 Mass. (18 Pick.) 57, 60 (1836); *Mixer* v. *Coburn*, 52 Mass. (11 Met.) 559, 562 (1846). The grandson cross-referenced *Oliver* v. *Sale*, *Reports*, 29, Case 13, *infra*, in which Otis argued that the implied warranty of merchantability was limited.

6 · NOTES

The outcome of this case made a sensible distinction between an ordinary customer, who deserved the "consumer protection" of an implied warranty, and a "contractor" buying large quantities by sample. The persistent Plaintiff, who appealed two lower determinations, was ordered to pay the Defendant's costs for each of the three hearings, a way to control vexatious suits!

CASE 3

INGRAHAM *v.* COOK.

Rec. 1762. Fol. 288.

A new Indorſer to a Writ will be ordered whenever it can be made to appear that the preſent Indorſer cannot anſwer Coſts.

Ingraham *verſ.* Cook & al.

IN this caſe, Ingraham, the Plaintiff, indorſed the Writ. It was urged by the Council for the Defendant, before the Trial, that Ingraham was gone in the Army, had no Eſtate, and could not anſwer the Coſts. It was ſaid *contra*, that a new Indorſer is never ordered but in the Caſe of abſconding inſolvent Debtors, and that the Plaintiff was in the Pay of the Government. But *the Court ruled*, that a new Indorſer ought to be found in every Caſe where it could be made to appear to the Court that there was Danger the preſent Indorſer could not anſwer Coſts. But a Witneſs was produced who knew the Plaintiff to have a conſiderable Sum of Money at Intereſt; upon which the Motion was ſilenced. (1)

---

(1) The Prov. Sts. of 1 Geo. 1 and 1 Geo. 2 (Anc. Chart. 406, 466) provided for the indorſement of all writs by the plaintiff or attorney, but contained no proviſion for finding a new indorſer in any caſe. The St. of 1784, c. 28, provided in addition, that where the plaintiff was not an inhabitant of the State, he ſhould procure a ſufficient indorſer who was, and alſo that where the writ was indorſed by plaintiff's attorney, if such attorney was ſhown to be of inſufficient ability, a new indorſer ſhould be ordered. This act was repealed by St. 1833, c. 50, which contains the proviſions ſubſtantially reënacted by the Rev. Sts. c. 90, § 10, (Gen. Sts. c. 123, § 20; c. 129, § 29,) viz., making the indorſement a condition precedent only where the plaintiff is not an inhabitant of the State, and giving the Court diſcretionary power to require it wherever it appears reaſonable. But it ſeems that mere poverty of the plaintiff will not be conſidered ſufficient cauſe for ſuch requirement, in the abſence of vexation or oppreſſion. Per *Shaw*, C. J., 21 Pick. 212. An indorſer will be required where the plaintiff removes from the State during the pendency of the action. 8 Mass. 272. 1 Gray, 114. But the removal of a foreign plaintiff into the State does not have the effect to diſcharge the indorſer. 8 Met. 149.

[PP. 4–5]

Ingraham v. *Cook & al.* (1762)
2 George III (Aug.) in the
Superior Court of Judicature

1 · BRIEF DESCRIPTION

In the previous case, *Baker* v. *Frobisher*, *Reports*, 4, Case 2, the Court demonstrated one control on vexatious litigation, the routine practice of ordering the unsuccessful party to pay costs. Here was the corollary concern, whether the Plaintiff had enough money to meet Defendant's costs, if necessary. The Court held that where a witness was produced who knew Plaintiff "to have a considerable Sum of Money at Interest," the Defendant's pretrial motion would be denied. See *Hallowell* v. *Daulton*, *Reports*, 33, Case 14, *infra*.

2 · COURT RECORDS

Available, Rec. 1762, fols. 387–88 (not 288, as in Samuel Quincy's notes).

The objection raised by the Defendant was more than academic in this case, because the Plaintiff lost in a suit for trespass in the Inferior Court of Common Pleas below and would owe the Defendant costs if he did not prevail in this appeal. In the suit below, the Plaintiff alleged that the four Defendants "with force and arms on the body of Ingraham . . . him did beat so that his life was despaired of," and prayed for damages in the amount of £100. After a trial de novo before the Superior Court of Judicature, the jury reversed the finding below and returned a verdict in the Plaintiff's favor, awarding him an amount of £20 plus costs.

Also available:

Ingraham v. *Cook* (same), July 8, 1761, No. 172547.

- Deposition by Eunice Hill in Wrentham, July 8, 1761.

Ingraham v. *Cook* (same), Aug. 25, 1761, No. 172361.

- Deposition of Robert Cook, Inferior Court, Suffolk.

Ingraham v. *Cook* (same), No. 174758.

- Jury Finding for Defendant. Full names of parties are Nathaniel Ingraham and Mary Cook.

3 · PROFESSIONALS INVOLVED

No indication.

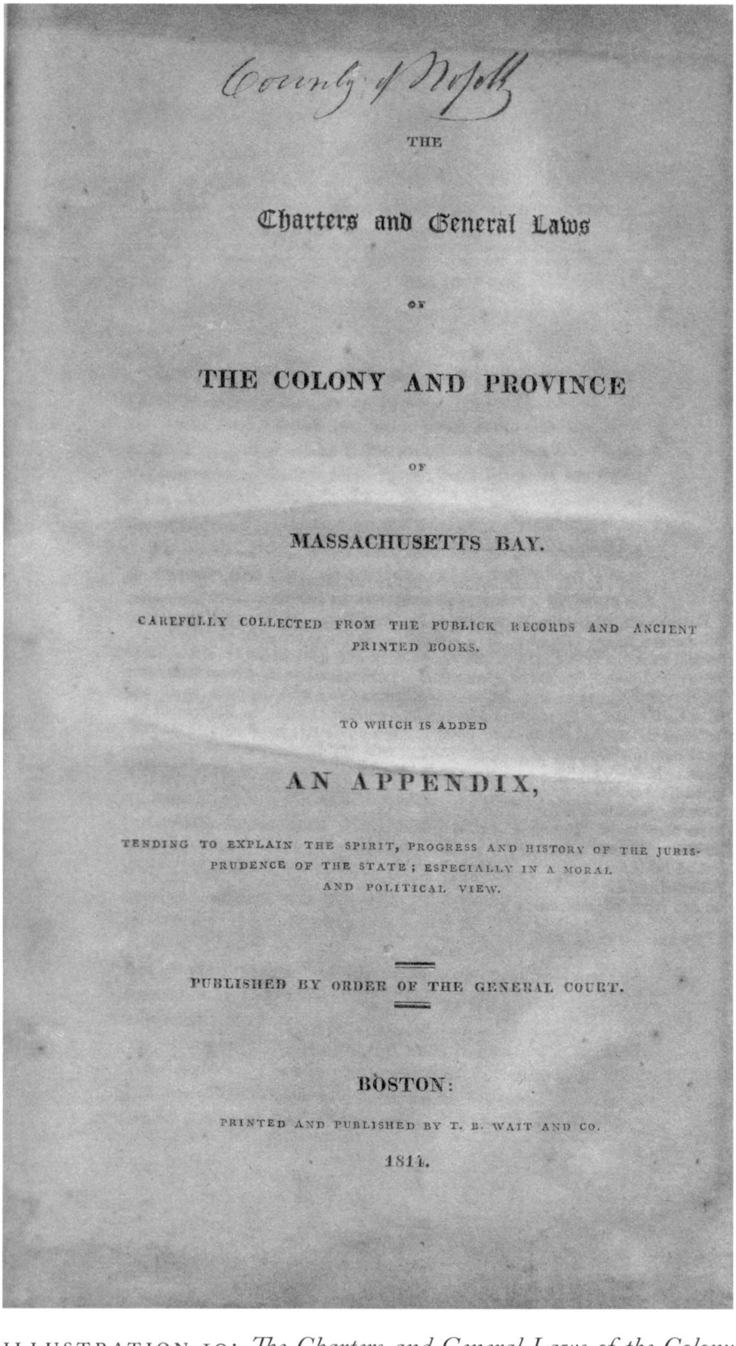

County of Norfolk

THE

Charters and General Laws

OF

THE COLONY AND PROVINCE

OF

MASSACHUSETTS BAY.

CAREFULLY COLLECTED FROM THE PUBLICK RECORDS AND ANCIENT PRINTED BOOKS.

TO WHICH IS ADDED

AN APPENDIX,

TENDING TO EXPLAIN THE SPIRIT, PROGRESS AND HISTORY OF THE JURISPRUDENCE OF THE STATE; ESPECIALLY IN A MORAL AND POLITICAL VIEW.

PUBLISHED BY ORDER OF THE GENERAL COURT.

BOSTON:

PRINTED AND PUBLISHED BY T. B. WAIT AND CO.

1814.

ILLUSTRATION 10: *The Charters and General Laws of the Colony and Province of Massachusetts Bay* (Boston, 1814) ("*Anc. Chart.*"). This was a fundamental source for Samuel Quincy, and all susequent colonial historians.

4 · AUTHORITY

None referenced by Quincy himself, although the grandson observes that the Provincial Statutes of I Geo. 1 (1714) and I Geo. 2 (1715) (*Anc. Chart.* 406, 466) made no provision for finding a new indorser in any case.

5 · LATER CITATIONS

The grandson cross-references the various statutes, enacted both before and after Massachusetts and the other colonies declared independence, requiring parties to answer costs in a civil action, and the gradual easing of this requirement. See Prov. St. of I Geo. I and I Geo. 2 (*Anc. Chart.* 406, 466); St. 1784, c.28; St. 1833, c.50; Rev. Sts. c.90, § 10 (Gen. Sts. c.123, § 20; c.129, § 29). The grandson also details early Supreme Judicial Court interpretations of the statutory requirement. See *Feneley* v. *Mahoney*, 38 Mass. (21 Pick.) 212 (1838); *Oysted* v. *Shed*, 8 Mass. (2 Tyng) 272 (1811); *Bartlett* v. *Holbrook*, 67 Mass. (1 Gray) 114 (1854); *Proprietors of the Locks & Canals on Merrimack River* v. *Reed*, 49 Mass. (8 Met.) 146, at 149 (1844).

6 · NOTES

Access to the courts was, and is, an important political and economic fact. Here the access of a soldier "in the pay of the government" was challenged on the grounds that he could not pay costs if he lost. His case, brought in trespass, alleged that he was cruelly beaten by the Defendant "so that his life, despaired of." Even allowing for the usual terms of art in trespass pleading, this was a serious case, and, indeed, the Plaintiff eventually received a large verdict of £20 plus costs. It was true the Plaintiff lost below, making the matter of costs for the Defendant a reasonable concern. But, nevertheless, precluding a poor soldier from this type of access to justice would have been significant. As it was, the issue was never squarely faced, for it turned out the soldier was not so poor after all. Later Massachusetts law eventually discarded these barriers to the courts, as Samuel Quincy's notes demonstrate.

CASE 4

Newman *verſ.* Homans.

NEWMAN *v.* HOMANS.

Rec. 1762. Fol. 383.

THE Queſtion was, whether Intereſt or Depretiation ought to be allowed by a Factor after any Period, otherwiſe than upon an Action of Account, in which he ſhews at what Time he received Pay for the Goods. (1)

After a reaſonable Time a Factor is liable for Intereſt on the Price received for Goods of his Principal. And ſuch Intereſt may be recovered in an Action of Aſſumpsit, as well as in Account.

The Court was of Opinion, that after a reaſonable Time he ought. (2)

(1) It appears by the record that this was *indebitatus aſſumpſit* for money had and received. The declaration alleged a promiſe to pay, with intereſt, to which the defendant demurred in the Court of Common Pleas, and the demurrer was ſuſtained. In the Superior Court this deciſion was reverſed, and the caſe ſent to a jury.

(2) S. P. *Dodge* v. *Perkins*, 9 Pick. 368. Where a factor, having received money, unreaſonably neglects to inform his principal, he is liable for intereſt for the time of ſuch unreaſonable delay.

Newman v. *Homans* (1762)
2 George III (Aug.) in the
Superior Court of Judicature

1 · BRIEF DESCRIPTION

This was a case brought by a Principal against his Factor for money paid to the Factor for goods belonging to the Principal. A "factor" was "[a] mercantile agent; a person who, in the usual course of his business has possession of the goods . . . of his principal, with authority to sell, etc. . . ." [See P. G. Osborn, *A Concise Law Dictionary* (London, 1964), 132. (Hereafter, "P. G. Osborn".)] The question was whether the Factor should be liable for interest if payment to the Principal is delayed. The Court concluded that "after a reasonable Time he ought."

2 · COURT RECORDS

Available, Rec. 1762, fol. 383.

The record here is of interest, because the action brought was *Indebitatus Assumpsit* for money had and received, not the action of Account, which was the common law action specially designed for holding agents accountable to principals. For that reason, the Court below sustained the Defendant's pleading objection. This is also why Quincy emphasized that this claim for interest was "otherwise than upon an Action of Account." The Superior Court here reversed that holding. See (6) "Note," below.

Also available:

Newman v. *Homans* (same), Aug. 1762, No. 172505.

- Bill of Costs

3 · PROFESSIONALS INVOLVED

No indication.

4 · AUTHORITY

None.

5 · LATER CITATIONS

As Samuel Quincy indicated at *Reports*, 6, his note 2, *Dodge* v. *Perkins*, 9 Pickering (26 Mass.), 368 (1830), essentially came to the same conclusion, where

was three Chaplains, be made Warden of the Cinque Ports, who may have a Chaplain as a part of his Office, yet he shall have but three. And so if a Baron hath three, and be made an Earl, yet he shall have but five in all, & *sic de cæteris.*

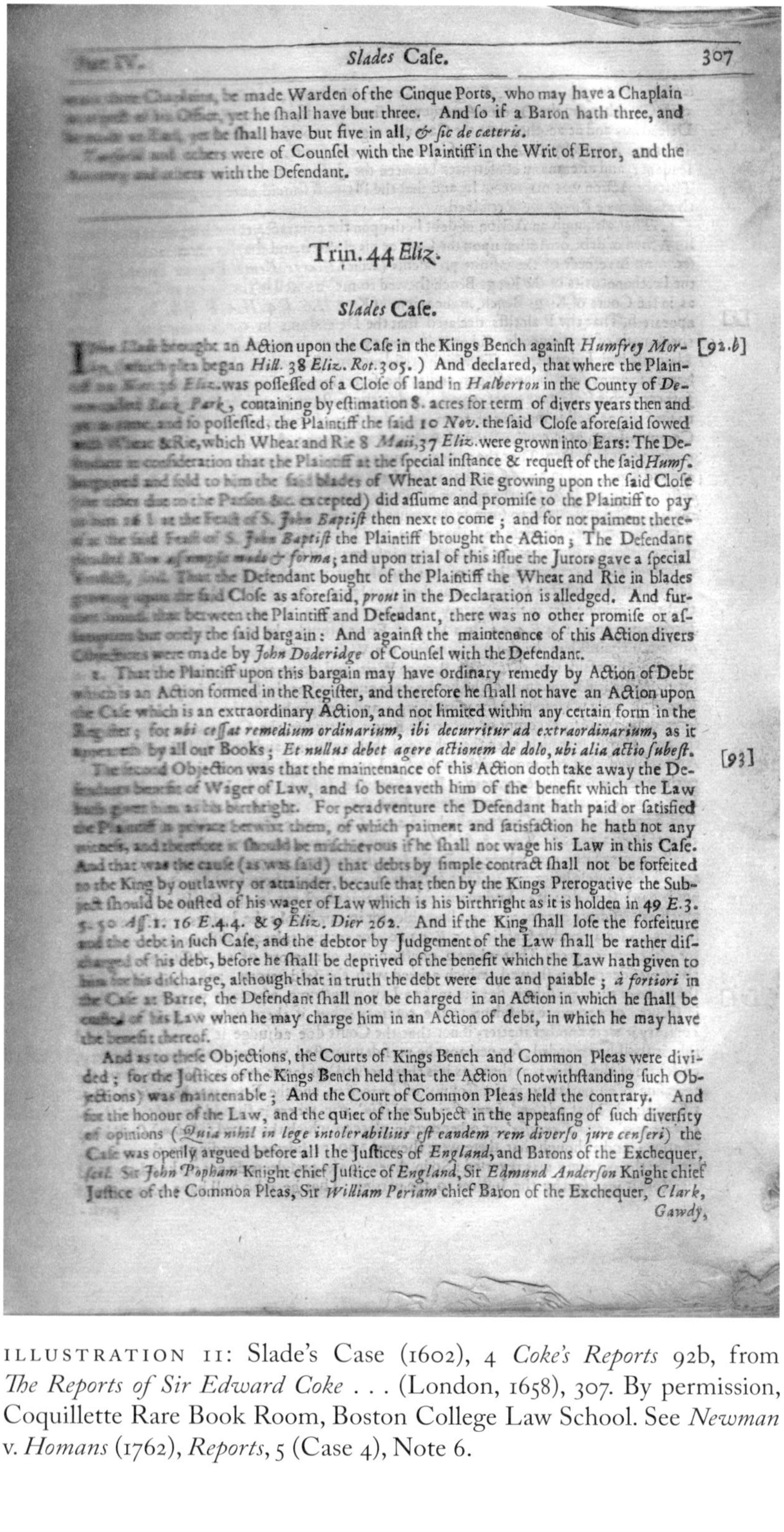

Tanfield and others were of Counsel with the Plaintiff in the Writ of Error, and the Attorney and others with the Defendant.

Trin. 44 *Eliz.*

Slades Case.

[92.b] John Slade brought an Action upon the Case in the Kings Bench against *Humfrey Morley*, which plea began *Hill.* 38 *Eliz. Rot.* 305.) And declared, that where the Plaintiff 10 *Nov.* 36 *Eliz.* was possessed of a Close of land in *Halberton* in the County of *Devon* called *Rack Park*, containing by estimation 8. acres for term of divers years then and yet to come, and so possessed, the Plaintiff the said 10 *Nov.* the said Close aforesaid sowed with Wheat & Rie, which Wheat and Rie 8 *Maii*, 37 *Eliz.* were grown into Ears: The Defendant in consideration that the Plaintiff at the special instance & request of the said *Humf.* bargained and sold to him the said blades of Wheat and Rie growing upon the said Close (the tithes due to the Parson &c. excepted) did assume and promise to the Plaintiff to pay to him 16 l. at the Feast of S. *John Baptist* then next to come; and for not paiment thereof at the said Feast of S. *John Baptist* the Plaintiff brought the Action; The Defendant pleaded *Non assumpsit modo & forma*; and upon trial of this issue the Jurors gave a special Verdict, *scil.* That the Defendant bought of the Plaintiff the Wheat and Rie in blades growing upon the said Close as aforesaid, *prout* in the Declaration is alledged. And further found, that between the Plaintiff and Defendant, there was no other promise or assumption but onely the said bargain: And against the maintenance of this Action divers Objections were made by *John Doderidge* of Counsel with the Defendant.

1. That the Plaintiff upon this bargain may have ordinary remedy by Action of Debt which is an Action formed in the Register, and therefore he shall not have an Action upon the Case which is an extraordinary Action, and not limited within any certain form in the Register; for *ubi cessat remedium ordinarium, ibi decurritur ad extraordinarium*, as it appeareth by all our Books; *Et nullus debet agere actionem de dolo, ubi alia actio subest.* [93]

The second Objection was that the maintenance of this Action doth take away the Defendants benefit of Wager of Law, and so bereaveth him of the benefit which the Law hath given him as his birthright. For peradventure the Defendant hath paid or satisfied the Plaintiff in private betwixt them, of which paiment and satisfaction he hath not any witness, and therefore it should be mischievous if he shall not wage his Law in this Case. And that was the cause (as was said) that debts by simple contract shall not be forfeited to the King by outlawry or attainder, because that then by the Kings Prerogative the Subject should be ousted of his wager of Law which is his birthright as it is holden in 49 *E.* 3. 5. 50 *Ass.* 1. 16 *E.* 4. 4. & 9 *Eliz. Dier* 262. And if the King shall lose the forfeiture and the debt in such Case, and the debtor by Judgement of the Law shall be rather discharged of his debt, before he shall be deprived of the benefit which the Law hath given to him for his discharge, although that in truth the debt were due and paiable; *à fortiori* in the Case at Barre, the Defendant shall not be charged in an Action in which he shall be ousted of his Law when he may charge him in an Action of debt, in which he may have the benefit thereof.

And as to these Objections, the Courts of Kings Bench and Common Pleas were divided; for the Justices of the Kings Bench held that the Action (notwithstanding such Objections) was maintenable; And the Court of Common Pleas held the contrary. And for the honour of the Law, and the quiet of the Subject in the appeasing of such diversity of opinions (*Quia nihil in lege intolerabilius est eandem rem diverso jure censeri*) the Case was openly argued before all the Justices of *England*, and Barons of the Exchequer, *scil.* Sir *John Popham* Knight chief Justice of *England*, Sir *Edmund Anderson* Knight chief Justice of the Common Pleas, Sir *William Periam* chief Baron of the Exchequer, *Clark*, *Gawdy*,

ILLUSTRATION 11: Slade's Case (1602), 4 *Coke's Reports* 92b, from *The Reports of Sir Edward Coke* . . . (London, 1658), 307. By permission, Coquillette Rare Book Room, Boston College Law School. See *Newman v. Homans* (1762), *Reports*, 5 (Case 4), Note 6.

the factor "neglects to inform his principal" of money had and received for an unreasonable period.

In *Ratner* v. *Hill*, 270 Mass. 249 (1930), the case of *Newman* v. *Homans* was cited as authority. The issue in *Ratner* was whether interest was due on a mortgage from the date of the sale of a property. *Newman* v. *Homans* was cited for the principle that the obligation to pay interest is imposed only by the terms agreed to by the parties, and that it is consideration for the use of the money. See *Ratner* v. *Hill*, *supra*, 270 Mass. at 254. The case was also cited in *Holmer* v. *Hunt*, 122 Mass. 505, at 513 (1877) to illustrate the change in Massachusetts from the common law action of account to the action of assumpsit. See *Appendix 5*, *infra*.

6 · NOTES

The holding of the case was practical and simple, but there was a concealed procedural issue of some importance. Assumpsit was the standard contractual remedy for damages for nonfeasance. See *Law Commonplace*, page [96], n.9 and page [123], n.8. But the older, and more specific remedy for misfeasance or nonfeasance of an agent was the Action of Account. Before *Slade's Case* (1602), 4 *Coke's Reports* 92b, it was uncertain whether *indebitatus assumpsit* ("being indebted, did undertake," a reference to a fiction designed to avoid perclusion by the writ of debt) would lie where an older, more specific writ, like Account, would provide a remedy. See J. H. Baker, *An Introduction to English Legal History* (4th ed., London, 2002) 337–365. But there were serious procedural problems with Account, even though the ancient trial of wager by law was denied to bailiffs and agents by 1600. *Id.*, 363–365. Here, the Superior Court was not troubled that the action was brought in *indebitatus assumpsit*, rather than Account. In doing this, it reversed the court below, the Court of Common Pleas, which sustained a demurrer to the *assumpsit* declaration, apparently because it was used instead of an Action of Account, which would have set out the time the factor received the money for the goods. (A "demurrer" being a pleading that alleged that the "other party showed no good cause of action or defense." P. G. Osborn, *supra*, 107.) The Court thus showed a relaxed view to the formality of the pleading. This would have encouraged the evolution of assumpsit as a general contract remedy, and, indeed, this was occurring in England after *Slade's Case*, *supra*.

CASE 5

ZUILL *v.* BRADLEY.

Rec. 1762. Fol. 388.

Where Father and Son of the ſame Name reſide in the ſame Town, *it ſeems* that the Omiſſion of "junior," in a Writ againſt the Son, is good Cauſe of Abatement. *It ſeems*, that Duplicity is no Objection to a Plea in Abatement.

Zuill *verſ.* Bradley.

THE Plaintiff ſues Bradley by the Name of Daniel Bradley, of Haverhill, &c., Trader.

Upon which the Defendant pleads as follows: "And Daniel Bradley, junior, of Haverhill, &c., "Innholder, whoſe Body was attached by this Writ, "comes and ſays he is the ſame Perſon who was ſued "by the ſaid John Zuill by the Name of Daniel "Bradley, of Haverhill, &c., Trader. And the ſaid "Daniel Bradley, junior, ſays this Writ ought to abate, "becauſe he ſays that at the Time of the Purchaſe "thereof *there were* two Men in ſaid Town of Haverhill known by the names of Daniel Bradley and "Daniel Bradley, junior, and that he hath been always called and known by the Name of Daniel "Bradley, junior, and not by the Name of Daniel "Bradley only, as in this Writ is ſuppoſed, and that "the ſaid Daniel Bradley, ſenior, is his the ſaid Daniel Bradley junior's Father, and all this the ſaid "Daniel Bradley, junior, is ready to verify; wherefore he prays Judgment of this Writ that it abate, "and for his Coſts.

"2. The ſaid Writ ought to abate, for that he the "ſaid Daniel Bradley, junior, was at the Time of the "Purchaſe of this Writ, and ſtill is, an Innholder, and "not a Trader, as in this Writ is ſuppoſed, and this "he alſo is ready to verify; wherefore he prays Judgment of this Writ that it abate, and for his Coſts."

O. Thacher.

Zuill v. *Bradley* (1762)
2 George III (Aug.) in the
Superior Court of Judicature

1 · BRIEF DESCRIPTION

This was the first of two cases focused on whether the Defendant was adequately described in the writ commencing the case. Here the writ said "Daniel Bradley of Haverhill, Trader." It was pleaded that the writ should abate for two reasons: 1) there were two Daniel Bradleys in Haverhill, father and son, and this was served on the son, "always called . . . Daniel Bradley, junior"; and 2) Daniel Bradley, junior, was "an Innholder, and not a Trader." The writ was abated, with the Chief Justice doubtful about the first ground, but apparently not the second.

Note, pleas in abatement "were pleas which, without either admitting or denying the existence of the cause of action, alleged some fact (such as non-joinder of a necessary party. . .) which would preclude the Plaintiff from recovering upon the writ as they framed." Earl Jowitt, *The Dictionary of English Law* (London, 1959), 6. (Hereafter, *Jowitt.*)

2 · COURT RECORDS

Available, Rec. 1762, fol. 388.

The record indicated that judgment was given "on the second exception," as Samuel Quincy notes. Also available:

- A receipt for Bradley's attendance of court which further states that he traveled 66 miles to get to court.
- Summons of Bradley to Superior Court of Judicature written by Hatch, Esq.
- A mysterious document that appears pertinent to the *Dunten* v. *Richards* case. (Case No. 28, *infra*, *Reports*, 67–68.)
- Order of Execution of Judgment in the amount of 365 pounds, 10 shillings, 10 pence plus costs of suit and perhaps interest, totaling 371.14:14.

3 · PROFESSIONALS INVOLVED

Oxenbridge Thacher (1714–1765) appeared for the Defendant. He was one of the elite of the Boston bar, and Josiah Quincy studied law in his office. See *Appendix 6, infra.*

To which it was objected, that there was a Duplicity which deftroyed it, for that he pleaded, that his Name was Daniel Bradley, junior, and not Daniel Bradley only, and alfo that he was an Innholder and not a Trader ; and Mod. was cited. But it was overruled. (1)

Upon a full Hearing, it was *ruled*, that as they were in the fame Town, and Father and Son, it was a Mifnomer sufficient to abate the Writ. (2) *Ch. Juft.* doubted of the Words "*there were.*" He thinks that the Latin Word "*habentur*" is of greater Extent, but fuppofes it is not fufficient to make it bad. (3)

---

(1) The Court would feem to have held duplicity to be no objection to a plea in abatement. The cafe of *Trevelian* v. *Seccomb*, Carth. 7, 8, feems to countenance fuch a view, but the miftake is explained in Steph. Pl. note (56). See alfo Bac. Ab. Abatement, (P); and 5 Pick. 223, where the objection of duplicity was overruled on the ground that one of the allegations was furplufage. It has been held in the Superior Court of Suffolk, that under the Practice Act of 1852, an anfwer in abatement may be objected to for duplicity, on motion. 20 Law Rep. 463. And this on the ground that the anfwer is fubject to the fame rules againft duplicity as was formerly the plea. But before the Pracice Act, duplicity could not be taken advantage of. St. 1836, c. 273, § 3. 1 Cufh. 137. And by § 13 of the act, "different confiftent defences may be ftated in the fame anfwer."

(2) "It feems to be only in the cafe of a father and fon of the fame names, that the addition is required to be ftated in a writ where the fon is made defendant." *Kincaid* v. *Howe*, 10 Mafs. 204. See alfo 5 Dane Ab. 705. To the point that "junior" is no part of a man's name, but an addition ufed to defcribe and defignate the perfon, fee 1 Pick. 388; 15 Pick. 7; 17 Pick. 200.

(3) It appears, however, by the record, that the judgment was finally given "on the fecond exception," perhaps on account of the Chief Juftice's doubt on this point.

The Chief Justice expressed doubts about the first ground of abatement, indicating some discourse on the bench, if not a formal dissent.

4 · AUTHORITY

Quincy indicated that *Modern Reports* (1669–1732) was cited, but did not give the case name and left the volume and page blank. See *Law Commonplace*, page [35], n.2, page [96], n.4. In any event, the authority of the case apparently was not followed.

5 · LATER CITATIONS

The opposing counsel's objection to Thacher's plea in abatement was based on "duplicity," i.e., that it "contains more claims, charges or defences than one." *Jowitt*, *supra*, 685. Later Massachusetts cases relaxed this requirement, and, as Samuel Quincy pointed out, Sec. 13 of the Massachusetts Practice Act of 1852 states that "different consistent defenses may be stated in the same answer." S. Quincy, n.1, *Reports*, 7. Later Massachusetts cases also revisited the "junior" question, and held that where the father and son had the same name, it was necessary to identify which was meant. *Kincaid* v. *Howe*, 10 Mass. 203, 204 (1813).

6 · NOTE

This case gives a good idea of the technicality of common law pleading in Massachusetts in Quincy's day. The Chief Justice's reference to the wording "'there were two Men in said Town," as different and less sufficient than the Latin "*habentur*" ("dwell") was certainly superfluous learning. The Court, however, rightly ignored the duplicity argument of the Plaintiff's counsel, another technical argument. Skilled counsel were needed when pleading became this complex.

CASE 6

BLOWER *v.* CAMPBELL.

Rec. 1763. Fol. 16.

Whether the Defcription "Blackfmith" includes a Nailor or not —*quære.*

Blower *verf.* Campbell.

THE Defendant was named in the Writ, Blackfmith, to which he pleaded he was a Nailor, and not a Blackfmith, and therefore prays Judgment for the Abatement of the Writ.

It was replied that Blackfmith was a general Name, including many Species, of which a Nailor was one.

The Defendant's Council anfwered that they were fo diftinct that the one knew Nothing of the other's Businefs, and a Forger, Gunfmith, &c., might as well be called Blackfmith.

The Court were unanimoufly of the Opinion that the Writ was good, but for different Reafons; fome becaufe the Defendant had at certain Times done fome Articles of Blackfmith's Work; others for the Reafon aforefaid.

Blower v. *Campbell* (1762)
2 George III (Aug.) in the
Superior Court of Judicature

1 · BRIEF DESCRIPTION

This is another plea in abatement, like *Zuill* v. *Bradley*, *Reports*, 6, Case 5, *supra.* This time the Defendant was described as a "Nailor," but claimed he was a "Blacksmith." (A "nailor" or "nailer" made nails, *Concise Oxford Dictionary*, 8th ed., 786.) This was too technical for the Court, which rejected the plea, some justices holding that the Defendant had been a blacksmith, others that a nailer was a kind of blacksmith.

2 · RECORD

Available at Rec. 1763, fol. 16.

3 · PROFESSIONALS INVOLVED

No indication. Quincy does indicate that the bench came to the same final result, but disagreed as to the reason.

4 · AUTHORITY

None.

5 · LATER CITATIONS

See *Zuill* v. *Bradley*, *Reports*, 6, Case 5, note 5, "Later Citations."

6 · NOTES

The Court would take technical pleading only so far!

CASE 7

Jones *verſ.* Belcher.

JONES *v.* BELCHER. Rec. 1762. Fol. 389.

DEBT upon a Bond given here, which it was ſuggeſted was for a Debt due in England. Moved that Engliſh Intereſt only ſhould be paid. Caſes in Eq. 288, cited.

A Bond given here for a Debt due in England to a third Party, draws New England Intereſt.

But *the Court* were of Opinion, as the Bond was given to a Perſon here, (not the Creditor in England,) and the Debt was become his, New England Intereſt ought to be granted. (1)

---

(1) This is according to the general rule of computing intereſt according to the *lex loci contractus*. *Winthrop* v. *Carleton*, 12 Maſs. 4. *Von Hemert* v. *Porter*, 11 Met. 210. But where intereſt is given as damages, the *lex fori* prevails. *Barringer* v. *King*, 5 Gray, 9, 12. *Eaton* v. *Mellus*, 7 Gray, 566.

2

Jones v. *Belcher* (1762)
2 George III (Aug.) in the
Superior Court of Judicature

1 · BRIEF DESCRIPTION

An interesting conflict of law case on a simple issue: if a bond (i.e., a Contract under seal to pay a sum of money) was to secure a debt due in England, but was executed to benefit a person here—not the original English creditor—should English or American interest rates apply? The Court held for American rates.

2 · RECORD

Available at Rec. 1762, Fol. 389.

3 · PROFESSIONALS INVOLVED

No indication.

4 · AUTHORITY

In support of the argument that English interest should be paid, citation was made to *Cases in Equity*. This refers to *A General Abridgment of Cases in Equity Argued and Adjudged in the High Court of Chancery*, first published in 1732 [see *Sweet & Maxwell's Legal Bibliography* (2nd ed., London 1955), vol. 1, p. 286; hereafter, "*Sweet & Maxwell*"]. Pages 288–289 of *Cases in Equity* state that "in all Cases Interest must be paid according to the Law of the Country where the Debt was contracted, and not according to that where the Debt is sued for."

5 · LATER CITATIONS

Massachusetts law continued to follow the *lex loci contractus* (i.e., law of the place of contract) rule, as Samuel Quincy indicated. See *Winthrop* v. *Carleton*, 12 Mass. 4 (1812). This is in contrast to the rule of *lex fori* (i.e., the law of the forum), which Samuel Quincy notes is applicable in cases where "interest is given in damages."

6 · NOTE

The result is still generally the law. It was interesting that the Court distinguished sharply between the Province and England, favoring the Province.

CASE 8

Minot *verſ.* Prout.

MINOT *v.* PROUT.

Rec. 1766. Fol. 78.

Suing and entering upon a Mortgage is no Bar to an Action upon the Bond ſecured thereby.

DEBT upon a Bond. Defendant pleads as follows: " The ſaid Timothy comes and de-" fends, &c., and prays Oyer of the Condition there-" of, and the ſame is read to him in theſe Words:

" The Condition of the aforewritten Obligation, " &c., (this Condition as uſuall,) which being read " and heard, the ſaid Timothy ſaith that the ſaid " Chriſtopher his Action aforeſaid againſt him the " ſaid Timothy ought not to have and maintain, " becauſe he ſaith that the ſaid Timothy, on the " Day of the Date of the ſaid Obligation, and col-" lateral thereto, at Boſton aforeſaid, made and exe-" cuted to the ſaid Chriſtopher a Deed of Mortgage " of a Meſſuage and Land, ſituate, &c., which " Mortgage was executed to the ſaid Chriſtopher " to be a collateral Security for the Payment of the " Sum in the Condition aforecited mentioned and " the Intereſt thereof, and afterwards, viz., at Boſ-" ton aforeſaid, on the 13th of December, 1758, he " the ſaid Chriſtopher by his Deed, ſealed with his " Seal, aſſigned and conveyed the ſaid Mortgage, " as well as the Obligation now ſued on, to one " William Brown, of, &c., and the ſaid William " afterwards, viz., the ſame Day, made his Election, " and for the Non-payment of the ſaid Sum en-" tered on the ſaid mortgaged Premiſes, and became " ſeiſed thereof in his Demeſne as of Fee, and ſtill " holds the ſaid mortgaged Premiſes; and all this " the ſaid Timothy is ready to verify, wherefore he " prays Judgment if the ſaid Chriſtopher his Action " aforeſaid againſt him the ſaid Timothy ſhall have " and maintain.

" *O. Thacher.*"

[PP. 9–10]

Minot v. *Prout* (1762)
2 Geo. III (Aug.) in the
Superior Court of Judicature

1 · BRIEF DESCRIPTION

This was an action for debt on a bond secured by a mortgage. The Defendant alleged that the Plaintiff entered on the mortgaged premises and therefore was barred to sue on the bond, having "elected" the mortgage remedy. The Court disagreed.

2 · RECORD

Available at Rec. 1766, Fol. 78.

3 · PROFESSIONALS INVOLVED

Richard Dana (1700–1772) for the Plaintiff and Oxenbridge Thacher (1719–1765) for the Defendant. Both were leaders of the bar. See short biographies in *Appendix 6*, *infra*.

4 · AUTHORITY

The Defendant argued that the Plaintiff's replication, i.e., the Plaintiff's answer to the Defendant's demurrer, *Jowitt*, *supra*, 1527, was a "negative pregnant," citing *Lea* v. *Luthell* (1619), 2 *Croke's Reports* (1582–1641) [Jac.], 559. See *Law Commonplace*, page [21], n.6. Also cited was Sampson Ewer's *Doctrina Placitandi* (London, 1677), 256. See *Sweet & Maxwell*, vol. 1, p. 268:58. A negative pregnant "in pleading, is where a person gives an evasive answer to an allegation of his opponent by answering it literally, without answering the substance of it. Thus, if it is alleged that A received a certain sum of money, and he denies that particular amount, this is a negative pregnant, because that substance of the allegation is the receipt of some money, and not the particular amount received." *Jowitt*, *supra*, 1215.

The defense theory apparently was that the Plaintiff's replication denied that the mortgage had been entered into, rather than denying that, had the mortgage been entered into, it would have barred the bond, as the Defendant's demurrer argued. Richard Dana rejected the Defendant's pleading argument

To which the Plaintiff replied: "And the ſaid "Chriſtopher ſaith, that for Anything above al- "ledged, he the ſaid Chriſtopher ought not to be "barred from having and maintaining his Action "aforeſaid, becauſe proteſting the ſaid William "Brown never made any Election as he the ſaid "Timothy above ſuppoſeth for Plea, the ſaid Chriſ- "topher ſaith *that the ſaid William Brown did not* "*enter into or upon the ſaid mortgaged Premiſes for* "*the Non-payment of the ſaid Sum mentioned in the* "*Condition aforeſaid, and the Intereſt thereof*, as the "ſaid Timothy in his Plea aboveſaid hath alledged, "and this the ſaid Chriſtopher prayeth may be in- "quired of by the Country.

"*R. Dana.*"

Upon Demurrer, Exception taken to the Replication, that it was a Negative Pregnant. *Doct. Placitandi*, 256, cited: That either the whole Plea ſhould have been traverſed, or he ſhould have ſet forth the particular Matter. Cro. James, 559.

Contra. They having demurred to our Replication, on that Demurrer we may take Exception to their Plea, which if bad we need not anſwer their Exception to our Replication. Their Plea is inſufficient; for though he had entered upon the Mortgage, yet that is not concluſive that the Bond may not be ſued.

Upon this it was largely debated whether a Mortgage being ſued and entered upon, the Bond could have Effect, and *e contra.*

Ruled unanimouſly, that it could, and that the Plea is bad. (1)

Bond to be chancered next Term. (2)

---

(1) S. P. *Amory* v. *Fairbanks*, 3 Maſs. 562. *Ely* v. *Ely*, 6 Gray, 439. See alſo 8 Pick. 336; 5 Cuſh. 231.

(2) A bill in chancery was accordingly filed praying that the penalty "be chancered down to the ſum of one penny." But the Court gave £176 10*s.*

on the grounds that if the underlying defense demurrer was bad, "we need not answer this Exception to our Replication." He then focused on the central issue i.e., "[t]heir Plea is insufficient; for though he had entered upon the Mortgage, yet that is not conclusive that the Bond may not be sued." *Reports*, 11.

The Court ignored the Defendant's pleading point, and the reference to the seventeenth-century English authority, and decided the case, as Dana had urged, on the central issue.

5 · LATER CITATIONS

The result was the later law in Massachusetts. See *Amory* v. *Fairbanks* (1793), 3 Mass. 562.

6 · NOTE

Once again the Court brushed aside a technical pleading point and did not address English authority on the point: i.e., the Defendant's "negative pregnant" argument. It focused on the central issue, and came up with a practical result.

CASE 9

Dudley *v.* Dudley.

Rec. 1762. Fol. 415.

Devise as follows: "I give to my Son W. my new Farm in R.," "from whence he shall annually supply and bring Home to his Mother her Firewood during her Life." "I also give him my Farm of 1000 Acres

Dudley *vers.* Dudley & al. (3)

THE late Governour Dudley, by his Will, devised as follows:

"I give my Wife One Hundred Pounds per "Annum, to be paid quarterly during her Life by "Paul Dudley my eldest Son, out of the Issues and "Rents of my Estates herein given him.

"I give to my Son, William Dudley, my new "Farm in the Woods in Roxbury, containing 150 "Acres with the Woodland there, purchased of "Devotion Craft, from whence he shall annually supply

(3) This was a review of a "plea of partition" brought by the younger children of William Dudley, against Thomas the eldest son. The special verdict found that the premises were the same called by the testator his "farm of a thousand acres at Manchaug," that William died intestate, and that Thomas then entered on the premises; "if therefore the said William, by force of the will aforesaid, took an estate in fee simple in the thousand acres aforesaid, then they find for the defendants costs; otherwise they find for the original defendant and now plaintiff."

Dudley v. *Dudley & al.* (1762)
2 Geo. III (Aug.) in the
Superior Court of Judicature

1 · BRIEF DESCRIPTION

Here was a case of the greatest importance, both legally and economically. It was a will contest about the will of the late Governor. The will was poorly drafted. The key clause read: "my Lands descend after the Manner of England forever; to the Male Heirs first, and after to the Females. If either of my Sons die without Male Issue, his Brother and his Male Issue shall inherit the Lands herein bequeathed," *Reports*, 13. Testator, the late Governor Dudley, devised to his younger son a farm in Roxbury, from which the son would be obligated to provide his mother with firewood, as well as a "Farm of one 1000 Acres at Manchaug and Three Hundred Pounds toward building him an House," *Reports*, 13.

At issue was whether the younger son, William, held the Manchaug farm as a fee simple or a fee tail. (A "fee tail" could always revert to the heirs of the grantor if there was a failure of issue, making it technically difficult to sell the property outright for more than a life estate. A fee simple delivered a clear title. See *Law Commonplace*, page [102], n.1. For a full discussion of banning entails in colonial Massachusetts, see *Baker* v. *Mattocks*, *Reports*, 234, (Case 29, 1763), Note 6. One could not bar an entail by will in Massachusetts until 1791). Opponents of the entail argued that the testator knew that the younger son would live in Roxbury, that the £300 was insufficient to build a house in Roxbury, and thus the devise of the farm in Manchaug was intended as a fee simple so that the son could sell the land to finance a home. The opponents also argued that the closing provision, although it hewed closely to the wording of a fee tail, failed to meet the necessary formalities, and a holding inimical to the free alienation of land should not be read into ambiguous wording. Whether the Superior Court of Judicature agreed with the narrow reading of this will, or the more sweeping rule of hostility toward finding estates of less than fee simple is unclear. The Court ruled that the will devised a fee simple estate in the farm, without comment or explanation.

2 · RECORD

Available at Rec. 1762, Fol. 415.

" ſupply and bring Home to his Mother her Fire-
" wood during her Life.

" I alſo give him my Farm of one 1000 Acres
" at Manchaug and Three Hundred Pounds toward
" building him an Houſe.

" I have already diſpoſed in Marriage of my
" Four Daughters, and paid them what I intended.

" I further give each of them 1000 Acres, to be
" taken out of my 6000 Acres in the Town of Ox-
" ford; and to my Nephew Daniel Allen, and my
" Niece Ann Hilton, 500 Acres, out of the ſame
" Dividend, to be equally divided between them;
" all thoſe Lands to deſcend to the Children ſev-
" erally, and the *Heirs of their Bodies.*

" To my eldeſt Son Paul I give the Inheritance
" of all my Houſes and Lands in Roxbury, Oxford,
" Woodſtock, Newtown, Brookline, Merrimack, or
" elſewhere, all my Stock, Debt, Money, and all
" Eſtate belonging to me whatſoever, except as
" above ſet down. *And my Will is that my Lands*
" *deſcend after the Manner of England forever; to the*
" *Male Heirs firſt, and after to the Females. If either*
" *of my Sons die without Male Iſſue, his Brother and*
" *his Male Iſſue ſhall inherit the Lands herein be-*
" *queathed,*" *&c.*

at M. and £300 toward building him an Houſe." After other Legacies and a Reſiduary Deviſe, the following: " And my Will is that my Lands deſcend after the Manner of England forever; to the Male Heirs firſt and after to the Females. If either of my Sons die without Male Iſſue, his Brother and his Male Iſſue ſhall inherit the Lands herein bequeathed." *Held*, that W. took a Fee Simple in the " Farm of 1000 Acres at M."

The Queſtion in this Caſe was, whether William Dudley took a Fee Simple by his Father's Will.

Mr.

[P. 13]

The action was originally brought by the younger children of William against the eldest son, Thomas, seeking partition of the land. William died intestate. If the land were an estate in fee simple, it would be inherited by all his children equally under Massachusetts law, "for here all Estates are partible," *Reports*, 14. If it were an entail, then it vested in Thomas as tenant in tail. See *Law Commonplace*, page [102], n.1.

3 · PROFESSIONALS INVOLVED

The best lawyers in the Colony were briefed on this case. James Otis Jr. (1725–1783) and Jeremiah Gridley (1701/2–1767) argued for the younger children and the fee simple. Robert Auchmuty (1723–1788), Benjamin Kent (1708–1788), and Edmund Trowbridge (1709–1793) argued for William's eldest son, Thomas, and for the entail. See *Law in Colonial Massachusetts*, *supra*, 348, 376–381, 345, 355. All five lawyers argued at length. See short biographies in *Appendix 6*, *infra*. Otis and Gridley frequently collaborated.

4 · AUTHORITY

Otis argued from *Coke on Littleton* (First Institute) (1628) and *Wood's Institute of the Laws of England* (1720), against favoring the entail. See *Law Commonplace*, page [2], n. 1; page [7], n. 3; page [7], n. 9. Kent answered, relying on *Fisher* v. *Nichols*, 3 *Salkeld's Reports* (1689–1712) 394, on general principles of will construction. See *Law Commonplace*, page [32], n. 7. The Court at this point asked for specific authorities. *Reports*, 15.

Gridley then cited three English cases and two treatises, which Trowbridge countered with two treatises and two English cases. None of these authorities were directly on point given the extraordinarily eccentric drafting of the will, but the Court expressed a clear interest in getting all the authorities "read now." *Reports*, 15. One reason might have been their suspicion that the losing party in a case this big was likely to try to appeal to the Privy Council in London pursuant to the Provincial Charter of 1691. See *Anc. Chart.*, 32. This was exactly what happened. See *Reports*, 25, S. Quincy n. 9.

5 · LATER CITATIONS

Except for Quincy's own cross-citation, none found. Later Massachusetts cases did not find entails unless clearly stated. There were obvious policy reasons to try to deliver a clear fee simple, unless that was an impossible reading. See "Introduction—The Reports," *supra*, notes 128, 129, and accompanying text.

Mr. Otis for the Fee Simple. (4) The Words upon which I ſuppoſe they build their Fee Tail are theſe, "*If either of my Sons die without Male Iſſue, his* "*Brother*," *&c.* There are no Words precedent to theſe which can be ſuppoſed in the leaſt to favour that Opinion, but on the contrary are inconſiſtent with it; he muſt have intended to have given him a Fee in the 1000 Acres, or his End, which was to build him an Houſe, could not be anſwered, for £300 can't be ſuppoſed any way ſufficient, and therefore we muſt ſuppoſe he deſigned William ſhould ſell the Land; and it is Law and Reaſon that a ſpecial Deviſe ſhould take Effect, which could not otherwiſe, a general Clauſe notwithſtanding, nor is the Law to be wreſted in favor of ſuch Eſtates; for however Eſtates Tail were once favoured and praiſed, as in the Statute *De Donis*, yet Ld. Coke tells us they were convinced of their Miſtake, and exclaims in pretty full Terms. Co. L. 20. Wood, Inſt. And here the Reaſon is greater than in England, for here all Eſtates are partable. (5)

Nay I don't think the Words give even Paul an Eſtate Tail. The Intention of the Teſtator is one of the grand Principles, and ſhall not be counteracted, and it is to be favoured as far as poſſible conſiſtent with the Rules of the Common Law; and unleſs there are ſome operative Words, Fee Simple muſt

---

(4) The MS. report of the arguments in this caſe bears evidence of being the original minutes taken in court. A little confuſion, and an occaſional defect in grammar, are thus accounted for.

(5) See *poſt*, *Baker* v. *Mattocks*.

6 · NOTES

In this "high-visibility" case, after hours of subtle argument, the Court delivered a one-line judgment, "The Chief Justice delivered the Judgment of the Court in Favor of the Fee Simple." The likelihood of an effort to appeal to the Privy Council, an effort which did in fact occur, may have inhibited the Court from giving explicit reasons. See *Reports*, 26, S. Quincy n. 9.

And reasons would have been important here, as there were two plausible grounds for the result. Was the Court convinced that the Governor had not intended an entail? In which case the wording of the will was extraordinarily misleading. Or was the Court adopting a rule of construction hostile to finding any but fully devisable estates, unless the wording was technically perfect to establish an entail. This latter ruling would have strongly supported the Colonial law of partible estates, essentially supporting the rights of younger children and women against "English style" primogeniture. Any reader of Jane Austen's *Pride and Prejudice* (1813) would appreciate the difference. See "Introduction—The Reports," notes 128, 129, and accompanying text. See also Richard B. Morris's classic discussion in *Study and History of American Law* (1959), which includes an extensive discussion of *Quincy's Reports*, including *Dudley* v. *Dudley*. See Richard B. Morris, *Study and History of American Law*, 95–97 and accompanying notes.

My reading of the will leads me to believe, with Samuel Quincy, that the Governor intended to give both brothers entailed estates, with cross remainders, also entailed. See *Reports*, 26, S. Quincy n. 9. This would make sense of words like "And my Will is that my Lands descend after the Manner of England, forever . . . If either of my Sons die without Male Issue, his Brother and his Male Issue shall inherit the Lands. . . ." (*Reports*, 13.) If so, the Court was seizing on the draftsman's incompetence to strike a bold stroke for a presumption of partibility. To say so openly, however, might tempt the Privy Council to interfere. As it was, the Court denied Thomas leave to appeal to England, probably on the grounds that such appeals were permitted for "personal" actions only, not "real" actions as here. See *Reports*, 25, S. Quincy n. 9. See also *The Charter of the Province of the Massachusetts Bay, 1691*, which reads, "And whereas we judge it necessary, that all our subjects should have the liberty to appeal to us . . . in any *personal action*, wherein the matter in difference, doth exceed the value of three hundred pounds sterling, . . ." *Anc. Chart.*, 32 [ital. added].

muſt be ſuppoſed to be given. Now here are no expreſs Words in Favour of a Fee Simple. "And "my Will is that my Land deſcend after the Man- "ner of England forever, to the Male Heirs firſt, "and after to the Females, &c." I think it manifeſt his Intention was, that they ſhould deſcend according to the Common Law, which knows no Eſtate Tail; and that being his Intention, the Law will not admit an Inheritance contrary to the known Law of the Country; and this being contrary to the Law deſcends as a Fee Simple, and the Word "Male Heirs, &c." ſhall be attributed to Unſkillfulneſs.

Mr. Kent for the Tail. Mr. Otis can't ſuppoſe an Eſtate Tail can't be made in this Province, ſo we need only inquire into the Teſtator's Intention. Cites 3 Salk. 394, *Fiſher* vs. *Nichols*, of the favourable Conſtruction of Wills. In Paul's Gift there was nothing enjoined him, but annual Payments which the Profits would ſecure. "To William I give "Manchaug Farm, and £300 towards building him "an Houſe," they are evidently ſeparate. He gives him Manchaug Farm, and moreover I give him £300 towards building him an Houſe. To Paul he gives the *Inheritance* of his Land, &c.; this Word is uſed in Tails. Vid. Caſes in Eq. Abr. 178, 179. 1 Salk. Tit. Deviſe, 234.

The Court aſked, as there had been no Authorities yet produced on the other Side, whether it would not be more regular to have them read now, before the Council in Favour of the Tail cloſed. Upon which *Mr. Gridley* produced his Authorities. 1 Inſt. 9 b, any Eſtate charged is a Fee Simple. 2 Peere Wms.

[P. 15]

Despite the denial of leave to appeal, it appears that an appeal to the Privy Council was taken by Thomas anyway. It was referred to Committee on May 5, 1765. An order for hearing was made on May 16, 1765, and on December 16, 1765, an appearance was entered by the respondents. See *Acts of the Privy Council, Colonial Series* (ed. W. L. Grant, J. Munro, Hereford, 1911), vol. 4, 688. No further entry has been found in the Privy Council records by the editors after that. My special thanks to my distinguished colleague, Sharon H. O'Connor. For a full discussion of Privy Council appeals involving Massachusetts real property, see *Banister* v. *Henderson* (1765), *Reports*, 119, Case 42, Note 6, *infra*.

Wms. 673. Siderfin, 312. Moore's Rep. 53. Viner, Tit. Devife, 82. 3 Mod. 82.

Mr. Trowbridge for the Tail. In his firft Devife to his Wife, he gives her £100, for Paul to pay out of the Rents and Iffues of his Eftate, which evidently exclude from his Intention to give Paul a Fee Simple; fo in the Gift of the Wood it is idle to fay that is greater or anything near equal to the yearly Rents of the 150 Acres. And as to the Manchaug Farm and £300; it is true £300 would not build him an Houfe at Roxbury, but does it appear that he meant fo? Perhaps, and moft probably, he intended on the Farm at Manchaug.

Ch. Juft. The words are build *him* an Houfe; not an Houfe fimply, but *him*, one whom he knew was to live at Roxbury.

Trowbridge continues. The firft Words in a Will may direct, but the laft fhall controul, and this is the Difference between Wills and Deeds. The Devife to his Couzins is in thefe Words, "*to defcend to* "*the Children feverally, and the Heirs of their Bodies.*" A Fee Tail *may defcend.* If in the firft Words he intended a Fee Simple, in the laft he altered his Mind, and intended to controul the firft. "If *either* "die without Male Iffue, then," &c. — *either.* A Devife of this Sort is as great an Eftate Tail as can be given, and the Word Body fhall be fupplied. Lilly, Tit. Devife. 6 Coke, 16, *Collier's Cafe.* Ventris, 230. Hawk. Abr. 17. Had he defigned it fhould defcend as Fee Simple in England, it would have defcended

deſcended to the Daughters of William before the Sons of Paul, &c., but here it is otherwiſe.

Mr. Gridley for the Fee. The Intent of the Deviſor is the only Thing your Honours will govern yourſelves by, (Vid. Peere Wms. *ut ſupra,*) and that Intention is to be ſpelt out by little Hints, by other Deviſes, &c. Viner, Tit. Deviſe, 182. Notwithſtanding 'tis a Deviſe he ſays 'ſhall *deſcend.*' He deſigned William ſhould ſell, and he muſt ſell, and that gives a Fee Simple, as much as expreſs Words. He deſigned William ſhould live in Roxbury, and £300 is not ſufficient to build him an Houſe there, a Dwelling Houſe. The Law takes Notice of the Rule of Grants, Words in the Beginning and End refer to the Whole. Sid. *ut ſupra.* It is not—I give 1000 Acres, I give him £300 towards building him an Houſe, but they are ſo coupled as to be the ſame; I give him 1000 Acres and £300 towards building him an Houſe. Vid. Moore's *ut ſup.* (*Ch. Juſt.* In the Authority you cite, they were each equally applicable to the Purpoſe, here not: Land does not ſeem ſo much ſo as Money.) In this Country we make our Real Eſtate almoſt Perſonal Eſtate by Act of Parliament, and our own Acts; beſides, Gov. Dudley did not perhaps leave a Sufficiency in Money. The Word *deſcend* I grant is uſed in Tails, but when it is uſed, there we always uſe the proper expreſs, Words of Tail; here it is—ſhall deſcend to him—not the Heirs of the Body, &c. Eſtates Tail can never be ſuppoſed by a Deviſe after the Manner of England, for being a minor Eſtate ſhould have been mentioned in expreſs Words. Suppoſing the Females deceaſe, there is

3 no

[P. 17]

no further Devife, if it is a Tail. The Law of this Province forbids his giving it as the Law of England: But if he meant fo, it could not be Tail, for it is the Common Law. I imagine Governor Dudley thought that was the Manner of England, that the Sons of the other fhould take exclufively of the Daughters of the other, and the Will is inaccurate throughout as to the Daughters. Shall what is underftood be fet afide by one infenfible Expreffion?

It was moved by *Mr. Kent*, and feconded by *Mr. Trowbridge*, that they might be heard again before Judgment, and *the Court* thinking it a Matter of Nicety and Confequence, defired a further Argument, and continued it to the next Term for Judgment. (4)

Mr. Otis. The fingle Queftion is, whether thefe Words, "I alfo give him my Farm of 1000 Acres at Manchaug and Three Hundred Pounds to build him an Houfe," compared with the whole Will, make a Fee Simple or a Tail. The Words of Acts executed in the Life are to be "to Heirs forever," in a Fee Simple, "Heirs of the Body" general, Male or Female, in a Fee Tail; greater Indulgence is to be given to Wills.

I fhall endeavour to fhow that from this Claufe by itfelf, or confidered with Refpect to the others, it muft

---

(4) The report of the cafe accordingly breaks off at this point in the MS., and is refumed between the cafes of *Gardner* v. *Purrington* and *Rogers* v. *Kenrick*, decided at the next term. For convenience, however, it is printed as a whole.

muſt be the Intention of Dudley to give his Son a Fee Simple; and ſeparately conſidered, there could be no Doubt; but 'tis the Clauſe "after the Manner of England, &c." which cauſes it. The Queſtion will be whether the laſt Words create a Tail in any, even to the Eſtate given Paul, and if it does, whether they extend through the Whole. Ld. Hobart ſays the two great Principles upon which all Deviſes hang, are the Intention of the Teſtator, which ſhall be indulged as far as the Rules of Law admit.

I think the Conſideration of the Intention, is the moſt rational Way of judging of any Will; and I think whoever does that will think any Eſtate Tail remote from the Teſtator's Intention. The firſt Words are only an Inheritance according to the Intent of the Common Law; his Intent was, I allow, to make a Common Law Deſcent, Spite of the Province Law,—to cut off his Daughters only. We ſhall conſider how far this Intent is to be indulged. No Man ſhall create an Eſtate contrary to the Laws of his Country; we know none according to the Courſe of the Common Law. As for the other Words of the Will, Manchaug Farm is given for ſuch a Purpoſe, as could not be anſwered by ſuch an Eſtate as they contend for; he has it given to build an Houſe, which he could not do, if he had only his Life in it. Co. Lit. 9, b. It is an old Principle, that paying is an Argument that the Land ſhall go. It has been ſaid that a Deviſe of Woodland formerly in this Country conveyed a Fee Simple, and that it has been adjudged ſo; any Words that can amount to an Intent that the Deviſee

visee ſhall have the Advantage of the Whole of it, ſhall have a Fee; it is not the firſt or laſt Part of a Will that ſhall ſtand, but the Whole together. Viner, 324, Tit. Deviſe. If he intended he ſhould reap the ſame Benefit, as he would if it had been a Fee, it ſhall be. Viner, 224, 13. Will to be taken altogether. Ibid. 182, 11, 12, 13. His Intent being contrary to Law, firſt Deviſees take a Fee Simple. Ibid. 229. Swin. 165, 141. Entails diſfavoured.—No Tail unleſs the firſt Words give a Fee Simple; none where it is given in any ſuch Manner. The firſt Words may be controuled, where it is a plain Fee Simple, here it is not; he tries to invent a new Conveyance, his Words are apt to convey according to the Law of England; he muſt either give it according to the Cuſtom of the Country, or in Fee Tail general or ſpecial. An implied Eſtate Tail has never been raiſed when the firſt Words were to give an Eſtate unknown to the Law of the Country. No Teſtator was ever interpreted to mean to give a Tail becauſe that came neareſt to his Intention.

Mr. Gridley's Authorities: Sid. 312—Rule that firſt and laſt Words relate to the whole; middle to the middle only. Moor, Caſe 153, p. 52. Plowd. Comment. 540. Viner, Tit. Deviſe, 182, 11. 3 Lev. 111. 4 Mod. 154. 3 Lev. 125. 3 Mod. 182. Styles, 276, 392.

Mr. Auchmuty. I ſhall conſider this by looking into the Words of the Will, collect the Intent, and compare it with the Rules of Law.—"His Brother and his Male Iſſue ſhall inherit." Theſe Words are

[P. 20]

are deſcriptive of an Eſtate Tail, and no other. The firſt Words are liable to be reſtrained, controuled, or defeated by the laſt; if a laſt Word contradict the firſt, the laſt ſhall ſtand. 1 Lilly, 449. Co. Lit. 112, b. The Words relate as well to William as Paul. Cro. Ja. 448. This is a Caſe Mr. Otis ſaid could not be found. Cro. Ja. 695, *Chadock* v. *Cowley*. It ſeems abſurd that an expreſs Eſtate may be controuled by latter Words, and yet that where there is no certain Eſtate given by the firſt Words, that they ſhall not; I ſhould think they might *a fortiori*. 9 Coke, 128, *Sonday's Caſe*. 1 Ld. Raymond, 185, *Baker* vs. *Wall*. Ib. 568, *Nottingham* vs. *Jennings*. Comyns, 539, *Brice* vs. *Smith*. I cite theſe to ſhow the firſt Words need not be expreſs, and that the laſt ſhall explain the firſt. I utterly deny that the giving Woodland could by Law give a Fee; but if that be the Caſe, when the Teſtator afterwards explains his Meaning, that muſt cauſe it to be otherwiſe. As to the Practice of the Court, the Rules of Law by being recollected would deſtroy it. I believe no Practice agreeable to that Rule of Woodland can be brought, and if there can, not where there are other ſuch Words as are here.

As to the Houſe, it does not appear that it was to build an Houſe at Roxbury; he was at that Time building an Houſe there, and the Deviſe, which takes no Effect till the Death of the Teſtator, might be ſome Years off.—Could he not have paſſed it by Deed, had that been his Intent? It is much more rational to conclude, that, as he had given him a Farm, he intended he ſhould live there, therefore gave him £300 to build him an Houſe there,

there, to encourage the Settlement: There are two Tracts given William and Paul much in the ſame Words. I can't find any Reaſon why they ſhould be confined to Paul; all the Lands therein bequeathed, in Caſe one died without Iſſue Male, are given to the other; he deſigning to entail all his Lands to the Survivor of his Sons, and his Male Iſſue, he has done it. I agree he intended to exclude the Daughters; could he then think he was giving a Fee Simple, when he expreſsly excludes them? He has not given a general Eſtate Tail, but confined it to Male Iſſue—They ſay he is making a new Eſtate, I ſay he has made an old one. In the Caſe of Raymond, 'tis ſaid he intended an Eſtate Tail, becauſe the Daughters were excluded. Take it as a Tail, all Purpoſes will be anſwered, the Daughters will be excluded, the Heirs Male will have it; and 'tis a Tail with Croſs Remainders, all which he ſeems to have had in View. The Heir-at-Law is favoured—ſo he is here: As to the paying, it is not always denotive of a Fee: The Wood is out of Roxbury, what is that to Manchaug? He has given that Farm, and ordered that Wood to be furniſhed; there is a Difference where a Sum in groſs is ordered, and where an annual Sum not exceeding the Rents. Co. Lit. 9, b. There is an Authority that ſays, where he gives it ſpecially, it is not an Inheritance. 2 Bacon. William could not be a Loſer by ſuch a Payment. Gilbert cites Cro. Eliz. 498. If the Deviſor orders A to pay B a Sum in groſs, this gives a Fee, though not even then, I ſuppoſe, if he afterwards explains it otherwiſe. As to the Authorities of Viner, they relate only to the Conſtruction of Wills, which we agree with them: As

[P. 22]

As for the Cafe from Moor, of the Coats, (5) they were to be paid forever: It would be inconfiftent, but that as the Incumbrance was perpetual, the Eftate fhould be perpetual alfo. The other Moor Cafe is only that all Parts of a Will are operative, we agree to it, if they can be reconciled. How can it be fuppofed the Land as well as £300 are to go towards building him an Houfe?—the other Words of the Will difpofe of the Land otherwife, this is in Anfwer to the Grammar Cafe (6); Plowden's Cafe is only the Say of Council. Moor's Cafe of the Item (7) is anfwered by Cro. Ja. 695. The Intention of the Will can be no otherwife anfwered than by Tail;—if a Tail not an Iota is loft.

Mr. Trowbridge. We all agree that the whole Will is to be taken together; that if the firft Words are doubtful, the laft may explain them, but if the firft are exprefs, the latter fhall not controul them. It muft be abfurd to fuppofe that the Farm as well as Money was given to build an Houfe; in fome Cafes the *Item* may couple, in fome not. 5 Co. 7, *Wyndham's Cafe.* 6 Co. 61, *Catesby's Cafe.* That the Word "*and*" is to be governed according to the Subject-Matter.—If there is any particular Eftate limited, paying does not make a Fee. 1 Vent. 227. Gilb. Law of Devifes. Comyn's, 539, *Brice* vs. *Smith.* Thofe Lands which he gives his Daughters, he expreffly entails, fo he does what he gives his Couzins, and ufes the Word *defcend* as he does here; as for the Word Inheritance, an Eftate Tail is

(5) Erroneoufly cited; the "Cafe of the Coats" is *Smith* v. *Tyndal*, 2 Salk. 685.

(6) Sid. 312.

(7) Moore, cafe 153.

is as much an Inheritance as a Fee Simple. As for the Manner of England, I deny that he meant Common Law, he only intended it ſhould be partable as here; If his Intent could not be anſwered according to the Rules of Law, the Law will mould it into ſuch one, as is moſt agreeable to his Will and Deſign.

Mr. Gridley. The Intent of the Deviſor ſhall be the Pole Star of the Will, and then every Iota ſhall have its Force, if it can conſiſtent with the reſt. I agree that the Subject-Matter muſt govern in all Caſes; the Subject-Matter here is a Supply to William to build him an Houſe. With Regard to Mr. Trowbridge's Authorities, I ſee not how they are applicable; the firſt is a Common Law Conveyance, to be judged by Common Law Maxims, to be taken moſt ſtrongly againſt the Grantor; here the Intent of the Deviſor is to be purſued;—If the £300 is given for the Houſe, the Lands are given; they are tied by an indiſſoluble Band, and can't be ſeparated, but by a Violence upon Common Senſe. The Moor Caſe has *Item*, here is none. We muſt conſider of our Country and Real Eſtate here: To a Perſon unacquainted with our Eſtate, this might ſeem ſtrange, but to us who know Real Eſtates are liable for the Payment of Debts, and are by Act of Parliament made Chattels Real, for the Payment of Debts, (8) that they are almoſt the only Things we have to trade upon, and that they continue in a Family ſcarce over three Generations, 'tis not ſtrange they ſhould be put upon the ſame Footing with Perſonal Eſtate. In this I take it, both muſt be ſupported

(8) Anc. Chart. 292.

ſuppoſed for the ſame Purpoſe, it is a Conſtruction ariſes from the Neceſſity of the Thing, and the Nature of Real Eſtate here. As for the Objection againſt our Conſtruction, that it is uncertain how long he would live; there was an Houſe for Paul, and one deſigned for William; if there was none erecting, 'twas for one hereafter to be built, if one was built, to finiſh it or to reimburſe him. As for the after Words; whether they ſhall deſtroy the Force of the Firſt — the Words "after the Manner of England," — it being unlimited, it muſt be Common Law; who would ſuppoſe Tail Male to mean the Manner of England?

"The Heirs Male, and after to the Female;" the whole Complexion is to the Creation of a new Eſtate; this laſt ought to be wholly laid aſide, this extraordinary, impoſſible Clauſe.

If this Clauſe operate at all, it can't take to the Manchaug Farm; if that can be ſatisfied elſewhere, it need not be applied here; let it go to the Roxbury Lands. 9 Mod. 154, *Adams* vs. *Clark.*

The Chief Juſtice delivered the Judgment of the Court in Favour of the Fee Simple. (9)

---

(9) This judgment is recorded as of September term at Worceſter, but the entry bears evidence of having been inſerted at a later date. The deciſion was undoubtedly given, as here reported, at February term in Suffolk. It alſo appears that "immediately upon entering up this judgment, the ſaid Thomas moved for an appeal to his Majeſty in Council, which the Court did not allow." The Province Charter provided for an appeal to the King in "perſonal actions" only. Anc. Chart. 32.

It is to be regretted that we have no means of aſcertaining on what ground this deciſion was given. If the Court were ſatisfied that the

 land,

CASE 10

JACKSON *v.* FOYE.

Rec. 1762. Fol. 385.

Evidence of Payment of full Rent by a Tenant, for thirty Years, and of the giving a Note of Hand for the Balance found due on a Settlement, is ſufficient Proof of a Contract to pay Taxes under the Province Law, which provides that " where no Contract is " the Landlord ſhall reimburſe half the Taxes. *Ruſſell, J., diſſentiente.*

Jackſon *verſ.* Foye.

MRS. JACKSON was upwards of thirty Years a Tenant to Mrs. Foye, paid her Rent without any Deduction but for Repairs, which were often made. A. D. 1758 they ſettled Accounts, and Mrs. Jackſon, owing Mrs. Foye, gave her a Note of Hand on Intereſt. The preſent Action was brought by Jackſon againſt Foye for half the Rates for Twenty Years.

The only Queſtion was, whether theſe Settlements, that Note of Hand given, when, if the Rates had been reckoned, there would have been a Balance due to Jackſon, amounted to Evidence of an expreſs Contract.

The

land, as well as the money, was given " toward building the houſe," it was evidently excepted from any operation of the ſubſequent general clauſe. But if the effect of that clauſe became neceſſary to be conſidered, a more difficult queſtion muſt have ariſen. The words directing a deſcent " according to the manner of England," &c., ſeem clearly to intend a common law deſcent, in oppoſition to the law of the Province. But the words which immediately follow, " If either of my ſons die," &c., would ſeem to import an indefinite failure of iſſue, and to give the brothers eſtates in tail male general, with croſs remainders, alſo in tail male. *Abbott* v. *Eſſex Co.* 18 How. 202. *Hall* v. *Prieſt*, 6 Gray, 18, and caſes cited. The queſtion cannot be better ſtated than in Mr. Otis's words, *ante*, p. 20 — " Can an implied eſtate tail ever be raiſed, when the firſt words give an eſtate unknown to the laws of the country ? " In the caſe of *Baniſter* v. *Henderſon*, *poſt*, 131, Mr. Auchmuty ſays that " the point of charge had weight " in this caſe. This ſeems hardly probable, as one was directly on the rents and profits, and the other a charge of wood to be furniſhed from the land itſelf. See 24 Pick. 139. And even a perſonal charge of a ſum in groſs will not enlarge a clear eſtate tail, though only ariſing by implication. 2 Jarman on Wills, (1st Am. ed.) 172. 5 T. R. 535. 2 B. & Ad. 318.

Jackson v. *Foye* (1762)
2 George III (Aug.) in the
Superior Court of Judicature

1 · BRIEF DESCRIPTION

Tenant brought suit against the landlord to recover half of the taxes paid on rental property over course of 20 years pursuant to the Annual Tax Acts of the Province. See *The Acts and Resolves . . . of the Province of the Massachusetts Bay*, vol. IV (1757–1768), Boston, 1881, chap. 12, "Province Laws – 1762–63," 596. "[W]here no contract is, the landlord to re-imburse one-half of the tax set upon such houses and lands; and to estimate Negro, Indian, and Mollatto servants proportionately as other personal estate . . . ." *Id.* (For one of the earliest examples of such a law, see Tax Act, Provincial Statute 6 William & Mary (1694). See also *Reports*, 39, S. Quincy n.3.) Special thanks to Mark Sullivan, research librarian beyond compare. The Tax Act provided that "where no Contract is" the Landlord shall reimburse half of the taxes. When the landlord and tenant settled accounts, the tenant, who believed she owed the landlord money, gave the landlord a "Note of Hand on Interest." The landlord argued that the note constituted evidence of an express contract extinguishing any claim by the tenant. The Superior Court of Judicature agreed, over the dissent of one member, and directed the jury to find for the defendant landlady.

2 · RECORD

Available at Rec. 1762, Fol. 385.

The Plaintiff tenant brought an action for trespass upon the case in the Inferior Court of Common Pleas, where the Defendant prevailed and recovered costs. The tenant appealed to the Superior Court of Judicature Court of Assize and General Gaol Delivery, where the judgment below was reversed. The Record of the appeal to the Superior Court of Judicature makes no note of the directed verdict, but records that the jury found for the Defendant landlord.

3 · PROFESSIONALS INVOLVED

James Otis Jr. (1725–1783), the patriot, represented the Plaintiff tenant. See *Law in Colonial Massachusetts*, *supra*, 348, and *Appendix 6*, "Brief Biographies."

The Court (*Juſtice Ruſſell diſſentiente*) gave it to the Jury as their Opinion, that it did, and directed them to give the Defendant Coſts, which they did. (1)

---

(1) This deciſion was under the following proviſion contained for many years in the annual tax acts of the Province: "Saving all contracts between landlord and tenant, and where no contract is, the landlord to reimburſe one half of the tax ſet upon ſuch houſes and lands." See *poſt*, *Derumple* v. *Clark*. The ſame proviſion in ſubſtance is contained in Rev. Sts. c. 7, § 8, by which the tenant was authorized to retain half the taxes out of his rent, unleſs there was an agreement to the contrary. By Gen. Sts. c. 11, § 9, he may ſo retain the whole taxes or recover the ſame by action.

Justice Chambers Russell dissented. This was one of his three dissents out of 78 cases. See *Appendix 1*, "Judicial Dissents."

4 · AUTHORITY

None cited.

5 · LATER CITATIONS

The grandson notes that the Commonwealth continued this policy for some time, see Rev. Sts. c.7, § 8, and ultimately, a tenant could retain all of the taxes paid on rental property, Gen. Sts. c.1, § 9. The grandson also cross-referenced *Derumple* v. *Clark*, *Reports*, 38, Case 17.

6 · NOTE

This is an important contract case, and it is easy to see why Russell dissented. The tenant of thirty years believed she owed the landlord money, and so—on an accounting for the last twenty years—gave the landlord a written promissory note at interest. But if the landlord had reimbursed half the taxes paid to the tenant, as required by the Province Law, then the *tenant* would be owed money. If we apply modern contract doctrine to this case, it is unclear what consideration the Plaintiff received for her promise to pay money to the landlord, even though she was actually owed money. Surely the tenant losing her rights to reimbursement of the tax was not a detriment to the landlord! A modern court would be unlikely to find an enforceable contract, unless the tenant was clearly aware of the effect of the agreement, and also received some benefit for it, i.e., "bargained for" consideration.

CASE II

Wiſwall *verſ.* Hall.

WISWALL *v.* HALL.

Rec. 1762. Fol. 385.

Referees cannot be admitted to teſtify that their Award that each Party ſhould bear his own Coſts, was made in Conſideration of a Promiſe by one Party never to enforce a certain Judgment againſt the other.

PLAINTIFF and Defendant had formerly ſubmitted Matters in Controverſy to certain Referees, who had reported thereon. This Action was brought by Wiſwall *vs.* Hall to recover the Coſts upon that former Suit, for though the Referees had reported that they ſhould bear the Coſts between them, yet Wiſwall alledged that it was upon a Promiſe of Hall to bear the whole Coſts. (2) To verify this he offered the Referees as Evidence. But *the Court ruled* unanimouſly that they could not by parol Evidence controul the Report which was of Record. (3)

---

(2) This is inaccurately ſtated. The declaration alleges that the promiſe by the defendant, but for which "the referees would have awarded the plaintiff coſts," was, never to enforce a certain other judgment for coſts previouſly recovered.

(3) Arbitrators cannot by parol teſtimony contradict their formal award in writing. 10 Met. 433. 4 Cuſh. 317, 399.

Wiswall v. *Hall* (1762)
2 George III (Aug.) in the
Superior Court of Judicature

1 · BRIEF DESCRIPTION

Parol evidence (i.e., oral or extrinsic) by way of referee's testimony is inadmissible to control, modify or contradict the referee's formal Report at arbitration. In his Report, the referee decreed that the Plaintiff and the Defendant share the costs of a matter submitted to arbitration. The Plaintiff then brought a separate suit to recover his costs at arbitration, contending that there was a parol, collateral promise to that effect. The Plaintiff sought to offer as evidence the testimony of the referee, but the Court refused to admit it.

This case was similar to *Poor* v. *Dougharty*, *Reports*, 1, Case 1, heard in the same term. There, a sharply divided Court did, in the end, admit evidence arguably barred by a formal legal rule to prevent a patent injustice.

2 · RECORD

Available at Rec. 1762, Fol. 385.

As Samuel Quincy notes (note 2), the record indicated that the actual promise argued by the Plaintiff was different from that set out by the report. Josiah Quincy Jr. states that it was a promise by "Hall to bear the whole Costs." The record indicates that it was a promise by Hall not to enforce another judgment for costs, without which "the referees would have awarded the plaintiff costs" (Declaration).

Also available:

Wiswall v. *Hall*, (same) Aug. 1760, No. 81064.

- Judgment and Order that Hugh Hall, Jacob Royall, & James Pitts are obliged to Samuel Wiswall of Bellingham for 750 pounds, Aug. 30, 1760.
- Notice of Appeal by Hall; saying that Hall will prosecute a Writ of Review with the Superior Court of Judicature, and setting out 12% interest on the judgment if he loses. No interest would apply if the judgment was recovered in part. Hall, Royall and Pitts signed it.

Wiswall v. *Hall*, (same) June 8, 1768, No. 88362. Note: Hall was a lawyer.

- Court Order concerning deed on swampland. Examined by Nathaniel Hatch. States that Hall will pay Wiswall 40.2:3 plus costs as final and full discharge. Mentions lawyers Josiah Edson and Joseph Scott. The itemized costs are as follows:

House Charge	0.18:0
Referee's Charge	5.14:0
Plaintiff's Travel	0.18:0 each
Attendance at 3 days	0.4:6
Witnesses travel and Attendance	0.12:0

Wiswall v. *Hall* (also "Hall v. Pond") Feb. 1755

- Contracts conveying farm.

3 · PROFESSIONALS INVOLVED

None indicated.

4 · AUTHORITY

None cited.

5 · LATER CITATIONS

This remained good Massachusetts law. See *Withington* v. *Warren*, 51 Mass. 433, 10 Met. 431, at 433 (1845); *Bigelow* v. *Maynard*, 58 Mass., 4 Cush. 317 (1849); *Clark* v. *Burt,* 58 Mass. 396, 4 Cush. 396, at 399. Case 11 was cited as authority in *Evans* v. *Clapp*, 123 Mass. 165 (1877). There the Court, in determining which questions were concluded by the award of a referee, held that the referee was a competent witness to establish the facts of what took place before him. His parol evidence, however, could not be used to vary or control a written award. The Court cited by example to *Wiswall* v. *Hall*, *Reports*, 27, Case 11. See *Evans* v. *Clapp*, *supra*, 123 Mass. 165, at 170.

6 · NOTE

One of the eternal issues of law is whether to strictly enforce technical rules, which give certainty to proceedings; or to bend these rules to prevent an injustice, or a "trap for the unwary." In a previous evidence case, *Poor* v. *Dougharty*,

Reports, 1, Case 1, *supra*, a sharply divided Court did bend the rules slightly to let in vital evidence. Here they did not, possibly because of the importance of being able to rely on a finished arbitrator's report. On the other hand, if the Plaintiff's account of the situation was correct, and he was eager to call on an arbitrator to confirm them, an injustice was done. The Plaintiff was trapped by failing to have the collateral agreement set out in the report. Rulings such as this indicate that formality in a colonial judicial system could outweigh "rough justice."

CASE 12

Sayer *v.* Thorp.

Rec. 1763. Fol. 17.

Whether the Owner and Hirer of a Veſſell can join in an Action of Treſpaſs for running away with the Veſſell — *quære.*

Sayer & al. *verſ.* Thorp & al.

THE only Queſtion of Law in this Caſe was, whether the Owner of a Veſſell and the Perſon who hired and freighted her could join in an Action of Treſpaſs for running away with the Veſſell. (1) It was not doubted that they might both have their Actions, (2) but whether they could join was the Doubt. It was ſaid on one Side, that Tenant

---

(1) There are ſeveral depoſitions on file in this caſe, from which it appears that the ſloop Proſperous was employed in freighting wood on the Chignecto River, Nova Scotia, for the uſe of Fort Cumberland, and that the party who ran away with her were deſerting ſoldiers of the fort. The defence was, the conſent or connivance of the maſter, who was alleged to have been paid for a ſimilar uſe of the ſloop on a former occaſion, and to have induced the attempt by telling the ſoldiers that there would be no reſiſtance, and that they were fools to ſtay in ſo bad a place after their time was up. And in his own depoſition he acknowledges having found forty-one dollars in his cabin, which he was told the ſoldiers had left, and which he was induced to put in his cheſt. There appears alſo among the papers a printed proclamation by Governor Pownall, bearing date March 17, 1759, and reciting that his Majeſty, having determined to make a general invaſion of Canada, called upon his faithful and brave ſubjects of New England for aſſiſtance; and that the Province, having reſolved to raiſe a number of men, "have made proviſion for the levying and ſupport of ſuch *to the firſt day of November next*, ſaid men to be then diſmiſſed." The words here in Italics are underſcored, ſhowing that the paper was offered to prove that the ſoldiers' term of enliſtment had expired before the running away with the veſſel. See 3 Hutchinſon's Hiſt. Maſs. 79. The verdict was for the defendants.

(2) It was formerly held that both owner and bailee might maintain treſpaſs, but that a recovery by one ſhould ouſt the other of his right of action. Bac. Ab. Treſpaſs, C. 2. It has been ſince decided, that general ownerſhip, without either poſſeſſion or right to poſſeſſion, is not ſufficient. *Ward* v. *Macauley*, 4 T. R. 488. *Muggridge* v. *Eveleth*, 9 Met. 233.

[P. 28]

Sayer & al. v. *Thorp & al.* (1762)
2 George III (Aug.) in the
Superior Court of Judicature

1 · BRIEF DESCRIPTION

Could a vessel owner and charterer join together in an action of trespass against Defendant for "running away with the vessel"? In this case, the alleged culprits were "deserting" soldiers from Fort Cumberland on the Canadian border. Although either the owner or charterer could pursue an action independently, the parties debated whether the two Plaintiffs could join in one action. Since the parties then agreed upon the issue, the Court did not decide the point.

2 · RECORD

Available at Rec. 1763, Fol. 17.

The depositions in the record give much more detail than Quincy's account. These are set out by Samuel Quincy's note 1. The Plaintiffs alleged the vessel was seized by "deserting" soldiers, and the defense was that the soldiers had actually paid the master of the vessel and had his consent. Also in the record is Governor Pownall's Proclamation of March 17, 1759, introduced, as Samuel Quincy indicated, to prove the soldiers' enlistment time was up. The verdict below was for the defense.

3 · PROFESSIONALS INVOLVED

Jeremiah Gridley (1701/02–1767), apparently for the defense, "Father of the Suffolk Bar." See Case 1, note 3, *supra*, and Anton-Hermann Chroust, *The Rise of the Legal Profession in America* (1965), vol. 1, 79. See also *Appendix 6.*

4 · AUTHORITY

None cited. Defense argued the English rule that the tenant of a freehold, say a life tenant, could not join with the owner of the underlying reversion (i.e., the base fee). Plaintiff counsel pointed out the obvious policy argument that, in cases like this, requiring two separate law suits just adds to the expense. Quincy notes Gridley's argument on the "two great Actions" (i.e., Trespass and Debt), requiring "Fullness of Evidence," but why this would make a difference in the pleading here is unclear.

ant and he in Reverſion of a Freehold ſhall never join; and on the other, that it would be a Cauſe of multiplying Actions. The Parties agreeing, this Point was not determined.

Mr. Gridley in this Argument ſaid: Treſpaſs and Debt are the two great Actions on which the Fullneſs of Evidence is required, and are Actions of the higheſt Nature.

[P. 29]

5 · LATER CITATIONS

The grandson observed that "[i]t has since been decided, that general ownership, without either possession or right to possession, is not sufficient." Citing *Ward* v. *Macauley*, 4 Term Reports (T. R.) 499 (1791). (His citation to page 488 is in error. These were reports of the King's Bench in England. See *Sweet & Maxwell,* vol. 1, 299:46); *Muggridge* v. *Eveleth*, 50 Mass. (9 Met.) 233 (1845).

6 · NOTE

The underlying case, which gave a picture of conditions along the Canadian border, was far more interesting than the technical issue before the Court. The rule that general ownership alone does not necessarily give standing as a Plaintiff is reasonable enough. In this case, for example, the Charterer—who had right of possession—may have been liable to the owner for all charges under the Charter, leaving the Owner with no damages.

CASE 13

Oliver *verſ.* Sale.

OLIVER *v.* SALE.

Rec. 1762. Fol. 385.

A Perſon who ſells a Negro as a Slave, whom he knows to be free, is liable to an Action by the Vendee for the Fraud. *Aliter*, where he tells the Vendee at the Time of Sale that he will not ſell the Negro as a Slave.

A Depoſition which comes up in a Caſe from the Inferiour Court may be read, though the Witneſs is alſo preſent in Court.

OLIVER ſues the Defendant for ſelling him two free Mulattos for Slaves. (1) There was no Bill of Sale, but only ſeveral Receipts of Money for two *Negro Boys ſold & delivered.* It was ſuggeſted on the other Side that the Defendant ſold them not as Slaves, but only his Right, if he had any, in them. (2) — The Caſe was thus argued.

Mr.

---

(1) The declaration was for deceit, in ſelling the mulattos to the plaintiff as ſlaves, knowing them to be free.

(2) Previouſly to the adoption of the State Conſtitution in 1780, negro ſlavery exiſted to ſome extent in Maſſachuſetts, and negroes held as ſlaves might be ſold; but all children of ſlaves were by law free. Body of Liberties of 1641, art. 91. Maſs. Colony Laws, (ed. 1660,) 5; (ed. 1672,) 10. Prov. Sts. 2 & 4 Anne. Anc. Chart. 52, 53, 745–749. 1 Hutchinſon's Hiſt. Maſs. 444. 2 Hildreth's Hiſt. U. S. 419. 1 John Adams's Works, 51, 55. James Otis's Rights of the Colonies, (1764,) 29, 37. 4 Maſs. Hiſt. Coll. 194 & *ſeq.* 2 Dane Ab. 413, 416, 426, 427. 3 Plym. Col. Rec. 27. 5 Ib. 216. Winſor's Hiſt. of Duxbury, 70, 71, & note. *Cutler* v. *March*, Rec. 1697, fol. 159. *Alliſon* v. *Cockran*, *poſt*, 94. 4 Maſs, 127, 128, & note. 13 Maſs. 551, 552. 16 Maſs. 75, 76. 10 Cuſh. 410. 2 Kent Com. (6th ed.) 252. 2 Palfrey's Hiſt. New England, 30 & note, 280 note, 370.

Slaves

Oliver v. *Sale* (1762)
2 George III (Aug.) in the
Superior Court of Judicature

1 · BRIEF DESCRIPTION

Action for deceit (fraud) by the Plaintiff for "selling him two free Mulattos for Slaves." *Reports*, 29. The Plaintiff argued that the receipt for "two Negro boys sold & delivered" demonstrated that the Defendant intended to convey property. *Id.*, 29, 30. Defense counsel argued that there should be an express warranty of freedom "in the Case of a Negro," and that any implied warranty should not be imputed to the Defendant in this matter. *Id.*, 31. Chief Justice Hutchinson then asked, "Is there not as palpable a Fraud, when a Man sells a Negro as a Slave whom he knows to be free, as when he sells a Bag of Feathers and assures them to be Hops?" *Id.*, 32. The Defendant then offered the deposition of a woman present at the time of the sale. (It was held that the Deposition could be read, even though the witness was in court.) The Deposition showed that the Defendant expressly refused to sell the boys as slaves because he knew they were to be free after some time, and only conveyed the Defendant's right and title in their services. The evidence "being clear," the Court then ordered the jury to find for the Defendant, with costs.

This case is of the greatest interest for what it reveals about the law of slavery in Massachusetts. For the lawyers arguing the case, however, the principal issue was warranty of merchandise and deceit, very much like that of the soap in *Baker* v. *Frobisher* (1762), *Reports*, 4, Case 2, *supra*. Of course, by Samuel Quincy's day in 1865, the Civil War had made slavery an issue of the greatest consequence, hence his extraordinary note 2, tracing the history of slave law in Massachusetts. At the time he was publishing the *Reports*, Samuel Quincy was commanding the Seventy-third United States Colored Troops at Port Hudson, north of New Orleans. See Daniel R. Coquillette, *Editor's Foreword*, *supra*, pp. 6–7.

2 · RECORD

Available Rec. 1762, Fol. 385.

Among the records are the depositions of Anna Bill and Lydia Whitaker, set out by Samuel Quincy in *Reports*, 32, note 4. One of the witnesses was in Court, and Josiah Quincy's pupil master Oxenbridge Thacher, for the Plaintiff,

Mr. Thacher, for Plaintiff. I think from the Words of the Receipt it may be learnt what was his Intent. *Sold & delivered* conveys the Property; and as he had really no Right to a Day's Service in the Lads, as they were free, he could not paſs any Property

---

Slaves were admitted to be church members at a period when church members had peculiar political privileges. 2 Winthrop, 26, & Savage's note. Anc. Chart. 117. 1 Bancroft's Hiſt. U. S. 360. Slaves were ſometimes required, ſometimes prohibited, to ſerve in the militia. 3 Maſs. Col. Rec. 268, 397. 4 Ib. pt. 1, 86, 257. Journals Maſs. Prov. Congreſs, (ed. 1838,) 29, 302, 553. They were enliſted in the army in the Old French War. 4 Maſs. Hiſt. Coll. 199, 203. 98 Maſs. Archives, 122. They were competent witneſſes, even in capital trials, *e. g.* in the trial of the *Britiſh Soldiers* in 1770, (ed. 1770, p. 111,) and in ſuits of other ſlaves for freedom, as appears by the files of court.

The right to marry was ſecured to them in 1705 by Prov. St. 4 Anne. Anc. Chart. 748. The ſubſequent records of Boſton and other towns ſhow that their banns were publiſhed like thoſe of white perſons. In 1745, a negro ſlave obtained from the Governor and Council a divorce for his wife's adultery with a white man. *Jethro Boſton's Caſe*, 9 Maſs. Archives, 248. In 1758, it was adjudged by the Superior Court of Judicature, that a child of a female ſlave, "never married according to any of the forms preſcribed by the laws of this land," by another ſlave, who "had kept her company with her maſter's conſent," was not a baſtard. *Flora's Caſe*, Rec. 1758, fol. 296. And the wife of a ſlave was not allowed to teſtify againſt him. MS. note by John Adams of *Cæſar* v. *Taylor*, in Eſſex, 1772, (Rec. 1772, fol. 91,) in the poſſeſſion of Hon. Charles Francis Adams; which alſo ſhows that the defendant in an action of falſe impriſonment was not permitted under the general iſſue to prove that the plaintiff was his ſlave.

Such actions, called "ſuits for liberty," were common as early as 1765. 2 John Adams's Works, 200. The lateſt inſtance of a verdict for the maſter is believed to have been in 1768. *Newport* v. *Billing*, Rec. 1768, fol. 284. But the caſe of *James* v. *Lechmere*, in Middleſex, a year later, which has been often ſpoken of as having determined the unlawfulneſs of ſlavery in Maſſachuſetts, is ſhown by the records and files of court to have been brought up from the inferior court by ſham demurrer, and, after one or two continuances, ſettled by the parties. Rec. 1769, fol. 196. The caſe mentioned by Dr. Belknap in 4 Maſs. Hiſt. Coll. 202, as "the firſt trial of this kind," may have been that of *Margarett* v. *Muzzy*, which was a writ *de homine replegiando*, ſued out and tried in Middleſex in 1768, and on review in 1770, in which, as appears by the

tried to prevent the deposition being read, thus giving him a chance to cross-examine her. The Court rejected his argument, and permitted the deposition to be read. Whether the witness could then be called, or was called, was not clear from the report. The Court did, however, accept the gist of both depositions as true, and that Captain Sale did not "sell them [i.e., the "two Negro Boys"] for Slaves . . . only his right & title in them, & Mr. Oliver said he would run the risk of their ever getting free."

Also available:

Oliver v. *Sale*, (same) Feb. 1762, Nos. 172435–36.

- Certificate of Attendance, Superior Court of Judicature, Boston.

Oliver v. *Sale*, (same) No. 174991.

- Jury finding for defendant with costs. Full names of parties are John Oliver and John Sale.
- Jury finding on back for a different case, *Hunt* v. *Proctor*.

3 · PROFESSIONALS INVOLVED

Oxenbridge Thacher (1719–1765), Quincy's pupil master, for the Plaintiff; James Otis, Jr. (1725–1783), for the Defendant. See *Reports*, Case 1, Note 3, "Professionals Involved," *supra*. See also *Appendix 6*, "Brief Biographies," *infra*. Otis and Thacher often worked as a team.

Chief Justice Hutchinson's comparison of a slave to a "Bag of Feathers" or a "Bag of Hops," see *Reports*, 32, *supra*, was not a high point in judicial humanity.

4 · AUTHORITY

Most striking, no authority was cited on the issue of slavery, despite the many cases and statutory provisions listed by Samuel Quincy in his famous note 2, *Reports*, 29–31. It was clear that there was slavery in Massachusetts, and that you could also assign an apprentice's indentures, as Otis observed. The successful argument was that Captain Sale sold whatever interest he had in the boys for any type of service, and Oliver assumed the risk that Sale had none.

Thacher also argued for the Plaintiff that Oliver, by "selling the Boys for Slaves" exposed himself to a "Writ of Replevin" and a "*Capias in Withernam*," and that this could result in "his own Body . . . subjected to Confinement till they are produced." *Reports*, 33. This was ostensibly added to support aggrava-

Property in them, and therefore muſt be ſuppoſed to have ſold them as Slaves, or meant from the firſt to have defrauded.

Ch. Juſt. Everything which is bought is ſold.

Witneſſes were produced who were preſent at the Time of the Sale, and heard Defendant ſay they were Slaves.

Mr. Otis, for Defendant. I hold in the Caſe of a Negro, there ſhould be an expreſs Warranty of their Freedom, and that the Rule of Merchandiſe which obliges the Vendor to anſwer for what he ſells without Warranty is confined to Manufactures of the Country which a Man muſt be ſuppoſed to know the Quality of; but in this Caſe it is impoſſible in moſt Caſes to know whether they are free or not.

Ch.

---

the depoſitions on file, there was much conflicting evidence, and the plaintiff prevailed. Rec. 1768, fol. 311; 1770, fol. 216. Slavery was certainly recognized by law in Maſſachuſetts after this; for in May, 1771, Hutchinſon wrote to Lord Hillſborough, "Slavery by the Provincial laws gives no right to the life of the ſervant; and a ſlave here is conſidered as a ſervant would be who had bound himſelf for a term of years exceeding the ordinary term of human life; and I do not know that it has been determined that he may not have a property in goods, notwithſtanding he is called a ſlave." 27 Maſs. Archives, 159, 160.

Slaves convicted of theft were ſentenced, like other perſons, beſides being whipt, to pay treble the value to the owner of the goods ſtolen, and, if unable to do ſo, were ordered to be "diſpoſed of in ſervice" for life, or for a term of years, "for payment of the ſame." *Hercules & Sharper's Caſes*, Rec. 1757, fol. 54, 55; Docket of February term, 1757, in Suffolk, *ad finem*. *Jeoffs's Caſe*, Rec. 1771, fol. 35.

By virtue of the firſt article of the Declaration of Rights, prefixed to the Conſtitution of Maſſachuſetts, if not before, ſlavery was entirely aboliſhed here. 2 Bradford Hiſt. Maſs. 124. 4 Maſs. Hiſt. Coll. 201–203. 31 Ib. 90. 34 Ib. 333. Willard Memoir, 153. 4 Maſs. 128. 9 Amer. Jur. 490. 18 Pick. 208–210. 7 Cuſh. 296. 7 Gray, 478. 5 Leigh, 622, 623. 20 Law Rep. 101, 108, 456.

tion of damages had the Plaintiff won which, of course, he did not. It was a curious, antique argument, particularly as there was no apparent difficulty in producing the boys. A "capias in withernam," from the Anglo-Saxon *withernam*, or "taking again," was used where the Defendant had hidden the goods, so that the sheriff could not replevy them on behalf of the Plaintiff. See *Jowitt*, *supra*, 308–309. In that case the Plaintiff could have a *capias in withernam*, a writ directing the sheriff to replevy equivalent goods of the Defendant. *Id.*, 308. Thacher added that where the sheriff returns "they are Essoigned" (i.e., excused), he could then seize the Defendant's person, until the goods were produced. See *id.*, 734. This argument, given the facts of the case, was an odd effort to invoke English common law doctrines to impress the Court. It apparently failed in this goal, but obviously impressed the young Quincy, who marked it "N.B." (*nota bene*). For the origins of the remedy of replevin, a personal action to recover possession in specific goods unlawfully taken, *id.*, 1526, see J. H. Baker, *An Introduction to English Legal History* (4th ed., 2002), (hereafter, *J. H. Baker*) 390–391, 538–539.

5 · LATER CITATIONS

As Samuel Quincy observed in his exhaustive "note 2," the adoption of the Massachusetts Constitution in 1780, Article 1, Declaration of Rights, ended slavery in the state. See S. Quincy, note 2, *Reports*, 31, *supra*.

Case No. 13 has been cited as authority for the right of slaves to marry prior to the 1780 Constitution, a point that could be important in disputes over inheritance. See *Merrick* v. *Betts*, 214 Mass. 223 (1913), which cites to *Oliver* v. *Sale* for this point at page 223.

6 · NOTE

This case remains an extraordinary window into the colonial consciousness about race and slavery. The two "Negro Boys sold & delivered," "free Mulattos" but sold "for Slaves," could have been mislabeled "Bag[s] of Feathers[!]" As the Chief Justice observed, "Is this not as palpable a Fraud, when a Man sells a Negro as a Slave whom he knows to be free, as when he sells a Bag of Feathers and assures them to be Hops." *Reports*, 32. But Quincy lived in a world where even free blacks were treated differently from whites. See, for example, the "negro woman being with Child . . . a free White Man being the father" who

Ch. Juſt. Is there not as palpable a Fraud, when a Man ſells a Negro as a Slave whom he knows to be free, as when he ſells a Bag of Feathers and aſſures them to be Hops? That he knew them to be free they muſt prove, or do not ſupport their Declaration. (3)

Mr. Otis offered a Depoſition lodged in the Caſe to be read.

Mr. Thacher demanded, as the Witneſs was there in Court, she might be examined orally. (4)

Court ruled, that when Depoſitions come up in the Caſe they may be firſt read. (5)

Mr.

---

(3) According to the rule now ſettled in this country, it ſeems that the *ſcienter* would be unneceſſary — the vendor being liable on the implied warranty of title in the ſale of a chattel. *Coolidge* v. *Brigham*, 1 Met. 547.

(4) Among the papers in this caſe are the depoſitions of Anna Bill and Lydia Whitaker, one of whom was undoubtedly the witneſs "there in Court." The depoſitions are ſubſtantially ſimilar, and the following is an exact copy of that of Lydia Whitaker: —

" Lydia Whitaker of Lawfull age teſtifies & ſays that ſhe was at the " houſe of Capt. John Sale when Mr Nath'l Brown & Mr John Oliver " came to buy two of his negro boys & Capt. Sale told them that he " would not ſell them for Slaves becauſe he underſtood they were to be " free after ſome time, & he would only ſell his right & title in them, " & Mr Oliver ſaid he would run the riſk of their ever getting free.

her
" LYDIA X WHITAKER
mark

" Sworn before the Court in Oct'r 1761

" Att. MIDDLECOTT COOKE *Cler.*"

(5) The cuſtom of uſing the depoſition in addition to oral teſtimony once prevailed in Maſſachuſetts. Compare Colony Law of 1647 and Prov. St. of 7 W. 3, (Anc. Chart. 209, 288,) with the St. of 1797, c. 35, reënacted in Rev. Sts. c. 94, § 25, and Gen. Sts. c. 131, § 28.

was unable to obtain the usual remedies of a white woman before the Justice of the Peace. See *Law Commonplace*, *infra*, page [91]. And even whites could be apprenticed for years, with greatly reduced freedoms. *Id.*, pages [19]–[21]. Thus if a woman apprentice married, she "must serve out her Time + her husband cannot take Her out of Her Master's service." *Id.*, page [20]. See also Quincy's extensive discussion of the curtailed rights of women. *Id.*, pages [25]–[28]. See, generally, the excellent articles by Sally E. Haddon, "The Fragmented Laws of Slavery in the Colonial and Revolutionary Eras," and by Holly Brewer, "The Transformation of Domestic Law," in *The Cambridge History of Law in America*, vol. 1, *Early America* (1580–1815), (ed. M. Grossberg, C. Tomlins, 2008), at 235, 289, respectively. Colonial Massachusetts had little consciousness of its racism, and assumed a hierarchical system that curtailed the rights of free blacks as well as slaves, and women generally, white as well as black.

Mr. Otis. When the Apprentice's Indentures are aſſigned, he may properly be ſaid to be ſold, but 'tis no Argument of his Slavery.

The Evidence being clear that Sale had ſaid he would not ſell them as Slaves, and told Plaintiff ſo when they were ſold, *the Court* directed the Jury to find Defendant Coſts.

N. B. In Aggravation of Damages, had they found for the Plaintiff, *Mr. Thacher* ſaid: "Oliver by ſelling theſe Boys for Slaves expoſed himſelf to a Writ of Replevin,* upon which if Sheriff returns '*They are Eſloigned,*' there ſhall go a *Capias in Withernam,*† and his own Body ſhall be ſubjected to Confinement till they are produced."

---

* *Homine replegiando.* Vid. F. N. B. 66. New Nat. B. 151, 152.

† If this is returned *non eſt invent.*, a *Capias* ſhall iſſue againſt the Defendant's Goods and Effects.

[P. 33]

ILLUSTRATION 12: Slave Quarters, Isaac Royall House, Medford, Massachusetts (1732–1739). Isaac Royall's will of 1778 and codicil of 1779 established the Isaac Royall Chair at Harvard Law School. His gift could be seen as the founding of that great law school. See Arthur E. Sutherland, *The Law at Harvard* (1967), pp. 32–42. That he was a major slaveholder in Antigua and brought slaves to Massachusetts, there can be no doubt. See the fascinating account by the present holder of the Royall Chair, Janet Halley, "My Isaac Royall Legacy," 24 *Harvard Black Letter Law Journal* 117 (Spring, 2008). Photograph courtesy Royal House Association. See *Oliver* v. *Sale* (1762), *Reports*, 29 (Case 13).

CASE 14

Hallowell *verſ.* Dalton.

HALLOWELL *v.* DALTON.

Rec. 1762. Fol. 390.

After Bond given to review, and before the Service of the Writ, the Depoſition of Witneſſes going to Sea may be taken

THIS Caſe was a Review of an Action brought by Dalton againſt Hallowell. The only Queſtion of Law was, whether after Bond given to review, before the Service of the Writ, there can be ſaid to be ſo much of Suit depending, and ſo much of Parties, as that a Juſtice may, out of Court, take the Evidence of Men going to Sea, according to the Province Law 7 W. 3, c. 11. (1) *Ruled*, there is.

---

(1) This law provided for the taking of affidavits of "witneſſes in civil cauſes," with a "notification to the adverſe party," but ſpecified no time as the commencement of a ſuit. Anc. Chart. 288. But the St. of 1797, c 35, provided for taking depoſitions only "when the writ, original ſummons, or complaint ſhall have been ſerved." This is in ſubſtance reënacted in Rev. Sts. c. 94, § 15, and Gen. Sts. c. 131, § 19.

Hallowell v. *Dalton* (1762)
2 George III (Aug.) in the
Superior Court of Judicature

1 · BRIEF DESCRIPTION

Actual service of the writ was not necessary for taking "the Evidence of Men going to Sea" by affidavit pursuant to a Province Law where a bond has been given.

2 · RECORD

Available at Rec. 1762, Fol. 390.

The case began as a suit by James Dalton, a "mariner," against Benjamin Hallowell, a "shipwright," over an unpaid bill for beef. Dalton won the judgment in the lower court, leading to Hallowell's appeal.

3 · PROFESSIONALS INVOLVED

According to the Record, Benjamin Kent (1708–1788) represented James Dalton. See *Appendix 6*. There is no indication of the Plaintiff's attorney.

4 · AUTHORITY

The sole authority cited was the Province Law itself, 2 William 3, chapter 11 (1701). It merely required that the affidavits be with a "notification to the adverse party," with nothing further about commencement of the suit. As Samuel Quincy pointed out, this ambiguity was remedied by Massachusetts Statute 1797, chapter 35, which permits depositions only after the service of the writ, original summons, or complaint.

5 · LATER CITATIONS

Today, most jurisdictions permit taking of depositions to preserve testimony before filing a complaint, so long as "expected adverse parties" are notified. See F. Rule Civ. P. 27(a). The practical reason is the same as recognized by the Court in this case, to preserve evidence that might otherwise be lost.

6 · NOTE

This case was a practical reading of an ambiguous statute to serve simple policy, preserving evidence that could be lost when men go to sea, a real danger in 1762.

CASE 15

GOULD *v.* STEVENS.

Rec. 1762. Fol. 383.

An Executor of his own Wrong is not liable to an Attachment of his Body or proper Goods on a Debt of the Teftator.

Gould *verf.* Stevens.

THIS Action was an Attachment againft Stevens as Executor of Somebody, a Debtor of the Plaintiff's. Plea in Abatement was made, that by the Law as Executor he fhould have been fummoned, and not his Body or proper Goods attached. The Replication to this was, that though he was named Executor in the Writ, he was not appointed by the Teftator, but was Executor of his own Wrong.

Mr. Thacker. The Province Law 2 Ann. c. 5,(1) directs the Manner of Suits againft Executors and Adminiftrators. Executor of his own Wrong takes the Duty and the Burden, he is by Wrong in the fame Manner as if by Right, and is anfwerable no further than as Effects come to his Hands. The Common Law is the fame with the Province Law.

Mr. Sewall, contra. An Executor in his own Wrong cannot maintain an Action certain. He is not favoured as Executor by Right. 4 Wm. & Mary, c. 2. 1 Salk. 297. 2 Ventris, 179. The Law knows Nothing of them but to reftrain and punifh them.

Judgment that the Writ abate.

---

(1) Anc. Chart. 377. St. 1783, c. 32, § 9. Rev. Sts. c. 110, § 1. Gen. Sts. c. 128, § 5.

[P. 34]

Gould v. *Stevens* (1762)
2 George III (Aug.) in the
Superior Court of Judicature

1 · BRIEF DESCRIPTION

Plaintiff was a creditor "of Somebody," who was deceased. Instead of suing Somebody's estate, Plaintiff summoned Stevens, as Somebody's executor, and attached Stevens's own body and goods. The Court held that the writ of attachment was no good.

2 · RECORD

Available at Rec. 1762, Fol. 383.

The Record reveals that three Goulds, John, Robert, and John Jr., were the Plaintiffs, and that Peter Stevens, the executor of John Stevens ("Somebody") was the Defendant.

3 · PROFESSIONALS INVOLVED

Counsel for the Plaintiff was Jonathan Sewall (1729–1796). See *Law in Colonial Massachusetts*, *supra*, 352–354 and Memorandum of 1762, *Reports*, 35, *infra*. Counsel for the Defendant was Oxenbridge Thacher (1719–1765). See Case 1, note 3, *supra*, and Memorandum of 1762, *Reports*, 35, *infra*. See also *Appendix 6*.

4 · AUTHORITY

Thacher relied heavily on the Province Law 2 Ann. c.5(1) (1704), which governs the duty of executors. An "Executor of his own Wrong," or "*Executor de son tort*" is "a stranger [who] takes upon himself the act as executor or administrator without any just authority . . ." *Jowitt*, *supra*, 759. The general common law rule is that such an executor is liable to suit, as if he were rightfully appointed, but only "to the extent of the assets which have come to him. . . ." *Id.*, 759. (He is not entitled to the "profits or advantages" or executorship. *Id.*, 759.) Sewall argued the contrary, but his statements were off the point. The "executor of his own wrong" cannot bring an action himself in the right of the deceased, it is true, but he cannot be sued personally, nor can his own goods be attached. See, today, the English Administration of Estates Act, 1925, ss 28, 29, 55(1) xi. *Id.*, 759. As authority, Sewall offered *Fouler* v. *Cooke* (1695), 1 *Salkeld's Reports* 297 (covering 1689–1712), see *Law Commonplace* p. [32], n. 7, and *Pyne* v. *Woolland* (1690), 2 *Ventris' Reports* 179 (covering 1668–1684), see *Law Commonplace*, p. [89], n. 7. Sewall's English cases were not on point, and the Court threw out his suit.

5 · LATER CITATIONS

The Court's holding remains the common and statutory law in most English and American jurisdictions, as Samuel Quincy noted.

6 · NOTE

Sewall tried to overcome direct Province statutory law by reference to English common law decisions. How the Court would have resolved a direct conflict between a Province statute and a leading English case would have been interesting, and, as we will see, such conflicts could occur. Here, however, "[t]he Common Law [was] the same with the Province Law," as Thacher argued. Sewall's citations were off point and showed a certain amount of pure braggadocio. The Court, however, was not fooled.

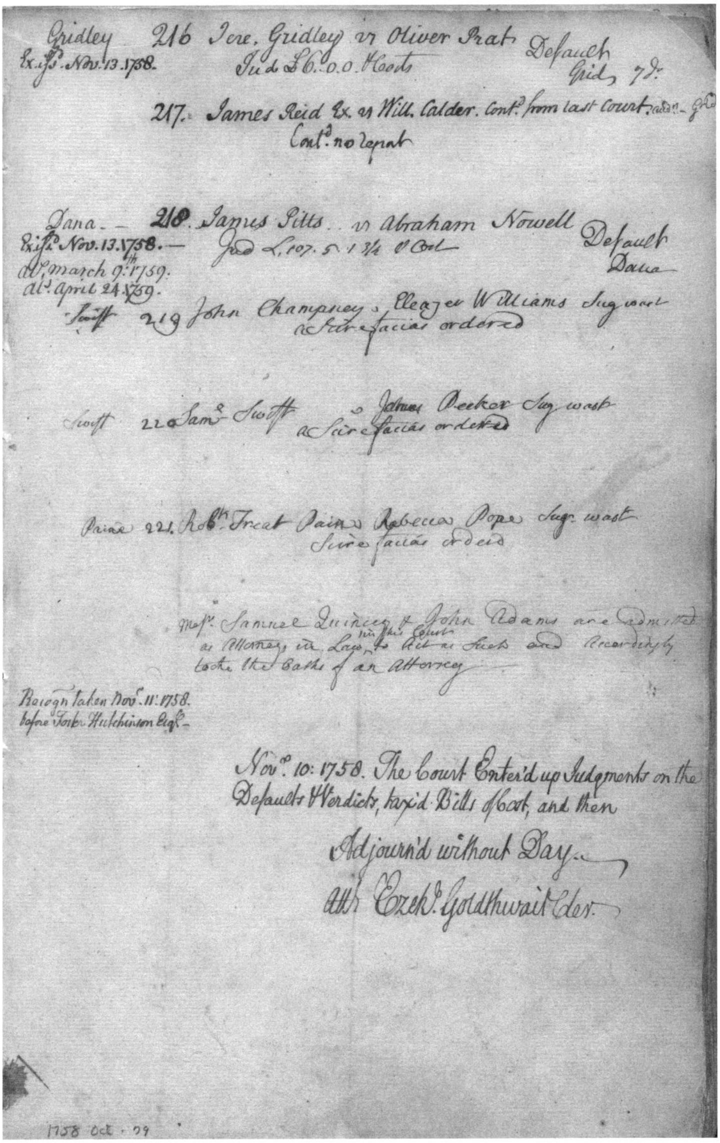

ILLUSTRATION 13: Docket Book, Inferior Court of Common Pleas, Suffolk, 1758 October, showing the admission of John Adams and Samuel Quincy, Josiah's older brother, as attorneys on November 6, 1758. Note the signature of Ezekiel Goldthwait, Clerk, and the names of Jeremiah Gridley, Foster Hutchinson, and Robert Treat Paine.

Josiah himself was admitted as attorney in 1766, but never the higher rank of "barrister," almost certainly for political reasons. See Neil L. York, "A Life Cut Short," *Quincy Papers*, vol. 1, pp. 17–18. See Quincy's own discussion at Memoranda, August Term, 1769, *Reports*, 317 (1769), *Quincy Papers*, vol. 5. Image courtesy Social Law Library, Boston.

MEMORANDUM

Barristers' Habits.

Memorandum. (1)

Rec. 1762. Fol. 400.

JAMES OTIS, Edmund Trowbridge, Jeremy Gridley, Richard Dana, Benjamin Kent, Daniel Farnham, John Worthington, James Otis, junr., James Putnam, Jofeph Hawley, John Chipman, Oxenbridge Thacher, Robert Auchmuty, Sam'l White, James Hovey, Samuel Fitch, Jonathan Sewall, William Cufhing, Robert Treat Paine, William Pynchon, William Read, Samuel Swift, Jofeph Dudley, Benja : Gridley, Samuel Quincy, and John Adams, having been called by the Court to be Barrifters at Law, the following Gentlemen, viz., Edmund Trowbridge, Jeremy Gridley, Benjamin Kent, James Otis, junr., Oxenbridge Thacher, Robert Auchmuty, Samuel Fitch, Jonathan Sewall, Robert Treat Paine, Samuel Swift, Samuel Quincy, and John Adams, Efquires, appeared accordingly this Term in Barrifters' Habits. (2)

---

(1) As this memorandum clofes the record of the term on the Suffolk docket, it is here inferted, although not a part of Mr. Quincy's reports.

(2) John Adams was fworn on the 14th of November, 1761. Rec. 1761, fol. 239. In a note to his diary at that date he fays : "About this time the project was conceived, I fuppofe by the Chief Juftice, Mr. Hutchinfon, of clothing the judges and lawyers with robes. Mr. Quincy and I were directed to prepare our gowns and bands and tie wigs, and were admitted barrifters, having practifed three years at the inferior courts according to our new rules." 2 John Adams's Works, 133. See alfo Adams's Letters to Tudor, 10 Ib. 233, 245.

The 1762 "Memorandum"

NOTE

John Adams recorded a major effort from 1762 to 1774 to impose a more formal structure on the Boston bar. See *Diary and Autobiography of John Adams* (hereafter, "*Adams Diary*") (L. H. Butterfield, ed., 4 vols., Cambridge, Mass., 1964) I, 136–137; III, 274; *Legal Papers of John Adams* (L. K. Wroth, H. B. Zobel, eds.), Cambridge, Mass., 1965 (hereafter, "*Adams, Legal Papers*"), I, lxxvii–lxxxiii. See also Daniel R. Coquillette, "Justinian in Braintree: John Adams, Civilian Learning, and Legal Elitism, 1758–1775" (hereafter, "Justinian in Braintree"), *Law in Colonial Massachusetts, 1630–1800* (D. R. Coquillette, R. Brink, C. S. Menand, eds., 1984), 395–400. It is unclear whether Adams supported the attempt by Chief Justice Hutchinson to establish a separate rank of barrister and to require gowns and wigs. *Id.*, 395–397.

In all events, listing the elite of the bar and inserting it into the Suffolk docket at Rec. 1762, fol. 400, was an important step. The list of 26 names seems to have been composed in order of seniority, with James Otis Senior as most preferred, going down to John Adams as "Mr. Junior," following the practice of the Inns of Court. The twelve that then "appeared accordingly this Term in Barristers' Habits" were apparently the most active, a fact confirmed by our Appendices I and 2. Biographies of all 26 appear in *Appendix 6*.

While assisting with the research on these cases in the Massachusetts Archives, my research assistants, Brandon Bigelow and Brian Sheppard, made an important discovery, additional lists of attorneys, with cases after each name. Apparently, these are the cases in which the attorneys appeared during a particular period, or signed pleadings. Not surprisingly, the most active attorneys are those that appear on the 1762 list. See *Appendix 6*. The only exceptions were our own Josiah Quincy, who was not yet "admitted" in 1762, and Benjamin Prat (1711–1763), who had left Boston in November of 1761 "to take his Seat as Chief Justice of that State." See *Adams Diary*, III, 274; "Justinian in Braintree," 377–379.

CASE 16

February Term

III Georgii Ter. in Sup. Cur.

Prefent:

The Honourable

Thomas Hutchinfon, Efqr., Chief Juftice.
Benja: Lynde,
John Cufhing,
Chambers Ruffell,
Peter Oliver,
Efqrs., Juftices.

WRENTHAM PROPRIETORS *v.* METCALF.

Rec. 1763. Fol. 17.

Proprietors of common and undivided Lands are incompetent Witneffes in a Suit where the Corporation is a Party.

Wrentham Proprietors *verf.* Metcalf. (1)

IT was moved that fome of the Proprietors fhould be admitted Witneffes in this Cafe, who were not of the Committee who brought this Suit. 2 Lev. 231,* was cited, where *Scroggs, Ch. Juft.*,

* *Quære* of this Cafe. Theory of Evid. 105, 106, and 2 Lilly's Abr. 702. 1 Str. 575, 1069. Vid. 2 Lev. 236. 2 Sid. 109. 1 Vern. 154. 2 Vern. 317. Vid. Cun. Law Dict'y, Will.

(1) This was an action of ejectment, originally brought in the Inferior Court againft Jofhua Daniels, who fuggefted that he held the premifes by deed of bargain and fale with warranty from Jonathan Metcalf, whom he prayed might be vouched in to defend the fuit, and who was fubfequently admitted for that purpofe. In the Superior Court the cafe was entitled as above.

Wrentham Proprietors v. *Metcalf* (1763)
3 George III (Feb.) in the
Superior Court of Judicature

1 · BRIEF DESCRIPTION

This was an action to eject the Defendant from real property. The sole issue here was whether those Proprietors who were not of the Committee who brought the case could be witnesses. (The usual common law rule was that parties in interest could not be witnesses, because they were not impartial. See J. H. Baker, *supra*, 91, 511; Lord Brougham's Evidence Act 1851, 14 & 15 Vict. c.99.) The answer here is "no," the Chief Justice "doubting whether in any Case, where the Interest was ever so small, if they were direct Plaintiffs they should be admitted [as witnesses]." *Reports*, 37.

2 · RECORD

Available at Rec. 1763, Fol. 17.

Further papers at Suffolk County Files under *Metcalf* v. *Wrentham Proprietors* (Aug. 1763).

Records also contain:

- Summons witnessed by Hutchinson and written by Nathaniel Hatch of Wrentham Prop. (At the bottom of the above document Auchmuty has written for Wrentham that he is now their counsel, and that he disagrees with the judgment.)

Wrentham Proprietors v. *Metcalf* ("Metcalf v. Wrentham Proprietors"), Aug. 1793, No. 84523.

- Summons to John Metcalf, Benjamin Pond, Michael Henry and Robert Hiardell(?) to Superior Court of Judicature to give evidence of plea review. (On the back of the summons is an indication that the summons was served and that the parties appeared in court signed by Nathaniel Hatch.)

Wrentham Proprietors v. *Metcalf* (same), Aug. 1763, No. 84517.

- Summons to Capt. Pond, Deacon Thurston, & Robert Blake to appear before Superior Court of Judicature signed by Nathaniel Hatch.

Wrentham Prop. v. *Metcalf* (same), No. 174885.

- A record of some kind, but it is barely legible.

Juſt., ſays, "that it ought not to be a general Rule "that Members of Corporations ſhall be admitted "or denied to be Witneſſes in Actions for or againſt "their Corporations: But every Caſe ſtands upon "its own particular Circumſtances, viz., whether "the Intereſt be ſo conſiderable as by Preſumption "to produce Partiality or not."

In this Caſe at Bar it was objected that they were liable to Coſts, and might each Member be taken for the Whole. A Guardian not admitted in Evidence in Favour of his Charge.

Ruled, that they be not admitted in this Caſe. *Ch. Juſt.* doubted whether in any Caſe, where the Intereſt was ever ſo ſmall, if they were direct Plaintiffs they ſhould be admitted. (2)

---

(2) The general rule ſeems to have been that only members of public or municipal, religious, and charitable corporations were competent witneſſes in ſuits where the corporation was a party or intereſted. 1 Greenl. Evid. §§ 331, 333. The St. of 1792, c. 32, provided for the admiſſibility of members of any "town, diſtrict, precinct, pariſh or other religious incorporate ſociety." Counties, ſchool diſtricts and mutual inſurance companies were afterward added to the liſt. Rev. Sts. c. 94, § 54. St. 1850, c. 34. By the practice acts of 1851 and 1852, all incompetency from intereſt was removed, except in caſe of parties to ſuits; and finally, by Sts. 1856, c. 188, and 1857, c. 305, parties themſelves have been admitted. Gen. Sts. c. 131, §§ 13, 14.

[P. 37]

Wrentham Prop. v. *Metcalf* (same), No. 174885.
- Jury finding, illegible.

3 · PROFESSIONALS INVOLVED

Robert Auchmuty (1723–1788) represented the Wrentham Proprietors. See *Appendix 6*, "Brief Biographies."

4 · AUTHORITY

Contemporaneous sources. *Rex* v. *Mayor, Citizens and Common Council of London* (1678), 2 *Levinz's Reports* 231 (covering 1660–1696), see *Law Commonplace*, [89], n. 7, cited by the Plaintiff's attorney. Josiah Quincy added a list of other cases and treatise descriptions he thought obtained, citing Theory of Evid. 105, 106, see *Law Commonplace,* [36], n. 6 (the cited pages refer to 2 *Levinz's Reports* 231); 2 *Lilly's Abridgment* 702, see *Law Commonplace,* [48], n. 3 (the cited section of the treatise deals with witness qualification, though p. 702 does not offer a close analogue to the instant case); *Ball* v. *Bastock* (1728), 1 *Strange's Reports* (covering 1716–1749), 575, and *Rex* v. *Robins* (1737), 2 *Strange's Reports* 1069, see *Law Commonplace* [21], n. 12; *Enfield* v. *Hills* (1679), 2 *Levinz's Reports* (covering 1660–1696) 236, see *Law Commonplace* [89], n. 7; *Dickson* v. *Williamson* (1658), 2 *Siderfin's Reports* (covering 1657–1670) 119, though this case does not appear to be on point (The case of *Le County De Salop* v. *Le County De Stafford*, 1 *Siderfin's Reports* 192, cited in 2 *Vernon's Reports, supra,* might have been intended. See *Sweet & Maxwell,* vol. 1, p. 319); *Gibbs* v. *Cotton* (1685), 1 *Vernon's Reports* (covering 1681–1720) 154, see *Law Commonplace* [19], n. 1 (this case is not on point, however); *Dowdeswell* v. *Nott* (1694), 2 *Vernon's Reports* (covering 1681–1720), 317, see *Law Commonplace* [19], n. 1; and volume 2 of Cunningham's *New and Complete Law Dictionary*, first published in 2 volumes in Dublin, 1764. See *Sweet & Maxwell,* vol. 1, p. 8. The fact that it was published after the case suggests the later reference and reevaluation inherent in the reporting method as a learning tool, assuming that the notation was in Quincy's hand. The entry under "Will" (on an un-numbered page near the end of vol. 2) offers extensive discussion of witnesses to wills.

5 · LATER CITATIONS

The grandson provides some interesting background concerning the scope of the rule barring members of a corporation from testifying where the corporation is an interested party, citing 1 Greenl. Evid. §§ 331, 333. Simon Greenleaf also provides subsequent statutory enactments that modified the rule against interested parties, citing St. 1792, c. 32; Rev. Sts. c. 94, § 54; St. 1850, c.34; St. 1856, c.188; St. 1857, c. 305, and ultimately lifted the bar to parties from testifying, see Gen. St. c. 131, §§ 13, 14.

6 · NOTE

Quincy challenged ("quare"), the English authority of Chief Justice William Scroggs (1623–1683), in the case of *Rex* v. *Mayor, Citizens and Common Council of London* (1678), 2 *Levinz's Reports* 231, cited by the Plaintiff. Chief Justice Hutchinson seems to have agreed. In this case, the Plaintiffs were proprietors of a common, undivided land, and the proposed witnesses were other non-party proprietors. Parties to an action, of course, could not testify in their own action in colonial Massachusetts. At issue was whether the testimony of non-party, interested witnesses should be admitted. The general rule vested great discretion in the trial court to determine whether the interest of the witness was so considerable that a presumption of prejudice ought to attach. Of particular interest to Josiah Quincy may have been a statement by Chief Justice Hutchinson from the bench expressing the view that he "doubted whether in any Case, where the Interest was ever so small, if they were direct Plaintiffs they should be admitted." Here, the "non-party" Proprietors might still have been liable to costs, and each member might have been liable for full costs, so they certainly had an interest in the case.

The case certainly demonstrates the relative independence of the colonial courts, at least in construing *dicta* in English decisions.

ILLUSTRATION 14: Sir William Scroggs (1623–1683), Chief Justice of the Common Pleas (1676–1678) and of the King's Bench (1678–1681). Portrait, possibly after John Michael Wright, oil on canvas (1678). Courtesy National Portrait Gallery. Chief Justice Scroggs' conduct during the Popish Plot trials was infamous, a "disgraceful exhibition of partiality." D. M. Walker, *The Oxford Companion to Law* (1980), 1121. He has been described as "coarse and unprincipled" and "undoubtedly one of the worst judges who ever disgraced the bench." *Id.*

CASE 17

DERUMPLE *v.* CLARK.

Derumple *verſ.* Clark.

Rec. 1763. Fol. 19.

Evidence of Payment of full Rent by a Tenant for five or ſix Years, without any Claim of Deduction for Taxes, ſuch being alſo the Cuſtom of the Town, is ſufficient Evidence of a Contract to pay Taxes under the Province Law, which provides that "where no Contract is" the Landlord ſhall reimburſe half the Taxes. *Ruſſell, J., diſſentiente.*

THIS Action was brought by the Tenant againſt the Landlord for the Recovery of half the Taxes, upon the Province Law called the Tax Act. (1) This Caſe was ſaid to differ from the Caſe of *Jackſon* v. *Foye*, (2) try'd before this Court in Auguſt Term laſt, as in that Caſe Jackſon had been Tenant to Foye ſo many Years, there had been many Settlements,—whereas here Derumple had been Tenant only five or ſix Years. The Rent had been paid, but there had been no regular methodical Settlement.

Mr. Auchmuty, for Plaintiff, urged, that the Law was very expreſs and particular—"Where no Contract is, the Landlord ſhall reimburſe the Tenant half the Taxes," ſo that the Payment of the whole Rent is no Argument of a Contract to pay half the Taxes, for the Tenant by the Law is not to keep back his Rent, but to have the Taxes reimburſed, which is an Argument that the Whole is firſt to be paid. I can have no Idea of an implied Contract in this Caſe; the Law evidently points out an expreſs one.

Mr. Thacker, for Defendant. It has been the uninterrupted Cuſtom of this Town for the Tenant to pay the whole Taxes, and though this Law is of very

---

(1) See *ante*, p. 27, note (1). (2) *Ante*, p. 26.

Derumple v. *Clark* (1763)
3 George III (Feb.) in the
Superior Court of Judicature

1 · BRIEF DESCRIPTION

This case involves the same contract issues as in *Jackson* v. *Foye* (1762), *Reports*, 26, Case 10, *supra*. Once again, the controversy is caused by the "Tax Act," which provided that "saving all contracts between the landlord and tenant, and where no contract is, the landlord to reimburse one half of the tax set upon such houses and lands." See Prov. St. 4 W. & M. (1692); *The Acts and Resolves . . . of the Province of the Massachusetts Bay*, vol. IV (1757–1768), Boston, 1881, chap. 12, "Province Laws – 1762–63," 596; and discussion at Case 10, *supra*. Here the Plaintiff was a tenant of "five or six years." There was no express contract to the contrary, and the Plaintiff sued the landlord for reimbursement of half of the tax. In a highly interesting decision, the Court found that there was an "implied" contract not to reimburse the tax, partly based on "the Custom of the Town." As in *Jackson* v. *Foye* (1762), *Reports*, 26, Case 10, *supra*, Justice Russell disagreed, stating: "I think the Law evidently means an express Agreement. However, I don't think we have here any Evidence of an implied Agreement, or any Agreement at all." *Reports*, 40. In *Jackson* v. *Foye*, *supra*, there was at least some evidence of an express contract, the tenant's note of hand. Here there was absolutely no evidence of an express contract.

2 · RECORD

Available at Rec. 1763, fol. 19.

Nothing in the Suffolk files.

3 · PROFESSIONALS INVOLVED

Robert Auchmuty (1723–1788) appeared for the Plaintiff tenant, seeking reimbursement. Oxenbridge Thacher (1719–1765) appeared for the Defendant landlord. These were "top" lawyers. See full description at *Appendix 6*, "Brief Biographies."

Justice Russell appears to have dissented from the outcome, which was supported by the Chief Justice, Justice Oliver, Justice Cushing, and Justice Lynde.

very antient Date, (3) we find no Action on it till 1752; ſo that it always ſuppoſed that ſuch a Contract is made. The Words of the Law are not — where no expreſs, — no written, — no verbal, — but "where *no Contract* is." And I think the continual paying Rent for ſeveral Years without any Demand of a Deduction, and ſeveral Receipts having been given by the Plaintiff to the Defendant in full of all Accounts, are full Evidence that ſuch was the Intention and Meaning of the Parties, which is a ſufficient Contract. To have this Point called in Queſtion would be big with the greateſt Inconveniences. If Landlords who from Year to Year have received their whole Rents, and given Diſcharges for them, are to be called to account for many Years' Taxes, it would be productive of an ample Harveſt of Suits, of which perhaps our Brotherhood might reap the Gleanings.

Mr. Auchmuty. As to the Cuſtom of the Town; if there had been no Law, that might have been an Argument of ſome Weight; but the Law is expreſs, and ſhall any pretended Cuſtom controul it? As for the Conſequences they muſt not be conſidered — if it is Law, it is Law, &c.

Juſtice

---

(3) The earlieſt ſtatute proviſion that we find on this ſubject is in the Prov. St. of 4 W. & M. in 1692. By this act however, as by the Gen. Sts. of 1860, c. 11, § 9, the landlord was to pay the whole taxes in the abſence of any particular agreement. The first proviſion for a contribution was in the Prov. St. of 6 W. & M. in 1694, and is as follows: "The fermer or occupier of any houſes or lands, being aſſeſſed for the ſame in his occupation, to be reimburſed the one half of what he ſhall ſo pay toward the ſaid aſſeſſment by the landlord or leſſor where there is no particular contract to the contrary, and ſhall be allowed to diſcount the ſame out of his rent." The laſt clauſe was omitted in ſubſequent acts. *Ante*, p. 27, note (1).

Justice Russell rarely dissented, and 58 out of the 78 opinions were unanimous. See *Appendix 1*, *infra*.

4 · AUTHORITY

None cited.

5 · LATER CITATIONS

Derumple v. *Clark* was cited in *Ammidown* v. *Freeland*, 101 Mass. 303, 310 (Mass. 1869), to provide an example of "provisions inserted in the tax acts of Massachusetts from an early period, taxing real estate either to the landlord or the tenant, and giving to the one who actually pays the amount of the tax the right to recover the same or a certain portion thereof from the other."

6 · NOTE

This is a fascinating case, because the Justices differed among themselves as to law, and there was disagreement on the law even among those who agreed on the outcome.

Justice Russell read the "Tax Act" as requiring reimbursement in the absence of an express contract, which certainly makes sense. Robert Auchmuty argued, rightly, that the "Law was very express and particular," and the mere fact his client paid the full rent could not give rise to an implied agreement, because the statutory right was for reimbursement only.

For the Defendant landlord, Oxenbridge Thacher (Quincy's pupil master) argued that it was "the uninterrupted Custom of this Town for the Tenant to pay the Whole Taxes." This impressed Justice Lynde ("I think the Custom of the Town is a Great Thing"), but not Justice Oliver ("As for the custom of the Town, I can't think it of any Weight"), *Reports*, 40. But Justice Oliver thought there was a "strong" presumption of a contract, as in *Jackson* v. *Foye*, *Reports*, 26, Case 10. Justice Cushing combined both the "Custom of the Town" and the "implied contract" argument. "[T]he Intention of these parties . . . may be collected from the Evidence joined to the Custom of the Town." *Reports*, 40.

This last argument was what impressed the Chief Justice. "Custom shall not be placed in Opposition to Law, but it may be a Circumstance going to interpret the Intention of the Parties." *Id.*, 41. The Chief Justice also thought

Juſtice Oliver. As for the Cuſtom of the Town, I can't think it of any Weight; but as the Law ſays " where no Contract is," you muſt confine it to an expreſs Contract. I ſee no eſſential difference between this and the Caſe of *Foye & Jackſon*, and can't but think the Evidence you have is a Preſumption of a Contract ſo ſtrong that you muſt find for the Defendant.

Juſtice Ruſſell. I think the Law evidently means an expreſs Agreement. However, I don't think we have here any Evidence of an implied Agreement, or any Agreement at all.

Juſtice Cuſhing. If there be Anything to ſhow the Intention of the Parties, I hold that Evidence of a ſufficient Agreement within the Senſe of the Law; and that the Intention of theſe Parties was that the Tenant ſhould pay the Whole, may be collected from the Evidence joined to the Cuſtom of the Town.

Juſtice Lynde. I always thought that the Intention of this Law was not to affect the Taxes in ſuch Towns as this, but merely where Farms are let to the Halves, where the Benefit of the Eſtate being divided, 'tis but juſt the Charges ſhould be divided too. I think the Cuſtom of the Town is a great Thing, and that the Parties are to be ſuppoſed to intend according to the Cuſtom. I think the Evidence ſufficient to prove a Contract within the Intendment of the Law.

Ch. Juſt. You are to go according to Law and Evidence.

[P. 40]

that the landlord had the better of the policy and fairness arguments, a point he expressed in terms of "equity." "Where the Law is in any Case doubtful and the Equity of it plain, you should verge towards Equity." *Id.*, 41. The reason for this may be that the law was rarely enforced. As Thacher observed, "[T]hough this Law is of very antient Date [1692], we find no action on it till 1752." *Id.*, 38–39.

Here the Justices, once again, "bend" a formal application of the law to achieve a "fair" result by invoking Custom, implied contracts, and equity arguments. What was so interesting in this case is that they each adopted slightly different rationales, and Justice Russell flatly disagreed.

It is notable that there was no appeal to English precedent, even in the arguments. Perhaps this was because of the "equitable" and "local" nature of the statutory dispute, although the legal principles involved were commonly debated in England. See J. H. Baker, *supra*, pp. 208–212.

Evidence. Where the Law is in any Cafe doubtfull and the Equity of it plain, you fhould verge towards Equity. Cuftom fhall not be placed in Oppofition to Law, but it may be a Circumftance going to interpret the Intention of the Parties. I fee Nothing to diftinguifh this from the Cafe of *Jackfon* v. *Foye.*

Verdict for Defendant.

[P. 41]

Several

ACTS

AND

LAWS

Paſſed by the Great and General Court or Aſſembly of Their Majeſties Province of the Maſſachuſetts-Bay, in

NEW ENGLAND.

Convened and Held at *Boſton*, the Eighth Day of *June*. 1692.

Anno Regni Gulielmi, et Mariæ. Regis et Reginæ Angliæ, Scotiæ, Franciæ, et Hiberniæ, Quarto

B O S T O N,

Printed by *Benjamin Harris*, Printer to His Excellency, the Governour and Council. 1692.

ILLUSTRATION 15: *The Acts and Laws . . . of New England* (Boston, 1692) containing an early "Tax Act," "an Act, for the Granting to their Majesties an Assessment upon Polls and Estates," pp. 4–5. Many thanks to Mark Sullivan.

CASE 18

Daniels *verſ.* Bullard.

DANIELS *v.* BULLARD.

Rec. 1763. Fol. 106.

The Fact that a Witneſs is immediately about to leave the Country will not authorize the taking his Depoſition without Notice to the oppoſite Party.

A DEPOSITION was offered; the Caption imported that the Witneſs was immediately going out of the Country, and therefore the oppoſite Party not notified. *Ruled* bad.

[P. 41]

Daniels v. *Bullard* (1763)
3 George III (Feb.) in the
Superior Court of Judicature

1 · BRIEF DESCRIPTION

The sole issue was whether a deposition was admissible when the opponent Party was not notified. The only grounds were that "the Witness was immediately going out of the Country." This was not sufficient to excuse lack of notice.

2 · RECORD

Available at Rec. 1763, fol. 106.

Numerous other depositions and papers are available in the Suffolk County Files, including:

vol. 494, fol. 58, index no. 83898
- (1) Attestation by justice of the peace
- (2) Deposition of Henry Bullard
- (3) Deposition of Jemima Bullard
- (4) Deposition of Nathan Partridge
- (5) Deposition of Josiah Rockwood

vol. 495, fol. 1, index no. 84041
- (1) Agreement to send dispute to referees (arbitration)
- (2) Notice to referees of agreement between parties
- (3) Deposition of Elijah Clark

3 · PROFESSIONALS INVOLVED

Not indicated.

4 · AUTHORITY

None cited.

5 · LATER CITATIONS

None.

6 · NOTE

This is still good Massachusetts and federal practice. See F.R. Civ. P. 27; Donald J. Savery, Frank C. Corso, William T. Harrington, *Massachusetts Practice*, vol. 46, *Federal Civil Practice*, 327–328 (1998).

CASE 19

BARNES *v.* GREENLEAF.

Rec. 1763. Fol. 23.

An Officer who difcharges a Defendant from Arreft in Confideration of the Promife of a third Perfon for his Appearance, can

Barnes *verf.* Greenleaf.

THE Queftion in this Cafe was, whether Mr. Wheelwright fhould be admitted as a Witnefs. The Action was brought againft Greenleaf (Sheriff) for an infufficient Service of a Writ upon which the Return ftood thus: "I have attached the Defendant, and taken Mr. Wheelwright's Word for his Appearance."(1) Mr. Wheelwright was offered

(1) The return as fet forth on record is as follows:

"Suffolk fs. Bofton, June 17, 1762. I attached the body of the within named Thomas Carnes, and Nathaniel Wheelwright Efq. gave his word for his appearance at Court.

BENJA: CUDWORTH,
Deputy Sheriff."

Barnes v. *Greenleaf* (1763)
3 George III (Feb.) in the
Superior Court of Judicature

1 · BRIEF DESCRIPTION

The Defendant Sheriff (Stephen Greenleaf) arrested one James Barnes and then released him, on the word of one Wheelwright that Barnes would appear in court. The issue, as in *Wrentham Proprietors* v. *Metcalf*, *Reports* 36, Case 16, *supra*, was whether Wheelwright was too interested in the outcome of a dispute between the Plaintiff and the Sheriff about the release of Barnes to appear as a witness. (The Sheriff argued that the prisoner was released with the Plaintiff's consent, and Wheelwright apparently would have supported this.) The Court held that the Sheriff would not have recourse against Wheelwright if the Sheriff was found to have deviated "from the Path of his Duty," therefore Wheelwright was not interested in the outcome and could testify.

2 · RECORD

Available at Rec. 1763, Fol. 23.

Nothing in the Suffolk Files.

3 · PROFESSIONALS INVOLVED

Not indicated.

4 · AUTHORITY

None cited. Quincy himself added a citation at *Reports*, 42, to that colonial favorite, [Matthew] *Bacon's Abridgement*, vol. 4, 462–463, which was on point. Volume 4 was first published in London in 1759. See *Sweet & Maxwell*, *supra*, vol. 1, 16.

5 · LATER CITATIONS

Samuel Quincy noted several subsequent cases on this issue: *Denny* v. *Lincoln*, 5 Mass. 385 (Mass. 1809); *Ayer* v. *Hutchins*, 4 Mass. 370 (Mass. 1808); *Foster* v. *Clark*, 36 Mass. 329, 19 Pick. 329 (Mass. 1837); and *Pollard* v. *Graves*, 40 Mass. 86 (Mass. 1839). *Reports*, note 2, page 42.

maintain no Action on fuch Promife; and fuch Perfon is therefore a competent Witnefs for the Officer in an Action for the infufficient Service.

offered to prove that at the Plaintiff's Confent the Prifoner was difmiffed. He was objected to, becaufe 'twas faid the Sheriff would recur to him, if he loft in this Action. But 'twas anfwered, there could be no fuch Recourfe, for the Sheriff deviating from the Path of his Duty muft expect the Confequence. (2) He was admitted and fworn.*

* Vid. 4 Bac. Ab. 462, 463, top. (4)

---

(2) S. P. *Denny* v. *Lincoln*, 5 Mafs. 385. In that cafe the officer forbore to arreft, upon a promife by a third party to deliver the debtor to him at a day named. *Parfons*, C. J. "It is to be regretted that officers having a plain path before them will not purfue it. If they deviate from it, it muft be at their own peril, and they cannot protect themfelves againft the damages arifing from a breach of official duty by any collateral ftipulation for indemnity." See alfo 4 Mafs. 370. But taking receipts for property attached, or notes in confideration of forbearing to attach, is confiftent with the officer's duty. *Fofter* v. *Clark*, 19 Pick. 329. And fuch receiptor has been held incompetent through intereft. 23 Pick. 86.

6 · NOTE

Another example, like *Reports* 36, Case 16 (*Wrentham Proprietors* v. *Metcalf*), of the old common law rule that persons could not testify in a case in which they were a party, or had a direct interest in the outcome, because of a likely bias. Here, the Plaintiff's lawyer was making aggressive use of the doctrine, and rightly lost.

CASE 20

ELWELL
v.
PIERSON.

Rec. 1763.
Fol. 56.

Devife of Land as follows: "To my Son S. and his Heirs forever, provided that my faid Son fhall maintain Myfelf and his Mother during our Lives with fufficient and convenient Maintenance." Afterwards: "Alfo whereas it is expreffed that my Son fhall have this my Living to him and his forever, my Will and Meaning is, and I do hereby appoint my Grandfon R.,

Elwell *verf.* Pierfon.

(From Effex.) (3)

THE Queftion in this Cafe was, whether Samuel, Son of the original Devifor, took an Eftate Tail,

---

(3) The eftate fued for is defcribed as "a neck of land in Glocefter Harbour now called Pierfon's Neck."

(4) Bac. Ab. Sheriff, O.

Elwell v. *Pierson* (1763)
3 George III (Feb.) in the
Superior Court of Judicature

1 · BRIEF DESCRIPTION

This is another case, like *Dudley* v. *Dudley*, *Reports* 12, Case 9, in which a poorly drafted will is challenged as to whether or not it established an entail. These are important cases, with much riding on the outcome. The direct heir could convey the land outright, if it was not entailed, but the land could be "locked in" if an entail existed. Here, the Court decided that the words technically established an entail, but that the duty in the will to "maintain Myself and his Mother during our Lives with sufficient and convenient Maintenance" resulted in a fee simple instead!

2 · RECORD

Available at Rec. 1763, Fol. 50.

Additional papers in Suffolk Files vol. 479, index no. 80289, and vol. 493, index no. 83617, including:

vol. 479, index no. 80289

- Court record and case description (2½ pages) from Essex County Superior Court of Judicature Court of Assize, dated 10/10/1759

vol. 493, index no. 83617

- Bill of costs from Essex County Superior Court, dated 1762.

3 · PROFESSIONALS INVOLVED

Oxenbridge Thacher (1719–1765), Quincy's pupil master, appeared for the Plaintiff, the eldest son of the direct heir, arguing for the entail. He was joined by Jeremiah Gridley (1701/2–1767). Robert Auchmuty (1723–1788) appeared for the Defendant, and argued against the entail. These were the "cream of the crop" of Boston's practicing bar. See *Appendix 6*. Thacher had studied law under Gridley, and the two occasionally collaborated.

4 · AUTHORITY

Thacher began his argument for the entail with a very important assertion, albeit directed at a side issue in the case. Apparently, it was "objected that

Tail, and if he did, whether the Plaintiff is ſole Heir in Tail of Samuel, being eldeſt Son of eldeſt Son all along.

Son of ſaid S., to be the next immediate Heir unto this my Living after his Father, to enjoy the ſame to him and his Heirs forever. And in Caſe that ſaid R. do die without Heir, it ſhall then fall to the next eldeſt of my Grandſons ſurviving, and ſo in like Caſe of Mortality, one from another to the next eldeſt of my Grandſons ſurviving." *Held*, that S. took an Eſtate in Fee Simple. *It ſeems*, that but for the Charge of Maintenance, S. would have taken an Eſtate Tail.

The Words of the Will are theſe: "I give to "Samuel Elwell the Houſe I now live in," &c.

Afterwards: "I give all my ſaid Houſing &c. "expreſſed, to him my ſaid Son Samuel, and *his* "*Heirs forever*, provided that my ſaid Son ſhall "maintain Myſelf and his Mother during our Lives "with ſufficient and convenient Maintenance."

Afterwards: "Alſo whereas it is above expreſſed "that my Son Samuel ſhall have this my Living "above ſaid to him and his forever, my Will and "Meaning is, and I do hereby appoint my Grand- "ſon Robert, Son of ſaid Samuel, to be the next "immediate Heir unto this my Living after his "Father, my ſaid Son Samuel, to enjoy the ſame to "him and his Heirs forever. And in Caſe that ſaid "Robert do die without Heir, it ſhall then fall to "the next eldeſt of my Grandſons ſurviving, and ſo "in like Caſe of Mortality one from another to the "next eldeſt of my Grandſons ſurviving."

Mr. Thacher for the Tail. It is objected that there were but two Witneſſes to the Will. At that Time the Law required but two. The Statute of Frauds was never ſuppoſed to extend here, till we made a like Law here. (5) Vid. Old Colony Laws, 158.

---

(5) Prov. St. 4 W. & M. Anc. Chart. 233.

there were but two witnesses to the will." *Reports*, 43. Thacher observed that at the time the will was made "the Law required but two" because "[t]he Statute of Frauds was never supposed to extend here, till we made a like Law here," citing Old Colony Laws (1672 ed.), 158. See Prov. St. 4 W.&M. *Anc. Chart.* 233 for the colonial statute, adopted in 1693. The Statute of Frauds was adopted in 1677, 29 Car. 2. c.3.

Thacher then went on to cite much English case authority on the central issue, as did Auchmuty on the other side. Characteristically, Gridley, also arguing for the tail, referring to relatively few English authorities, but rather arguing from a general law of construction, i.e., "every Word shall be operative if possible." *Reports*, 45.

The nature of the cases cited demonstrated extensive research, and excellent libraries, available to both sides. *Sonday's Case* from 9 *Coke's Reports* 128 [1572–1616], first published in 1613 (*Sweet & Maxwell*, vol. 1, 296:31), was cited by Thacher for the distinction between a remainder over to a stranger, as opposed to kin, as were two cases from *Croke's Reports* (Jacobean) (covering 1542–1641), first published in 1657 (*Sweet & Maxwell*, vol. 1, 298:37). More recent cases were cited from 1 *Lord Raymond's Reports* 569 (covering 1694–1732), first published in 1743 (*Sweet & Maxwell*, vol. 1, 307:105, and *Law Commonplace,* p. [70], n. 2) and *Lord Talbot's Reports* 1 (covering 1730–1737), first published in 1741 (*Sweet & Maxwell*, vol. 1, 345:12). Auchmuty also appealed to *Coke* and *Croke's Reports*, arguing that once a fee simple is given "nothing by implication shall take it away." *Reports*, 45. Auchmuty and Gridley also referred to *Bacon's New Abridgment of the Law*, vol. 2, title "Devise." See *Reports*, 46–47. This large, useful legal encyclopedia was published in installments from 1736 to 1766, vol. 2 appearing in 1736. Quincy referred to *Bacon's Abridgment* frequently in his *Law Commonplace*, and possessed copies of *Croke's Reports* in his library at his death in 1775. See *Appendix 8*, *infra*, "Catalogue of Books Belonging to the Estate of Josiah Quincy jun: Esq: Deceas'd," item 80.

5 · LATER CITATIONS

This case has never been cited by later Massachusetts courts, and probably for the reason noted by Samuel Quincy, *Reports* 48, S. Quincy n. 9. According to Samuel Quincy, Gridley's textual argument was correct, and "never was any

158. (6) The Queſtion is, whether Samuel took an Eſtate Tail, by the Words of the Will. Great Condeſcenſion is given to Wills, and Words, which in Acts executed in the Lifetime would not make Eſtates Tail, will make them in Wills, becauſe Teſtators are ſuppoſed to be *inops conſilii*, and Lord Holt obſerves that there were no ſuch Conveyances at Common Law, but by Statute. The Teſtator's Intent is to be the Rule of Conſtruction, if agreeable to Rules of Law. The firſt Deviſe is an Inheritance; then he explains his Grandſon Robert to be the next immediate Heir of his ſaid Son Samuel; he does not retract, but only directs how that Inheritance ſhall go. The Intent appears from this alſo — He ſays, the next eldeſt Brother ſhall inherit for want of Heirs; now he could not die without Heirs, while he had any Brothers, whence it appears he excluded Brothers from his Idea of Heirs in this Caſe, and ſo could only mean Heirs of the Body. There is a Difference between the Remainder over being given to a Stranger, and to one of Kin; in the firſt Caſe it cannot be explanatory of what Heirs are meant; in the laſt it is. 9 Co. 128, *Sonday's Caſe.* Cro. Ja. 415, *Webb & Hearing.* Id. 448, *King* vs. *Rumball.* Id. 695, *Chaddock* vs. *Cowley.* 1 Ld. Raym. 569, *Nottingham* vs. *Jennings.* Comyns, 539, *Brice* vs. *Smith.* Ld. Talbot, 1, *Tyte* vs. *Willis.*

The only Queſtion remaining is, whether this Eſtate Tail firſt veſted in Samuel the Son, or Robert

(6) Col. Laws, ed. of 1672. Anc. Chart. 204, § 2.

maintenance construed to make a fee-simple when a clear tail was," citing T. Jarman's *Treatise on Wills*, vol. 2, 172 (1841, 1844) originally published in two volumes, the second appearing in 1844 (*Sweet & Maxwell*, vol. 2, 185). As Jarman noted, "[F]or where the direction to pay is imposed on a person to whom there is given . . . an estate tail whether limited in express terms, or arising constructively by implication . . . the charge is inoperative to enlarge such . . . estate tail, to a fee simple." *Id.*, 172–173. Samuel charitably suggests that "the Court must have considered the intent of the testator to be doubtful," but the Chief Justice actually said the opposite. *Reports*, 48. As a point of law, the case appears wrongly decided.

6 · NOTE

This case is important for two reasons. First, it shows the reliance by the best advocates in the colony on reported English cases, some over two hundred years old, in arguing a complex legal issue. Ironically, the second reason for its importance is because the Court, in the end, paid little attention to these authorities.

The best argument for finding an entail was thoroughly supported by the English authorities. The maker of a will cannot explain what he meant to do after his death. In attempting to discover his intent, the Court should try to make every word used "operative," as Gridley argued: "[E]very word shall be operative if possible . . . if he [Samuel, the son] took a Fee, the Last Words go for Nothing." *Reports*, 45. The Chief Justice's questions during argument show him using such a textual approach. See *Reports*, 46, 47.

The Court clearly had trouble with this case, however, and adjourned judgment. On announcing the opinion, the Chief Justice said it "was unanimous that Samuel by the Words would have taken a Tail," i.e., the textual approach, but that "the Burden and Duty of Maintenance made it a Fee Simple." *Reports*, 48. In short, the Court acknowledged the validity of the textual argument, but found it trumped by the practical concerns of the son's duty to maintain his Mother "with sufficient and convenient Maintenance." *Reports*, 43. Whether the Court was also expressing a covert hostility to entails, whose validity in Massachusetts was challenged in other leading cases such as *Dudley* v. *Dudley* (1762), *Reports* 12, Case 9, is open to conjecture.

ert the Grandſon; I think in Samuel, firſt, becauſe Samuel had an Inheritance by the firſt Words; Secondly, becauſe the Teſtator appoints Robert his next immediate Heir; this is ſurely ſhowing how the Inheritance ſhall be limited, and it is as it would be limited by Law, ſuppoſing it an Eſtate Tail. The Inheritance of Samuel ſhall by no means be taken away, if the Will can be conſtrued otherwiſe, as in this Caſe the Words do not make an Eſtate for Life only, but a Limitation.

Mr. Gridley. The Queſtion is, whether Samuel took a Fee Simple or Tail; the firſt Words of the Will give him a Fee, but afterwards ſay Robert ſhall be his Heir: We all agree as to the Fee—we ſay the other Words ſhew the Intent. If Samuel had a Fee, he could convey it, and Robert would not be his Heir; in the ſecond Place, every Word ſhall be operative if poſſible; whereas on their Suppoſition the laſt Words are of no Force. Robert on their Suppoſition ſhould take only as the Law gave him, and Robert took as a Purchaſer, which he could not do unleſs Samuel took an Eſtate for Life: If a Fee, he could not—if he took a Fee, the laſt Words go for Nothing.

Auchmuty againſt the Tail. Their Authorities do not reach this Caſe, the Intent of the Teſtator is to be followed, but the Intent muſt be clear and muſt be agreeable to the Rules of Law. The Fee is at firſt plainly given; and where an expreſs Eſtate is given, nothing by Implication ſhall take it away. 1 Salk. 236, *Popham* vs. *Banfield.* Cro. Cha. 368, *Spirt* vs. *Bence.* 6 Co. 16, *Wild's Caſe.* Where an an Implication affects an Heir at Law, that Implication muft be very ftrong. 2 Bac. 66, Tit. Devife.

I'll confider the Force of the Words in the Will, and whether thofe Words operate fo ftrongly as to turn the plain Fee Simple into a Tail. If Robert died and left Iffue, well — but if not, then to the next eldeft Grandfon, which is not the Courfe of Tails; fo that the Teftator's meaning cannot be collected from thefe Words; and if a Man fhall try to make fuch an Eftate as the Law never made, I take it to be utterly void. I fhall fhew the Words, pointing out the next immediate Heir a meer Nullity. The Grandfon of an younger Son may be an elder Grandfon than thofe of an elder, which is not agreeable to Tail.

Ch. Juft. Quære — Whether the fecond Son of an eldeft Son may not be called an elder Grandfon, than an elder Grandfon of a younger Son?

Mr. Auchmuty. This with vulgar Minds would not be a natural Thought. I think if he has any Eftate, it is a Fee Simple. Cro. Jam. 590, *Pells* vs. *Brown.* (This Cafe he largely compared with the Cafe at Bar.) The ordering him to maintain his Mother amounts to his ordering him to pay her a Sum in grofs, which is allowed to caufe a Fee Simple. 2 Bacon, 54. (7) 3 Rep. 31, a. 1 Lill. 451. The true Diftinction is between a Sum to be paid out

(7) Bac. Ab. Devife, C.

out of the Rents, and a Sum in grofs, which may be greater. But fuppofing the Cafe to be doubtful, as they are the Plaintiffs, I take it to be incumbent upon them to make out a clear Title.

Mr. Gridley. 2 Bacon, 62. (8) With Regard to the Difherifon of the Heir, that is not in this Cafe to be confidered — if it is the Mind of the Teftator, that is the Rule. By the firft Part Samuel was to have had a Fee Simple, but fo as not to exclude Robert; 'tis plain he intended Robert fhould have the Eftate. Samuel muft either have a Fee Simple, Tail or an Eftate for Life: If for Life, how is it to him and his Heirs? — if in Fee, what has Robert? The laft Claufe confirms my Opinion, it muft be fuppofed that by eldeft Grandfon he intended Grandfon by Samuel; this is the natural Courfe, that if Robert died, it fhould go to the Brothers of Robert, other Children of Samuel.

Ch. Juft. Is it not better firft to make it an Eftate Tail in Samuel, that it fhould rather go to thefe, than other Grandfons, than becaufe it is thus divided, that therefore it is an Eftate Tail?

Mr. Gridley. Cafes in Equity, 184, Cafe 28, *Shaw* vs. *Weigh.* Cro. Cha. 57. As for the Cafe *Pells & Brown*, here is nothing like a Limitation; Upon his Suppofition it tends to fuch a Perpetuity as the Law abhors, it fhould have been "if Samuel die without Iffue;" here it is "if Robert." With

(8) Bac. Ab. Devife, D.

With Regard to the Maintenance, if there is a Doubt, what the Eſtate is, it ſhall be a Fee Simple, but never was any Maintenance conſtrued to make a Fee Simple, when a clear Tail was: Maintenance in ſome Tails is good.

The Court choſe to conſult upon the Matter, and ſo Judgment was adjourned to Auguſt Term, where the *Chief Juſtice* delivered the Opinion of the Court, which he ſaid was unanimous that Samuel by the Words would have taken a Tail; but that the Burden and Duty of Maintenance made it a Fee Simple. (9)

---

(9) It would ſeem, however, that the Court muſt have conſidered the intent of the teſtator to be doubtful, as otherwiſe it would be difficult to anſwer Mr. Gridley's poſition that "never was any maintenance conſtrued to make a fee-ſimple when a clear tail was." 2 Jarman on Wills, 172.

[P. 48]

CASE 21

Ruſſel *verſ.* Oakes.

RUSSEL *v.* OAKES.

(From Middleſex.)

Rec. 1763. Fol. 91.

Payment by the Maker to the Promiſee of a Note on Demand is a good Defence againſt a ſubſequent Indorſee for Value without Notice. *Hutchinſon, C. J., diſſ.*

THIS was an Action of the Caſe on a Note of Hand which was indorſed to the Plaintiff, and appeared to have been paid before the Indorſement. The Queſtion was, whether the Plaintiff ſhould recover in this Action or be barred by the Payment. (1)

Mr.

(1) It appears by the declaration that the note in ſuit bore date, October 19, 1759, and was payable on demand to one James Webber or

Russel v. *Oakes* (1763)
3 George III (Feb.) in the
Superior Court of Judicature

1 · BRIEF DESCRIPTION

This is an important case about negotiable commercial papers. "A note of hand," payable to "James Webber or order," is indorsed to the Plaintiff, but the promisor, the Defendant, had already paid the indorser. The Plaintiff did not know of the payment when he took the note. The Court found for the Defendant, but the Chief Justice was in dissent. The problem, of course, is that good faith holders for value of such notes, without notice of such a payment, can be left with only an action against the indorser, who may be judgment proof. As the Chief Justice observed, "If this Action be barred, it seems to me that one half of the Trade must be extremely precarious, for it rests upon such Bills, whose Credit must be destroyed." *Reports*, 50.

2 · RECORD

Available at Rec. 1763, Vol. 91. See also the file, August 4, 1761, No. 82195 which contains:

Russell v. *Oakes*, (same) Aug. 4, 1761, No. 82195.

- Jury Findings—jury found that the note at issue was made and given by Oaks for valuable consideration, and after the giving of the note, but before its endorsement, the sum of the note was paid by Oaks to Webber in order to discharge it, and Webster accepted it thereafter; and Plaintiff at the time of endorsement did not know that it had already been paid on Aug. 11, 1761, so the Plaintiff ought to recover the sum of 2.12:8 with costs.
- Fragment of Recognizance to Prosecute Appeal from Dec. 1761.

3 · PROFESSIONALS INVOLVED

Counsels in this case were among the most distinguished of the bar. Edmund Trowbridge (1709–1793) appeared for the Defendant, as did Jeremy Gridley (1701/2–1767). See biographies in *Appendix 6*. Gridley, John Adams's pupil master, became Attorney General in 1767. Trowbridge was Attorney General

Mr. Trowbridge for Defendant. Strange, 674. It is always held when Payment is once made, a Promiſe is of no Force. Lucas, 287. (2) After the Promiſee had once received it he could not recover himſelf; he cannot give a greater Power than he has himſelf. Skinner, 410. In a Declaration on inland Bills 'tis ſaid "then wholly unpaid." 2 Show. 495.

Mr. Gridley. This Caſe muſt appear evident on our Side to any Perſon who is at all acquainted with the Nature of Bills of Exchange. To pay him *or* his Order, is there any Intereſt to transfer? Is not the Intereſt gone? The Indorſer is guilty of a Fraud againſt the Indorſee, who has his Action for it. There is an entire Difference between this and in Caſe it had not been paid till after the Indorſement, for by this the Property is changed and in the Indorſee. Trade would be rendered very precarious, if ſuch negotiable Notes can't be diſcharged but by taking up of the Note.

Mr. Kent. Cunningham on Bills of Exchange cites Comyns. It was formerly ſettled Law that the Conſideration ſhould not be called in Queſtion — they are upon the ſame Footing as Inland Bills.

Ch. Juſt. If this Action ſhould be barred, it ſeems

---

order, and by him indorſed to the plaintiff. The queſtion of law was raiſed by a ſpecial verdict, which ſhowed that the plaintiff took the note by indorſement on the 4th of Auguſt, 1761, after it had been paid, but without knowledge of the payment.

(2) —— v. *Ormſton*, 10 Mod. 287.

from 1749–1767, and became a Justice of the Superior Court in 1767. They were opposed by Benjamin Kent (1708–1788), for the Plaintiff, who became Attorney General in 1776. See his biography in *Appendix 6*. Thus all the counsels in this case either were, or would become, Attorney General!

4 · AUTHORITY

Trowbridge cited four English cases, *Jefferies* v. *Austin* (1725), 1 *Strange*'s *Reports* 674 (1716–1749), 2 vols., 1755 (*Sweet & Maxwell*, vol. 1, 309:124, *Law Commonplace,* p. [21], n. 12); *Anonymous* v. *Ormston*, *Lucas*' *Reporter* 286 at 287—part 10 of *Modern Reporter* (covering 1702–1710), eds. in 1736, 1741, 1769 (*Sweet & Maxwell,* vol. 1, 305:88); *Hill* v. *Lewis* (1694), *Skinner*'s *Reports*, 410 (covering 1681–1697), 1728 (*Sweet & Maxwell*, vol. 1, 309:121); and *Claxton* v. *Smith* (1686), 2 *Showers' Reports* 494, at 495, (covering 1678–1694), pt. 2, 1720 (*Sweet & Maxwell*, vol. 1, 309:119, *Law Commonplace,* p. [82], n. 1). Gridley cited to no English authority, but argued the policy implications of requiring the promisor to actually find and destroy the note if he wants to pay it. Kent, in opposition, cited to Cunningham's *The Law of Bills of Exchange* etc. London, 1760, with further editions in 1761 and 1766 (see *Sweet & Maxwell,* vol. 1, 521:30) which he stated also cited *Comyns Reporter* (covering 1695–1741), 1744 (see *Law Commonplace*, p. [32], n. 2).

5 · LATER CITATIONS

This was good law in Massachusetts until the statutory reforms of 1839. See *Baker* v. *Wheaton*, 5 Mass. 509, at 512 (1809); *Hemenway* v. *Stove*, 7 Mass. 58 (1810); Mass St. 1839, c. 121, § 1; Gen. Sts. C.53, § 10. It was actually cited as authority in *Quincy's Reports* itself. See *Tuttle* v. *Williston*, *Reports*, 333, Case 70, at 336.

6 · NOTE

This case demonstrates a major division of the Court about a very important topic, and a willingness to pick and choose among many English precedents in a matter highly important to the law of trade. The Chief Justice was right that applying a defense between the original parties to a note against a *bona fide* purchaser for value without notice damages free negotiability. In his words,

ſeems to me that one half of the Trade muſt be extremely precarious, for it reſts upon ſuch Bills, whoſe Credit muſt be deſtroyed. It deſtroys the Diſtinction between Notes negotiable and not.

Juſt. Ruſſell. There is no Difference between them till the Indorſement.

Judgment was rendered at Cambridge in Auguſt Term, 1763, for Defendant.* (3) *Ch. Juſt. diſſentiente.*

* *Qu.* If the Reaſon of the Judgment in Strange, 1155, would not have been pertinent in this Caſe. Vid. Salk. 344; Carth. 356; L'd Raym'd, 87.

---

(3) S. P. *Baker* v. *Wheaton*, 5 Maſs. 512. *Hemmenway* v. *Stone*, 7 Maſs. 58. But see St. 1839, c. 121, § 1; Gen. Sts. c. 53, § 10.

The caſe on the next page, argued and decided at Auguſt term, 1761, ſeems to have been copied into the book here from notes taken at that time. That the notes were Quincy's own appears from the memorandum prefixed to the argument of Otis, *poſt*, 55; and at the end of the caſe in the MS. is a reference to "Law File C," which probably contained his original notes, now loſt. It ſeems ſtrange that this argument ſhould not have been mentioned by the hiſtorians. Even John Adams, who was admitted to the bar only four days before, (*ante*, 35,) and to whom we are indebted for a report of the firſt argument upon Writs of Aſſiſtance in February 1761, (*post*, 469,) does not appear to have left any notice of this one, except in a letter of October 4, 1780, to Mr. Calkoen, in which he ſays that the queſtion "was ſolemnly and repeatedly argued before the ſupreme court by the moſt learned counſel in the Province." 7 John Adams's Works, 267. But Adams's diary contains only one entry between his admiſſion and June 5, 1762. 2 John Adams's Works, 133, 134. And his autobiography and his letters to William Tudor were written many years afterwards. *Vid. poſt*, 409, 417. Hutchinſon, having received his inſtructions from England ſince the firſt argument, (*poſt*, 415, note,) probably conſidered the ſecond argument a mere form. For copies of the papers, and other information about the Writs of Aſſiſtance, ſee Appendix I.

"It destroys the Distinction between Notes negotiable and not." *Reports*, 50. On the other hand, it puts the original promisor in a practical dilemma. How can he discharge the note without getting possession of the actual note itself, which may have circulated through dozens of hands? This was the core of Gridley's argument for the Defense. While both Trowbridge and Kent relied on English authority, it was ignored by both Justice Russell and the Chief Justice, who appear to have relied solely on policy arguments.

In the end, Gridley's policy argument seems to have prevailed, i.e., that the innocent *bona fide* purchaser of the note could always sue the indorser for fraud, as indorsing a fully paid note is clearly a deceit. Whether Justice Russell was correct in responding to the Chief Justice's concerns about negotiability that "there is no difference between them [notes negotiable and not] till the Indorsement" is a different matter. The note in this case was made out to the promisee "or order." It was clearly meant to be negotiable, and was, therefore, not the same as a non-negotiable note, even before indorsement. The outcome of the case would make such negotiable notes less safe in the Commonwealth, which doubtless led to the later statutory changes.

Today, Article 3 of the *Uniform Commercial Code* generally provides that payment would not be a defense against a holder in due course, so that makers of negotiable notes should never pay unless the note is surrendered. My distinguished colleague, James Rogers, has pointed out that the issue still arises in the disorganized market for second mortgages, where a person pays off a mortgage without ensuring that the original note is surrendered. This has permitted the dishonest sale of such prior mortgage notes. The drafters of American Law Institute's *Restatement of the Law of Mortgages* argued that third parties holding such mortgages should not have automatic recourse against the original parties to the mortgage, resulting in much controversy, including a proposed revision to UCC sec. 3-605 to permit the defense of payment if the obligor has not been notified that the mortgage note has been transferred. My thanks to James Rogers.

CASE 22

August Term (1)

Georgii Ter. in Sup. Cur.

1761. PAXTON'S CASE. Rec. 1761. Fol. 225.

Paxton's Cafe of the Writ of Affiftance.

CHARLES PAXTON, Efq., applied to the Superiour Court for the Writ of Affiftants, as by Act of Parliament to be granted to him.

This Court has Power to iffue general Writs of Affiftance to Officers of the Cuftoms.

Upon this, the Court defired the Opinion of the Bar, whether they had a Right and ought to grant it.

Mr. Otis & Mr. Thacher fpoke againft.

Meffrs. Gridley & Auchmuty (2) for granting it.

Mr. Thacher firft read the Acts of 14 Car. 2, ch. 22, and 7 & 8 of Wm. & Mary, upon which the Requeft for this Writ is founded. (3)

Though this Act of Parliament has exifted 60 Years, yet it was never applied for, nor ever granted, till

(1) Auguft term 1 Geo. 3, which was adjourned without day on Thurfday, November 19th, 1761. Rec. 1761, fol. 239. The argument and decision, here reported, were made upon Wednefday, the 18th of November. Bofton Gazette of November 23, 1761.

(2) Auchmuty was foon after appointed Advocate General, in the place of Otis, who had refigned to avoid arguing for these Writs. Wafhburn's Jud. Hift, Mafs. 185, 186.

(3) Sts. 13 & 14 Car. 2, c. 11, § 5; 7 & 8 W. 3, c. 22, § 6; quoted in Gridley's firft argument, *poft*, 480, 481.

I D O N, June 16.
tance of a Series of repeated Acts
nd benevolence reflects great honour
concerned in it.
f an honest tar, whose husband
in the late expedition, being
er leave of him at Portsmouth,
don, in order to proceed from
amptonshire, where her friends
reduced very low, and being not
endure travelling, she applied
the Northampton stage, intreat-
her credit for an outside passage,
et down to her friends, and be
him. Perceiving her to be very
e made her an offer of an inside
ch, gratis, which was to set out
That very night, however, the
to lay at the inn, was delivered
—Thus disappointed of her pas-
critical circumstance, her dis-
greater than before; but the af-
he ears of some gentlemen who
o be in the inn, they formed a
them to the amount of between
satisfied with this, they sent for
dens of the parish, who contri-
rds conveying the mother and
Added to this, two worthy sai-
ed to come into the inn, hear-
of a brother tar was in distress,
ite of all they had about them,
to about 3s. 6d.—This money
osited in the landlord's hands,
oth for the woman an infant
tion and oeconomy purchased
odging for the whole time was

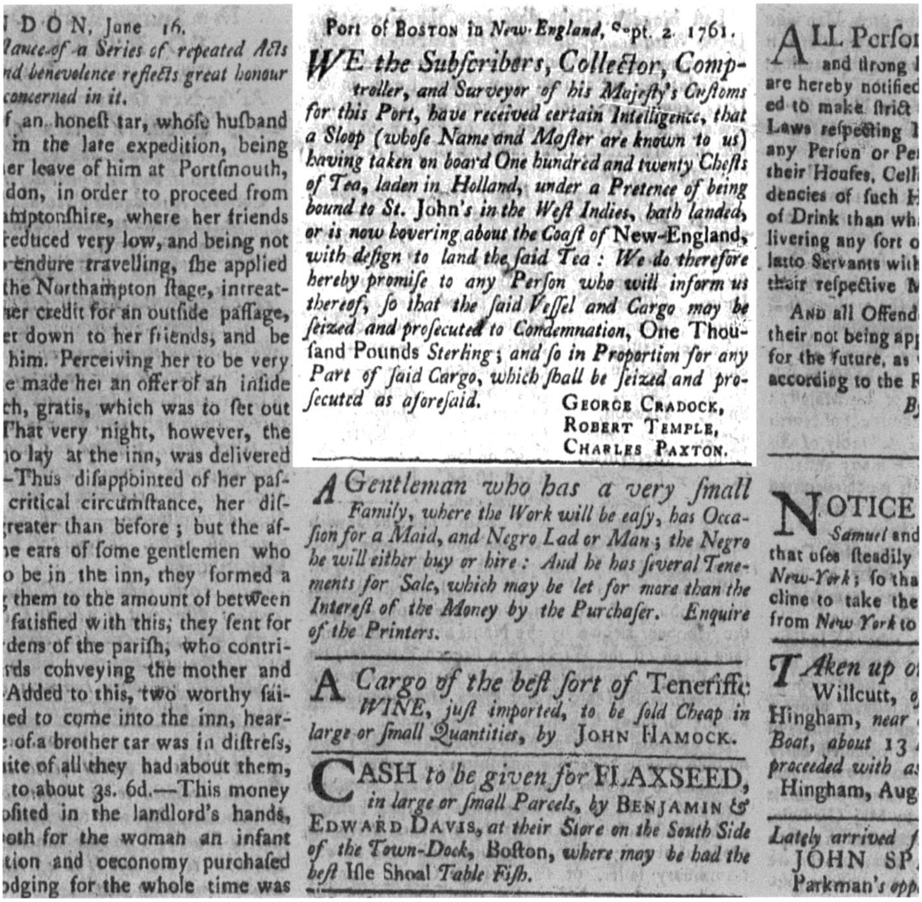

Port of BOSTON in *New-England*, Sept. 2. 1761.

WE the Subscribers, Collector, Comptroller, and Surveyor of his Majesty's Customs for this Port, have received certain Intelligence, that a Sloop (whose Name and Master are known to us) having taken on board One hundred and twenty Chests of Tea, laden in Holland, under a Pretence of being bound to St. John's *in the West Indies, hath landed, or is now hovering about the Coast of* New-England, *with design to land the said Tea: We do therefore hereby promise to any Person who will inform us thereof, so that the said Vessel and Cargo may be seized and prosecuted to Condemnation,* One Thousand Pounds *Sterling; and so in Proportion for any Part of said Cargo, which shall be seized and prosecuted as aforesaid.*

GEORGE CRADOCK,
ROBERT TEMPLE,
CHARLES PAXTON.

A Gentleman who has a very small Family, where the Work will be easy, has Occasion for a Maid, and Negro Lad or Man; the Negro he will either buy or hire: And he has several Tenements for Sale, which may be let for more than the Interest of the Money by the Purchaser. Enquire of the Printers.

A *Cargo of the best sort of* Teneriffe *WINE, just imported, to be sold Cheap in large or small Quantities, by* JOHN HAMOCK.

CASH *to be given for* FLAXSEED, *in large or small Parcels, by* BENJAMIN & EDWARD DAVIS, *at their Store on the South Side of the Town-Dock,* Boston, *where may be had the best* Isle Shoal *Table Fish.*

ALL Perso
and strong
are hereby notified
ed to make strict
Laws respecting
any Person or Pe
their Houses, Cell
dencies of such
of Drink than wh
livering any sort o
latto Servants with
their respective
AND all Offend
their not being ap
for the future, as
according to the

NOTICE
Samuel and
that uses steadily
New-York; so tha
cline to take the
from *New York* to

TAken up o
Willcutt,
Hingham, *near*
Boat, about 13
proceeded with a
Hingham, Aug

Lately arrived
JOHN SP
Parkman's *opp*

ILLUSTRATION 16: *Boston Evening Post*, Sept. 14, 1761, 4. See the Notice signed by Charles Paxton, top center, of Sept. 2, 1761. See also *Paxton's Case of the Writ of Assistance* (1761), Reports, 51 (Case 22). Courtesy of Early American Newspapers, and Archive of Americana Collection. Published by Readex (Readex.com), a division of NewsBank, inc.

till 1756;(4) which is a great Argument againſt granting it; not that an Act of Parliament can be antiquated, but Non-uſer is a great Preſumption that the Law will not bear it; this is the Reaſoning of Littleton and Coke. Knight Service, p. 80, Sect. 108.(5) Moreover, when an Act of Parliament is not expreſs, but even doubtfull, and then has been neglected and not executed, in ſuch a Caſe the Preſumption is more violent.

Ch. Juſtice. (6) The Cuſtom Houſe Officers have frequently applied to the Governour for this Writ, and have had it granted them by him,(7) and therefore, though he had no Power to grant it, yet that removes the Argument of Non-uſer.

Mr. Thacker. If this Court have a Right to grant this Writ, it muſt be either *ex debita Juſtitia* or diſcretionary. If *ex debita Juſtitia*, it cannot in any Caſe be refuſed; which from the Act itſelf and its Conſequences, he argued, could not be intended. It can't be diſcretionary; for it can't be in the Power of any Judge at diſcretion to determine that I ſhall have my Houſe broken open or not. As ſays Juſt. Holt, "There can be no diſcretionary Power whether a Man ſhall be hanged or no."(8)

He moved further that ſuch a Writ is granted and muſt iſſue from the Exchequer Court, and no other

---

(4) *Paxton's caſe*, Auguſt term, 1755; *poſt*, 402–404, & notes.
(5) Co. Lit. 81 a, 81 b. S. P. 11 Met. 291.
(6) Hutchinſon, appointed November 13th, 1760. *Poſt*, 410, 411.
(7) S. P. 3 Hutchinſon's Hiſt. Maſs. 92. *Post*, 401.
(8) *Armſtrong* v. *Liſle*, (1697) Comb. 410. *S. C.* J. Kel. 95, 105; Skin.

Paxton's Case of the Writ of Assistance (1761)
1 George III (Aug.) in the
Superior Court of Judicature
Note: This case is out of chronological order, but the notes are Quincy's, probably copied in from notes taken in August term, 1761. See S. Quincy, unnumbered note, *Reports*, 50.

1 · BRIEF DESCRIPTION

This is the famous second argument of the "Writ of Assistance" case, a case of the greatest political importance. In June of 1755 Charles Paxton, in his capacity of "Surveyor of all Rates, Duties and Impositions arising and growing due to his Majesty at Boston," sought a "Writ of Assistants" under "the Seal of this Superiour Court in the Legal form & according to Usage in his Majestys Court of Exchequer & in Great Britain." See *Reports, Appendix I*, p. 402. (The correct historical name for the writ, as Gridley would later argue, is "*Assistants*, not assistance." See *Reports*, 56–57.) Samuel Quincy's original edition of *Quincy's Reports* in 1865 contained two "Appendices" related to this case, prepared by Horace Gray, Jr., who became Chief Justice of the Supreme Judicial Court and a Justice of the Supreme Court of the United States. (For a full account of Gray's involvement with the *Reports*, see Mark G. Sullivan, "Phantom References to *Quincy's Reports* in the Massachusetts Supreme Judicial Court *Reports*," *Appendix* 5, *infra*.) Gray's *Appendix I* addressed the issue "What are writs of assistance?" and other legal issues. See *Reports*, 395–540. *Appendix II* contained Gray's accounts of *Gray, Treasurer of the Province of Massachusetts Bay* v. *Paxton* (1761), *Province of Massachusetts Bay* v. *Paxton* (1762), and *Erving* v. *Cradock* (1761), related civil actions. See *Reports*, 541–572. As to other contemporary accounts, see *The Legal Papers of John Adams* (eds. L. Kinvin Wroth, Hiller B. Zobel), Cambridge, 1965 vol. 2, 106–107; Samuel A. Green, *James Otis's Argument Against The Writs of Assistance*, 1761 (Cambridge, 1890), 4–8; and James M. Farrell's excellent account "The Writs of Assistance and Public Memory: John Adams and the Legacy of James Otis," 79 *New England Quarterly* (2006), 557. See also the general account of the controversy in *The Boston Gazette and Country Journal*, November 23, 1761, 3.

The Writ here was being sought pursuant to Statute 13 & 14 Car.2 c. 14, sec. 5, which authorized "the Officers of our Customs & their Deputies . . . to

other can grant it; 4 Inſt. 103; and that no other Officers but ſuch as conſtitute that Court can grant it.

Skin. 671; Holt, 63; 12 Mod. 109, 157; Carth. 395; 1 Salk. 63. The deciſion in that caſe was, that a conviction of manſlaughter and allowance of benefit of clergy were a bar to an appeal of murder by the heir of the deceaſed; and that the defendant was entitled to be allowed his clergy at once, without waiting for the trial of the appeal, on which, if convicted, he might be hanged. S. P. 3 Inst. 130; *Smith* v. *Taylor*, (1771) 5 Bur. 2778.

Benefit of clergy in Maſſachuſetts.

Benefit of clergy does not appear to have been allowed in the Colony of Maſſachuſetts. 1 Hutchinſon's Hiſt. Maſs. (3d ed.) 388, note. At a later period, it was allowed in the Province in caſes of manſlaughter and burglary. *Trial of the Britiſh Soldiers*, (ed. 1770) 209. Waſhburn's Jud. Hiſt. Maſs. 194. But it was not ſettled to what other crimes it extended. Reſolution of General Court in February, 1768, 14 Maſs. Archives, 507. 2 John Adams's Works, 534. Opinion of Trowbridge on "Benefit of Clergy reſpecting Rape," Keith MS. No. 11. (*Vid. post*, 478.) It was aboliſhed here by St. 1784, c. 56.

Appeal of death in England.

The appeal of death was by Lord Holt "eſteemed a noble remedy, and a badge of the rights and liberties of an Engliſhman." *Rex* v. *Toler*, 1 Ld. Raym. 557; 12 Mod. 375; Holt, 483. See Barrington on Sts. (5th ed.) 27. In the early part of the laſt century in England, persons who had been acquitted on indictments for murder, were often tried, convicted and executed on appeals. Kendall on Trial by Battel (3d ed.), 44–47. In 1770 its abolition was ſuggested in the Houſe of Commons, but not preſſed. 2 Cavendiſh Debates, 13. 20 Howell's State Trials, 716. An appeal of murder was brought in England as lately as 1817, but defeated by the appellant's declining to accept the wager of battel. *Aſhford* v. *Thornton*, 1 B. & Ald. 403. Such appeals, as well as all trials by battel, were then aboliſhed by St. 59 G. 3, c. 46.

Appeal of murder in the other Colonies.

The Engliſh Sts. of 9 H. 3, c. 34, & 6 Edw. 1, c. 9, concerning appeals of murder, were in force in the Provinces of Pennſylvania and Maryland. Report of Judges, 6 Binn. 599, 604. Kilty on Maryland Sts. 141, 143, 158. It is ſaid that no ſuch appeal was ever brought in Pennſylvania. Roberts on British Statutes in Pennſylvania, 59, 60. But in Maryland in 1765 a negro was convicted and executed upon ſuch an appeal. *Soaper* v. *Tom*, 1 Har. & McHen. 227. The St. of 9 H. 3 was expreſſly adopted in South Carolina in 1712; and Mr. Cooper, the ſtate editor of its ſtatutes, doubts whether trial by battel and appeal of death were not both ſtill in force there in 1837. 2 Sts. at Large of South Carolina, 401, 403, 715.

In Maſſachuſetts Bay.

On the debate in the Houſe of Commons in 1774 on the bill "for the better adminiſtration of Juſtice in Maſſachuſetts Bay," a clauſe ſuſpending

go & enter aboard any ship or vessel outward or inward bound" or "to enter & go into the vaults cellars warehouses shops . . ." then "to seize and from thence to bring any kind of goods or merchandise whatsoever prohibited & uncustomed . . ." See *Reports*, 419–421, *Appendix I*. Such a general warrant was, naturally, resented by Boston merchants, who bitterly opposed it. See "Petition of the Merchants," February 1761, *Reports*, 412–413. Very significantly, the Court sought "the Opinion of the Bar, whether they had a right and ought to grant it." *Reports*, 51. Despite eloquent arguments against the Court issuing such a Writ, made by James Otis and Oxenbridge Thacher, the Writ was approved by a unanimous court. *Reports*, 57.

2 · RECORD

Available at Rec. 1761, fol. 225. Many additional legal records from related cases were set out by Horace Gray, Jr., in *Appendix I* to the 1865 1st edition of the *Reports*, as indicated above.

3 · PROFESSIONALS INVOLVED

The case was argued because the Court "desired the Opinion of the Bar." *Reports*, 51. Whether counsel were retained by interested parties, or were speaking their own views, is unclear on the record. All four advocates were leaders of the Bar. See *Appendix 6*, "Brief Biographies." Certainly, historical events would show Otis, arguing against the Writ, to be a fervent patriot, and Auchmuty arguing for the Writ, to be a firm Tory. This was most certainly one of the two arguments that made the professional reputation of James Otis, Jr. (1725–1783). He was joined by Oxenbridge Thacher (1719–1765), Quincy's pupil master and another senior member of the bar. Otis had been Advocate General in Admiralty since 1756, but resigned to avoid arguing for the Writ, as Samuel Quincy noted. *Reports*, 51, n. 2. See *Appendix 6*. Arguing to grant the Writ were the two most respected members of contemporary bar, Jeremy Gridley (1701/2–1767) and Robert Auchmuty (1723–1788). See *Appendix 6*. Gridley died within months of being appointed Attorney General in 1767. Perhaps mercifully, he never saw the Revolution. Auchmuty, on the other hand, was proscribed in 1778, after replacing Otis as Advocate General and then serving as Judge of the Crown-dominated Vice Admiralty Court from 1767–1776. Interestingly, Otis,

it. 2 Inſt. 551. That this Court is not ſuch a one, vid. Prov. Law. (9) This Court has in the moſt ſolemn Manner diſclaimed the Authority of the Exchequer; this they did in the Caſe of McNeal of Ireland & McNeal of Boſton. (10) This they cannot do in Part; if the Province Law gives them any, it gives them all the Power of the Exchequer Court; nor can they chuſe and refuſe to act at Pleaſure. But ſuppoſing this Court has the Power of the Exchequer, yet there are many Circumſtances which render that Court in this Caſe an improper Precedent; for there the Officers are ſworn in that Court, and are accountable to it, are obliged there to paſs their Accounts weekly; which is not the Caſe here. In that Court, there Caſes are tried, and there finally; which is another Diverſity. Beſides, the Officers of the Cuſtoms are their Officers, and under their Check, and that ſo much, that

---

ſuſpending the appeal of murder was vigorouſly aſſailed by Dunning, Burke, Fox, and others, and withdrawn. 17 Parl. Hiſt. 1291, 1292, 1296. And Mr. Kendall thinks, it exiſted in the Colonies. Kendall, 248, 249, 272. But Mr. Dane ſays, the appeal of felony did not exist here. 7 Dane Ab. 336. And ſee Conſtitution of Maſſachuſetts, c. 6, art. 6; Declaration of Rights, arts. 12, 15; U. S. Conſtitution, amendment 5.

Trial by battel.

In England, the last joinder of iſſue for trial by battel was on a writ of right in 1638; but the judges deferred the combat from time to time for error in the record until 1641, when the Houſe of Commons, upon the petition of the tenant, "ordered a bill to be brought in to take away trial by battel." *Claxton* v. *Lilburne*, 2 Ruſhw. Hiſt. Coll. 788, 790; 3 Ib. 356. Commons & Lords Journals 1620–1641, quoted in Kendall, 135, note. 3 Bl. Com. 337 *& ſeq.* But no ſuch bill was paſſed in England until 1820, *ut sup.* This mode of trial is not ſuppoſed to have been introduced in America, unleſs in South Carolina, *ut sup.* *Poſt*, 178. 3 Wilſon's Works, 142. 3 Dall. 350. 2 Sumner, 68.

(9) Prov. St. 11 W. 3, Anc. Chart. 330, 331.

(10) *McNeal* v. *Brideoak*, *post*, 470, note.

Thacher, Gridley and Auchmuty all collaborated with each other in arguing regular cases.

4 · AUTHORITY

Both sides relied heavily on Edward Coke, the great authority of the English common law. Arguing that "non-user is a great Presumption that the Law will not bear it," Thacher relied on *Coke on Littleton* (*First Institutes*) (London, 1628), 81a–81b. Thacher also relied on Holt, another great English Common lawyer, for the proposition that this Writ cannot be discretionary, but must either be required by law or not, quoting Holt, "There can be no discretionary Power whether a Man shall be hanged or no." *Armstrong* v. *Lisle* (1697), *Comberbach Reports*, 410 (covering 1685–1698), London, 1724. Thacher also appealed to Coke's *Fourth Institutes*, 103, London, 1644, for the proposal that the Writ must issue from the Exchequer Court, and to Coke's *Second Institutes*, 551, London, 1642, for the proposition that no other court could issue it.

Quincy was absent for most of Otis's great argument. "Mr. Otis was of the same side [as Thacher], but I was absent while he was speaking, most of the Time, and so have but Few Notes." *Reports*, 55. Nevertheless, the authorities noted for Otis are fascinating. There was a predictable reliance on English criminal law authorities, Hawkins, Coke and Viner, *Reports*, 56, but also extensive citation to Rapin's *History of England* (2nd ed.) London, 1732, as Samuel Quincy noted, *Reports*, 55, S. Quincy n. 14.

Gridley and Auchmuty's arguments for the Writ also cited to English authorities, including Bacon's *Abridgment* and Coke's *Fourth Institutes*, *supra*, but the core of these arguments were largely a matter of strict application of the words of the statute. Auchmuty also argued that these were earlier grants of the writ in the colony "in Chief Justice Sewall's time." *Reports*, 56. For this assertion, there as no citation of authority. Gridley also argued that "every other Plantation Court" had given "their Superiour Court" power to issue the Writ of Assistants. This argument was in at least Samuel Quincy's view—wrong. See *Reports*, 57, S. Quincy n. 27.

5 · LATER CITATIONS

One of the greatest of all pre-revolutionary legal cases, *Paxton's Case* has been widely cited ever since, including seven times by the Supreme Court of the

that for Mifbehaviour they may punifh with corporal Punifhment. 3 & 4 Car. 2, § 8. (11) 7 & 8 W. & M. does not give the Authority. (12)

(*Mr. Otis* was of the fame Side, but I was abfent, while he was speaking, moft of the Time, and so have but few Notes.)

Mr. Otis. 12 Car. 2, 19. (13) 13 & 14 Car. 2, p. 56. Let a Warrant come from whence it will improperly, it is to be refufed, and the higher the Power granting it, the more dangerous. The Exchequer itfelf was thought a Hardfhip in the firft Conftitution. Vid. Rapin, Vol. 1ft, p. 178, 386, 403, 404. (14) Vol. 2, 285, (15) 375. (16)

It

---

(11) St. 13 & 14 Car. 2, c. 11, § 8.

(12) St. 7 & 8 W. 3, c. 22, § 6.

(13) St. 12 Car. 2, c. 19, *poft*, 395, note.

(14) Rapin's Hift. of Eng. (2d ed.) London, 1732. The pages referred to in the firft volume relate to the Court of Exchequer and proceedings therein.

(15) Where Rapin fays, that in 1629 the privy council of Charles 1 gave orders, " impowering the officers of the cuftoms to enter into any fhip, veffel, or houfe, and to fearch in any trunk or cheft, and break any bulk whatfoever, in default of the payment of cuftoms. But befides that this had never been practifed before, another inconvenience arofe. Thefe officers, under colour of fearching, ufed many oppreffions and rogueries, which caufed the people ftill the more to exclaim." See alfo 1 Rufhworth's Hift. Coll. 665, 668, 669; 2 Ib. 8, 9. *Breaking of houfes, &c., by officers of cuftoms in England in 1629:*

Before writs of affiftance were iffued in Maffachufetts, the officers of the customs, " merely by the authority derived from their commiffions, had forcibly entered warehoufes, and even dwelling-houfes, upon information that contraband goods were concealed in them." But " the people grew uneafy under the exercife of this affumed authority," and refifted or fued the officers. 3 Hutchinfon's Hift. Mafs. 92. *In Maffachufetts before 1755.*

(16) The articles of impeachment againft the Earl of Strafford in 1641, beginning with the ninth article, which charged him with iffuing general warrants of arreft. *S. C.* & *S. P.* in Rufhw. Hift. Coll. 65, 236–240; 3 Howell's State Trial 1391, 1404, 1427. *Impeachment of Strafford.*

United States. The most recent example is Justice O'Connor's dissent, joined by Justices Brennan, Marshall and Stevens, in *Illinois* v. *Krull*, 480 U.S. 340, 363 (1987). It has also been widley discussed by historians. Horace Gray's *Appendix I* is a good early example. See *Reports,* 395–540, and *Appendix* 5, "Cases Citing to Quincy's Reports," *infra*. Paxton's case has also been cited by the Supreme Judicial Court itself and by other state and federal courts, including courts in Indiana, Pennsylvania and Maine, and the Court of Military Appeals. See *Appendix* 5, *infra*, for a full list.

6 · NOTE

The Writ of Assistants (more correct than "Assistance," see Note 1, *supra*) was used by the Court of the Exchequer pursuant to 14 Car. 2, ch. 22 (the "Act") as a powerful general warrant to secure goods on which tax was owed to the government. Smuggling in the colony led, in June of 1755, to an effort by the customs officers in Boston to use the Writ under the seal of the Superior Court, to enter boats and houses without the usual common law procedures.

There were essentially three arguments against this. First, as Thacher argued, the Writ had never been issued by the Superior Court in Massachusetts, despite 60 years since the passage of the Act. Why? The "non-user" suggested a wise presumption against the validity and wisdom of the act itself. *Reports*, 52. Otis put it more strongly, "[i]t is worthy consideration whether this Writ was constitutional even in England." *Reports*, 56. As Samuel Quincy noted, Otis's first argument in February 1761 stated that "An act of Parliament against the Constitution is void." *Reports*, 56, S. Quincy, n. 17. By "Constitution" Otis, according to Samuel Quincy's notes, was referring to the famous section of the *Magna Carta*, conventionally numbered c.39 in the 1215 original, that "[n]o freeman shall be captured or imprisoned or disseised or outlawed or exiled or in any way destroyed, nor will we go against him or send against him except by the lawful judgement of his peers or by the law of the land." See J. C. Holt, *Magna Carta* (2d ed., 1992), 461. Samuel Quincy also cited to Coke's assertion in *Coke on Littleton*, *supra*, that statutes should be construed "by the rule and reason of the common law." *Reports*, 56, S. Quincy, n. 22.

Otis's second argument was that the Act was passed after the First Massachusetts Charter and, hence, "not there invented until after our Constitution

It is worthy Confideration whether this Writ was conftitutional even in England; (17) and I think it plainly appears it was not; much lefs here, fince it was not there invented till after our Conftitution and Settlement. (18) Such a Writ is generally illegal. Hawkins, B. 2, ch. 1, Of Crim. Jur. (19) Viner, Tit. Commiffion, A. (20) 1 Inft. 464. (21) 29 M. (22)

Mr. Auchmuty. Bacon. (23) 4 Inft. 100. From the Words of the Law, this Court may have the Power of the Exchequer. Now the Exchequer always had that Power; the Court cannot regard Confequences, but muft follow Law. As for the Argument of Non-ufer, that ends whenever the Law is once executed; and this Law has been executed in this Country, and this Writ granted, not only by the Governor, but alfo from this Court in Ch. Juftice Sewall's Time. (24)

Mr. Gridley. This is properly a Writ of Affift-

ants,

---

(17) An indication of the pofition, more diftinctly ftated in Otis's firft argument in February, 1761: "An act of Parliament againft the Conftitution is void." *Vid. poft*, 474, & Appendix I, J.

(18) *Qu.* Whether Otis here intended to deny that Acts of Parliament bound the Province. See Appendix I, J.

(19) 2 Hawk. c. 1, §§ 7, 8.

(20) "If commiffion iffues to take J. S. and his goods, without indictment, or fuit of the party, or other procefs, this is not good; for it is againft the law."

(21) Probably 1 Inft. 272 b, note to Lit. § 464: "The fureft conftruction of a ftatute is by the rule and reafon of the common law."

(22) Probably c. 29 of Magna Charta: "*Nullus liber homo capiatur, vel imprifonetur*," *&c.* 2 Inft. 45 *& feq.* See Appendix I, E.

(23) Bac. Ab. Court of Exchequer.

(24) 1755–1759, *poft*, 403–406.

and Settlement." *Reports*, 56. This would bring in question all subsequent English Statutes. In addition, the Chief Justice had already ruled that such writs had already been issued in the colony by the Governor, even if improperly. *Reports*, 52.

A final argument was that the Writ was designed to be issued by the Court of Exchequer, and the Superior Court lacked the safeguards of the English Court of Exchequer, "for there the Officers are sworn . . . and are accountable to it, are obliged there to pass their Accounts weekly, which is not the Case here." *Reports*, 54. The Exchequer had direct supervisory power over the customs officers and could punish them directly. *Reports*, 55.

Early on, the Chief Justice had interrupted Thacher to attack the "non-user" argument, because the writs had been issued by the Governor in the past. Auchmuty and Gridley both argued that the Superior Court had all the power of the English Exchequer in Massachusetts, citing "728 Wm 2 M. ch.18." (By this they must have meant "St. 7. 28. William 3, c.22, rec. 6," as Samuel Quincy points out.)

As for the "constitutionality" argument, it was ignored. But Gridley did point to the fact that the Writ did not give customs officers unlimited power. "This is properly a Writ of Assistants, not Assistance; not to give the Officers a greater Power, but as a Check upon them. For by this they cannot enter into any House, without the Presence of the Sheriff or civil Officer, who will be always supposed to have an Eye over and be a Check upon them." *Reports*, 57.

Gridley concluded by saying: "Quoting History [clearly referring to Otis] is not speaking like a Lawyer. If it is Law in England, it is Law here. . . ." *Reports*, 57.

Ironically, this case really was more about history than law. The Court unanimously granted the Writ, with no discussion. Gridley was lucky to die before the Revolution and, again, his colleague, Auchmuty, was proscribed in 1778. Writ of "Assistants" (or, if you will, "Assistance") were to be specifically barred by the Bill of Rights. Otis's argument, as Gridley correctly observed, was not to this Court or to the legal issues, but to a future political order and, indeed, it ensured his place in history. How unlucky Quincy must have been to have be absent from Otis's argument "most of the Time." *Reports*, 55.

ants, not Affiftance; not to give the Officers a greater Power, but as a Check upon them. For by this they cannot enter into any Houfe, without the Prefence of the Sheriff or civil Officer, who will be always fuppofed to have an Eye over and be a Check upon them. Quoting Hiftory is not fpeaking like a Lawyer. If it is Law in England, it is Law here; it is extended to this Country by Act of Parliament. 7 & 8 Wm. & M. ch. 18. (25) By Act of Parliament they are entitled to like Affiftants; (26) now how can they have like Affiftants, (26) if the Court cannot grant them it; and how can the Court grant them like Affiftance, if they cannot grant this Writ. Pity it would be, they fhould have like Right, and not like Remedy; the Law abhors Right without Remedy. But the General Court has given this Court Authority to grant it, and fo has every other Plantation Court given their Superiour Court. (27)

The Juftices were unanimoufly of Opinion that this Writ might be granted, and fome Time after, out of Term, it was granted. (28)

---

(25) St. 7 & 8 W. 3, c. 22, § 6.

(26) Altered in the MS. from " Affiftance " to "Affiftants." The words of St. 7 & 8 W. 3, c. 22, § 6, are " like affiftance."

(27) But it is faid that in other colonies the writs were refufed. 7 John Adams's Works, 267. 4 Bancroft's Hist. U. S. 431, note.

(28) Judgment was given at the conclufion of the argument on the 18th of November, 1761. Bofton Gazette of November 23, 1761. And it appears by the court files that the writ was iffued on the 2d of December, 1761. See App. I, C.

For a report of another cafe of public intereft, decided foon after, to which Paxton was a party, fee *Province of Maffachufetts Bay* v. *Paxton*, App. II.

8

ILLUSTRATION 17: James Otis Jr. (1725–1783), by Joseph Blackburn (c. 1700–1780). Dated 1755. Courtesy Harvard Law School Art Collection.

CASE 23

February Term

III Geo. 3.

1763.
RUDDOCK *v.* GORDON.

Rec. 1763. Fol. 22.

Ruddock *verſ.* Gordon.

A Collector of Taxes cannot maintain an Action to recover them where the Remedy given by Statute is by Diſtreſs.
The Want of Power to maintain ſuch Action is not Matter of Abatement.

RUDDOCK was a Collector of Taxes in the Town of Boſton, and brought his Action, which was Treſpaſs upon the Caſe, for the Defendant's Tax, upon a general *Indebitatus Aſſumpſit.*

There were three Exceptions to the Writ, and Pleas in Abatement. Firſt, to the Looſeneſs of the Account, which was only in general for Tax for the Year 1761; and 'twas ſaid that the Account was Part of the Declaration, and that the Action would not be a Bar to another which might be brought hereafter for each Tax in particular. Secondly, that the Collector has no Right or Authority to bring ſuch Actions, the Law having pointed out another Way, viz., by Diſtreſs. Thirdly, that if any Action lay at all, it ſhould be Debt, and not Caſe. (1)

It

(1) The Rev. Sts. c. 8, § 15, provide that in certain caſes the collector "may maintain an action of debt or aſſumpſit." And by the St. of 1859, c. 171, the right of action is extended to all caſes of a neglect to pay for the ſpace of one year after the tax has been committed to the collector. Gen. Sts. c. 12, § 19.

Ruddock v. *Gordon* (1763)
3 George III (Feb.) in the
Superior Court of Judicature

1 · BRIEF DESCRIPTION

The Plaintiff, collector of taxes in Boston, brought an action against the Defendant in the standard contractual form of a trespass on the case "*indebitatus assumpsit*" (*Law Commonplace*, p. [96], n. 9). It was objected: (1) that the collector's account was too general and might not bar future, more specific actions for back taxes; (2) that the collector had no right to bring such a civil action, but should use distress instead; and (3) that the action, if proper at all, should be in debt. The Court held that the collector's authority should not be decided in connection with a plea in abatement, but at trial on the merits. Nevertheless, "being asked by both parties on that point," the Court held that the tax collector had no power to bring such actions, but apparently must proceed by distress.

2 · RECORD

Available at Rec. 1763, fol. 22.

3 · PROFESSIONALS INVOLVED

No indication.

4 · AUTHORITY

None cited.

5 · LATER CITATIONS

None. As Samuel Quincy noted, later Massachusetts statutes gave the collector an explicit power to maintain "an action of debt or assumpsit." See *Reports*, 58, S. Quincy n. 1, citing Mass. Rev. Sts. C.8 § 15. Massachusetts courts also later would hear a disability that "destroys the plaintiff's right of action" either "in abatement or bar," *Langdon* v. *Potter*, 11 Mass. 313 (Mass. 1814), a much more sensible approach. See *Reports* 59, S. Quincy n. 2.

6 · NOTE

This is a very odd case. Having ruled that the issue of the tax collector's right to bring this action should not be decided at the pleading stage by a writ of abatement, but rather later at trial, the Court then ignored its own ruling and

It was anſwered to the firſt, that in the Town of Boſton all the Taxes were made up together, and that Tax was a Noun collective, including all, and would be a Bar; that as for the Collector's Right of bringing this Action, that ought to be conſidered upon the Merits and not in Abatement; and as for its being Debt, it is merely a Matter *in Pais.*

The Court ruled unanimouſly, that the Objection to the Collector's Power is not Matter of Abatement, but to be try'd upon the Merits. (2) But the Opinion of *the Court* being aſked by both Parties upon that Point, *the Court* were of Opinion that they had no ſuch Power, and that this Action can't be ſupported. (3)

---

(2) The general principle has ſometimes been ſtated to be, that a perpetual diſability in the plaintiff is to be pleaded in bar, but if only temporary, then in abatement. 5 Dane Ab. 693. But this rule has many exceptions; and it ſeems to be now ſettled that a perpetual diſability, which forever deſtroys the plaintiff's right of action, is pleadable either in abatement or bar, (*Langdon* v. *Potter*, 11 Maſs. 313,) the rule that a plea in abatement muſt give a better writ having ſo many exceptions that it can hardly be called a general rule of law. 6 Pick. 369.

(3) S. P. *Crapo* v. *Stetſon*, 8 Met. 393. "A collector of taxes cannot maintain an action to recover them in any caſe beſides thoſe in which an action is given to him by Rev. Sts. c. 8, § 15." See alſo 6 Maſs. 44.

decided the issue anyway, just because the parties urged it to do so. The ultimate decision certainly seems reasonable, as the tax collector always had the power of "distress," i.e., to seize possession of personal chattel to force payment of back taxes, in the same way usually allowed for back rent. See *Bouvier's Law Dictionary* (8th ed., F. Rawle, 1914), vol. 1, 872–898. (Hereafter, *Bouvier's*.) While a common law action for money might be more effective in some cases, that power was not explicitly given by statute until after the Revolution.

It is disappointing that the Court never had to reach the issue of whether the tax collector could use trespass on the case *indebitatus assumpsit*, or would be required to sue in debt. Debt was the ancient remedy for a sum certain in money, but at least since *Slade's Case*, 9 *Coke's Reports* 57(b) (1611), the Plaintiff would normally have an election between debt and an action on the case *indebitatus assumpsit* ("being indebted, did undertake"). The latter cause of action, originally based on the fiction of a subsequent promise, permitted jury trial and damages, as opposed to the old wager of law process and simple restitution. See A.W.B. Simpson, "The Place of Slade's Case in the History of Contract," 74 *Law Quarterly Review* (1955), 381. Whether these distractions made any difference in Massachusetts law a century and a half later would have been interesting. The arguments on behalf of the tax collector that uncollected taxes were "merely a Matter *in Pais*," i.e., lacking the legal formality or certainty for establishing a debt, does not really answer the question. See *Bouvier's*, *supra*, vol. 1, 1523. In theory, action on the case in *assumpsit* lay "as well where it is certain," while debt lay where the sum due "is certain or ascertained in such a manner as to be readily reduced to a certainty." *Id.*, vol. 1, 787.

In any event, this case demonstrates the Court's willingness to overlook pleading formalities to reach a quick resolution of underlying issues. The irate tax collectors later took their cause to the legislature in a "Memorial of John Ruddock . . ." to the Governor, Council, and General Court, set out in the *Boston Evening Post* of Sept. 12, 1763, in which they attacked the "ruled case in the superior court of judicature." *Id.*, 2. The "Memorial" sought legislation to permit the tax collectors to bring an "action of Debt before . . . any Court of Record." The committee charged to consider the "Memorial" were not entirely sympathetic. The report, by Edmund Trowbridge, observed that "said Collectors are already duly and sufficiently empowered to collect the taxes in almost all cases" and "[t]hat it would not be advisable to impower them to recover the money by action." *Id.*, 3.

CASE 24

Gardiner *verſ.* Purrington.

GARDINER *v.* PURRINGTON.

Rec. 1763. Fol. 22.

In Trover for Trees, the Plaintiffs' Title to Land in another County, on which they were cut, cannot be given in Evidence where the Action might have been brought in that County.

THIS is an Action of Trover brought to the Inferiour Court in *Suffolk* for a Quantity of Timber cut in the County of *Cumberland.*

The

[P. 59]

Gardiner v. *Purrington* (1763)
3 George III (Feb.) in the
Superior Court of Judicature

1 · BRIEF DESCRIPTION

The sole issue in this case was whether, in a case to recover the value of cut timber, evidence of title of the land could be given in a proceeding other than one in the county where the land was located. The Court held that, in the absence of "necessity" or reason why a case could not be tried in that county, the evidence of title was not admissible.

2 · RECORD

Available at Rec. 1763, fol. 22

3 · PROFESSIONALS INVOLVED

The argument for the Plaintiff was by Jeremy Gridley (1701/2–1767), John Adams's pupil master and arguably "the greatest New England lawyer of his generation." See *Appendix 6*. He was opposed by his distinguished peers, Robert Auchmuty (1723–1788) and Benjamin Kent (1708–1788). See *Appendix 6* for descriptions of all three. Gridley and Auchmuty combined on the same side in arguing for the Writs of Assistance. See *Reports*, 51, Case 22, *Paxton's Case of the Writs of Assistance* (1761).

This case is remarkable for recording a candid discussion between Justice Russell and the Chief Justice, as they "worked out" a solution in open court.

4 · AUTHORITY

Both sides cited a variety of English law cases: *Brown* v. *Hedges* (1708), 1 *Salkeld's Reports* (covering 1689–1712), 290, see *Law Commonplace*, p. [32], n. 7; *Walrond* v. *Van Moses* (1724), *Modern Cases* (Part 8 of *Modern Reports*) 321, see *Law Commonplace*, p. [35], n. 2; and *Rogers* v. *Dove* (1652), *Style's Reports* (covering 1646–1655), 331, see *Sweet & Maxwell*, vol. 1, p. 310. There is also a citation to Lilly's *Abridgment*, which addresses transitory tort actions on page 20 of volume 1. See *Sweet & Maxwell*, vol. 1, p. 273. Both sides also appealed to *Bacon's New Abridgment of the Law*, a common multi-volume legal encyclopedia first

The Queſtion was, whether the *Title* of Land can be given in Evidence in Trover in *another* County than where the Land lies.

1 Bacon, 35; 1 Salk. 290, *Brown* vs. *Hedges;* Mod. Caſes, 322, *Walrond* vs. *Van Moſes*, (1) were cited in Favour of the Action; and it was ſaid by the Council on this Side, that the giving Title under this Action did not bar or affect an Action of Ejectment brought in the County where the Land lies.

Gridley. There is no ſpecial Pleading in Trover, except a Releaſe, which admits the Converſion. The Title is often given in Treſpaſs where the Poſſeſſion is not clear, 'tis what the Law calls incidental; yet 'tis neceſſary in Treſpaſs; juſt ſo in Trover. The Man cuts down the Timber—I may bring Treſpaſs; ſo I may Trover. The Timber is mine after it is cut down; the Tort never ſhall give him Property. It is mine in the Timber as it is mine in the Tree, and I may bring my Action: Now how can I prove my Property, unleſs I can give my Title in Evidence? When the Poſſeſſion ſeems mutual, it can never be determined, and though my own, (the Thing may be,) if I may not be admitted, I may never recover my own. In the Admiralty, many Things that are not naturally within its Juriſdiction may be tried there. Difference between an Inconvenience and a Miſchief—whenever the Law has once conſidered of this, it vaniſhes;

(1) *Anon.*, cited in *Walrond* v. *Van Moſes*, 8 Mod. 322.

published in London in 1736 through 1766, in parts. Volume 1, here referred to by both parties, was first published in London in 1736.

The Court considered the cited English cases in its conclusion that evidence of title could not be admitted, observing that cases to the contrary were "only cases of necessity."

5 · LATER CITATIONS

Samuel Quincy observed that later Massachusetts cases did agree with the Court's decision that when title to land becomes involved, the case becomes "real," and then should be tried in the county where the land lies. *Reports*, 62, S. Quincy n. 4. But he questions whether this case really involves title to land, as it is "only offered as a means of proving a right to possession of the trees." *Id.* Samuel Quincy specifically refers to the cases of *Lord* v. *Tyler,* 31 Mass. 156, 15 Pick. 156 (Mass. 1833); *Blood* v. *Kemp,* 21 Mass. 169, 4 Pick. 169 (Mass. 1826); and *Boynton* v. *Willard*, 27 Mass. 166, 10 Pick. 166 (Mass. 1830).

6 · NOTE

As Samuel Quincy noted, this was a problematic case. Assume the issue did not involve title to land, but rightful possession of trees that were chopped down by a trespasser. If so, Gridley's argument that this is an unreasonable burden on the Plaintiff seems compelling. But suppose, as Auchmuty argued, the title of the land itself was "not determined," and his client was claiming rightful possession of the trees because he, not the Plaintiff, owned the land. See *Reports*, 61. If so, title was a paramount issue, and it should be tried in the county where the land was located, unless there were exceptional circumstances.

vanifhes ; in determining what is an Inconvenience, the Law is fettled.

Juft. Ruffell. Whether this Cafe is not different from the Cafe of Mod. Cafes, (2) where it was admitted for the Inconvenience, and is it not the fame in Effect as if the Title was determined ?

Ch. Juft. Whether it will not operate againft another Rule of Law about Titles of Land coming in Queftion in another County ?

Auchmuty. The Title is not determined.

Ch. Juft. As my Brother Ruffell obferves, is it not the fame Thing ? It is not whether Trover is a tranfitory Action, (3) but whether that which is of the Nature of a real one fhall be given in Evidence.

Mr. Gridley cites Styles, 331.

Mr.

---

(2) The cafe cited in *Walrond* v. *Van Mofes*, *ub. fup.*, is as follows : " *Nota.* At the trial of this caufe a cafe was cited that trover lay in England for timber taken away and converted in Ireland ; and this was by the opinion of the late Chief Juftice Holt, though it was objected that it might bring the title of lands in Ireland in queftion, which could not be tried here ; but he anfwered that as trover was a tranfitory action it might be brought here for a converfion in Ireland ; nor fhall any incident queftion which may arife on the fame bar the plaintiff of fuch action ; for if it fhould, then a perfon being in England can have no remedy here when the defendant is guilty of a trover in Ireland, and comes from thence into this kingdom."

(3) Trover for cutting down trees is a tranfitory action. Steph. Nifi Prius, 2695. *Brown* v. *Hedges*, *ub. fup.* So alfo an action of trefpafs *de bonis afportatis* for burning down a fmall houfe erected for a temporary purpofe, and without a cellar. 15 Pick. 156.

Mr. Kent. 1 Bacon, 32. Mod. Cafes, . A perfonal Action may grow into a real one as here. 1 Lilly, 20.

The Court were of Opinion that the Cafes cited in Favour of this Evidence refpected only Cafes of Neceffity, and where they could not be tried in the fame County, which not being the Cafe here, they determined that in this Cafe it could not be admitted. (4)

---

(4) Actions, perfonal in form, which involve or bring in iffue the title to land, have been held to become thereby real, within the meaning of the ftatutes concerning cofts and the jurifdiction of juftices of the peace. 4 Pick. 169. 10 Pick. 473. But the point here decided appears to be, not that the action becomes local, but that the title to real eftate in another county fhall not incidentally be given in evidence to fupport a tranfitory action which might have been brought in that county. This feems a difficult pofition to fupport, as the title to the land is only offered as a means of proving a right to poffeffion of the trees when converted, on which latter point alone is the judgment conclusive.

CASE 25

ROGERS *v.* KENWRICK.

Rec. 1763. Fol. 46.

It is no Objection to an Award that it settles the Boundary Line between adjacent Lands of the Parties without ordering Releases. *Hutchinson, C. J., & Oliver, J., diss.*

Rogers *verf.* Kenwrick.

(From Barnstable.)

THIS Action was Debt upon an Arbitration Bond. No Award pleaded. Award was read as follows: "We do determine and settle the northwest Corner Bound as settled by us is an Heap of Stones," &c., "which appears to be the reputed known N. W. Bound for many Years, and nothing appears

[P. 62]

Rogers v. *Kenwrick* (1763)
3 George III (Feb.) in the
Superior Court of Judicature

1 · BRIEF DESCRIPTION

The sole issue in this case is whether determining a boundary line in an arbitration also determines a title of freehold. If so, it was agreed by both parties that the arbitrators exceeded their powers. The sharply divided Court held that the arbitrators did not determine the freehold, and thus action on an arbitration bond was valid. The Chief Justice and Justice Oliver dissented, the Chief Justice dissented "very warmly." *Reports*, 64.

2 · RECORD

Available at Rec. 1763, fol. 46.

3 · PROFESSIONALS INVOLVED

Two great patriots argued this case. Robert Treat Paine (1731–1814), a signer of the Declaration of Independence and later a Justice of the Supreme Judicial Court, argued for the Defendant, against the powers of the arbitrators. James Otis, Jr. (1725–1783), the patriot who argued against the writ of assistance in Paxton's Case, *Reports* 51, Case 22, was for the Plaintiff. See *Appendix 6* for brief biographies of both.

The closely split Court was unusual. Fifty-eight of the seventy-eight decisions reported by Quincy were unanimous. Among the most frequent dissenters was the Chief Justice, and he dissented with Oliver twice. See *Appendix 1*.

4 · AUTHORITY

Paine cited a variety of English Yearbook cases and English reporters, including *Rolle's Abridgment*, published in London in 1668. See *Sweet & Maxwell*, vol. 1, 19:18, *Law Commonplace,* p. [8], n. 9. He also cited *Bacon's Abridgment*, vol. 1, p. 132, first published in London in 1736. See *Sweet & Maxwell*, vol. 1, 16:1. See "Authority" in Cases 20 and 22, *Reports* 42, 51, *supra*. All of this authority was for the proposition that "parties themselves cannot pass corporeal Inheritance without solemn Livery [or by appropriate releases]." *Reports*, 63. Here no act was done by a party, so the arbitrators exceeded their powers if they determined title of freehold.

appears but was always ſo," &c., "and that the ſaid Kenwrick pay," &c. (1) Now 'twas anſwered by

Mr. Paine. That the Arbitrators had taken upon them to determine a Title of Freehold, and therefore the Arbitration void and no Award. Where the Right of Freehold is in Debate, the Property cannot be transferred by an Award; the Arbitrators only are in Stead of the Parties, and can do no more than can be done by them. Now the Parties themſelves cannot paſs corporeal Inheritances without ſolemn Livery. 1 Roll. Abr. 242. 14 H. 4, 19, 24. 9 H. 6, 6. 3 H. 4, 6. 11 H. 4, 12. Keilw. 99. 1 Leon. 228. 1 Roll. Abr. 244. 1 Bacon, 132. But if Condition of the Obligation is to ſtand to Award of Arbitrators, who award the Land to one, and that the other ſhall releaſe, who does not, the Penalty of the Obligation is forfeited, but if no Act to be done by the Party, as releaſing, is awarded, it is not forfeited though the other do not convey to him a good Title. (2)

Mr. Otis, contra. I grant the Award to be void if

---

(1) The replication further alleged that the defendant had not kept up to the tenor of the award, but had broken over the line by cutting wood on the land of the plaintiffs. And among the papers on file appeared the depoſition of Jonathan Kenwrick, ſealed up and directed, "For the Clerk of ye Superiour Court of Judicature" &c. This being opened by the preſent Clerk of the Supreme Judicial Court, it appeared that the deponent teſtified to ſeeing the defendant "cutting wood about ſix rods to ye weſtward of ye range that was ſettled by ye arbitrators."

(2) Among the papers on file appears one which would ſeem to have been part of Mr. Paine's brief, ſince it contains the above argument and liſt of authorities almoſt *verbatim;* the whole being taken from Bac. Ab. Arbitrament, A.

Otis also relied on *Bacon's Abridgment, supra*, vol. 1 on "Arbitrament and Award," for the proposal that setting a boundary is "but a mathematical line without Breadth or Thickness" and, thus, "does not affect the Freehold." *Reports*, 64.

5 · LATER CITATIONS

Josiah Quincy himself questioned the outcome of this case, citing to one of his last manuscript volumes. "Quare, if this Case is not agreeable to law." *Reports*, 64.

But in *Searle* v. *Abbe*, 79 Mass. 409, 13 Gray 409, 412 (1859), a case concerning the effect of an arbitrator's decision in a boundary dispute, the successful arguments of James Otis in *Rogers* v. *Kenwrick* were quoted by Justice Metcalf. This citation is particularly interesting in that the case was decided before Quincy's *Reports* were published in 1865. See the discussion in the excellent note by Mark Sullivan to *Appendix 5*, "Phantom References to *Quincy's Reports* in the Massachusetts Supreme Judicial Court *Reports*," *infra*. Samuel Quincy, citing additional cases, pointed out that an arbitrator's boundary decision may not actually convey lands, but could operate by estoppel to prevent parties from later disputing the title. *Reports*, 64, S. Quincy n. 3.

6 · NOTE

It is hard not to agree with the dissenters here, the obviously agitated Chief Justice and Justice Oliver. Josiah Quincy also apparently felt the dissenters were in the right. Otis's argument about how a line has no significance is simply bogus; shifting the boundary line shifts the area of the freehold. If this should have been done by releases by the parties, then enforcing an arbitration bond was unjust. The strongest argument for the case's outcome, picked up in the later Massachusetts cases, was simple expediency.

if the Arbitrators have determined the Freehold; but here they have not, they have only determined the Line; the real Boundary is but a mathematical Line without Breadth or Thicknefs, the fettling that does not affect the Freehold. 1 Bacon, Tit. Arbitra. I think then a Bond conditioned to abide by fuch Award is good, and the Award good, and if not complied with, the Obligation fhould be forfeited.

Paine. When they fettle the Line, they fay to whom the Land on each Side belongs. They have awarded Nothing to be done; they fhould have ordered Releafes.

Judgment for the Plaintiff. (3) *Ruffell, Cufhing, Lynde,* againft *Oliver & Ch. Juftice.*

Ch. Juft. very warmly againft the Determination.*

* *Quære,* if this Cafe is not agreeable to Law? Vid. Vol. 1, (4) p. 18, and the Authorities there cited.

---

(3) S. P. *Jones* v. *Bofton Mill Corp.* 6 Pick. 148. *Goodridge* v. *Duftin,* 5 Met. 363. In this cafe the previous decifion in *Whitney* v. *Holmes,* 15 Mafs. 152, was partially overruled, and the rule ftated by Mr. Juftice Hubbard to be, that an award which fettles a boundary, "although it will not have the direct effect of conveying lands, will yet conclude the parties from difputing the title or boundary which is diftinctly fettled by the award, and that it fhall operate by way of eftoppel." See alfo *Searle* v. *Abbe,* 13 Gray, 409.

(4) This volume is miffing. Many other references to miffing volumes are omitted. See Preface.

ILLUSTRATION 18: Robert Treart Paine (1731–1814). Portrait by Edward Savage and John Coles Jr., c. 1796–1801. Courtesy, Massachusetts Historical Society. Paine was a signer of the Declaration of Independence. He served as Massachusetts Attorney General (1777–1790) and as a Justice of the Supreme Judicial Court (1790–1804). See brief biography in *Appendix 6*, *infra*.

CASE 26

Gridley *verſ.* Balſton & al.

GRIDLEY *v.* BALSTON.

Rec. 1763. Fol. 15.

The Eſtate of a Teſtator is not liable for the Negligence of Executors in carrying out and executing a Conſignment made to the Teſtator in his Lifetime.

BALSTON and others were Executors of Palmer of London, who was Agent for the Plaintiff in his Lifetime. A Ship was conſigned to Palmer by the Plaintiff, but Palmer died before her Arrival or Knowledge of it. The Executors undertook the Buſineſs and tranſacted it, and are now ſued as Executors to Mr. Palmer for Breach of Truſt. (1)

The Queſtion was, as Conſignment was made in Mr. Palmer's Life, and the Executors proſecuted it, whether they ſhould anſwer as Executors, and Palmer's Eſtate be liable in their Hands. 2 Bacon, 144. (2)

It was ſaid, if the Breach of Truſt was in Mr. Palmer — being a Tort, it dies with him; if not, he can't be chargeable.

On the other Hand that it was but a Continuance of the ſame Affair, and they acted in his Stead. Viner, Tit. Executor, P. 4, Plea 39, 43. 1 Lill. 778, Let. H. Dyer, 324.

The

(1) The declaration alleged that the teſtator, being factor of the plaintiffs, procured inſurance on the freight of the plaintiff's galley from Jamaica to London; that when ſhe arrived the teſtator died; and that the executors undertook to ſettle and manage the ſaid truſt, but managed it ill, and "perfunctorily acted with great negligence" in ſettling a leakage of ſugars.

(2) Bac. Ab. Executor, P. 2. "The taking up of an executorſhip doth not embark executor in the perſonal truſts of the deceaſed."

9

[P. 65]

Gridley v. *Balston* (1763)
3 George III (Feb.) in the
Superior Court of Judicature

1 · BRIEF DESCRIPTION

The sole issue in this case was whether executors of the deceased Defendant, who had been an Agent for the Plaintiff, would be liable in tort for breach of trust for mishandling the deceased's agency after his death. The Court's unanimous opinion was that breach of trust was a tort action against the Agent, and died with him.

2 · RECORD

Available at Rec. 1763, fol. 15. The files at the Massachusetts Archives contain the following:

Gridley v. *Balstone*, Jan. 1762, No. 170982.
- Bill of Costs for Court of Common Pleas.

Gridley v. *Balstone*, (same) Feb. 1763, No. 171010.
- Fragment of Judgment for Superior Court of Judicature.

Gridley v. *Balstone*, (same) Aug. 1763, No. 171131.
- Writ of Review for Superior Court of Judicature at Suffolk County.

Gridley v. *Balstone*, (same) Nov. 1762, No. 171142.
- Bill of Costs for Superior Court of Judicature, Boston.

3 · PROFESSIONALS INVOLVED

No indication.

4 · AUTHORITY

Bacon's *Abridgment*, vol. 2, p. 144, "Executor," part 2, (London, 1736), was again cited. See Cases 20, 22, 24 "Authority," *Reports* 42, 51, 59, *supra*. This was for the proposition that the executors did not, simply by "taking up of an executorship," undertake "the personal trusts of the deceased," as Samuel Quincy correctly noted. See *Id.*, vol. 2, p. 144; *Reports*, 65, S. Quincy n. 2.

Other English authority was cited for the opposite proposition: that the

The Court unanimous that theſe Authorities are not in Point, and the Aₒtion will not lie.

[P. 66]

executor's actions were "but a Continuance of the same Affair," including *Viner's Abridgment* under the title "Executor and Plea" (first published in London between 1741–1753 in 23 volumes); Lilly's *Practical Register*; a *General Abridgment of the Law*, vol. 1, 778 (just published in two volumes in London, 1719); and *Dyer's Reports*, which are of the earliest of the English law reports, first published in 1585 with a substantially increased 6th edition in 1688 (the case cited is *Ligeart* v. *Wiseman*, which begins on page 323b of vol. 3). See *Sweet & Maxwell*, vol. 1, 299: 47. The Court rightly said "these authorities" were "not in Point."

5 · LATER CITATIONS

None.

6 · NOTE

This case demonstrates the Court's critical use of English authority, as it correctly rejected a wide range of citations as irrelevant. *Bacon's Abridgment*, vol. 2 (1st ed., London, 1736), widely used by the Court in other cases, was relied on as correct.

The declaration shows the Plaintiff was shipping sugar from Jamaica to London, and the deceased was his Agent in London. But before the deceased even learned of this particular shipment, he died. His executors undertook the business when the ship arrived, allegedly with "great negligence." The essence of the case was that the executors never agreed to do this business, and it was not automatically part of their duties. In the absence of fraud, the Plaintiff had no recourse. As a matter of policy, it might have been regarded as unfair to require a standard of care of people who never agreed to a business, but who tried to transact it as an emergency measure. The alternative would be no agency at all.

CASE 27

BROWN *v.* CULNON.

Rec. 1763. Fol. 10.

Brown *verſ.* Culnon.

(From Middleſex.)

A Town may recover of an Individual Money advanced by the Overſeers of the Poor for the neceſſary Support of his Wife and Children.

UPON a ſpecial Verdict, which was: "The "Jury find that the Overſeers of the Poor in "the Abſence of the Defendant and without his "Requeſt advanced for the neceſſary Support of the "Defendant's Wife and Children a certain Sum, and "if by Law the Plaintiff as Treaſurer of the Town "ought to recover the ſame back from the Defend-"ant, they find for the Plaintiff—otherwiſe, for the "Defendant."

Judgment that the Defendant is liable. (1)

---

(1) S. P. *Hanover* v. *Turner*, 14 Maſs. 227. *New Bedford* v. *Chace*, 5 Gray, 28. But the town cannot recover for ſupplies ſuitable to the wife's condition in life, beyond her neceſſary ſupport as a pauper. *Monſon* v. *Williams*, 6 Gray, 416.

[P. 66]

Brown v. *Culnon* (1763)
3 George III (Feb.) in the
Superior Court of Judicature

1 · BRIEF DESCRIPTION

The sole issue in this case was whether the Overseers of the Poor could collect, from the Defendant, "the necessary Support" paid by the Overseers to the Defendant's wife and children. The Defendant was absent, and had not requested the support. Held, yes.

2 · RECORD

Available at Rec. 1763, fol. 10.

3 · PROFESSIONALS INVOLVED

No indication.

4 · AUTHORITY

None cited.

5 · LATER CITATIONS

As Samuel Quincy observed, this remained good Massachusetts law, but only for the wife's "necessary support as a pauper." *Reports*, 66, S. Quincy n. 1. He cited the cases *Hanover* v. *Turner*, 14 Mass. 227 (1817); *New Bedford* v. *Chace*, 71 Mass. 28, 5 Gray 28 (1855); and *Monson* v. *Williams*, 72 Mass. 416, 6 Gray 416 (1856).

6 · NOTE

The case came to the Court on special verdict of a jury, i.e., they found the necessary facts but requested guidance on the law. The Massachusetts "safety net" for poverty was local, and put the burden on local authorities. To recover from an absent husband "necessary support" would be reasonable. See Douglas Lamar Jones, "The Transformation of the Law of Poverty in Eighteenth-Century Massachusetts," *Law in Colonial Massachusetts* (eds. Coquillette, Brink, Menand, 1984), 153, 158–164. The most common device to provide for destitute single parents with a family was use of a custodial family, which received payments from Overseers. This could lead to serious disputes between the parent and the authority. If the father was in debtor's prison, the local authority could be in a particularly hard bind. *Id.*, 162–163.

CASE 28

Dunten *verſ.* Richards.

DUNTEN *v.* RICHARDS.

Rec. 1763. Fol. 12.

(From Cambridge.)

A Guardian who has executed his Ward's Indentures of Apprenticeſhip has no Power to releaſe the Maſter from his Covenant of Payment to the Ward, in Settlement of a Claim againſt himſelf for Deceit, grounded on the Ward's alledged Incapacity of performing his Covenants of Service.

PLAINTIFF was an Apprentice bound by his Guardian to the Defendant, who covenanted among other Things to pay the Plaintiff £80 (1) at the Expiration of the Time of his Service. This Action was Covenant broken. Oyer of the Indenture, upon which Defendant pleads that Plaintiff was not capable of ſerving him as he covenanted, and that in Conſideration thereof the Guardian had releaſed the Payment of the £80. The Queſtion was, whether the Guardian had Authority to make ſuch Releaſe.

It

---

(1) The declaration alleged that the plaintiff bound himſelf with the conſent of the guardian, and that the defendant covenanted to diſmiſs him at the end of the term "with two ſuits of apparell, one for the Sabbath and one for every day, and to give him eighty pounds in bills of public credit of the old tenor, or the value thereof in ſuch money as ſhall then be current," which value was alleged to have been £10 13*s.* 4*d.* The plea ſet forth that the defendant was deceived and impoſed upon by the guardian in binding the minor, whom he found deficient in underſtanding, and not capable of learning or ſerving him, wherefore he inſiſted that the apprentice ſhould be taken back, and, after much diſpute and controverſy, it was finally agreed that the maſter ſhould releaſe all demands on account of the impoſition, and that the guardian ſhould releaſe the £80 as aforeſaid, which was accordingly done. To this plea there was a "replication in writing, as on file, concluding to the country," and a rejoinder, after which the caſe was ſent to a jury, who found for the plaintiff "three pounds money damage and coſts." The caſe was continued for argument on the ſpecial plea, and judgment was finally entered for the full amount of £10 13*s.* 4*d.* It would ſeem that this argument muſt have been on a motion for judgment *non obſtante veredicto*, but as all the Middleſex files of court for 1763 are miſſing, no information can be obtained except from the record.

Dunten v. *Richards* (1763)
3 George III (Feb.) in the
Superior Court of Judicature

1 · BRIEF DESCRIPTION

This was an action on a covenant between an apprentice, a minor, and his master which included an "£80" payment (or same value in "current" money) at the expiration of service (found by the Middlesex Jury to be worth £10,13s.4d. in current money). The covenant was entered into by the Plaintiff's guardian, on the Plaintiff's behalf. Allegedly, the guardian agreed with the master to forgo the payment, and the master, in turn, released the Plaintiff from apprenticeship, because the Plaintiff was "deficient in understanding" and was "not capable of learning or serving him." *Reports*, 67, S. Quincy n. 1, containing the Declaration. Held, unanimously, the guardian had no such authority, and the master had to pay the money.

2 · RECORD

Available at 1763, fol. 12. The Middlesex files of court for 1763 are missing, as Samuel Quincy noted. *Reports*, 67, S. Quincy n. 1.

3 · PROFESSIONALS INVOLVED

No indication.

4 · AUTHORITY

None cited. The Plaintiff cited one English case, the only one cited in the report, for the principle that "Guardians have no Right to release or give Discharge but for Sums received." The case was *While* v. *Hall* (1616), *Moore's Reports* (covering 1512–1621), 852. See *Sweet & Maxwell,* vol. 1, p. 305.

5 · LATER CITATIONS

As Samuel Quincy noted, Massachusetts law has consistently held that "contracts beneficial to a ward cannot be avoided by the guardian." *Oliver* v. *Houdlet,* 13 Mass. 237, at 240 (1816). *Reports*, 68, S. Quincy n. 2. It would have been interesting had the master sued the guardian on the subsequent

It was ſaid by the Plaintiff that Guardians have no Right to releaſe or give Diſcharge but for Sums received. Moore, 852, *White* vs. *Hall.*

On the other Hand, the Guardian was a Party by their own ſhewing, and releaſed no other Contract than he made himſelf.

Court were unanimouſly of Opinion that the Guardian had no Right to Releaſe. (2)

---

(2) From the pleadings in this caſe it would ſeem that there was no attempt to affect the guardian with any liability on the covenants of the indenture, but that the maſter's claim was on the ground of deception and impoſition in inducing him to enter into it. See *Blunt* v. *Melcher*, 2 Maſs. 228. In that caſe it was held, that where a ward binds himſelf with the aſſent of his guardian, the words deſcribing his duties are not the covenants of the guardian, though he ſigns and ſeals the indenture. But in an indenture between father, ſon, and maſter, under 5 Eliz. c. 4, the father is anſwerable in covenant for what is to be performed by the ſon. Com. Dig. Covenant, A 2. Doug. 518. 8 Mod. 190. 3 Dane Ab. 588. Whether a father or guardian liable on a broken covenant for ſervice would have any power to releaſe the maſter from a covenant beneficial to the minor, is not here decided. It is a general rule that contracts beneficial to the ward cannot be avoided by the guardian. See 13 Maſs. 240.

[P. 68]

"understanding," rather than try to avoid the covenant. Samuel Quincy suggests that the common law would not hold the guardian to the covenants of the indenture, although he signed it on behalf of the minor, but a father might be held to an indenture signed on behalf of his son. *Reports*, 68, S. Quincy n. 2.

In *Hunting* v. *Stafford*, 183 Mass. 157 (1903), this case was cited to show that guardians in Massachusetts have long been held to have fiduciary obligations to minors, including an obligation not to release contracts beneficial to the minor. *Id.*, 160.

6 · NOTE

Quincy's *Law Commonplace* was full of cases involving apprentices and masters. See *Law Commonplace*, [19]–[20]. In general, these cases made it difficult for either party to easily extract himself from the covenant. Almost certainly, the Defendant master in this case would have found it difficult to dissolve the relationship on the traditional grounds of dereliction, without paying the promised sum. To permit the guardian to release the minor, without the minor's consent, would permit an evasion of the mutual duties. In addition, there were social security issues. Assume the minor here really was, as the Declaration alleged, "deficient in understanding," perhaps to the point of mental retardation. The close-knit system of social welfare, based on "custodial families" compensated by local officials, would hardly be benefited if boys, like the Plaintiff in this case, could be too easily "released" from beneficial apprenticeships. They would simply become charges on the public. See Douglas Lamar Jones, "The Transformation of the Law of Poverty in Eighteenth-Century Massachusetts," *Law in Colonial Massachusetts* (eds. Coquillette, Brink, Menand, 1984), 153, 157–160.

CASE 29

Auguſt Term

III Georgii Ter. in Sup. Cur.

Preſent:

The Honourable

Thomas Hutchinſon, Eſqr., Chief Juſtice.
Benja: Lynde,
John Cuſhing,
Chambers Ruſſell,
Peter Oliver,
Eſqrs., Juſtices.

1763.
BAKER *v.* MATTOCKS.
Rec. 1763. Fol. 118.

Baker *verſ.* Mattocks. (1)

THE Queſtion in this Caſe was, whether Eſtates in Tail are partable in this Province, by the Province Law.

The Prov. St. of 4 W. & M. by which Lands deſcend to all the Children, and which empowers the Anceſtor to convey or deviſe them at his Pleaſure, does not extend to Eſtates Tail, but leaves

Mr.

(1) *Formedon in the deſcender.* The declaration alleged a gift in tail to Samuel and Conſtance Mattocks, and a deſcent according to the form of the gift to Samuel, the ſon of the donees, and to the ſaid Samuel's eldeſt ſon, who died leaving the plaintiff and another daughter, who died leaving a ſon, who died without iſſue, "after whoſe death the whole right to the demanded premiſes came to the plaintiff according to the form of the gift." The ſpecial verdict found that Samuel, the grandfather of the plaintiff, made a deed of the premiſes to the defendant, one of his younger ſons, and that there were many other deſcendants

[P. 69]

Baker v. *Mattocks* (1763)
3 George III (Aug.) in the
Superior Court of Judicature

1 · BRIEF DESCRIPTION

This was one of the most important cases reported by Quincy. The issue was whether an entail estate was "partible," i.e., could be split "to all the children alike," or should go only to the eldest male, if one existed. English common law only gave inheritance to the eldest son—i.e., "primogeniture"—unless the lands were governed by some special custom, such as "gavelkind," which made the lands partible.

Primogeniture had been abolished in Massachusetts as to fee simple estates by a provincial statute, 4 William & Mary Chap. 8, in 1692. Charter and General Laws of the Colony and Province of Massachusetts Bay (Boston, 1814), 230–236. The statute recited the "assistance" of the younger children in "subduing" the land and the unfairness of excluding them. See *Reports*, 70, S. Quincy n. 2. But the statute only mentioned "fee simple," an estate held by what today we would describe as "outright" ownership. A "fee tail" was held by the tenant entail, and then went to his or her children, who were "remainder men." If there were no "heirs of the body," the fee reverted to the heirs of the original donor, the "reversioners." This device, since the Statute *De Donis* of 1285, had been important in preserving great English landed estates, and through the wide use of the settlements inspired by the "entail male," ensured male social dominance. See J. H. Baker, Introduction to *English Legal History*, *supra*, 273–277, 280–283; Daniel R. Coquillette, *Anglo-American Legal Heritage*, *supra*, 95–115.

Thus this case presented a major "choice of law" decision with profound social and gender implications. This was recognized at the time, as Justice Cushing put it, "This point is of great consequence to the Province." *Reports*, 73. By a narrowly split court, three to two, it was decided that fee tails were not partible, a victory for reactionary ideas.

2 · RECORD

Available at Rec. 1763, fol. 118. The Declaration and special verdict are particularly important. See *Reports*, 69–70, n.1.

them as at the Common Law. *Cuſhing, J., & Hutchinſon, C. J., diſſ.*

Mr. Fitch in Favour of the Partability. The Deſign of the Province Law (2) was to alter the Common Law Deſcent. All Eſtates Tail at Common Law were Fee Simple conditional. Co. Lit. 20 a. 'Tis the Statute of Weſtminſter that forms Eſtates Tail. This Statute does not alter the Courſe of the Common Law Deſcents, it only limits them. Co. Lit. 19 a. Co. Lit. 110 b. This is the Caſe of Gavelkind Lands. Vin. Tit. Gavelkind, B.

Juſtice Ruſſell. The Common Law never took Place with Regard to Gavelkind Lands, but the Common Law takes Place here unleſs in Caſe of particular Eſtates.

Mr. Gridley. The Tail is only cut out of Fee Simple,

---

ants of the original donees beſides the parties to this caſe; "and if it ſhall appear to the Court upon the whole that the ſaid Samuel and Conſtance, the donees, took an eſtate in tail, and that the ſaid eſtate tail is not made partible by the law of this Province, then the jury find for the appellant poſſeſſion of the premiſes ſued for and coſts; otherwiſe they find for the appellee coſts."

(2) Prov. St. 4 W. & M. This was the law by which the right of primogeniture was firſt aboliſhed in the Province, for the reaſons ſet forth in the preamble as follows:

"Whereas eſtates in theſe plantations do conſiſt chiefly of lands which have been ſubdued and brought to improvement by the induſtry and labour of the proprietors, with the aſſiſtance of their children, the younger children generally having been longeſt and moſt ſerviceable unto their parents in that behalf, who have not perſonal eſtate to give out unto them in portions, or otherwiſe to recompenſe their labour.

"Sect. 1. Be it therefore enacted," &c., "that every perſon lawfully ſeiſed of any lands, tenements, or hereditaments within this province, in his own proper right in fee ſimple, ſhall have power to give, diſpoſe, and deviſe as well by his laſt will and teſtament in writing as otherwiſe by any act executed in his life, all ſuch lands, tenements, and hereditaments to or among his children or others as he ſhall think fit at his pleaſure, and if no ſuch diſpoſition, gift, or deviſe be made," then preſcribing the rules of deſcent to all the children. Anc. Chart. 230.

3 · PROFESSIONALS INVOLVED

The informal dean of the bar, Jeremy Gridley (1701/2–1767) and Samuel Fitch (1724–1799) argued for partibility. (While Fitch was, in 1763, relatively junior to Gridley, he later became Advocate General of the Admiralty [1768–1776].) Arguing against partibility was Quincy's pupil master, Oxenbridge Thacher (1719–1765) and the great James Otis, Jr. (1725–1783). For biographies of all four, see *Appendix 6*.

It remains curious that the advocates for partibility, a relatively egalitarian idea, were known to be conservative Tories. Indeed, Fitch was proscribed in 1778. Those arguing for the hierarchical entail without partibility were relatively Whig. Otis, of course, was a great patriot, and Thacher's seat in the House was taken by Sam Adams on Thacher's death in 1765.

In the oral argument, Otis attacked the idea that there was a "Natural Right of Descent to all Children alike," and advocated following the English entail, rather than expanding the colonial exception! See "Note 6," *infra,* for a further discussion.

The Justices were closely split. There, too, the votes were curious. Chief Justice Hutchinson and Justice Cushing voted for partibility, with Justices Oliver, Russell and Lynde forming the majority. *Reports*, 72–74. Hutchinson and Oliver were politically Tory, while Cushing was a moderate Whig. But these categories are always overly simplistic. Hutchinson was a complex man, whose loyalty to the crown was balanced with a deep identification with the colony and its institutions, political and legal. See generally Bernard Bailyn, *The Ordeal of Thomas Hutchinson* (1974), 9–18; William Pencak, *America's Burke: The Mind of Thomas Hutchinson* (1982); Andrew S. Walmsley, *Thomas Hutchinson and the Origins of the American Revolution* (1999). See also John A. Denehy, "Thomas Hutchinson: Chief Justice of the Massachusetts Superior Court of Judicature," 8 *Massachusetts Legal History* (2002), 1, 8–15. In any event, the fundamental issues presented by *Baker* v. *Mattocks* did not split the Justices on political grounds, but on jurisprudential beliefs about statutory construction and the correct relationship between colonial law and English common law. See "Note 6," *infra*.

4 · AUTHORITY

For such an important case, very little authority was cited. Reference was obviously made by the lawyers and judges on both sides to the Provincial statute, 4 William & Mary, Chap. 8 (1692). Fitch also cited to *Coke on Littleton* (London,

Simple, it is only excluding others to whom it would otherwiſe deſcend.

Mr. Thacher. But for the Province Law, neither Fee Simple or Tail would be partable. The Queſtion then is, whether this Law is extended to Eſtates Tail; by this Law, every Perſon ſhall have Right of Diſpoſition, and if no ſuch be made, then follow the Rules of Deſcent. 'Tis certain the Legiſlature had Fee Simple only in Contemplation; both would have gone according to the Common Law of England, but our Fee Simple is by this Act taken out of that Courſe, while the Fee Tail is not. The Statute of Weſtminſter left Gavelkind as it found it. Lilly, 648. 'Tis otherwiſe with Regard to our Province Law, which ſhall alter no further than its Deſign to alter.

Mr. Otis. The Manner of Succeſſion, if traced to its Original, is merely arbitrary; the Law of Nature is a Stranger to it; by that, no Man has a Right to more than his Life. States have an undoubted Right to ſettle it as they pleaſe: I ſay this in Anſwer to the Argument of the Natural Right of Deſcent to all the Children alike. When once any State has ſettled the Courſe of Deſcents among them, 'tis of great Importance that the Principles ſhould be kept to. The Method of Deſcent in England to the eldeſt Son is 700 Years—nay, as old as the Common Law itſelf. I conclude that before the Conqueſt the Right of Primogeniture did not take Place; ſomewhere between William 1 and Henry 1 it aroſe, but that does not affect the Caſe; it is now, and long has been ſo ſettled. Now as the

Province

[P. 71]

1628) three times for the proposal that the Statute Westminster "did not alter the Course of Common Law Descents by creating entails, only by limiting them." He also looked to *Viner's Abridgment* (London, 1742–1753) under "Gavelkind," for the proposition that gavelkind, the custom of partibility in certain English lands, was another relevant precedent, particularly since entails were usually partible in gavelkind lands. (In this he was corrected by Justice Russell, who observed that the common law never applied to gavelkind lands, while the common law did apply here, "unless in the case of particular Estates." *Reports*, 70.)

Thacher, arguing against partibility, referred to *Lilly's Collection of Modern Entries* (London, 1723, English trans., 2d ed., 1741), 648, for the proposal that "the statute of Westminster left Gavelkind as it found it," while it was otherwise with the province law, "which shall alter no further than its Design to alter," *Reports*, 71, a weak argument as to the authority cited.

In any event, the most powerful arguments by the opposing senior lawyers, Otis and Gridley, made no specific references to authority at all, but argued instead in terms of historical and legal generalities, of varying accuracy. See the discussion at "Note 6."

5 · LATER CITATIONS

As Samuel Quincy correctly observed, later Massachusetts law followed the majority opinion, and did not permit partibility when land was entailed. See *Corbin* v. *Healy*, 37 Mass. (20 *Pickering*) 514, 516 (1838); *Wright* v. *Thayer*, 67 Mass. (1 *Gray*) 284, 286 (1854). This was of limited importance, once entails could be broken by statute, through a common deed, but, as Samuel Quincy also pointed out—even in 1865 it couldn't be done in a will, leaving a drafting "trap for the unwary." See Mass. Statutes 1791, c.60. This would be no joke for an accidentally disinherited younger child. See *Reports*, 74, S. Quincy n. 4.

6 · NOTE

This case provides a fascinating insight into the legal minds of 1763 Massachusetts. At stake was the application of a Province statute with clear policy goals. It began by pointing out the differences between Massachusetts and England, "[w]hereas estates in these plantations do consist chiefly of lands which have been subdued and brought to improvement by the industry and labour of the proprietors with the assistance of their children, the younger

Province Law has altered this Rule of Defcent with Regard to the Fee, the Queftion is, whether of Confequence it has alter'd the Courfe of Tails. No Statute can alter the Courfe of the Law further than the exprefs Words of the Statute. Viner, Tit. Tail. It has been doubted whether any Alteration at all by our Province Law is good; it has been determin'd to be good at Home in the Cafe of Fee Simple, and for the Reafon given in our Law, which does not hold with Regard to Tails.

Mr. Gridley. The Queftion is, whether as Fee Simple is partable by Cuftom or by Law of the Land, Tail is not alfo partable; that is the Cafe in the Cuftom of Gavelkind. Fee Simple contains in it Fee Tail, which is a Part of it; as it was in the Fee Simple, fo muft be the Courfe of Defcent in the Fee Tail. Heirs in Fee Simple are Heirs in Fee Tail; only certain Heirs are excluded, cut out, and 'tis an univerfal Interpretation of thefe limited Eftates, that they fhould follow the Rule of Fee Simple. Now fhall we take the Courfe of our Eftates Tail from our own Fee Simple, out of which they are created, and interpret the Rule of their Defcent by it, or to interpret our Tails fhall we have Recourfe to the Fee Simple of England to judge of our Tail?

Juftice Oliver. Till the Statute *De Donis*, Tails were Fee Simple Conditional; by that, Eftates Tail were created. We brought over both the Common Law and Statute with us. (3) This Law of ours relates

---

(3) S. P. 1 Mafs. 60, 61. 2 Mafs. 534. 8 Pick. 316. 13 Met. 68.

children generally having been longest and most serviceable unto their parents in that behalf [because older parents are more likely to have land?] who have not personal estate to give out unto them in portions, or otherwise to recompense their labor." *Reports*, 70, S. Quincy n. 2; Prov. St. 4 William & Mary, Chap. 8 (1692). The statute concluded by ensuring free divisibility by will by all persons "lawfully served any lands . . . in his own proper right in fee simple" and, in default, to all the deceased; children equally. By statute, therefore, Massachusetts had the same rules of inheritance for fee simples as prevailed in England in land governed by the curator of gavelkind, i.e., originally much of East Anglia and, until 1926, much of the land in Kent, with major difference, gavelkind land went to all sons equally, not to all children equally, unless there were only daughters. See J. H. Baker, *An Introduction to English Legal History*, *supra*, 265–266. (Note: many of the original settlers in Massachusetts came from East Anglia.) For two other helpful accounts of the laws of primogeniture and entail in the colonies, see Robert Morris, "Primogeniture and Entailed Estates in America," *Columbia Law Review*, vol. 27 (1927), 24–51, and George L. Haskins, "The Beginnings of Partible Inheritance in the American Colonies," *Essays on the History of Early American Law*, ed. David H. Flaherty (Chapel Hill, 1969).

In gavelkind lands, the "partible" quality of the custom extended to estates tail, "for if a person died seized in tail of lands held in gavelkind, all his sons inherited together as heirs of his body," rather than just the oldest son, as in common law primogeniture. See Justice Cushing at *Reports*, 73. Thus one of the major arguments for why the same should be true in Massachusetts was that the effect of the 1692 statute was to make Massachusetts land like those held in gavelkind in England. See the arguments of Fitch and Gridley for partibility, *Reports*, 70–72.

A second argument for partibility was based on the nature of a fee tail estate. The term "estate tail" or "entail" derives from the Latin "*feudum talliatum*" and the French "*entaille*; *tailler*, to cut." See Earl Jowitt, *The Dictionary of English Law* (ed. C. Walsh, 1959), 715–716. (Hereafter, "*Jowitt*"). The idea is that an entail is a "cut down" fee simple, as that can only be inherited by "heirs of the body," i.e., blood descendants—as opposed to a fee simple, which could be inherited by any heir. ("In tail male" could only be inherited by blood male heirs.) If there was a failure of suitable issue, the statute of Westminster II,

relates particularly to Fee Simple, and I think does not affect Eſtates Tail, but leaves them as in England. I am againſt the Partability.

Juſtice Ruſſell. The very Intent of Tails was to ſecure Eſtates in Familys, and keep them together. The Intent ought to be obſerved, but would be deſtroyed by ſuch a Conſtruction of the Law. I am therefore againſt the Partability.

Juſtice Cuſhing. This Point is of great Conſequence to the Province, and it would be attended with great Difficulty at this Day to determine, that Eſtates Tail were partable, the general Tenor having been otherwiſe, yet if the Law is plain, as I hold it is, I don't ſee how it can be help'd. If there was no other than Fee Simple intended by the Prov. Law; yet as it was there ſettled, who were Heirs, that ſettled Eſtates of Inheritance, all being made out of Fee Simple, and being a Limitation, not an Alteration. This is the Manner of Conſtruction of the Law at Home: Where Fee Simple is partable, ſo are Eſtates Tail; and where Fee Simple deſcends to the eldeſt Son, ſo does Tail.

Juſtice Lynde. Had there been no particular Law of our Province, I ſhould have thought Fee Simple and Tail would have gone alike, but now I think by our Law, Fee Tails are exempted and left at Common Law. Fee Eſtates only are directed to deſcend to all the Children, and with Reaſon. It ſeems directly againſt the Reaſon and Intent of Eſtates Tail that they ſhould be partable, and that they

c. 1 "*De donis conditionalibus*" (1285), provided that the land revert back to the heirs of the original grantor. These heirs of the grantor always had a right to prevent the tenant in tail from alienating the land by a "writ of foremedon" (from "*de forma donationis*" or form of the gift), than defeating their right of reversion. This was the cause of action used here. See *Reports*, 69, S. Quincy n. 1. Such heirs of the grantor were called "reversioners." Likewise, the tenant in tail's children also had an expectation to inherit, which they could also enforce by the writ of formedon. They were called "remaindermen." See *Jowitt*, *supra*, 715–716, 827.

By 1763 various mechanisms had evolved in Massachusetts to permit a tenant in tail in possession to bar the entail during his or her life. But one could not bar an entail in Massachusetts by will until after 1791, as Samuel Quincy noted at *Reports*, 74, S. Quincy n. 4.

If an entail was just a "cut down" fee simple, and if fee simples in Massachusetts had been made partible by the 1693 Provincial statute, then—so it would seem to follow—entails were also partible, and so Gridley argued. "Fee simple contains in it Fee Tail, which is a Part of it . . . and 'tis an universal Interpretation of these limited Estates, that they should follow the Rule of Fee Simple." *Reports*, 72.

Thacher responded to this argument that, in Massachusetts, "neither Fee Simple or Tail would be partible" except for the 1692 Act. "[O]ur Fee Simple is by this Act taken out of that course, while the Fee Tail is not." *Id.*, 71.

But the most interesting argument was that of Otis, directed against partibility. He answered an argument never made by his opponents, that partibility was required by the Law of Nature . . . i.e., "the Natural Right or Descent to all the Children alike." *Reports*, 71. To this Otis answered "The Manner of Succession, if traced to its Original, is merely arbitrary; the Law of Nature is a Stranger to it; by that, no Man has a Right to more than his Life." *Id.*, 71. What an extraordinary argument for a patriot, who had argued two years before against the Writs of Assistance, and would support a Revolution founded on "inalienable rights," including an attack on taxation without representation! See *Paxton's Case*, *Reports* 48, Case 22, Note 6.

Justice Oliver was convinced by the statutory argument to decide against partibility. His reasoning was that the Statute *De Donis* (Westminster II, c.2) (1285), created the "Estates Tail," an inaccurate historical view, and "[w]e

they are not made partable by this Law, is my Opinion.

Ch. Juſtice. It ſeems evident to me that it is the Spirit of the Engliſh Law, that all Inheritances ſhould follow the Method of Fee Simple: If it was now a thing intirely upon the Law I ſhould not have the leaſt Difficulty of thinking Fee Tail, as well as Fee Simple, was partable; but it has been ſo long thought otherwiſe here, and this has been the uninterrupted contemporaneous Expoſition of the Law, and many Judgments of Court founded on it, that it creates a great Difficulty, and I am glad that the Point is determined without me, for how ſuch a Cuſtom can prevail againſt plain Law, I doubt. (4)

---

(4) Judge Trowbridge, in an opinion given upon the will of Shute Shrimpton Yeomans, who died in 1769, (for an opportunity of examining which we are indebted to Edmund Trowbridge Dana, Eſq.,) took the ſame view of the law as the Chief Juſtice and Juſtice Cuſhing in this caſe. But the law in this State has ſince been ſettled in accordance with the deciſion of the majority of the Court. *Corbin* v. *Healy*, 20 Pick. 516. *Wight* v. *Thayer*, 1 Gray, 284, 286. It was not until after the Revolution that the proviſions for barring entails by common deed of warranty were enacted. St. 1791, c. 60. And even at the preſent day this cannot be done by will. Gen. Sts. c. 92, § 1. 6 Gray, 24.

brought over both the Common Law and Statute with us." Since the Provincial Law "does not affect Estates Tail" it "leaves them as in England." i.e., Not partible—*Reports*, 72–73.

Justices Russell and Lynde voted the same way, but for more policy-oriented reasons. Entails were designed to keep land in the family, and to keep them from being broken up. "The very Intent of Tails was to secure Estates in Familys, and keep them together." This would be "destroyed by such a Construction of the Law." *Reports*, 73. Lynde also made a policy argument. "It seems directly against the Reason and Intent of Estates Tail that they should be partible." (i.e., estates tail are to hold lands together, not divide them). *Reports*, 73.

Cushing and the Chief Justice seemed convinced by Gridley's "chopped down fee" argument. As Cushing observed, "This is the Manner of Construction of the Law at Home [i.e., England]: Where Fee Simple is partible, so are Estates Tail; and where Fee Simple descends to the eldest Son, so does Tail." *Reports*, 73. But both were somewhat relieved to lose. Cushing pointed out that there would be "great Difficulty at this Day to determine . . . Estates Tail were partible, the general Tenor having been otherwise . . ." *Reports*, 73. The Chief Justice agreed "it has been so long thought otherwise here [i.e., fee tails not partible] . . . I am glad that the Point is determined without me, for how such a Custom can prevail against plain Law, I doubt." *Id.*, 74. As Richard Morris has observed "[t]he admission of the dissenting judges in *Baker* v. *Mattocks* that the rule they favored was opposed to the practice then current" is evidence that, in practice at least, the entail had prevailed "up to that time," *Study and History of American Law* (Philadelphia, 1959), 97. (Although I would not go so far as to agree with Morris that it was also supported by "the weight of authority," as there is so little before *Quincy's Reports*. See *id.*, 97.)

Thus the majority decided to limit the social goals of fairness and egalitarianism articulated by the 1692 Act, to the fee simple, and to permit the cruel unfairness of the entail, so well known to readers of Jane Austen (1775–1817). (See particularly, *Pride and Prejudice*, 1st ed., 1815.) For such an important case, the arguments were oddly technical and focused on the 500-year-old history of the statute *De Donis*, rather than the immediate policy effects in 1763 Massachusetts, although two of the Justices affirmed the relatively elitist social and economic goals of the entail, preserving intact family estates. *Reports*, 73. This case was surely a window into the 1763 Massachusetts judicial mind.

CASE 30

SCOLLAY *v.* DUNN.

Rec. 1763. Fol. 107.

An Hoſtage ſent by the Maſter for the Ranſom of a Ship taken by the Enemy cannot maintain Admiralty Proceſs *in Perſonam* againſt the Owners for refuſing to pay the Money for his Liberation. *Oliver, J., diſſentiente.*

Scollay *verſ.* Dunn.

DUNN brought a Libel in the Admiralty againſt Scollay, for that he was a Mate on board a Veſſell of Scollay's, which was taken, and ranſomed by the Maſter, and Dunn went as an Hoſtage. He was

Scollay v. *Dunn* (1763)
3 George III (Aug.) in the Superior Court of Judicature

1 · BRIEF DESCRIPTION

This is one of the most extraordinary cases in *Quincy's Reports*, and it is also of great importance legally. Dunn was a mate on the *Peggy*, a ship owned by Scollay and consigned to a London merchant, William Sitwell. It was captured by a French privateer. The French were persuaded to ransom the ship, "the captain of the Peggy drew a ransom bill on the consignee," keeping Dunn as hostage to ensure payment. *Reports*, 187, S. Quincy n. 1. Scollay refused to pay. Eventually Dunn was ransomed by his friends. He brought a libel in Admiralty against Scollay, for reimbursement. Scollay in turn sought a prohibition from the Superior Court, which was granted on February 12, 1763, asserting that the Admiralty court had no proper jurisdiction, at least as to a process "against the Owners' Persons." *Reports*, 75. The issue in this case was whether the prohibition was properly granted. Held, by a split decision, "the Affair of Ransom" was not "a Contract upon the High Seas" and, therefore, outside the jurisdiction of the Admiralty. *Reports*, 78–79.

Following that decision, Gridley, appearing for Dunn, claimed an "appeal to the King and Council." The Justices then closely examined the 1691 Second Charter, reviewing whether an appeal had to be a matter over £300, or whether it was discretionary, or whether the Admiralty jurisdiction was entirely excepted. The Court refused to allow the appeal to England. *Reports*, 81–83. See discussion at Note 6, *infra*. The ground was apparently that the 1691 Charter, while it provided for appeals "in cases that may deserve the same," modified that clause by a subsequent requirement that "the matter in difference doth exceed the value of three hundred pounds of sterling." See *The Charter and General Laws of the Colony and Province of Massachusetts Bay* (Boston, 1814), 32. This was despite doubts by both the Chief Justice and Justice Lynde that this case might exceed £300, as the Chief Justice observed, "As for this Case, whether it exceeds £300 or no, there is the Difficulty." *Reports*, 83. In any event, no mention of an appeal has yet been found in the Privy Council records. See discussion at Note 6, *infra*.

There was a further note concerning this situation in August Term, 5 George 3 (1765), where it is described as "Dunn vers. Scollay" and as "Case of Hostage

was long Prifoner, and at laft releafed by the Money raifed by fome of his Friends, and now returned to Bofton. Libels againft Scollay and others, Owners of the Veffell. A Prohibition was granted, and the prefent Queftion was, whether the Prohibition ftand or a Confultation ordered; The Point was, whether the Procefs in the Admiralty againft the Owners' Perfons was good. (1)

No Appeal lies to the King in Council from a Decifion of this Court granting a Prohibition to the Admiralty in a Caufe wherein the Matter in Controverfy is lefs than £300.

Mr.

---

(1) The writ of prohibition is addreffed "to Chambers Ruffell Efq., Judge of our Court of Vice-Admiralty, Charles Paxton Efq., Marfhal, Andrew Belcher Efq., Regifter, and all the officers of faid Court." The libel is alleged to have fet forth as follows: "That the libellant was mate of the brigantine Peggy belonging to John Scollay and Thomas Fletcher, and Ifaac Freeman was mafter of her, and that fhe was taken on the high feas as prize by a private French fhip of war called the *Entreprenante*, belonging to Monfieur Boutellier at Nantes, and that the faid Ifaac ranfomed her and her cargo for 5000 livres, to be paid in fix months, and that the faid John, at the faid Ifaac's requeft and direction, became hoftage for fecuring the payment, and was by Peter Thibaut, the French captain of faid fhip, carried to Nantes," &c., "and that the libellant was finally obliged to pay the fum of £213 10*s*. of his own money to obtain his liberty." The petition further alleged that "the brigantine was not then here, and that the faid Court of Admiralty could not award any procefs againft her, and that the libellant did not allege that fhe ever came to the petitioners' poffeffion, or that they ever agreed to the faid contract of ranfom, but that the defign of the libellant was to make the petitioners' perfons and eftates liable for the default of the mafter, whereof they were wholly unknowing." After reciting the petition at length, the writ concludes as follows:

"We therefore willing to maintain the Laws and Rights of our Judi-
"catories and Courts of Record, and being unwilling our liege people
"with delays to hurt, Command and firmly Enjoin you that you meddle
"not further in the faid Plea or Caufe, nor moleft or caufe to be molefted
"the faid John Scollay and Thomas Fletcher or either of them in the
"Caufe aforefaid in the faid Court of Vice Admiralty neither attempt or
"prefume to attempt anything more therein: Untill our faid Juftices have
"advifed and confulted therein at our Superiour Court of Judicature
"Court of Affize, and general Goal Delivery to be holden at Bofton,
"within and for our County of Suffolk on the third Tuefday of Feb-
"ruary inftant, when and where you the faid Chambers Ruffell and the
"faid John Dunn or any other perfons may be prefent, if you or they
"pleafe

ILLUSTRATION 19: John Scollay (1711–1790), original Defendant in *Scollay* v. *Dunn*, *Quincy's Reports*, p. 74 (Case 30, 1763), by John Singleton Copley (1738–1813). Dated 1764. Image courtesy of the Pennsylvania Academy of the Fine Arts. Property owned by his family would take their name and become known as Scollay Square, Boston, now Government Center. My thanks to Kevin Cox.

Mr. Auchmuty for the Jurifdiction. The firft being taken upon the High Seas, Facts arifing afterwards in Confequence in the Body are within the Jurifdiction of the Court of Admiralty. Mafters may make Contracts that bind the Owners. Molloy, B. 2, C. 1, § 10; Ch. 2, §§ 14 & 16. Ib. B. 2, Ch. 2, § 2. Hardres, 183, *Sparks* vs. *Stafford.* In Salkeld the Cafe is not fo well reported as the fame in Mod. Rep. 'Tis unneceffary to fet forth Order to redeem; as the Mafter may juftify throwing over Goods in Cafe of a Storm to fave a greater Lofs, fo may he redeem, as otherwife the Whole would be loft. 2 Ld. Raym. 931, *Tranter* vs. *Watfon.* As for the Cafe of *Johnfon* vs. *Shippin* in Salkeld, that the Mafter by his Contracts cannot make the Owners liable, 6 Mod. 79 is the fame Cafe, and not fo reported, befides there the Contract appeared to have been made at Land; as for the Veffell's being loft, 'tis of no Avail — the Owners muft be bound inftantly or not at all; if the Mafter has a Right to bind the Owners by his Contract, they are bound, and the Contract cannot be refcinded but by the Parties, and not depend upon fuch a Contingency as the Arrival of the Veffell.

Mr. Gridley. If the Admiralty has Jurifdiction of the Principal, it has of the Incidents; if of the Thing, it has of the Perfon; as in the Cafe of Damage

---

" pleafe to fhow forth and maintain if you or they can, that the aforefaid " Plea or Caufe is cognizable in the faid Court of Vice Admiralty.

" Witnefs, Thomas Hutchinfon Efq. at Bofton this twelfth day of " February in the third Year of our Reign *Annoque Domini* 1763.

" NATH'L HATCH, Cler."

[P. 76]

ILLUSTRATION 20: Episode in Place du Bouffay, Nantes, 1859 (oil on canvas), by Auguste Hyacinthe Debay (1804–65). The Bouffay Prison in the background was where John Dunn, original Plaintiff in *Scollay* v. *Dunn*, *Quincy's Reports*, p. 74 (Case 30, 1763), was imprisoned for six years until his ransom was finally paid in 1762. My thanks to Kevin Cox. Courtesy Bridgeman Art Library.

age done by one Ship againſt another. Molloy, B. 2, C. 2, p. 2.

Thacher. Whether the Owners muſt anſwer in their Perſons for the Act of the Maſter at Sea, of which they were utterly unknowing, is the Queſtion; I take it not the Owners perſonally, for the Thing itſelf is bound. Every Ranſom is a new Purchaſe, and if the Owners are liable in this Caſe, they would be liable if the Maſter had contracted with the Captors for another Ship, and ſent an Hoſtage as a Pawn.

Ch. Juſtice. It differs from a new Purchaſe, for a new Purchaſe from an Enemy is void; 'tis a Redemption, a Saving it from being the Enemy's Property.

Thacher. If the Veſſell be liable for the Ranſom, and the Maſter may retain her for the Ranſom Money, then ſhe can't remain ſo abſolutely the Owner's Property as ſhe was before the Capture. 2 Ld. Raym. 932, *Tranter* vs. *Watſon.*

Ch. Juſtice. The Queſtion ſeems to me to be, whether the Contract of the Maſter upon the *High Sea* is the Contract of the Owner; and whether, if it is, there is any Inſtance of Suit in the Admiralty againſt the Perſons of the Owners.

Otis. The very Idea of Hypothecation is that the Maſter may bind the Owners, ſo far as that Intereſt of theirs goes, with what he is intereſted. Molloy, 15, 2, Ch. 11, § 11.

It

[P. 77]

ILLUSTRATION 21: Title page, *De Jure Maritimo et Navali or a Treatise of Affaires Maritime, and of Commerce* (1676), by Charles Molloy (1645/6–1690). Molloy is repeatedly cited as authority in *Scollay* v. *Dunn*, *Quincy's Reports*, p. 74 (Case 30, 1763). See description of Molloy's importance in Daniel R. Coquillette, *The Civilian Writers of Doctors' Commons, London* (Berlin, 1988), pp. 124–146.

It is now ſettled that Owners ſhall not be liable for the Barratry of the Maſter further than the Ship and Freight. 7 G. 2.

The Power of the Maſter is confined to the Ship and Cargo. Holt's Rep'ts, 48. Viner, Tit. Court of Admiralty. The Caſe of Hardres is conſiſtent with the above Rule.

Gridley. There are ſome Things though tranſacted upon the High Sea are not of a Maritime Nature, are not within the Juriſdiction of the Court of Admiralty. Things of a Maritime Nature tranſacted at Sea are undoubtedly within its Juriſdiction. So there are ſome Things of a Maritime Nature, though not tranſacted upon the High Seas, that are within the Juriſdiction of the Admiralty; ſuch are Wages of Seamen. There is Nothing that Owners are not liable for, which is neceſſary for the Support of the Voyage; it is no Argument that becauſe the Veſſell is liable, the Owners are not alſo; Veſſell, Maſter, and Owners are all liable for Wages. Viner, Tit. Hypoth. 329, bot.

Otis. This is Nothing but Hypoth. Viner, Tit. Mariner, 236; Tit. Maſter of a Ship, 348.

Mr. Juſtice Oliver delivered his Opinion in Favour of the Juriſdiction of the Admiralty.

Juſtice Lynde. I take the Affair of Ranſom to be a Matter upon Sea, and therefore if the Libel was on the Ship or Cargo, I ſhould hold it good; but

[P. 78]

& Ransom." See *Reports*, 187, set out in *Quincy Papers*, vol. 5, 478. This subsequent proceeding was really an appeal of a second case, brought by Dunn against Scollay in the Court of Common Pleas, following the prohibition against his libel in Admiralty that was upheld in this first case. See *Reports*, 187–188. That action was successful for Dunn, and he obtained a judgment of £700 against Scollay. Scollay appealed that judgment to the Superior Court. Quincy's report simply sets out the authorities involved on both sides, which were very similar to those involved in this case. See Note 4, "Authority," *infra*. Dunn apparently lost the appeal, and his judgment, on the issue of whether a ship's master could "bind the owner by a contract of ransom, without special orders to that effect." See *Reports*, 188, S. Quincy n.1, and the full discussion of second case, described as Case 30[B], *Reports*, 187–188, set out in *Quincy Papers*, vol. 5, 478–481, *infra*.

2 · RECORD

Available at Rec. 1763, fol. 107. The writ of prohibition itself is particularly important. See *Reports*, 75–76, n.1. The Suffolk files also contain the following:

Scollay v. *Dunn*, (same) Oct. 21, 1765, Nos. 86627 and 87801.

- See Attached Sheet.
- No. 87801, a printed blank form of a Writ of Assistance for collection of customs, 29 Sept. 1770.

Scollay v. *Dunn*: (listed as *Dunn* v. *Scollay*, Sept. 12, 1758)

- A letter to Dunn from William Sitwell, the London merchant to whom the *Peggy* was consigned, dated March 3, 1758. Sitwell expresses regret that a bill was not paid, and that the confinement continued. Sitwell also says that he visited France during the previous summer. Lastly, he promises that the business with the underwriters will be taken care of.
- A letter in different handwriting which is nearly identical to the other letter.
- Another letter to Dunn from Sitwell dated Sept. 12, 1758. Like the other letter, this letter serves as an apology from Sitwell. Sitwell claims that he has been unable to get a discharge for Dunn, but that he was encouraged about Dunn's release because some of the underwriters had agreed to release Dunn with a partial payment. Unfortunately, the letter continues, the remaining two underwriters absolutely refused to comply. Sitwell claims that the only way to compel these two underwriters is by law

but as it is not, I cannot but be for the Prohibition ſtanding.

Chief Juſtice. Ranſom as far as it reſpects Maſter and Hoſtage maritime, ſo far as Owner and Maſter does not appear to be a Contract upon the High Seas. None of the Authorities maintain the Juriſdiction in this Caſe; and where it is doubtfull, I think 'tis a Rule that common Juriſdiction ought to be maintained, and that the Admiralty Juriſdiction ought to be made plain and clear, which I think is not the Caſe now.

Prohibition ſtands. (2)

Mr.

---

(2) There cannot be much doubt that the contract between the owner and the hoſtage who pawns himſelf for the ranſom, is maritime, and within admiralty juriſdiction. See the caſes cited above; alſo 3 Doug. 166; 1 Ld. Raym. 22. The concluſion arrived at by Mr. Juſtice Lynde is, that although the contract be maritime, yet that only the remedy *in rem* can be ſought in the admiralty. The oppoſite doctrine may now be conſidered as eſtabliſhed in this country, "if indeed," as ſays Mr. Juſtice Sprague, (21 Law Rep. 605,) "anything as to admiralty juriſdiction can now be deemed ſettled." See *Andrews* v. *Wall*, 3 How. 573, *Story*, *J.*—"Over maritime contracts the admiralty poſſeſſes a clear and eſtabliſhed juriſdiction capable of being enforced *in perſonam* as well as *in rem.*" *New Jerſey Steam Navigation Co.* v. *Merchant's Bank*, 6 How. 392, *Nelſon*, *J.*—"If the cauſe is a maritime cauſe, ſubject to admiralty cognizance, juriſdiction is complete over the perſon as well as over the ſhip; it cannot be confined to one of the remedies on the contract, when the contract itſelf is within its cognizance." Alſo *De Lovio* v. *Boit*, 2 Gallis. 462; Clerke's Praxis, Tit. 1. But that it was once ſo confined to one remedy in ſome caſes by the Engliſh law, ſee the diſſenting opinion of Mr. Juſtice Johnſon in *Allegre* v. *Ramſay*, 12 Wheat. 614. The reſolutions of 1632 gave the admiralty juriſdiction *in rem*, but not *in perſonam*, over contracts for "building or mending, ſaving or neceſſary victualling of a ship." And Mr. Juſtice Johnſon, *ub. ſup.*, contends that the only inſtance of admiralty juriſdiction *in perſonam* upon contracts was for ſeamen's wages, which was allowed on the principle of *communis*

error

—which is uncertain because no such case has been tried before and it would take a long time. The letter further states that Sitwell attempted to get the agent of one Mr. Boutail [Mons. Boutellier, owner of the privateer?] to pay the remaining portion and that seemed promising until Mr. Boutail's wife died, and Sitwell was unable to contact him. Thereafter, Sitwell received a settlement offer from Scollay, but for some reason could proceed no further. As a final resort, Sitwell said that he had asked for a prisoner swap in order to get Dunn out, but after three requests, the Commissioner has failed to respond. Apparently, Dunn was considered a prisoner of war. Lastly, Sitwell says that he would have continued his payments, but has ceased because of the settlement letter from Scollay. In a bit of an about face, Sitwell then becomes defensive and claims that he will not give more money because he has already given a good deal of money at his own risk. In the end, however, Sitwell reiterates that he is Dunn's friend.

3 · PROFESSIONALS INVOLVED

This case was argued by the leaders of the colonial Bar, with Robert Auchmuty (1723–1788) and Jeremy Gridley (1701/2–1767) arguing for the jurisdiction of the Admiralty and, when that was denied, for appeal to the Privy Council. In opposition on both issues were Oxenbridge Thacher (1719–1765) and the patriot, James Otis, Jr. (1725–1783). See brief biographies for all four in *Appendix 6.* Assuming that Tories would favor the Admiralty, with its lack of jury trial, and also would favor broad supervision of colonial courts through appeal to the Privy Council, *Reports*, 80, then the advocates were true to type. Gridley had defended the Writ of Assistance against Otis, and Robert Auchmuty actually became Judge of the Massachusetts Vice Admiralty (1767–1776) and was proscribed in 1778. Auchmuty's father had also served as the Judge of the Vice Admiralty court, from 1733 to 1747. Otis, of course, was a famous patriot, and Thacher's seat in the House passed to Sam Adams on Thacher's death in 1765. See *Appendix 6.*

4 · AUTHORITY

This case is particularly important for the use of statutory and English case law authority on both sides, although the crucial question as to the right of appeal from the Court's decision upholding the prohibition—involving a fundamen-

Mr. Gridley then claimed an Appeal to the King and Council: Reafon of Government requires that they fhould have Power of final Judgment in Cafes of Importance; at Home, in Cafe of *Ejectione Firmæ* on a Leafe, Appeal lies.

Auchmuty. This is a Matter that deferves Appeal. Vaughan Rep. 290, 402. That Writs of Error lie in all inferiour Dominions, Ib. 418. Admiralty Jurifdiction is expreffly excepted from our Charter; (3) and if no Appeal lies in this Cafe, it feems to me that Exception is of no Value. 1 Peere Wms. 330, *Chriftian* vs. *Corren.*

Mr. Thacher. The laft Claufe of the Charter relative to this Matter of Appeals feems evidently explanatory

---

error facit jus. But fee 3 Burr. 1740, where Dunning, *arguendo*, "admitted that actions had been brought in the admiralty by the hoftage againft the owners who refufed to ranfom him." Alfo 5 Rob. 104, where it is ftated that in fuits for ranfom on the part of the enemy, "proceedings were always carried on againft the owner in the name of the hoftage fuing for his liberty." Whether the claim of the hoftage againft the owners is in the nature of falvage, and therefore dependent on the fafe arrival of the veffel, or whether, as argued here, the owners are bound inftantly by the act of redeeming her from her prefent peril — *quære.* A recapture of a fhip from the enemy or from pirates is falvage. *The Trelawney*, 4 Rob. 227. And where the poffeffion has been parted with for the benefit of the owner, proceedings *in perfonam* may be fuftained. *The Hope*, 3 Rob. 216.

(3) "Provided always, and it is hereby declared, that nothing herein fhall extend or be taken to erect or grant or allow the exercife of any admiral court, jurifdiction, power or authority, but that the fame fhall be, and is hereby referved to us and our fucceffors, and fhall from time to time be erected, granted and exercifed, by virtue of commiffions to be iffued under the Great Seal of England, or under the feal of the high admiral, or the commiffioners for executing the office of high admiral of England." *Province Charter*, Anc. Chart. 36.

[P. 80]

tal construction of the words of the Second Charter—was done without any citation to authority. That could be because the question of appeal was a purely colonial issue, whereas the scope of the admiralty jurisdiction had attracted much attention in England. In any event, the next page of the manuscript after the case report lists the authorities for either side, including several not included in Quincy's account of the arguments themselves. See *Reports*, 83, S. Quincy n. 7.

Among the authorities cited by the distinguished professional team attacking the prohibition, Gridley and Auchmuty, were some very familiar sources, such as *Lord Raymond's Reports*, *Modern Reports* and the appropriate subheadings of *Viner's Abridgment*, such as "Hypothecation." These sources also frequently appear in Quincy's *Law Commonplace*. See *Law Commonplace*, [35], n. 2, [96], n. 4 (*Modern Reports*); p.[32], n. 7 (*Salkeld's Reports*); [26], n. 2 (*Lord Raymond's Reports*) and [16], n. 2 (*Viner's Abridgment*). Other sources cited were more unusual, with heavy reliance on Charles Molloy's *De Jure Maritimo et Navali: Or a Treatise of Affaires Maritime and of Commerce*, first published in London in 1676, and frequently republished, with the "new" edition of 1744 mentioned in Quincy's "authority" note. *Reports*, 83, S. Quincy n.7. See *Sweet & Maxwell*, vol. 1, 511:64. See also the full discussion of Molloy's importance as a "bridge" between common lawyers and the civilian law of the sea and commerce in Daniel R. Coquillette, *The Civilian Writers of Doctors' Commons, London* (Berlin, 1988), 140–146. According to Quincy's "authority" note, Gridley and Auchmuty also referred to "Sea Laws, 128." This is probably William Welwood's famous *Abridgment of all Sea-Laws*, first published in 1613 and republished in 1636, although the page reference seems uncertain. See *Sweet & Maxwell*, vol. 1, 516:100 and Coquillette, *The Civilian Writers*, *supra*, at 128. At the very least, these sources demonstrated the strength of Gridley's famous library and the breadth of learning of the advocates.

Their opponents, Thacher and Otis, were more prosaic. Essentially, they tried distinguishing cases such as *Tranter* v. *Watson* (1703), 2 *Ld. Raymond's Reports*, 932, cited by their opponents, as being about security in the ship, rather than a personal action against the owner. (Security in a vessel, usually secured by a lien on the vessel in Admiralty, was known as "hypothecation." See *Jowitt*, *supra*, 932.) They also cited Molloy, *supra*, and *Viner's Abridgment*, "Tit. Mariner, 236; Tit. Master of the Ship, 348" to show that "this is Nothing but Hypoth. [hypothecation]," i.e., security in the vessels only, and further cited the statute

explanatory of the firſt, (4) the Matter in Difference only is what is to be conſidered in giving Juriſdiction, and not the Suggeſtion of Damages.

Otis. It appears to me that by the plain Conſtruction of the Words of the Charter, the Matter in Difference muſt neceſſarily be £300. Courts have conſtantly denied Appeals where there has has been no Judgment for more than that Sum; this has been the contemporaneous Expoſition of it.

Gridley. The Charter ſhould be liberally conſtrued in Favour of Appeals. I hold, this Court, by the Clauſes in our Charter relative to this Matter, is to judge of the Limitations of Appeals. "In all Matters deſerving the ſame," are the Words upon which my Opinion is founded. It ſeems to be ſettled that the Subject has a Right in all Cauſes to appeal; therefore even the King cannot abridge it. "All Matters deſerving the ſame" ought to have a liberal Conſtruction in Favour of the Subject. "We think it neceſſary that our Subjects ſhould have Liberty of Appeal to us in all Caſes that may deſerve the ſame." The Conſtruction, the Gentlemen on the other Side would give, ſeems to be providing Appeals only for the Defendant; upon their Principles,

(4) "And whereas we judge it neceſſary that all our ſubjects ſhould have liberty to appeal to us, our heirs and ſucceſſors, in caſes that may deſerve the ſame, we do by theſe preſents ordain, that in caſe either party ſhall not reſt ſatisfied with the judgment or ſentence of any judicatories or courts within our ſaid province or territory, in any perſonal action, wherein the matter in difference doth exceed the value of three hundred pounds ſterling, that then he or they may appeal to us, our heirs and ſucceſſors, in our or their privy council." *Province Charter*, Anc. Chart. 32.

11

7 George 2 (1733) for it being "now settled that Owners shall not be liable for the Barratry [i.e., a wilfull, unauthorized act] of the Master further than Ship and Freight." *Reports*, 78. See *Jowitt*, *supra*, 215.

As to the issue of appeal, Auchmuty cited to *Vaughan's Reports* 290, *Craw* v. *Ramsey* (1670), beginning on 274, 402 (Process out of Courts at Westminster into Wales, beginning on page 395), another commonly cited report in the colony (see *Law Commonplace*, [50], n. 2), and to *Christian* v. *Corren* in 1 *Peere William's Report* 330, a rather unusual report of cases in Chancery, and [special cases] in the King's Bench, between 1695–1735, published in London in installments between 1740–1749. See *Sweet* & *Maxwell*, vol. 1, 347–348:33. Their adversaries cited no authority except, in Otis's words, "the plain Construction of the Words of the Charter. . . ." *Reports*, 81.

5 · LATER CITATIONS

This case has never been cited by the Supreme Judicial Court for the principal holding, and for good reason. As Samuel Quincy observed, in light of later cases, "[t]here cannot be much doubt that the contract between the owner and the hostage who pawns himself for ransom, is maritime, and within admiralty jurisdiction." *Reports*, 79, S. Quincy n. 2. Further, later American cases made it clear that the hostage could proceed *in personam* against the owner as well as *in rem* against the boat. *New Jersey Steam Navigation Co.* v. *Merchant's Bank*, 47 U. S. 394, 6 How. 392 (1848) (Nelson J.). *Reports*, 79, S. Quincy n.2. (Although earlier English cases may have supported the decision in *Scollay* v. *Dunn*, see *Reports*, 79–80, S. Quincy n. 2.)

This case has been cited for the proposition that a writ of prohibition may issue against the state, see *Connecticut River R. Co.* v. *Franklin County Commissioners*, 127 Mass. 50, 58 (1879), and as to the colonial record of issuing writs of prohibition to admiralty courts in Massachusetts. See *The Underwriter*, 119 F. 713, D.C. Mass. (1702).

6 · NOTE

This is a highly important case for four reasons. First, it sheds vivid light on the practices and risks of Massachusetts commerce. See *Introduction*, *supra*, 52–57. John Scollay's brigantine, the *Peggy*, was on consignment to a London merchant in Atlantic trading operations. See *Quincy*, 187, S. Quincy n.1. It was captured at sea on October 26, 1756, by a French privateer, the *Entreprenante*. The

Principles, a Demurrer being to the Declaration, and Judgment againſt the Plaintiff, how can he ever appeal?

Juſtice Oliver. I take the firſt Clauſe in the Charter relating to Appeals to be only introductory to the ſecond, and that there can be no Appeal where the Matter in Difference is leſs than £300; and upon that ſecond Clauſe I am againſt granting an Appeal in this Caſe.

Juſtice Cuſhing. I take, the ſecond Clauſe is explanatory, and ſo I am againſt it.

Juſtice Lynde. With Regard to the firſt Clauſe, it appears to me to be only introductory, and therefore on that I am of the ſame Opinion; as to the ſecond I am doubtfull, but as I am in general againſt Appeals, I am againſt it in this Caſe.

Chief Juſtice. Firſt, whether the Subject Matter comes within the Clauſe of the Charter relative to Appeals, as it is an Affair begun in the Admiralty and brought here only by Prohibition; and for this we muſt look into the Charter, which entirely reſerves and excepts it, and 'tis by a ſubſequent Act we have any Right to iſſue Prohibitions to it; (5) and

(5) The Province Law of 11 W. 3, which gave the Superior Court general juriſdiction "as fully and amply to all intents and purpoſes whatſoever as the Courts of King's Bench, Common Pleas and Exchequer within his Majeſty's Kingdom of England, have or ought to have." Anc. Chart. 331. "The rights of the courts of common law within the Province of the Maſſachuſetts to reſtrain the exceſſes of the Admiralty Juriſdiction, are not derived from their charter, but from ſubſequent

ILLUSTRATION 22: Chief Justice Benjamin Lynde Jr. (1711–1780), Justice, Superior Court of Judicature, 1745–1769, Chief Justice, 1769–1771, attributed to John Smibert (1688–1751) or possibly to his son, Nathaniel. Dated about 1738. See Henry Wilder Foote, *John Smibert, Painter: With a Descriptive Catalogue of Portraits* (Cambridge, Mass., 1950), pp. 73, 219–220, 263–264. Lynde's father, Benjamin Lynde Sr. (1666–1745) was also a Justice of the Superior Court of Judicature, 1712–1729, and Chief Justice, 1729–1745. Lynde presided at the Boston Massacre trial, and would have heard John Adams and Josiah Quincy argue for the Defendants. See *Editor's Foreword* to Volume 4, *supra*. In 1774, he was one of the signers of the Salem address to Gen. Thomas Gage. See *id.*, p. 219. See also Sally E. Hadden, "Benjamin Lynde, Jr., Servant of the Commonwealth," 9 *Massachusetts Legal History* (2003), p. 1. Lynde voted to grant the writ of prohibition in *Scollay* v. *Dunn*, *Quincy's Reports*, pp. 74, 82 (Case 30, 1763). Image courtesy of the Library of Congress. Special thanks to Kevin Cox and Charles Riordan.

and if we have any Right to judge, I think it is the fame as if the Matter came originally before this Court. Under the old Colony Charter, there was no Mention of Appeals; this was Objection againft that Charter. One while in the Quo Warranto, that Claufe in the new Charter was looked upon as a great Priviledge; (6) had it ftood without any Claufe, all Caufes would have been appealable: I take it therefore to be a Priviledge in our Charter; "all Caufes which deferve it," is explained to be above £300, but fhould it be admitted to be within the Difcretion of the Court to grant Appeals, whether lefs or more, I fhould be againft it, in Favour of Priviledge. As for this Cafe, whether it exceeds £300 or no, there is the Difficulty. I am confidering the Allegations, &c., in Favour of Appeal. (7)

---

fubfequent laws of the Province, confirmed afterwards by the Crown." Dummer's Defence of the New England Charters, (Bofton ed. 1745,) 26.

(6) Under the Colony Charter no appeals to England were allowed. See the remonftrance of the legiflature to the Long Parliament — "We have not admitted appeals to your authority, being affured they cannot ftand with the liberty and power granted us by our charter." 1 Bancroft's Hift. U. S. 441. Afterwards in the reign of Charles 2, the colony "joined iffue with the King by denying the right of appeal." 2 Ib. 74. And this was one of the principal caufes of the fubfequent iffuing of the Quo Warranto, by which the charter fell.

(7) The appeal was not granted.

On a fubfequent page in the MS. is the following memorandum: "*Dunn* v. *Scollay*, Cafe of Hoftage & Ranfom: Authorities in Favour of the Plaintiff were Molloy, (Old Edit.) 205 § 10, 212 § 14, 213 § 14. Molloy, (New Edit. 1744,) 358, 237, 8; 244, 5. 2 L'd Raymond, 931; Lord Holt's Opinion relied on; Sea Laws, 128. In Favour of the Defendant were 2 Chancery Cafes, 239; 1 Salk. 35; 3 Bacon, 592, 595.

ILLUSTRATION 23: Chambers Russell (1713–1766), who served both as a judge for the Vice Admiralty Court and as a Justice of the Superior Court of Judicature (1752–1760), arguably by Joseph Blackburn (circa 1700–1780), although also attributed to Gilbert Stuart (1755–1828) and others. See *Sibley's Harvard Graduates*, vol. IX (1731–1735), p. 83. Russell recused himself from *Scollay* v. *Dunn*, *Quincy's Reports*, p. 74 (Case 30, 1763), to avoid voting on whether the Superior Court of Judicature should prohibit him from hearing Dunn's suit in the Court of Vice Admiralty. See Kevin W. Cox, "Scollay v. Dunn: The Conflict and Confluence of Colonial Admiralty and Common Law Jurisdiction in 1760's Boston" (2007), unpublished paper on file with editor, p. 13. Many thanks to Kevin Cox. Image courtesy of The Frick Collection.

captain, Isaac Freeman, persuaded the French to take a ransom note, secured by a hostage, the Mate and Plaintiff in this case, Dunn. Neither Scollay nor the London merchant, William Sitwell, paid the note, and Dunn languished in prison at Nantes until rescued by his own family and friends. See *Introduction*, "First Flower," Section IV B, 52–57, *supra*. Ransom notes of this kind were fairly common in the latter half of the eighteenth century, but this was a very graphic example. Of course, Dunn, on his return, promptly sued Scollay.

The second important issue in this case concerned the jurisdiction of colonial courts. Initially, Dunn's lawyers chose to file libels against Scollay and other owners of the *Peggy* in the Court of Vice Admiralty, certainly on the theory that this was a contract entered into on the high seas. The relationship between the jurisdiction of common law courts and admiralty courts was a major point of contention on both sides of the Atlantic. See F. L. Wiswall, *The Development of Admiralty Jurisdiction and Practice Since 1800* (Cambridge, 1970), 1–39; E. S. Roscoe, *Studies in the History of Admiralty and Prize Courts* (2nd ed., London, 1932). The standard means used by courts to control admiralty jurisdiction was the powerful prerogative Writ of Prohibition, see Daniel R. Coquillette, *Anglo-American Legal Heritage*, *supra*, 246–247. By a split Court, with Justice Oliver in dissent, such a writ was issued here, preventing Dunn from further proceedings in Admiralty.

The decision was thus an important one, both in light of admiralty jurisdiction's contested past and for its future, as the first federal courts of the new American republic would have admiralty jurisdictions. See Henry J. Bourguignon, *The First Federal Court* (Philadelphia, 1977), 3–78. Scope of admiralty jurisdiction became an important issue as such courts sought to expand their power. See Daniel R. Coquillette, "'Mourning Venice and Genoa': Joseph Story, Legal Education, and the *Lex Mercatoria*," *From Lex Mercatoria to Commercial Law* (V. Piergiovanni, ed., Berlin, 2005), 11–51. The decision was also important in determining the possible effect of political ideology on the justices, as the Vice-Admiralty Court was free of pesky colonial juries, and was often favored by the English in controversial cases. See, for a powerful example, John Adams's defense in *Rex* v. *Corbet*, *supra*, vol. 11, 275–276, described in D. R. Coquillette "Justinian In Braintree: John Adams, Civilian Learning, and Legal Elitism, 1758–1775," *Law in Colonial Massachusetts* (eds. Coquillette, Brink, Menand), 392–394.

One of the Superior Court judges, Chambers Russell, did not participate in the decision, most certainly because he was also the Vice-Admiralty Judge and would have been considering a prohibition against his own jurisdiction—a most awkward position. Oliver, a staunch Tory, predictably voted for an expanded view of the Vice-Admiralty jurisdiction, but Lynde and the Chief Justice did not. Lynde refused to find admiralty jurisdiction beyond a libel "on the Ship or Cargo," even though he found "the Affair of Ransom to be a Matter upon Sea." *Reports*, 78. Here, of course, Dunn was trying to sue Scollay personally, rather than proceeding against the ship, which may have been very difficult to locate and attach.

Chief Justice Hutchinson voted with Lynde, although he disagreed with Lynde's rationale, finding that "Ransom as far as it respects Master and Hostage maritime, so far as Owner and Master does not appear to be a Contract upon the High Seas." *Reports*, 79. The Chief Justice relied on the absence of authority directly in point, "[n]one of the Authorities maintain the Jurisdiction in this Case . . ." and on a general rule that "common [law] Jurisdiction ought to be maintained" unless "the Admiral Jurisdiction ought to be made plain and clear, which I think is not the case now." *Reports*, 79. As Samuel Quincy demonstrated, later American courts, led by Joseph Story, rejected the rationale of both Lynde and Hutchinson, and consistently found for a broader admiralty jurisdiction. See *Reports*, 79, S. Quincy n. 2. Bolstered by Story's sweeping view of admiralty jurisdiction, Justice Nelson wrote in 1848 that "[o]ver maritime contracts the admiralty possesses a clear and established jurisdiction capable of being enforced *in personam* as well as *in rem*." *New Jersey Steam Navigation Co.* v. *Merchant's Bank*, 47 U. S. 394, 6 Howard 392 (1848), cited at *Reports*, 79, S. Quincy n. 2. Thus, the colonial judges' earlier loyalty to the common law jurisdiction was remarkable!

The Chief Justice's reference to the "authorities" brings in a third point of significance for this remarkable case—the use of sophisticated English authority. As discussed in Note 4, "Authority," *supra*, both sides made use of extensive English sources, including unusual treaties such as Charles Molloy's *De Jure Maritimo et Navali* [1676] and William Welwood's *Abridgment of all Sea-Laws* (1613). Molloy, in particular, was a "bridge" between Roman and Civil law continental sources and the Common law of England. See Daniel R. Coquillette, *Civilian Writers of Doctors' Commons, London*, *supra*, at 140–146. These citations demonstrated the depth of the colonial law libraries and some sophistication about civilian law, a trend also reflected, more strongly, by John Adams's law practice. See D. R. Coquillette, "Justinian in Braintree: John Adams, Civilian Learning, and Legal Elitism, 1758–1775," *Law in Colonial Massachusetts* (eds. Coquillette, Brink, Menand), 382–418. That some of these authorities were used in a rather loose manner, as Chief Justice Hutchinson implied in his ruling, should not detract from the scholarly level of the argument, which would have been respectable in London. See Note 4 "Authority," *supra.* It was also remarkable that, in such an important case, there was no reference to colonial law at all with regard to the substance of the dispute. Quincy doubtless found this to be an incentive to create colonial law reports.

Finally, there was the important legal issue of the appeal to the Privy Council, the "King and Council" in London. Here the Court was required to make colonial law, as the issue had to be determined by reference to Section 4 of the Second Charter. The wording of the Charter was badly drafted, and left it open to debate whether the words "cases that may deserve the same" [i.e., "liberty to appeal to us"] were limited by the subsequent provision allowing appeals "in any personal action, wherein the matter in difference doth exceed the value of three hundred pound sterling." See *Reports*, 81, n. 4 and *The Charter and General Laws of the Colony and Province of Massachusetts Bay* (Boston, 1814), 32. One could certainly argue that the first clause gave the Court *discretion* to grant appeals to deserving cases, whereas the second clause *required* that appeals be granted in cases with contested amounts over £300. Justice Oliver, however, read the first clause to "be only introductory to the second" and, therefore, that "there can be no Appeal where the Matter in Difference is Less than £300." In this case "upon that second Clause," Oliver was "against granting an Appeal," because he was of the view that less than £300 was involved. *Reports*, 82. Justice Cushing agreed that the "second Clause is explanatory," and that the amount was under £300. *Reports*, 82.

Justice Lynde agreed that the amount had to exceed £300, but "as to the second I am doubtful" [i.e., he was not sure that the £300 amount had not been exceeded by this case.] "[B]ut," he continued, "as I am in general against Appeals, I am against it in this Case." *Reports*, 82.

Chief Justice Hutchinson was also unsure whether the case was worth more than £300. "As for this case, whether it exceeds £300 or no, there is the Difficulty." *Reports*, 83. He was also concerned that "it is an Affair begun in the Admiralty and brought here only by Prohibition," because the 1691 Charter originally excepted admiralty from all its provisions, including the appeals clause. See *The Charters and General Laws of the Colony and Province of Massachusetts Bay* (Boston, 1814), *supra*, 36. The ability to issue prohibition to the Admiralty was based on a subsequent statute, Province Law, 11 William 3 (1699). Finally, the Chief Justice was concerned whether the Court had discretion under the "all Causes which deserve it" language, to deny appeals exceeding £300. While the language of the Report is unclear, the Chief Justice apparently opposed such discretion, in favor of an appeal exceeding £300 being a privilege under the Charter. "I take it therefore to be a Priviledge in our Charter; 'all Causes which deserve it,' is explained to be above £300, but should it be admitted to be within the Discretion of the Court to grant Appeals, whether less or more, I should be against it, in Favour of Priviledge." *Reports*, 83.

In all events, the appeal was denied. All the justices, except the Chief Justice, expressed clear opposition. As Justice Lynde put it, "I am in general against Appeals." Given the importance of the case and the difficulty of the legal issues involved, the resistance of the Court to appeals to London was striking.

In addition, the Chief Justice was quite right to wonder if the case did not exceed £300 after all. When Dunn brought his action later in the Common Pleas, he was awarded a judgment of £700. See *Scollay* v. *Dunn* (1766), *Reports*, 187, Case 30 [B], S. Quincy n. 1. In any event, no evidence of an appeal has yet been found in the Privy Council records, and the case was mentioned by Joseph Smith as an example of limitations on such appeals. See Joseph H. Smith, *Appeals to the Privy Council from the American Plantations* (New York, 1956), 166. My thanks to my distinguished colleague, Sharon H. O'Connor. See the discussion at *Banister* v. *Henderson* (1765), *Reports*, 119, Case 42, Note 6, *infra*.

There is an excellent paper, "*Scollay* v. *Dunn*: the Conflict and Confluence of Colonial Admiralty and Common Law Jurisdiction in 1760s Boston," on file with the Editor. It was prepared by my brilliant research assistant, Kevin W. Cox, Harvard Law School Class of 2005, who also was invaluable in assisting with these annotations.

All in all, *Scollay* v. *Dunn* was a great colonial case, involving compelling human and economic factors, difficult issues of jurisdiction, sophisticated authorities, and a major decision about right to appeal to under the Charter. Even in London, it would have been a "major league" case.

CASE 31

ANGIER *v.* JACKSON.
Rec. 1763. Fol. 93.

It ſeems, that a new Trial may be granted where the Verdict is againſt Law and Evidence, but not where there is Evidence on both Sides.

Angier *verſ.* Jackſon.

MOTION was made for a new Trial. This Cauſe was from Middleſex. It ſeems the Jury gave a Verdict for Damages in Favour of Jackſon, original Plaintiff, contrary to the Mind of the Court.

Trowbridge. When the Jury give a Verdict againſt Evidence, the Court may grant a new Trial. That Jury are not abſolute Judges of Evidence and Damages, ſee Holt's Rep. 701, 702, *Aſh* vs. *Lady Aſh.* Jurys are to try Cauſes with the Aſſiſtance of Judges. Lucas's Caſes of L. & Eq. 202. (1) Miſtake of Judge or Jury good Cauſe for new Trial. Strange, 1105. Ibid. 584. Evidence doubtfull no new Trial ſhould be granted, but here 'twas againſt direct Evidence. New Trial granted after Trial at Bar, is conceded. This Caſe is not like Ejectment — he may have a new Ejectment; not ſo here.

Auchmuty. If ever any Caſe was excepted from new Trials, this is. Trial at Bar is more favoured than Trial otherwiſe, becauſe of its Solemnity. I confeſs I wiſh for a Power in the Court to ſet aſide Verdicts, but not for an unlimited one. This Caſe was not againſt Evidence. I allow there was Evidence againſt Evidence; and two Verdicts, though no Rule of Controul, is yet of ſome Weight. (2) Strange,

(1) 10 Mod. 202, *The Queen* v. *Helſton.*
(2) S. P. 7 Maſs. 301. 9 Maſs. 450. 18 Pick. 15. 8 Gray, 46.

Angier v. *Jackson* (1763)
George III (Aug.) in the
Superior Court of Judicature

1 · BRIEF DESCRIPTION

This an important case on the power of juries. A Middlesex jury gave a verdict for damages in favor of the Plaintiff Jackson, contrary "to the Mind of the Court." Angier, the Defendant, now moves for a new trial. Held, motion denied, because there was "Evidence on both sides" and the Court below was "not clear" that the verdict was "against Law and Evidence." *Reports*, 85.

2 · RECORD

Available at Rec. 1763, fol. 93.

3 · PROFESSIONALS INVOLVED

Edmund Trowbridge (1709–1793) argued for the new trial. He was later to become a Justice of the Superior Court (1767–1775). Arguing for the power of the jury was Robert Auchmuty (1723–1788), who became Judge of the Massachusetts Vice Admiralty Court (1767–1776), where—ironically—jury trial was not allowed. Auchmuty was also proscribed as a loyalist in 1778. This is another example where lawyers certainly argued legal positions that were not "knee-jerk" assertions to their politics—here a Tory who was already Advocate General in Admiralty (1762–1767) was arguing for the inherent power of a common law jury. See brief biographies in *Appendix 6.*

4 · AUTHORITY

Trowbridge relied on a series of English cases, including the famous *Ash* v. *Lady Ash*, *Holt's Reports* 701, 702 (K.B. 1688–1710), together with *Strange's Reports* (covering 1716–1749), 584 (the 1724 case of *Musgrave* v. *Nevinson*), 1105 (the 1739 case of *Smith* v. *Parkhurst,* vol. 2), and *Lucas's Cases in Law and Equity*, which was part 10 of the *Modern Reports* [1709–1725], first published in 1736. The case from *Lucas's Reports* is *Regina* v. *Corporation of Helston* in Cornwall (1714), 202. Quincy's *Law Commonplace* has extensive notations to *Strange's* and *Modern Reports*. Significantly, the *Law Commonplace* directly cross-references to *Angier*

Strange, 1105. Evidence doubtfull. Ibid. 1142. Salk. 648, *Sparks* vs. *Spicer*. The Court is not to be Judge of the Law and Fact too abſolutely; if it ſhould be, it takes away all Verdicts but ſuch as are agreeable to the Mind of the Court. It would be opening a Door to great Inconveniences to the Subject, even if Attaints did not lie; but here Attaint lies. (3)

Ch. Juſtice. Are you not agreed, that, were it evidently againſt Law and Evidence, there the Court may grant a new Trial, but not where there is Evidence on both Sides. (4)

Trowbridge. It can never be ſuppoſed that a Verdict will be given againſt direct Evidence, without Shadow of Evidence to ſupport it. This differs from the Caſe of *Fuller & Clark* at Cambridge — there was plainly Evidence againſt Evidence. I hold, this Court always have Right to grant new Trials when they think Injuſtice like to be done.

Juſtices Oliver, *Cuſhing*, *Ruſſell & Lynde* againſt a new Trial, becauſe the Court were not clear in the former Trial.

---

(3) It ſeems however that attaints had long been obſolete. See 3 Bl. Com. 390 — "The attaint is now as obſolete as the trial by battel which it ſucceeded, and we ſhall probably ſee the revival of one as ſoon as the revival of the other." But in *Aſhford* v. *Thornton*, 1 B. & Ald. 460, wager of battel was ſuſtained by the Court in 1818.

(4) See 20 Pick. 289, *Shaw*, *C. J.* — "For a long time it was conſidered that a new trial could only regularly be granted, where the verdict was without evidence or againſt the whole evidence. It has however been extended to caſes, where the verdict is clearly againſt the weight of evidence, although evidence was given on both ſides."

v. *Jackson* in a section on new trials, demonstrating the interconnectedness of the *Reports* and the *Law Commonplace* in Quincy's legal training. See *Law Commonplace,* [90], n. 4. The authorities stand for new trial only where the jury verdict was against direct evidence.

Auchmuty argued that "[t]his case was not against Evidence," although there was "Evidence against Evidence." *Reports*, 84. He also evoked another case in *Strange's Reports* where the jury verdict was permitted to stand though the "[e]vidence [was] doubtful." See *Ashley* v. *Ashley* (1740), *Strange's Reports, supra*, 1142. He also cited to *Sparker* v. *Spices* in *Salkeld's Reports* (1689–1712), first published in 1717; for the proposition that the Court should defer to a jury if the evidence is arguable.

The use of English reports on either side to decide the inherent power of a colonial jury certainly must have encouraged Quincy's ambitions to publish a colonial law report. Even more interesting was Trowbridge's citation to "the Case of *Fuller & Clark* at Cambridge," where the jury verdict had been upheld, but where there was "plainly Evidence against Evidence." *Reports*, 85. That case was never reported.

5 · LATER CITATIONS

As Samuel Quincy noted, later Massachusetts law permitted a new trial where "the verdict is clearly against the weight of evidence, although evidence was given on both sides." *Miller* v. *Baker* (1838), 37 Mass. Reports 285, 20 Pickering 285, 289 Mass. (Shaw, C. J.). See *Reports*, 85, S. Quincy n. 4.

More recently, however, the extent to which eighteenth-century common law jury verdicts could be set aside by reviewing judges has taken on much significance. This is because the so-called "Re-Examination" Clause of the Seventh Amendment of the U.S. Constitution provides that "no fact tried by a jury, shall be otherwise re-examined in any court of the United States, than according to the rules of the common law." U.S. Const. Amendment VII. The meaning of this important clause requires knowledge of what the "rules of common law" were at the time the Seventh Amendment was adopted in 1791. Cases like *Angier* v. *Jackson* are important evidence of what these rules were, occurring only 28 years before. For a full review of this importance in the context of two major, and recent, Supreme Court cases, see *Honda Motor Co. Ltd et al.* v. *Oberg*, 512 U. S. 415, 424 (1994), "Brief of Legal Historians Coquillette, Hager, Mann and McEvoy as *Amici Curiae* in Support of Respondent," No. 93–6444, March 31, 1994; *Gasperini* v. *Center for Humanities*, 518 U. S. 415, 432–3 (1996), "Brief of Federal Jurisdiction and Legal History Scholars Amar, Chemerinsky, Coquillette, McEvoy and Miller and of Trial Lawyers for Public Justice as *Amici Curiae* in Support of Petitioner," No. 95–719, March 1, 1996.

6 · NOTE

Even as an advocate for jury power, Auchmuty did not argue for an unlimited power. He stated that "I confess I wish for a Power in the Court to set aside Verdicts, but not for an unlimited one." *Reports*, 84. The Court unanimously agreed, refusing to set aside a verdict "where there is Evidence on both Sides." *Id.*, 85. In the Chief Justice's words, a common law jury verdict should stand unless it were "evidently against Law *and* Evidence." *Id.*, 85. [Italics added.] It should be noted that he used "and," not "or," above, as the key issue was whether there was at least some evidence to support the verdict. This standard remains of great importance in American constitutional cases arising under the Seventh Amendment Re-examination Clause. See Note 5, "Later Citations," *supra*.

ILLUSTRATION 24: Justice Edmund Trowbridge (1709–1793), Justice, Superior Court of Judicature, 1767–1775. See *Appendix 7, infra*. Etching courtesy Supreme Judicial Court of Massachusetts.

CASE 32

POOR
v.
DOBLE.

Rec. 1763.
Fol. 113.

An Action on the Case for a Rescue cannot be brought in a County where the Conspiracy to rescue, but not the Rescue itself, took Place. *One Judge dissenting.*

Poor *vers.* Doble.

POOR brought an Action against one Jutsham, and, it being suggested to the Admiralty that Jutsham was on board a Vessell in the Harbour, the Writ was committed to a Water Bailiff, who entered the Vessell and took him. Doble interposed, went up to Boston, and upon his Return forced the Defendant Jutsham from the Officer and carried him off; upon this the present Action was grounded. There were several Exceptions in Abatement of the Writ taken. The first was, "Not within the Jurisdiction of the Court;" it was said they conspired at Boston, but the Act was done below.(1)

Mr.

---

(1) The declaration set forth the original cause of action, the purchase of the writ, and the subsequent issue of a warrant from the Court of Admiralty, by virtue of which the deputy marshal "went on board the sloop Pompey, being then within the jurisdiction of the said Court of Admiralty, and there found the said Samuel Jutsham and him detained as a prisoner till he should convene him to justice or deliver him to the sheriff of this county or his deputy, that the said writ of attachment might be duly served on him." And it was further alleged that the defendants having conspired and agreed to rescue the prisoner, "in pursuance of the said unlawful conspiracy and agreement," "procured a boat at Boston and went down to the said sloop Pompey, then lying at anchor in Nantasket Bay, so called, about a quarter of a mile from the shore," that they rescued the prisoner, forced the officer to return to Boston without him, and the sloop Pompey to put to sea and carry him off, "whereby the plaintiff hath wholly lost the benefit of the writ of attachment and his debt aforesaid."

The defendants pleaded in abatement "that the said Patrick hath not in said declaration shown forth that the cause of the said action arose within the county of Suffolk;" and the writ was abated "upon the first exception."

[P. 86]

Poor v. *Doble* (1763)
3 George III (Aug.) in the
Superior Court of Judicature

1 · BRIEF DESCRIPTION

Poor had a writ of debt against one Jutsham, who was on board the sloop *Pompey* lying off Nantasket Bay. A warrant was obtained from the Court of Admiralty to arrest Jutsham on the sloop, and a water bailiff duly tried to arrest him aboard the sloop. Allegedly, the Defendant Doble, with others, got a boat in Boston, went out to the *Pompey*, and forced the water bailiff to return without his prisoner. The *Pompey* then put to sea with Jutsham, a good escape from the creditor, Poor.

The creditor Poor now sues Doble in tort in Suffolk County (i.e., Boston) for procuring the escape, claiming that he, Poor, was a victim of a conspiracy that arose in Boston. Held, 3 to 1 with the Chief Justice dissenting, that the cause of action arose from the rescue, not the conspiracy, and the rescue was outside the jurisdiction of a court in Suffolk County.

2 · RECORD

Available at Rec. 1763, fol. 113. The declaration is of particular intent. See *Reports*, 86, S. Quincy n. 1.

3 · PROFESSIONALS INVOLVED

Quincy's pupil master, Oxenbridge Thacher (1719–1765), argued for the writ being good. His mentor and John Adams's pupil master, Jeremy Gridley (1701/2–1767), the informal dean of the bar, argued for the other side, and won. See brief biographies in *Appendix 6*.

The split Court was given as "3 vs. 1." The dissenter appears to be the Chief Justice. See the discussion at Note 6, *infra*. Given that the potential jurisdiction of the Vice Admiralty Court was also questioned, it is possible that Chamber Russell recused himself, because he served concurrently as the judge of the Vice Admiralty Court. For a similar conflict, see *Scollay* v. *Dunn*, *Reports*, 74, Case 30, *supra*.

4 · AUTHORITY

None cited.

Mr. Thacher, in ſupport of the Writ ſaid, that the former Writ was ſaid to be purchaſed in Boſton, Complaint made there, Warrant procured there and Contrivance there.

Ch. Juſt. If Conſpiracy be in one County and Reſcous in another, could the Courts in both have Juriſdiction?

Mr. Gridley. Juriſdiction of inferiour Courts muſt be ſhewn. This is a Court of a limited Juriſdiction; they have ſhewn the Conſpiracy to be within, but 'tis the Reſcue, and not Conſpiracy, which is the Cauſe of Action.

Writ abated, 3 *vs.* 1. (2)

---

(2) It appears to have been aſſumed that a civil action for a reſcue was local, and could only be brought in the county where the cauſe of action or ſome part thereof aroſe, and the deciſion was ſimply to the point that a conſpiracy alone within a county was not ſufficient to authorize the action to be brought there. No queſtion of admiralty juriſdiction could have ariſen, becauſe even if a ſhip "in Nantaſket Bay a quarter of a mile from ſhore" was not *infra corpus comitatus*, (12 Met. 387,) yet of torts upon the high ſea the common law had concurrent juriſdiction. 2 Gallis. 422.

For a ſomewhat analogous deciſion in a caſe in which the locality of the tort was the limit of juriſdiction, ſee *Adams* v. *Haſſard*, 20 Pick. 127, where it was held, that an impriſonment on ſhore, in purſuance of orders given on the high ſea, did not conſtitute a cauſe of action within admiralty juriſdiction.

But whether an action on the caſe againſt reſcuers is local at common law, *quære*. An action of eſcape againſt the officer is tranſitory. Bac. Ab. Eſcape, F. 2 Chit. Pl. (6th Am. Ed.) 736, 737, & note (d).

5 · LATER CITATIONS

Samuel Quincy questioned whether this case was correctly decided, citing both contemporary and later authority that "an action on the case against rescuers" is not "local at common law" but "transitory." See *Reports*, 87, S. Quincy n. 2. As Samuel Quincy further noted, *Bacon's Abridgement*, a favorite of the contemporary Massachusetts bar and first published in London in 1736, made the same argument under "Escape, F." The corollary assertion, that imprisonment on shore pursuant to high seas orders was not within the Admiralty jurisdiction, is quite distinguishable. See *Adams* v. *Haffard*, 37 Mass. 127, 20 Pickering 127 (1838). The Admiralty jurisdiction was strictly limited to high seas matters, whereas the common law had concurrent jurisdiction with the Admiralty of torts upon the high seas, as Samuel Quincy observed. Samuel Quincy also offers the example from a later case of a ship 'in Nantasket Bay a quarter of a mile from shore' "that was not judged *infra corpus comitatus* [i.e., "within the body of the county," as opposed to the high seas]." See *Commonwealth* v. *Henry Peters*, 53 Mass. 387, 12 Met. 387 (1847). Even in this situation, Samuel Quincy argued, concurrent tort jurisdiction would lie. See *Reports*, 87, S. Quincy n. 2.

6 · NOTE

As a matter of law, the Chief Justice was right when he asked "If Conspiracy be in one County and Rescous (Rescue) in another, could the Courts in both have Jurisdiction?" *Reports*, 87. Indeed, why not? In this case, the rescue was certainly within the Court's concurrent tort jurisdiction with Admiralty. So why three votes to abate Poor's writ?

Readers of today's Patrick O'Brian novels about seamen of Quincy's time get a sense of the public sympathy for certain debtors. There was clearly a story behind this Declaration and the rescue itself. The majority of the Court was probably happy to duck this case, relying on Gridley's artful argument that, "'tis the Rescue, and not Conspiracy, which is the Cause of Action." *Reports*, 87. Better use of contemporary authority by Thacher, such as arguing from the favorable provisions of that reliable "stand by," *Bacon's Abridgement*, *supra*, might have changed the Court's mind.

CASE 33

LOVELL *v.* DOBLE.

Lovell *verſ.* Doble.

Rec. 1765. Fol. 129.

THIS was for the ſame Cauſe, and the Declaration was the ſame.

Exceptions to the Declaration ſhould be taken by Special Demurrer, and not by Plea in Abatement.

Firſt Exception was, that it was not alledged in the Declaration that they ſet forth to the Admiralty that Jutſham had abſconded and concealed himſelf on board ſome Veſſell from the Service of the Writ.

A Plea in Abatement to the Declaration, which does not point out a better Declaration, cannot be ſupported as in the Nature of a Special Demurrer.

Second Exception. They have not alledged that the Admiralty had Juriſdiction of the Matter of ſaid Complaint. *Given up.*

Auchmuty. Theſe Pleas are all negative; they find Fault with this, but do not point out a better. Pleas muſt be certain—not ſupported by Argument or Implication. 3 Doct. Plac. 54.

Gridley. They are defective in a material Point in their Declaration, your Honours will not ſupport it; our firſt Plea being over, and having been argued upon in Subſtance, they are too late to take Exceptions to this.

Auchmuty. The firſt Plea had no Exception to Form, but Subſtance; they are all ſeparate and diſtinct. All they verify is, that we have not done ſo and ſo—they do not verify it to be neceſſary. As for conſidering theſe Pleas as Special Demurrers, I think it cannot be intended here. He muſt conform to Rules of Abatement, and cannot avail himſelf

Lovell v. *Doble* (1763)
3 George III (Aug.) in the
Superior Court of Judicature

1 · BRIEF DESCRIPTION

This is the same case as the last, *Poor* v. *Doble*, Case 32, with the same Declaration as set out at *Reports*, 86, S. Quincy n. 1. It is a pleading squabble about whether an action for causing an escape of a debtor from an arrest by the water bailiff off Nantasket could be heard in Suffolk County. The case for jurisdiction apparently was that the escape was within the traditional Admiralty jurisdiction, and thus could be heard in Suffolk. Here, the lawyers for the Defendant, seeking to evade the jurisdiction, raise two more pleading exceptions, i.e., 1) that the Plaintiff's Declaration did not set forth that the escaped debtor "concealed himself on board the Vessel" and 2) did not allege that "the Admiralty had Jurisdiction." *Reports*, 89–90. A "Declaration" was a statement of claim, the first pleading delivered by a Plaintiff. It included the cause of action, the purchase of the writ and in this case, the Admiralty warrant to the Deputy Marshall. See *Reports*, 89, S. Quincy n. 1. Both of these exceptions were rejected by the Court, which nevertheless found no jurisdiction for the rather weak reasons stated in *Reports*, 86, Case 32, *supra*.

2 · RECORD

Available at Rec. 1765, Fol. 125.

3 · PROFESSIONALS INVOLVED

As in Case 32, Jeremy Gridley (1701/2–1767) was in opposition to the writ and Declaration. Now he is joined by Samuel Fitch (1724–1799), who will become Advocate General of the Admiralty (1768–1776).

Oxenbridge Thacher (1718–1765), who argued for the validity of the writ in Case 32, has been replaced by Robert Auchmuty (1723–1788), who will become Advocate General of the Admiralty (1762–1767) and then Judge of the Massachusetts Vice Admiralty Court (1767–1776). He is joined by the great patriot James Otis, Jr. (1725–1783), who served as Advocate General of the Admiralty from 1756 to 1760. The two opponents with the special admiralty experience,

ſelf of what he might upon Special Demurrer; in Demurrer it might have been final againſt them, but in Abatement they plead over.

Fitch. Abatement is regularly to the Writ; Exceptions to Form of Declaration is by Special Demurrer. Here they are generally taken in Abatement, not at Home, therefore we ought not to be taken up for conforming: However there are Inſtances of the like Pleas in Abatement; Lilly Ent. p. 9, Tit. Abatement; and many other Inſtances in Special Demurrer where the Plea is negative without pointing out a better. Lilly, Tit. Demurrer, 106, 186. (1)

Gridley. Theſe Pleas are in the Nature of Special Demurrer, but according to Cuſtom we have concluded in Abatement. When we have ſaid that there is an Omiſſion, do they ſay Anything new? Will your Honours go on with a Writ materially faulty, becauſe we have not pointed out?

Otis. They might have demurred, but have choſen Abatement, and ſo have entitled themſelves to all the Disfavour of Abatement.

Ch. Juſt. Plea in Abatement muſt be to the Writ, not Declaration. (2)

Otis.

---

(1) See 6 Pick. 369, *Wilde, J.*—"The exceptions to this rule [that the plea muſt give a better writ] are ſo numerous that it can hardly be called a general rule of law."

(2) A plea in abatement which concluded to the writ and declaration has been ſuſtained, on the ground that ſo much of the declaration as

12 would

Fitch and Auchmuty, will both be proscribed in 1778. See the brief biographies in *Appendix 6.*

Why were the two advocacy teams "beefed up" by lawyers with a special admiralty interest? If the purpose was to improve the initial attack on the writ and Declaration, it was of little value. The two new exceptions were weak, and quickly rejected.

4 · AUTHORITY

This is a pleading struggle. In arguing that attacks on the writ must "point out a better," Auchmuty relied on the old text *Doctrina Placitandi; or the art and science of pleading* (vol. 3, 54), written by "S.E." (Sampson Ever) and published in London in 1677. See *Sweet & Maxwell, supra*, vol. 1, 268:58. Fitch countered with "many other Instances in Special Demurrer where the Plea is negative without pointing out a better," pointing to *Lilly's Collection of Modern Entries*, 9, title "Abatement," and to pages 106 and 186, title "Demurrer," of *Lilly's Entries*, which reported "Select Pleading" in the common law courts and was published in Latin in 1723 and 1741, and then in English in 1741 and 1758. See *Sweet & Maxwell, supra*, vol. 1, 273:97. Quincy used *Lilly's Entries* in his *Law Commonplace*, 38, n.5, and he owned a copy at his death. See his *Estate Catalogue*, no. 24, set out in *Appendix 8.*

5 · LATER CITATIONS

This case was never cited by the Supreme Judicial Court. The one statement of law set out, the Chief Justice's view that a "Pleas in Abatement must be to Writ, not Declaration," was rejected by *Ilsley* v. *Stubbs*, 5 Mass. 280, 285 (1809), as Samuel Quincy points out. *Reports*, 89–90, S. Quincy n. 2. Later Massachusetts pleadings permitted a plea is abatement to both together, on the sensible ground that "so much of the declaration as would be necessary to make a perfect writ, is a part of the writ. . . ." *Id.*, 89–90, n. 2. *Ilsley* v. *Stubbs*, *supra*, at 585.

6 · NOTE

The most interesting argument, in this technical squabble, was Fitch's answer to Auchmuty's argument that the opposition to the Declaration should have been by special Demurrer, rather than pleas in abatement, because only the

Otis. They may plead Matter of Fact in Abatement.

Exception not well taken.

Another Plea in Abatement was that they had not alledged the Admiralty to have had Jurisdiction of the Matter of the Complaint. Salk. 404, Tit. Jurisdiction.

Fitch. They have not alledged they had any Cause of Complaint to the Admiralty. Hobart, 129.

Auchmuty. We have set forth that he was concealed within their Jurisdiction. (3)

---

would be necessary to make a perfect writ, is a part of the writ, and may be excepted to in abatement. *Ilsley* v. *Stubbs*, 5 Mass. 285.

(3) The second exception was given up, and the case entered "Neither Party."

former are appropriate to attack a Declaration, rather than the writ. Fitch, Auchmuty, and Otis further argued that pleas in abatement must point out a better writ, and that having "chosen Abatement" the opposition "have entitled themselves to all the Disfavour of Abatement." *Reports*, 89. Fitch pointed out that "Here" exception to the Declaration "are generally taken in Abatement," not "at Home" (i.e., England). Thus, "we ought not to be taken up for conforming." *Reports*, 89. Chief Justice Hutchinson rejects this "colonial practice" argument out of hand, "Plea in Abatement must be to the Writ, not Declaration." *Reports*, 89.

Technical pleading arguments, now abolished by "notice pleading" systems such as the Federal Rules of Civil Procedure of 1934, were a mystery to lay people and an arcane specialty of the common law bar. The Superior Court, as in *Reports*, 86, Case 32, frequently reached results with little regard for technicalities, but the Chief Justice was not going to permit local pleading errors to become official practice "Here," i.e., in the Commonwealth, as opposed to "Home," i.e., England. In any event, both pleading exceptions were rejected, although the creditor still lost, for the reason given in *Reports*, 86, Case 32.

CASE 34

REX *v.* DOAKS.

Rec. 1763. Fol. 110.

In Support of an Indictment for keeping a Bawdy House, Evidence of Acts of Lasciviousness by the Defendant while a Lodger, and before she was Mistress of the House, is inadmissible.

On Trial of an Indict-

Dom. Rex *vers.* Doaks.

DOAKS was indicted before the Sessions for keeping a Bawdy House, found guilty there and fined; from thence she appealed, and it appeared that Part of the Time she was indicted for, she was only a Lodger, and not Mistress of the House.

The King's Attorney offered to give Evidence of some Acts of Lasciviousness before the Time in which

Dom. Rex v. *Doaks* (1763)
3 George III (Aug.) in the
Superior Court of Judicature

1 · BRIEF DESCRIPTION

Doaks was indicted for keeping a Bawdy House and was convicted. She appealed because "for part of the Time she was Indicted for, she was only a Lodger, and not Mistress of the House." The Court agreed that there was a defect in the indictment, and that additional evidence of Doaks's "lasciviousness" before when she was proved "Mistress of the House" was not admissible to remedy the defect. Nor was proof of "general ill Character" admissible, as the Defense had not put her character in issue. *Reports*, 91.

2 · RECORD

Available at Rec. 1763, fol. 110.

3 · PROFESSIONALS INVOLVED

The King's attorney, John Worthington (1719–1800), was the prosecutor. See brief biography in *Appendix 6*. There may have been no one for the defense, but the arguments are sophisticated.

4 · AUTHORITY

None cited.

5 · LATER CITATIONS

As Samuel Quincy noted, this case was good later Massachusetts law. Character evidence cannot be introduced by a prosecutor unless "the defendant has voluntarily put his character in issue." *Commonwealth* v. *Hardy*, 2 Mass. 318 (1807) (Parsons, C. J.). *Rex* v. *Doaks* was cited with approval in *Commonwealth* v. *Kozlowsky*, 238 Mass. 379 (1921), where the question was raised whether the Attorney General, or his assistant, may be present in his official capacity during grand jury deliberations. Proof of the Attorney General's chief role as prosecuting officer during the provincial period was shown by the King's Attorney's appearance in court in this case, and the court cited *Rex* v. *Doaks*,

which ſhe was proved to have been Miſtreſs of the Houſe. He ſaid it was by Way of Inducement, but *the Court ruled*, that no Evidence before ought to be admitted.

ment for keeping a Bawdy Houſe, Evidence of the Defendant's general Character is inadmiſſible for the Government, until the Defendant has attempted to ſupport it.

He likewiſe offered to prove her of general ill Character, but *the Court*, on that Point too, *ruled*, that he could not enter into that, before the other Side attempted to ſupport it. (1)

The Jury, by Direction of the Court, brought in their Verdict "*Not Guilty*."

---

(1) S. P. *Commonwealth* v. *Hardy*, 2 Maſs. 318, *Parſons*, *C. J.*—"It is not competent for the proſecutor to go into this inquiry until the defendant has voluntarily put his character in iſſue."

Reports, 90. See also, *Dom. Rex* v. *Mangent* (1765), *Reports*, 162, (Case 44), where the Attorney General appeared. The case was also cited by the Supreme Court of the United States in *Marshall* v. *Lonberger*, 459 U.S. 422, 448 (1983) by Justice Stevens, in dissent, as an example of how the common law deemed it unfair to consider past crimes when determining the probability of whether a person committed a similar crime later. See *Appendix 5*, *infra*.

6 · NOTE

This case is of obvious sociological interest, and provides an insight into efforts to control colonial prostitution. More important is the Court's careful concern for the law of evidence, even in a case such as this, and for specificity in indictments. It was no good for the King's Attorney to try to remedy a defective indictment by later offering to introduce evidence of bad character or lewd behavior. *Reports*, 90–91.

CASE 35

Dom. Rex *verſ.* Gay.

Rex *v.* Gay.

Rec. 1763. Fol. 132.

A Juſtice has no Power to iſſue a Capias to bring before him a Perſon charged with Neglect in mending Highways.

A Warrant irregular on its Face is no Juſtification of the Officer.

GAY was indicted for aſſaulting and beating the Sheriff in the due Execution of his Office. The Caſe appeared to be this: Gay by Virtue of the Province Law relative to Highways, 5 W. & M. c. 8, & 11 G. 1, c. 3, (2) was warned to mend the Highways, and upon Complaint to a Juſtice that he had neglected his Duty therein, the Juſtice made out a Warrant to bring Gay before him to anſwer for

(2) The proviſions of theſe ſtatutes are that in caſe of neglect "upon complaint and proof thereof before the next juſtice of the peace, without reaſonable excuſe made, and allowed by ſuch juſtice, he ſhall cauſe to be levied of every ſuch offender's goods the ſum or penalty of two ſhillings and ſixpence," &c. Anc. Chart. 268, 440.

Dom. Rex v. *Gay* (1763)
3 George III (Aug.) in the
Superior Court of Judicature

1 · BRIEF DESCRIPTION

The Defendant, Gay, concededly assaulted the Sheriff when the latter tried to arrest Gay for failing to "mend the Highways," as required by the Province Laws. The arrest was pursuant to a defective warrant issued by a Justice. The sole issue was whether that warrant, which was illegal on its face, could be given in evidence of the Sheriff's right to arrest Gay. In a 3-to-2 split decision, the Court held that an illegal warrant could not be admitted. Gay was, therefore, acquitted, because the Sheriff had "made the first assault." *Reports*, 92.

2 · RECORD

Available at Rec. 1763. Fol. 132.

3 · PROFESSIONALS INVOLVED

James Otis, Jr. (1725–1783), the patriot, appeared for the Defendant, Gay. Oxenbridge Thacher (1719–1765), Quincy's pupil master, appeared for the Sheriff. Comparing Thacher with Otis, John Adams observed, "Thacher has not the same strength and elasticity; he is sensible but slow of conception and communication; he is queer and affected. . . ." See "Thacher," *Appendix 6*.

There was no indication which of the three Justices were against admitting the warrant, and which were "doubtful." Closely split decisions were rare, and those with no reasons noted, even more scarce. See *Appendix 1*.

4 · AUTHORITY

Otis invoked William Hawkins's multi-volume *Pleas of the Crown*. Published in London in 1716–21, 1724–26, 1739 and 1762, this treatise was one of the most commonly invoked authorities in England and the colonies on criminal law. See *Sweet & Maxwell*, vol. 1, 362–363:37. Quincy referred to it in the *Law Commonplace*, see [35], n. 5. He also owned a copy at his death. Catalogue of Estate, n. 23, *Appendix 8*. The correct citation is to vol. 2, 81 of the first edition (1721), and Samuel Quincy, note 4 is erroneous. The section discussed unauthorized arrest by officers, but does not directly support Otis's position.

for the Neglect. Dean, the Sheriff, having the Warrant, took Gay, who refcued himfelf and beat the Sheriff. The Queftion was, whether that Warrant fhould be given as Evidence of Dean's Right to take Gay, the Affault being confeffed and juftified.

Otis. The Juftice had no Right to iffue a Capias in this Cafe, and if fo, Dean made the firft Affault. A Warrant from an inferiour Court is lefs refpected than from a fuperiour, yet even a Warrant iffuing from this Court, illegally, would be a Trefpafs in the Perfon granting, and alfo in the Perfon executing it. It falls within that Rule, that the Officer executes at his Peril. This Court will not iffue previous Procefs againft the Body, when Execution can only go againft the Goods; this is the Reafon why original Summons iffues againft Executors and Adminiftrators and Truftees of abfconding Debtors. Difference between this Cafe and that of Affeffors who have Authority of the Perfon. (3) Every Officer is bound to know what is within the Jurifdiction of the Court. Hawkins's Plea, 81. (4)

Thacher. The Juftice has a Right to convene, and this Capias iffued for that Purpofe, &c.

Warrant not admitted, (5) 3 Judges againft it, 2 doubtful. In Confequence of this,

Defendant acquitted.

N. B.

---

(3) Prov. Law, 4 G 2, Anc. Chart. 477. Gen. Sts. c. 12, § 13. 8 Met. 102.

(4) 1 Hawk. c. 10, § 4.

(5) An illegal warrant is a juftification only when regular on its face, and

Samuel Quincy noted that Thacher "says that in a Case at Barnstable" the Chief Justice held "an irregular Warrant might be admitted in Justification," and that the Court was wrong in this case. The case was *Bassett* v. *Mayhew*, May Term, 1763. See *Reports*, 93, S. Quincy n. 6. It is unclear if Thacher cited the case to the Court in the later *Gay* case. If so, the majority paid no attention.

5 · LATER CITATIONS

None. Later Massachusetts cases held that an illegal warrant is justification "only when regular on its face and apparently within the jurisdiction of the court or magistrate issuing it." *Fisher* v. *McGirr*, 67 Mass. (1 *Gray*) 1, 45 (1854); *Clark* v. *May*, 68 Mass. (2 *Gray*) 410, 413 (1854). See *Reports*, 92–93, S. Quincy n. 5.

6 · NOTE

The Superior Court was very careful about the right of defendants who resisted irregular arrests. See also *Poor* v. *Doble* (1763), *Reports*, 86, Case 32. Beating police who come with illegal warrants is not recommended today. See, e.g., *Commonwealth* v. *Gomes*, 59 Mass. App. Ct. 332 (2003) (absent the use of unnecessary force by police on his person, an individual may not forcibly resist even an unlawful entry into his residence by one who he knows or has good reason to believe is a police officer engaged in the performance of his duties); see also *Commonwealth* v. *Moreira*, 388 Mass. 596 (1983).

N. B. Mr. Thacher ſays that in a Caſe at Barnſtable (*Mayhew & Wadſworth,*) the *Ch. Juſt. held*, an irregular Warrant might be admitted in Juſtification of the Officer, and that the Court were wrong in the Caſe of Gay on the other Side. (6)

---

and apparently within the juriſdiction of the court or magiſtrate iſſuing it. *Fiſher* v. *McGirr*, 1 Gray, 45. *Clark* v. *May*, 2 Gray, 410, 413.

(6) The caſe referred to is *Cornelius Baſſett* v. *Wadſworth Mayhew & al.* May Term 1763, which was an action of treſpaſs for ſhooting the plaintiff, a deputy ſheriff, in the leg, while he was endeavoring to arreſt the defendant by virtue of the following warrant:

"Dukes County ſs: To the Sherriff of ſaid County, his Under Sher-"riff or Deputy, Greeting. Whereas Robert Allen of Chill-
[SEAL.] "mark in ſaid County, Gent[n]. Has this Day appeared before "the Juſtices of our Lord the King at His Majeſty's Court of "General Seſſ:[s] of The Peace, and made Complaint That he being in "the Execution of his office as Corroner, at the Houſe of Zacheus "Mayhew Eſq in Chillmark in the County aforeſaid: Lawfully au "thorized by a Mittimus to carry one Jeruſha Mayhew to his Majeſty's "Goal in Edgartown in ſaid County, he was there oppoſed in his ſaid "Office by one Wadſworth Mayhew of ſaid Chillmark by violently "ſeizing the body of the ſaid Jeruſha & holding her, and Prevented his "Carrying ſaid Jeruſha to his Majeſty's Goal: Which Doings of ſaid "Wadſworth is Contrary to Law, &c. Theſe are therefore in His "Majeſty's Name, To Require You or Either of You forthwith to "take the Body of the ſaid Wadſworth (if he may be found in your "Precinct), Againſt all Oppoſition to enter any Houſe where you ſhall "ſuſpect him ſaid Wadſworth to be, & to bring him forthwith before "the Juſtices of Our Lord the King at his Majeſty's Court of Gen[ral] "Seſſ:[s] of the Peace now Sitting in Seſſ:[s] at Tiſbury: So that he may "be Dealt with According to Law in the Premiſes. Hereof fail not "& make Return of this Writ with your Doings therein into ſ'd Court.

"Dated at Tiſbury The 26th Day of Octo[r]. Anno Dom: 1762 & In "the Third Year of his Majeſty's Reign.

"Per Order of Court

"JAMES ATHEARN *Cler.*"

[P. 93]

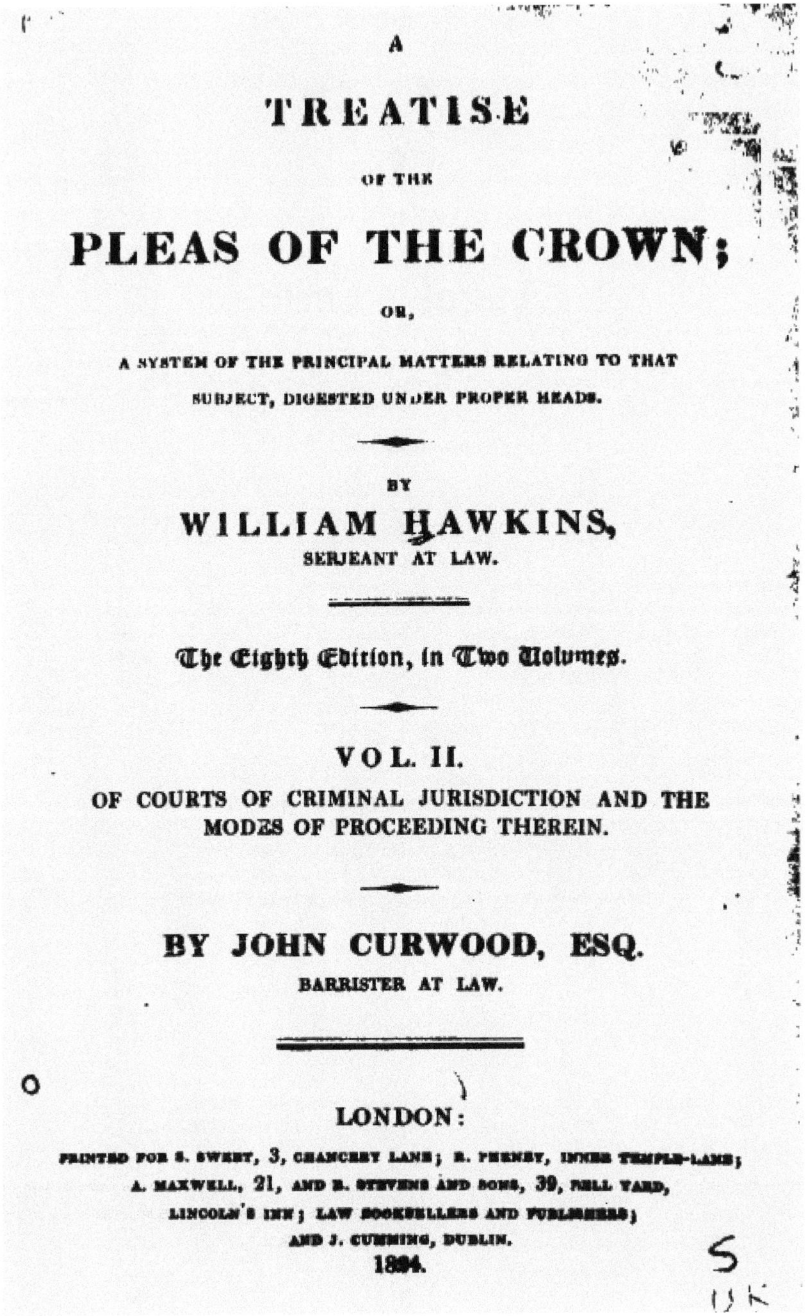

A

TREATISE

OF THE

PLEAS OF THE CROWN;

OR,

A SYSTEM OF THE PRINCIPAL MATTERS RELATING TO THAT SUBJECT, DIGESTED UNDER PROPER HEADS.

BY

WILLIAM HAWKINS,

SERJEANT AT LAW.

The Eighth Edition, in Two Volumes.

VOL. II.

OF COURTS OF CRIMINAL JURISDICTION AND THE MODES OF PROCEEDING THEREIN.

BY JOHN CURWOOD, ESQ.

BARRISTER AT LAW.

LONDON:

PRINTED FOR S. SWEET, 3, CHANCERY LANE; R. PHENEY, INNER TEMPLE-LANE; A. MAXWELL, 21, AND R. STEVENS AND SONS, 39, BELL YARD, LINCOLN'S INN; LAW BOOKSELLERS AND PUBLISHERS; AND J. CUMMING, DUBLIN.

1824.

ILLUSTRATION 25: William Hawkins, *Pleas of the Crown*, Book 2 (London, 1721). See citations to this volume in *Dom. Rex* v. *Gay* (1763), *Reports*, 91 (Case 35) and *Dom. Rex* v. *Pourksdorff* (1764), *Reports*, 104 (Case 38). This was a major authority on criminal law for colonial lawyers.

CASE 36

Auguſt Term

IV Georgii Ter. in Sup. Cur.

Preſent:

The Honourable

Thomas Hutchinſon, Eſqr., Chief Juſtice.
John Cuſhing, Peter Oliver, } Eſqrs., Juſtices.

1764.
ALLISON *v.* COCKRAN.

Rec. 1764. Fol. 103.

Adminiſtrators are incompetent Witneſſes in Matters affecting the Eſtate of their Inteſtate, except where ſuch Eſtate is inſolvent.
The Report of the Commiſſioners is the only legal Evidence of ſuch Inſolvency

Alliſon *verſ.* Cockran.

TROVER* for a Negro. (1) The Adminiſtratrix of one Cockran, (Father-in-Law to the Defendant,)

* *Qu.* if this Action is well brought, for Trover lies not for a Negro. 2 Salk. 666. Ld. Raym. 1274, 146. Caſes in the Time of Holt, 495.

---

(1) In 1677, the Court of King's Bench, conſiſting of *Rainsford, C. J., Twiſden, Wild & Jones, JJ.*, expreſſed an opinion that trover would lie for negroes, who had been found, by ſpecial verdict, to be "infidels," and "uſually bought and ſold in America," [or, as other reporters have it, "in India,"] "as merchandiſe, by the cuſtom of merchants." *Butts* v. *Penny*, 2 Lev. 201; 3 Keb. 785; Freem. 452. But the record ſhows that the negroes in that caſe were "in India;" 20 Howell's State Trials, 52; and the deciſion, as reported by Freeman, was put upon

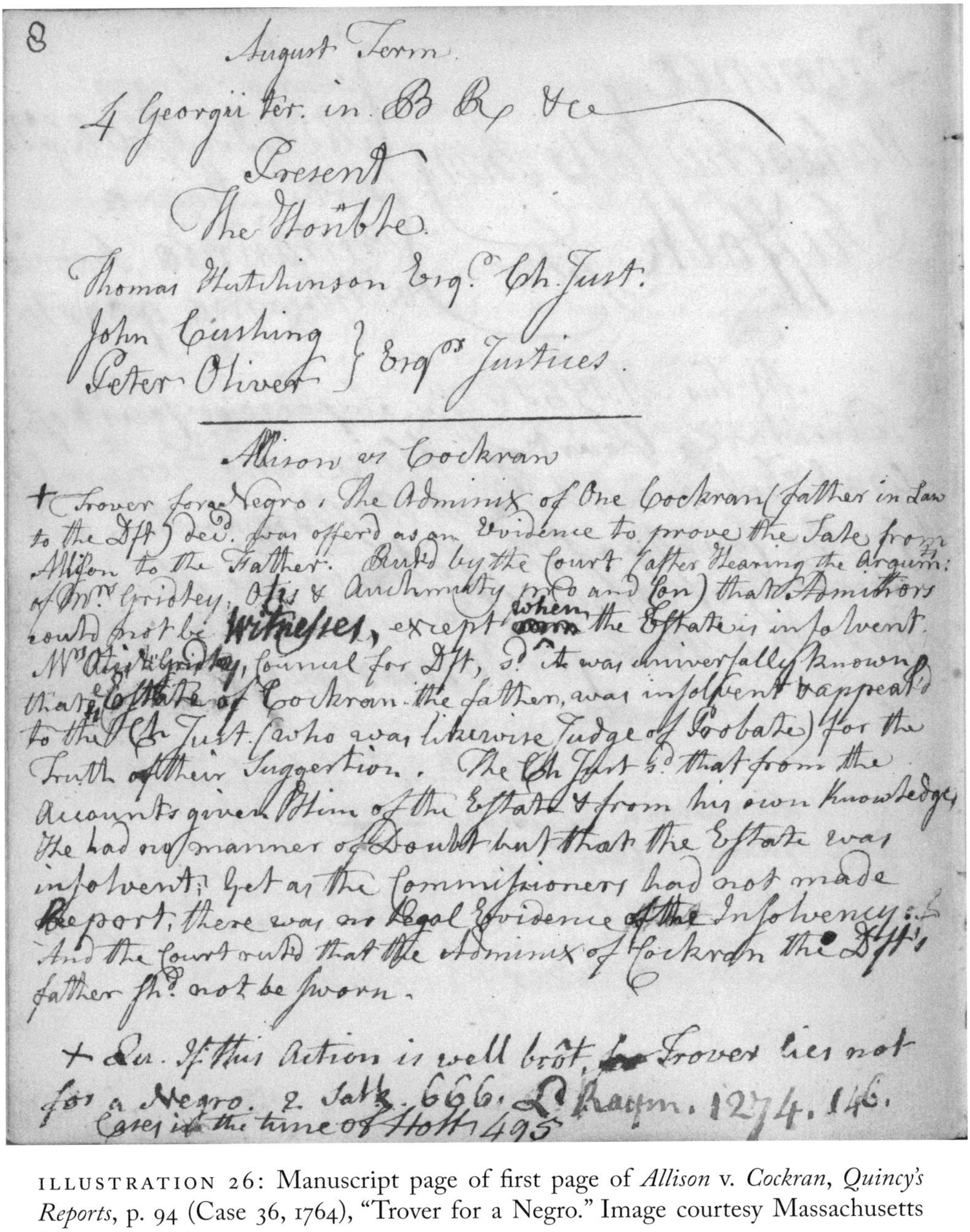

8 August Term.

4 Georgii Ter. in B R &c

Present

The Honble.

Thomas Hutchinson Esqr. Ch. Just.

John Cushing } Esqrs. Justices
Peter Oliver }

Allison vs Cockran

+ Trover for a Negro. The Adminx of One Cockran (Father in Law to the Dft) decd. was offerd as an Evidence to prove the Sale from Allison to the Father. Ruled by the Court (after Hearing the Argumt. of Mrs. Gridley, Otis & Auchmuty pro and Con) that Admitors could not be witnesses, except when the Estate is insolvent. Mr. Gridley, Counsel for Dft, sd. it was universally known that the Estate of Cockran the father, was insolvent & appeald to the Ch. Just. (who was likewise Judge of Probate) for the Truth of their Suggestion. The Ch. Just sd. that from the Accounts given Him of the Estate & from his own knowledge, He had no manner of Doubt but that the Estate was insolvent; yet as the Commissioners had not made Report, there was no legal Evidence of the Insolvency: And the Court ruled that the Adminx of Cockran the Dft's father shd. not be sworn.

+ Qu. If this Action is well brot, Trover lies not for a Negro. 2 Salk. 666. L Raym. 1274. 146. Cases in the time of Holt 495

ILLUSTRATION 26: Manuscript page of first page of *Allison* v. *Cockran*, *Quincy's Reports*, p. 94 (Case 36, 1764), "Trover for a Negro." Image courtesy Massachusetts Historical Society.

Defendant,) deceafed, was offered as an Evidence to prove the Sale from Allifon to the Father. *Ruled*

which can eftablifh the Competency of the Administrator.

Whether Trover lies for a Negro — *quære.*

---

upon that ground only — " Held *per Curiam*, that although by the law with us a man cannot have an abfolute property in the body of another, yet the cuftom of India concerning buying and felling of flaves being found, a trover and converfion would lie well enough." Freem. 452. This does not appear to have been known to the fucceffors of thofe judges, (Freeman's Reports not being yet published,) when they " denied the opinion in the cafe of *Butts & Penny.*" 2 Ld. Raym. 1275.

In the fame court in 1680, *Dolben, J.*, faid that trover, brought by one tenant in common " for half a negro," " has been allowed." 2 Show. 177. But it does not appear where that negro was. The decifion referred to may have been in *Butts* v. *Penny, ub. fup.*, which is reported by Keble as " trover of 10 negroes and a half;" 3 Keb. 785; (although the record of that cafe only mentions ten; 20 Howell's State Trials, 51, note;) or, more probably, the cafe thus quoted in the Court of Chancery in 1687: " *Mr. Sergeant Maynard's cafe* was cited, who recovered a debt contracted here againft the executor of an owner of a plantation in Barbadoes, and by his advice an action of trover was brought, and judgment obtained for the fourth part of a negro." 1 Vern. 453.

In 1689, Lord *Holt, & Rokeby & Turton, JJ.*, (three of the four judges who afterwards decided *Chamberlain* v. *Harvey, infra*,) joined in an opinion, given to the King and Council, that negroes were merchandife in the colonies. 1 Burge Col. & For. Laws, 736, note.

It is faid to have been afterwards adjudged in the Common Bench that trover will lie for negroes. *Gelly* v. *Cleve*, (1693,) 1 Ld. Raym. 147, *ex rel.* Place. 3 Lev. 337. But it muft be prefumed that thofe negroes too were in the colonies; for if they were in England, the decifion is inconfiftent with a feries of cafes in the King's Bench, (cited in Quincy's note, *fupra*, 94,) by which it was very foon afterwards eftablifhed as the law of England, that " as foon as a negro comes into England, he becomes free; one may be a villein in England, but not a flave." 2 Salk. 666; Caf. temp. Holt, 495.

In thofe cafes, it was held, that trefpafs would not lie for taking a negro in England, without declaring (as in the cafe of the taking away of any other fervant) *per quod fervitium amifit*; *Chamberlain* v. *Harvey*, (1696,) 1 Ld. Raym. 146; 3 Ib. 129; 5 Mod. 182, 186; Carth. 397: Nor *indebitatus affumpfit* for the price of a negro, without averring that at the time of the fale he was in a country by the laws of which he might be fold as a chattel; *Smith* v. *Brown*, 2 Salk. 666; Caf. temp. Holt, 495: Nor trover. *Smith* v. *Gould*, (1706,) 2 Ld.

Allison v. *Cockran* (1764)
4 George III (Aug.) in the
Superior Court of Judicature

1 · BRIEF DESCRIPTION

The case was argued on the narrow issue of whether the administratrix to the Defendant's father's estate could certify that a negro had been sold by the Plaintiff to the Defendant's father. Administrators were only competent witnesses when the estate was insolvent. Although the Chief Justice had personal knowledge of insolvency, the only legal evidence that the estate was insolvent was a Commissioners' Report, and that had not yet been received.

The larger significance of the case was that it was an action in "trover for a negro." Trover, from the French "trouver," to find, was a common law action to recover the value of goods that had been wrongfully converted. See J. H. Baker, *An Introduction to English Legal History*, *supra*, 397–399. Josiah Quincy noted, "*Qu* [*quare*, query], if this Action is well brought, for Trover lies not for a Negro," citing English authorities. Whether Massachusetts permitted such an action for a human being was a most important issue. This implies that such actions were permitted, whereas Josiah Quincy's queries argue that they were not. In a long note, Samuel Quincy argued that the Court was right. *Reports*, 94–98, S. Quincy n. 1.

2 · COURT RECORDS

Available at Rec. 1764, Fol. 103.

3 · PROFESSIONALS INVOLVED

Robert Auchmuty (1723–1788) appeared for the Plaintiff. Jeremy Gridley (1701/2–1767), the acknowledged "Dean" of the bar, and the patriot James Otis, Jr. (1725–1783) appeared for the defense. See biographies at *Appendix 6*.

4 · AUTHORITY

None cited.

5 · LATER CITATIONS

None cited.

Ruled by the Court, (after hearing the Arguments of *Meſſrs. Gridley, Otis & Auckmuty, pro & con,*) that Adminiſtrators

---

Ld. Raym. 1274; 2 Salk. 666. That the converſion alleged in the laſt caſe was in England is manifeſt from the grounds given for the deciſion by Lord *Holt* — "The common law takes no notice of negroes being different from other men. By the common law no man can have a property in another, but in ſpecial caſes, as in a villein," &c. "There is no ſuch thing as a ſlave by the law of England." 2 Ld. Raym. 1274, 1275. The ſtatement at the end of Salkeld's report of this caſe — "the Court ſeemed to think that in treſpaſs *quare captivum ſuum cepit* the plaintiff might give evidence that the party was his negro and he bought him" — appears to be an unwarranted inference of the reporter, inconſiſtent with Lord Raymond's report, and with the caſe of *Chamberlain* v. *Harvey, ub. ſup.*

There is no Engliſh adjudication ſince, which conflicts with theſe deciſions of Lord *Holt*. In *Pearne* v. *Liſle*, (1749,) Ambl. 75, Lord *Hardwicke* refuſed a writ of *ne exeat* againſt one who owed the plaintiff for the hire of certain negroes, upon the ground that it was a legal demand on which the defendant might be arreſted at law, ſaying: "As to the nature of the demand, it is for the uſe of negroes; a man may hire the ſervant of another, whether he be a ſlave or not, and will be bound to ſatisfy the maſter for the uſe of him." This paſſage accords with the ſuggeſtion in *Chamberlain* v. *Harvey, ub. ſup.*, that treſpaſs *per quod ſervitium amiſit* might be maintained in England for enticing away a ſlave; and concluſively ſhows that, even if the writ of *ne exeat* had been granted, the caſe would have involved no deciſion of the queſtion of what property one might have in a negro. The additional remark of the Lord Chancellor — "I have no doubt that trover will lie for a negro ſlave; it is as much property as any other thing" — is therefore wholly extrajudicial; and is moreover accompanied by a miſrepreſentation of the grounds of Lord *Holt's* deciſion, and by a manifeſt deſire to confirm the opinion given by Lord *Talbot* and himſelf in 1729 as attorney and ſolicitor general, in favor of holding ſlaves in England, of which Lord *Mansfield* ſaid that it "was upon a petition in Lincoln's Inn Hall, after dinner; probably, therefore, might not be taken with much accuracy." Lofft, 8; 20 Howell's State Trials, 70.

Lord *Hardwicke's* opinion on this ſubject has never been recognized as law by any court in England. In 1762, a bill in equity, filed by an adminiſtrator to recover back money given by his inteſtate to a negro who had been brought to England as a ſlave, (which was apparently founded on the ſuppoſition that the negro was ſtill a ſlave, and therefore incapable

[P. 96]

6 · NOTES

This was a fairly harsh and technical evidentiary ruling, as the Chief Justice admitted that "he had no Manner of Doubt but that the Estate was insolvent. . . ." *Reports*, 99.

The real importance of the case was that the Court took for granted that trover could lie for a Negro in Massachusetts. That exact issue had been decided by the Superior Court in *Goodspeed* v. *Gay*, Barnstable, Rec. 1763, Fol. 47. See *Reports*, 98, S. Quincy n. 1. Samuel Quincy's lengthy review of the English law concluded that, despite the free status of slaves physically in England, as described by Lord Mansfield in *Sommersett's Case* in 1772, *Lofft's Reports* (London, 1776), 17–79, 20 *Howell's State Trials* 79–82, "[b]y the English authorities . . . the right to maintain trover for a negro would seem to depend . . . whether he may be held and sold as a chattel by the law of the country where his master's possession of him is interfered with." *Reports*, 98, S. Quincy n. 2. Cases such as *Oliver* v. *Sale*, *Reports*, 29, Case 13, *supra*, leave little doubt that slaves were bought and sold as merchandise in Massachusetts. Thus it is not surprising that the Court assumed that "trover" would lie for "a Negro." (More startling today was the Court's easy equation of race with slavery.) Quincy's "query" note shows a familiarity with the English law, but was not an accurate statement of Massachusetts law. See *Introduction*, "*First Flower—The Earliest American Law Reports and the Extraordinary Josiah Quincy Jr. (1744–1775)*," *supra*, 59–61. See generally, on *Sommersett's Case*, Steven M. Wise, *Though the Heavens May Fall* (Boston, 2005). It is striking that Samuel Quincy's notes were most likely written while he was in command of the Seventy-third United States Colored Troops at Port Hudson, Louisiana! See *Editor's Foreword*, *supra*, 5–7.

Adminiſtrators could not be Witneſſes, except when the Eſtate is inſolvent.

Meſſrs.

---

incapable of receiving a gift,) was diſmiſſed by Lord *Northington*, who ſaid: " As ſoon as a man ſets foot on Engliſh ground, he is free; a negro may maintain an action againſt his maſter for ill uſage, and may have a *habeas corpus* if reſtrained of his liberty." *Shanley* v. *Harvey*, 2 Eden, 127.

It appears by *Granville Sharp's* MS. that Lord C. J. *Wilmot*, in 1768, held, that a female negro slave, married in England to a negro man who had alſo been brought from the Weſt Indies as a ſlave, could not be carried back without the conſent of the huſband; and that Lord C. J. *De Grey*, about the ſame time, more than once expreſſed the opinion, that there could be no property in the perſon of a ſlave by the law of England. Sharp's Memoirs, (2d ed.) 72, 110. The ſame book contains a full account of Lord *Mansfield's* evaſions of a deciſion of the general queſtion in the caſe of *Rex* v. *Stapylton*, in 1771. Ib. 82, 89-92.

It is clear from theſe authorities, (without relying on the caſe of the *Ruſſian Slave* in 1569, mentioned in 2 Ruſhw. Hiſt. Coll. 468,) that Lord *Mansfield's* reluctant diſcharge of the *Negro Sommerſett* in 1772, (Lofft, 17–19; 20 Howell's State Trials, 79–82,) was but a re-affirmance of the law of England, as previouſly determined by Lord *Holt* and other eminent judges — notwithſtanding the ſubſequent ſtatement of Lord *Mansfield*, in *The King* v. *Thames Ditton*, (1785,) 4 Doug. 301, that " the caſe of *Sommerſett* is the only one on this ſubject; " and the aſſertion of Lord *Stowell*, in the caſe of the *Slave Grace*, (1827,) 2 Hagg. Adm. R. 106, 114, that Lord *Mansfield*, in *Sommerſett's caſe*, " made a change in the law." For an examination of ſome of the *obiter dicta* of Lord *Stowell*, ſee 20 Law Rep. 99, 105–107. That learned civilian does not manifeſt any knowledge that one of his predeceſſors, Sir *George Hay*, almoſt as ſoon as *Sommerſett's caſe* was decided, twice held, upon full argument, that, before as well as ſince that deciſion, negroes could not lawfully be held or ſold as ſlaves in England. *Cay* v. *Crichton*, (1773,) in the Prerogative Court; *Rogers* v. *Jones*, (1776,) in the High Court of Admiralty; both reported in Granville Sharp's " Juſt Limitation of Slavery," (London, 1776,) App. 10 & 11, pp. 77–86.

Sir *William Blackſtone's* oſcillations in this matter are too characteriſtic to be paſſed by, notwithſtanding the length to which this note has already extended. In the firſt edition of his Commentaries, publiſhed in 1765, founding himſelf upon Lord *Holt*, (" Salk. 666,") he wrote: " This ſpirit of liberty is ſo deeply implanted in our Conſtitution and rooted in our very ſoil, that a ſlave or a negro, the moment he lands in England, falls under the protection of the laws, and, with regard to

Meſſrs. Otis & Gridley, Council for Defendant, ſaid it was univerſally known that the Eſtate of Cockran, the Father, was inſolvent, and appealed to the Chief Juſtice (who was likewiſe Judge of Probate) (2) for the Truth of their Suggeſtion.

The

---

all natural rights, becomes *eo inſtanti* a freeman." In his third edition, publiſhed in 1768, after the queſtion had begun to be re-agitated in England, he altered the laſt clauſe of his ſtatement to this: "and ſo far becomes a free man; though the maſter's right to his ſervice may probably ſtill continue." Againſt which Quincy has written, in the margin of his copy, "Curious!" In the fourth edition, publiſhed two years later, "*poſſibly*" was ſubſtituted for "probably." 1 Bl. Com. 127. After the paſſage had aſſumed this ſhape, Hargrave truly ſaid of it, "There appears to be ſomewhat of very ſubtle diſtinction, if not rather of contradiction." 20 Howell's State Trials, 30, note.

Treſpaſs will lie in England for taking ſlaves on the high ſeas, or in a country where ſlavery is not prohibited by law, from one who is not prohibited by the laws of his own country from trading in ſlaves. *Madrazo* v. *Willes*, (1820,) 3 B. & Ald. 353. *Buron* v. *Denman*, (1848,) 2 Exch. 167. But the commander of a Britiſh veſſel is not liable to an action for refuſing to deliver up to their maſter ſlaves who have eſcaped from a foreign country where ſlavery is recognized by law, and got on board his veſſel, and are unwilling to return. *Forbes* v. *Cochrane*, (1824,) 2 B. & C. 448; 3 D. & R. 679.

By the Engliſh authorities, therefore, the right to maintain trover for a negro would ſeem to depend upon the queſtion whether he may be held and ſold as a chattel by the law of the country where his maſter's poſſeſſion of him is interfered with. The fact ſuggeſted by Hargrave, *arguendo*, in 20 Howell's State Trials, 53, that "the maſter's power over the ſlave doth not extend to his life, and conſequently the maſter's property in the ſlave is in ſome degree qualified and limited," would ſeem to be no valid objection to the maintenance of the action; for trover lies by one who has any ſpecial property in a chattel, with the right to immediate poſſeſſion. 2 Saund. 47, & note.

At the time of the trial of the caſe here reported by Quincy, negro ſlaves were held and ſold as property in Maſſachuſetts. *Ante*, 29, note (2) to *Oliver* v. *Sale*, and authorities there cited. And in 1763 trover had been maintained in this court for a negro. *Goodſpeed* v. *Gay*, in Barnſtable, Rec. 1763, fol. 47. But it has been ſaid, that in Connecticut, while ſlavery exiſted there, trover would not lie for a ſlave. Reeve Dom. Rel. 340.

(2) By the Province Charter the juriſdiction in matters of probate was

The *Ch. Juſt.* ſaid that from the Accounts given him of the Eſtate, and from his own Knowledge, he had no Manner of Doubt but that the Eſtate was inſolvent; yet as the Commiſſioners had not made Report, there was no legal Evidence of the Inſolvency. And *the Court ruled*, that the Adminiſtratrix of Cockran the Defendant's Father ſhould not be ſworn. (3)

---

was veſted in the Governor and Council as a civil law court, who appointed judges of probate in each county as their delegates or ſubſtitutes. Anc. Chart. 32. Governor Pownall's Meſſage to the Council in February, 1760, App. III. 3 Hutchinſon's Hiſt. Maſs. 451, note. 2 Maſs. 154. 8 Cuſh. 541. 21 Law Rep. 78, 79.

(3) It is not eaſy to ſee why an adminiſtrator, not a party to the ſuit, and without any beneficial intereſt in the truſt fund, ſhould not be a competent witneſs for the eſtate, without regard to its ſolvency or inſolvency. 2 Stark. Evid. (2d Amer. ed.) 775. 3 Dane Ab. 420. 12 Maſs. 358. But it is probable that, in practice, adminiſtrators were paid by a commiſſion on the amount collected, as was afterwards expreſſly provided by the Rev. Sts. c. 67, § 8 — which might require a releaſe to make them competent witneſſes. 11 S. & R. 208. 15 Ib. 235. 7 Ib. 116. See alſo 16 Maſs. 118.

CONSTANTINOPLE, Aug. 3.

THE 12th ult. the Porte received the melancholy News of the total Deſtruction of their Fleet. The Engagement began the 5th at Ten in the Morning, and laſted till the 7th. The bad Diſpoſition of our Fleet was owing to our Captain Bacha, who neglected the Advice of Zeffer Bey and Haſſan Bey. The Captain Bacha has been ſince depoſited, and Zeffer Bey named Great Admiral in his Stead. Moldavangi Pacha has received Orders to defend the Strait of the Dardanelles, where, beſides ſtrong Garriſons in the four Caſtles, there are in that Canal four Ships of War, and a great Number of Tranſport Veſſels chained together, and furniſhed with Cannon, to defend that Place to the utmoſt.

The Populace have been very turbulent, and demanded Proviſions from the Magazines; the Government, to quiet them, hath agreed to diſtribute Rice and Oil, but in ſmall Quantities.

Letters from Smyrna inform us, that on their receiving News of the above Defeat, the Soldiers and Sailors had murdered a great number of Franks, and that the latter had requeſted the Ruſſians not to approach that Place, as they feared the Maſſacre would be general if they did.

LONDON, Sept. 24.

We hear that Lord Hillſborough was not expected home till the month of November, and that his ſudden return was owing to an earneſt requeſt value upon his counſel and advice in all ſtate affairs.

It is apprehended, that the blow is ſtruck before this time at Falkland's Iſland.

A rupture is, we hear, likely to commence very ſpeedily between the King of Sardinia and the republic of Genoa; owing to ſome infringement on the treaties by the latter.

We are aſſured, that for ſome time paſt a very Great Perſonage has been cloſely employed in reading Sidney, Locke, and ſome other celebrated Writers on Government.

Dublin, Sept. 22. Tueſday Night four Sailors, belonging to the Boyne, Captain Wilſon, bound for Philadelphia, and four Paſſengers, going in a Boat down to ſaid Ship, were drowned in Poolbeg. The Captain was with Difficulty ſaved.

Canterbury, Sept 8. We learn from Deal, that the Duke of Newcaſtle, Thomlinſon, from Piſcataqua, with Maſts for Portſmouth, is loſt off Scilly, & all the Crew drowned.

PHILADELPHIA, Nov. 22.

By Captain Daviſon from Briſtol, we have a Confirmation of the Engliſh being diſpoſſeſſed of Faulkland Iſland, in the South Seas, by the Spaniards, and that the Garriſon, in a Frigate, had arrived at Cadiz: That there was the hotteſt Preſs, perhaps ever known in England: That every warlike Preparation was carrying on with the utmoſt Expedition: And that it was tho't a War with Spain was inevitable.

We hear from Paxton, in Lancaſter County, the laſt Week, at the Raiſing of a Barn there, in hoiſting a Log, it broke in the Middle, killed three Men on the Spot, and hurt five others.

They write from Liverpool, that the Demand for Check Linen from New-York, &c. was ſo great there, that the Merchants have been obliged to buy ſingle Pieces in little Retail Shops.

Great-Britain and Spain; but not having received a Confirmation of this Report, we believe it to be premature.

S A L E M, *November* 27.

Yeſterday Morning the Lady of JOHN FISHER, Eſq; His Majeſty's Collector for this Port, was delivered of a Daughter.

Laſt Thurſday Mr. ISAAC WINSLOW, jun. of Boſton, Merchant, was married to Miſs PEGGY SPARHAWK, Daughter of the late Reverend Mr. SPARHAWK, of this Place, deceaſed, and Neice of the Hon. NATHANIEL SPARHAWK, Eſq; of Kittery.

P O R T S M O U T H, *November* 16.

We hear from Rye, that the Day before the Storm on the 22d of laſt Month, there went out from that Town two Fiſhing Schooners, which were ſeen off in the Bay about Sun-ſet, and they have not been heard of ſince, and there is no Hopes but they are loſt.—— There was on board one Schooner, ſix Men and two Boys; the Men's Names were, John Sanders and John Sanders, junr. Son of John Sanders, John Yeaton, William Thomas, and two others, with the two Lads. On board the other, were Samuel Sanders, Joſhua Foſs, and Samuel Sanders, with two Boys.— They have left Six ſorrowful Widows, and a Number of Fatherleſs Children.

Boſton, December 3.

Capt. Reeves in 18 Days from Quebec, arrived at New-York, informs, That on the 19th of October they had the moſt violent Gale of Wind at that Place ever known in the Memory of the oldeſt Man living there, which laſted about 6 Hours, and had it continued but a few Hours longer, every Veſſel then in the Harbour muſt inevitably have been ſplit to Pieces; as it was ſeveral Veſſels received conſiderable Damage, and a Whaler from Nantucket, and two French Veſſels, were entirely loſt with their Cargoes, within two Leagues of Quebec, and the Crews of the two latter, conſiſting of about 14 Souls, among which were ſome Women and Children, all periſhed.

Extract of a Leter from Gibralter, Auguſt 20.

" We have juſt received Advice here, that the Daniſh Squadron before Algiers has been reinforced by three Ships of the Line, three large Frigates, and ſeveral Bomb-ketches; that they ſoon after began to bombard Algiers afreſh; that they had made a Breach, knocked down ſome Battlements, and diſmounted ſeveral of the Guns; that the Dey had ſent to the Admiral freſh Propoſitions, on which Account they ceaſed firing, and called a Council of War to deliberate upon them, and after a ſhort Time rejected them; on which the Firing was again renewed very briſkly, and continued ſo when the Advice-boat came away."

Tueſday came on at the Superior Court in this Town, the Trial of the Soldiers, indicted by the Grand Jury for the Murder of the People on the Evening of the 5th of March laſt. The Trial is not yet finiſhed.

Saturday laſt died after a few Days Illneſs Mrs. Abiel Wingfield, Conſort to Capt. William Wingfield.

Tueſday laſt a Negro Lad belonging to Samuel Quincy, Eſq; going into a Cellar, drop'd inſtantly dead.

On Thurſday the 8th ult. was ordained to the work of the Goſpel Miniſtry, at Lenox, in the Province of Maſſachuſetts-Bay, the Rev. Mr. ...

ILLUSTRATION 27: *Boston Post Boy*, Dec. 3, 1770, 3. With notices regarding the Boston Massacre Case, see *Petition of the Jurors in the Trial of Captain Preston and the British Soldier Reports*, (1771), *Reports*, 382, (Case 77), and with regard to the death of a slave belonging to Josiah Quincy's brother, Samuel (1734–1789). See *Appendix 6*, *infra*, for a brief biography. Courtesy of Early American Newspapers, and Archive of Americana Collection. Published by Readex (Readex.com), a division of NewsBank, inc.

CASE 37

Hanlon *verſ.* Thayer.

HANLON *v.* THAYER.

Rec. 1764. Fol. 109.

Articles of Apparell and Ornament of a Wife, owned by her before her Marriage, (except neceſſary wearing Apparell,) are liable to Attachment for the Debts of the Huſband.

THE Plaintiff (Hanlon's Wife) (1) brings Trover againſt Thayer (a Sheriff) for attaching her Apparell. (2) There were two Queſtions in this

(1) Mark Hanlon was the plaintiff. The writ, however, was indorſed by Mary Hanlon, his attorney, who may have conducted the caſe, and thus occaſioned the miſtake.

(2) The common law proceeding by attachment was merely to compel the defendant's appearance where he failed to answer the ſummons. The Colony Law of 1644 gave plaintiffs the power to take out either ſummons or attachment in the firſt inſtance. Anc. Chart. 49. But the attachment

[P. 99]

Hanlon v. *Thayer* (1764)
4 George III (Aug.) in the
Superior Court of Judicature

1 · BRIEF DESCRIPTION

This is a "trover" [conversion] action by Hanlon's wife against a sheriff, Thayer, for attaching her clothes to pay her husband's debts. The two issues were: (1) whether clothes bought *before* the marriage could be attached and (2) whether the clothes attached were "necessary . . . Apparell" exempt from attachment by Prov. St. 13 William Chap. 3 (1702), Sec. 367, Com. Sts. C.123, § 42. Held: by a split Court, clothes bought before the marriage could be attached, and that included all but that apparel really necessary for protection from the weather, not clothes "necessary" for one's "Station in Life." *Reports*, *supra*, 100–103.

2 · COURT RECORDS

Available at Rec. 1764, fol. 109. There is a schedule in the record showing that, among the attached goods were, "earrings, necklaces, laces, ribbons, fans, etc." and, including "Gloshoes" [goloshes] and an "embrillo." See *Reports*, 101, n. 5, as well as a "list of necessary articles" which the Defendant Sheriff "tendered back" before the law suit. See *Reports*, 100–101, S. Quincy n. 3.

3 · PROFESSIONALS INVOLVED

For the Plaintiff wife appeared Robert Auchmuty (1723–1788) and James Otis, Jr., the patriot (1725–1783). For the Defendant Sheriff appeared a "Mr. Chardon," who does not appear on the list of barristers of August Term, and Jeremy Gridley (1701/2–1767), the informal "dean" of the bar. Chardon is likely Peter Chardon, whom John Adams described as a "promising Youth" pursuing a legal career. Chardon died in 1766. See *Diary and Autobiography of John Adams* (L. H. Butterfield, L. C. Faber, W. D. Garret, eds., Cambridge, MA, 1961), vol. 1, 47; see also *Law Commonplace*, vol. 2 of *Quincy Papers*, "Introduction," 15. See short biographies at *Appendix 6*.

4 · AUTHORITY

No English authorities were cited by counsel for the wife. Chardon cited the English statute 4 George II, c.1 as an example of the narrow meaning of "necessary" at English law. Gridley also cited to Chief Justice Holt's decision in

this Cafe; one, whether, as the Apparell attached was the Property of Hanlon's Wife before the Intermarriage, it did not make a Difference in the Law from Cafes where Apparell after the Marriage came to the Wife; the other, whether the feveral Articles in the Schedule annexed were *all neceffary* wearing Apparell.

Mr. Auchmuty, taking no Notice of the firft Queftion, endeavoured to prove the Apparell mentioned was neceffary, by obferving, what was neceffary for one Station in Life was not fo for another, and faid the Law never meant the Word "Neceffary" in its ftricteft Senfe.

Mr. Chardon for Defendant. The Argument *ab Inconvenienti* is of very great Weight in the Law, and by admitting all thefe Things (in the Schedule) as *neceffary* wearing Apparell, would be putting it in the Power of almoft every Debtor to defraud his Creditor. (3) To explain and fhow the Senfe in which

---

attachment being difcharged by an appearance, as at common law, or at moft by a judgment, twelve hours before execution, it was afterwards provided in 1650 that goods fo attached fhould "ftand engaged" until the judgment fhould be fatisfied. Ib. 51. By the Prov. St. of 13 W. 3, the duration of the liability was limited to thirty days after judgment. Ib. 367. Gen. Sts. c. 123, § 42. The chattels liable to attachment have always been held to be fuch only as may legally be taken on execution, and where this latter right is left at the common law, "fo muft the right to attach depend upon the common law." 6 Mafs. 244. By the Colony Law of 1647, officers were prohibited from levying execution on "any man's neceffary bedding, apparell, tools or arms, neither implements of houfehold which are for the neceffary upholding of his life." Anc. Chart. 155.

(3) The fchedule comprifes earrings, necklaces, laces, ribbons, fans, &c.,

Hardistey v. *Barney*, *Comberbach's Reports*, London (1724), 356. The Chief Justice was not pleased by the arguments, or the scanty nature of the Authorities, "I should have been extremely glad if this Case had been argued a little more largely by the Gentlemen of the Bar, and more Authorities cited, in Matter of so great Consequence." *Reports*, 102.

5 · LATER CITATIONS

Hanlon v. *Thayer* was cited in *Nolin* v. *Pearson*, 191 Mass. 283, 284 (1906) for the precedent that a wife could not alienate or devise her property during coverture without the assent of her husband.

Later Massachusetts statutes allowed a widow all her apparel against auditors of the husband's estate, Statutes of 1838, c. 145, General Statutes, c. 96, § 4, and later Massachusetts cases defined the word "necessary" in a more lenient way. As Samuel Quincy pointed out, the quaint Chief Justice Lemuel Shaw observed that "This word [necessary] is not used in its most rigid sense, as something absolutely indispensable, and without which a debtor cannot live." *Davlin* v. *Stone,* 58 Mass. (4 *Cushing*) 359, 361 (1849). See *Reports*, 103, S. Quincy n. 7.

6 · NOTES

This case was sometimes called the "Naked Wife Case," from the Chief Justice's observation: "for one Gown can never be supposed sufficient—must she go naked when that is washing?" *Reports*, 103. It has traditionally been used to illustrate the severe hardships that women suffered by their subordinate legal status in the colony. This was felt most painfully when a woman brought ample personal resources by marriage into the grasp of the creditors of a penniless husband. One of my excellent students, Sally Ann Carter, Harvard Law School Class of 1997, did a detailed reexamination of the record, and came to a different conclusion. "My research into the 1764 Massachusetts case *Hanlon* v. *Thayer* has opened up possible scenarios and interconnections instead of yielding clean truths. Yet I am comfortable stating that this case is not merely about what it at first glance seems to be: whether 'a woman with assets who marries a bankrupt husband loses all her belongings to his creditors, including her clothes.'" See Sally Ann Carter, "An Exploration of *Hanlon* v. *Thayer*," May 10, 1997, unpublished paper on file with the Editor, 1.

which the Law ufes the Word *Neceffary*, I cite 4 G. 2, c. 1. (4)

Mr. Gridley. Nothing is *neceffary* in the *Law* but what is neceffary to defend from the Inclemency of the Weather, (5) or neceffary to the Degree: But before they can talk highly of Degree they muft pay their Debts. If any befides what is barely neceffary is allowed for Comfort, it is not the Law, but Humanity. The Law here wifely ufes the Word *Neceffary*, for the Boundary of Neceffity is determinate, but Conveniency not, — Conveniency! What is convenient? &c. (a little Rhetorick and concludes.) *Mr. Gridley* alfo faid: If a Judge of Probate grant to the Wife of an Inteftate whofe Eftate is infolvent, two Beds, where *one only* was neceffary, the other immediately became liable to be attached, and he cited *Hardiftey & Barney*, (Comber. 356,) where *Holt* fays if the Party have two Gowns, Sheriff may take one.*

Mr. Otis relied chiefly on the Evidence that proved Hanlon never bought or paid for a fingle Rag

* *Qu.* if 1 Inft. 351 b, top, would not have been a good Authority?

&c. There appears alfo a lift of neceffary articles which the defendant tendered back to Mrs. Hanlon before the date of the writ.

(4) Anc. Chart. 481.

(5) "1 Pr Glofhoes" (golofhes) and "1 Green Embrillo" appear upon the fchedule, but were not among the articles tendered back as neceffary. About this time, "Umbrillos" were firft advertifed in the papers, and were doubtlefs then confidered articles of luxury. See Drake's Hiftory of Bofton, p. 660.

In particular, Ms. Carter argues that the case really "illustrates the effect on legal process of the system of formalistic pleading still in use in 1764" and that "there was no particular reason to believe the husband was bankrupt." *Id.* The underlying records, instead, show that the case was really about defenses to collecting a judgment, taking its present form as "the result of the necessity in 1764 of using legal fiction in order to navigate the legal system." *Id.* Ms. Carter is right. The record shows that both Quincy and Chief Justice Hutchinson oversimplified the case on appeal, not the first or last time that has happened in the history of the law.

Rag of his Wife's Cloaths, but that ſhe brought all with her at the Marriage, and ſaid it had been the Cuſtom univerſally, never to take Cloaths ſo brought, for the Debts of the Huſband.

Juſtices Oliver & Cuſhing both ſaid the Caſe was very hard upon the Wife, who brought all theſe Cloaths at Marriage, yet "as they are perſonal Property, they become the Huſband's on Marriage, and therefore liable."

Ch. Juſt. I ſhould have been extremely glad if this Caſe had been argued a little more largely by the Gentlemen of the Bar, and more Authorities cited, in Matter of ſo great Conſequence. I always took it to have been the Cuſtom in ſuch Caſes as this, for the Wife to have her Cloaths; in Caſes that have come before me as Judge of Probate I never knew it denied to the Wife where the Eſtate was inſolvent. (6) In the Caſe cited (by Mr. G.) I ſuppoſe the Woman was a Party, and the Debt contracted

(6) The Prov. St. of 9 Anne reserved only "the neceſſary bedding, utenſils and implements of houſehold," where the eſtate was inſolvent. Anc. Chart. 390. At common law, however, there ſeems to have been a queſtion to what extent the widow's "paraphernalia," beyond neceſſary wearing apparel, was liable to creditors of the huſband's eſtate. Bac. Ab. Baron & Feme, C. 3. 1 Dane Ab. 364. And the practice of allowing the widow her apparel in all caſes was afterwards confirmed by Sts. 1783, c. 36; 1802, c. 93; 1816, c. 95. The Reviſed Statutes, c. 65, § 5, excepted from the inventory of the eſtate "all the articles of apparel or ornament of the widow, according to the degree and eſtate of her huſband," "although his eſtate ſhould be inſolvent." The St. of 1838, c. 145, omits the limitation as to the huſband's degree, and provides that the articles aforeſaid ſhall be conſidered as excluſively belonging to the widow. Gen. Sts. c. 96, § 4.

contracted by her; this alters the Cafe much, but yet I apprehend (here *Ch. Juft.* makes an Apology for what follows) that this may be one of thofe Cafes where the Juftice fays a Thing *obiter*, or fuddenly; for one Gown can never be fuppofed fufficient — muft fhe go naked when that is wafhing? Upon the Whole I think it would be very hard upon the Wife, fhould fuch a Precedent as this take Place, that her *Cloaths* which fhe *brought* in *Marriage* muft go to difcharge the Hufband's Debts. I fhould think it fafer to verge towards Conveniency than to ftrain the Word *Neceffary*. (7)

The *Ch. Juft.* in the Courfe of this Cafe afked if it would not have been better to have brought Detinue.

N. B. The Jury found for the Defendant Cofts.

Adjourned to September 11th — and then met
Chief Juftice.
Lynde, Ruffell, } Juftices.

(7) Somewhat fimilar opinions have been fubfequently expreffed. See 4 Cufh. 361, *Shaw, C. J.* — "This word is not ufed in its moft rigid fenfe, as fomething abfolutely indifpenfable, and without which a debtor cannot live." And the exemption of "neceffary wearing apparel" has been held to extend to cloth in the hands of a tailor. *Richardfon* v. *Bufwell*, 10 Met. 506.

CASE 38

Rex *v.* Pourksdorff.

Rec. 1764. Fol. 125.

A Conviction of Petit Larceny and Judgment thereon do not deftroy the Competency of a Witnefs.

Dom. Rex *verf.* Pourkfdorff.

INDICTMENT vs. Pourkfdorff for Stealing. A Woman offered as Evidence who at the fame Term had pleaded guilty to an Indictment of the fame Nature. (1)

The Attorney General objected to her, that fhe pleaded guilty to an infamous Crime, and therefore no Witnefs, and cited Hawkins's Pleas of the Crown, B. 2, ch. 33, § 129; ch. 37, §§ 48 to 53.

Mr. Kent for the Prifoner. Law of Evid. 145. Judge Raymond, 32. 2 Sid. 51. (2)

The Attorney General then moved for Judgment; and

Granted.

The Queftion then arofe, whether, when there is a Judgment, and not an infamous Judgment,* it bars the Perfon on whom Judgment is paffed, from being a Witnefs.

Attorney General & Mr. Kent cited as above.

Ch.

* It is the Crime and not the Punifhment that makes a Man infamous. Theory of Evid. 107, *q.v.*

---

(1) *Rex* v. *Pourkfdorff & al.*, Rec. 1764, fol. 123.

(2) Where it is decided that a conviction without judgment thereon is not fufficient to difqualify a witnefs.

Dom. Rex v. *Pourksdorff* (1764)
4 George III (Aug.) in the
Superior Court of Judicature

1 · BRIEF DESCRIPTION

The sole issue was whether a woman, who had pleaded guilty to stealing, was competent to be a witness for the Defendant, Pourksdorff. Conviction of felony destroyed the competency of a witness at common law, but the Court here held that she could testify, as "the Crime is not of such a Nature as the least to invalidate the Credit of the Witness's *Oath*." *Reports*, 105. She then testified that she had stolen goods in question, not the Defendant, and Pourksdorff was acquitted on "[t]his Evidence alone." *Reports*, 106.

2 · COURT RECORDS

Available at Rec. 1764, Fol. 125.

3 · PROFESSIONALS INVOLVED

Counsel were very distinguished, at least for a thievery case. The Attorney General, Edmund Trowbridge (1709–1793), Attorney General, (1749–1767), appeared for the prosecution. Benjamin Kent (1708–1788), who himself became Attorney General in 1776 and served as Suffolk County Attorney General from 1777–1785, appeared for the Defendant. See *Appendix 6* for brief biographies.

4 · AUTHORITY

The Attorney General relied heavily on William Hawkins's popular *Pleas of the Crown* (London, 1716–21); see full description in *Dom. Rex* v. *Gay*, *Reports*, 90, Case 35, Note 4, "Authority," *supra*. The selections cited hold that a pardon can enable a convict to "be a good witness," which is not really in point. Kent cited "Law of Evidence," almost certainly referring to *Law of Evidence by a Late Learned Judge* [G. Gilbert], 145, first published in Dublin in 1754 and London in 1756, with subsequent editions in 1760 and 1769. See *Sweet & Maxwell*, *supra*, vol. 1, 379:5. He also cited [Sir Thomas] *Raymond's Reports*, 32 [the case of *Fitch* v. *Smalbrook* (1661)], a case about a prior conviction on perjury being entered into evidence "to weaken the credit of a witness," thus not really on point. Sir Thomas Raymond's *Reports* covered all the common law courts from 1660–83,

Ch. Juſt. When the Crime is ſo great and of ſuch a *Nature* (for Inſtance the *Crimen Falſi* in Law) as it is to be ſuppoſed that the Perſon guilty has loſt all Senſe of Truth, and would not heſitate at violating his Oath, in ſuch Caſe no Doubt not to be admitted, but even where the Judgment is infamous, (as that a Perſon ſhall ſit in the Pillory for writing a Libel,) yet if the Crime is not of ſuch a Nature as the leaſt to invalidate the Credit of the Witneſs's *Oath*, (as in the Caſe I mentioned, and that of the Witneſs now offered,) no Doubt they may be admitted.

Attorney General. Theft is infamous.

Kent. Petit Larceny is not.

Attorney General. There is no Difference between grand and petit Larceny.

Ch. Juſt. Do you ſuppoſe, Mr. Attorney, every Perſon convicted of petit Larceny at the Old Baily is ever after barred from being a Witneſs?

Attorney General. I don't know.

The Court unanimouſly *held*, No; (3) and ordered the

(3) It ſeems to have been aſſumed that the conviction in this caſe was for petit larceny. But the only indictment againſt a woman for larceny, on the record of this term, is againſt Margaret Knodle, joined with Pourkſdorff on a former indictment for grand larceny, to which ſhe pleaded guilty. In either caſe, however, the deciſion appears unaccountable, in view of the well-known rules of the common law on this ſubject, at that time unaltered by ſtatute. A conviction of felony de-

14 ſtroyed

and were first published in London in 1696. See *Sweet & Maxwell*, *supra*, vol. 1, 308:106. He also cited [Sir Thomas] *Siderfin's Reports*, vol. 2, 51 [the case of *Foster* v. *Ramsy* (1657)] which involved disability of felons, but was not directly on point. *Siderfin's Reports* covered the King's Bench from 1678–94, and was published in London in 1683–84 with Part 2 in 1689. See *Sweet & Maxwell*, *supra*, vol. 1, 309:120. Many thanks, as always, to Mark Sullivan.

At one point, the Chief Justice speculated on what English Practice would be in such a case. "Do you suppose, Mr. Attorney, every Person convicted of petit Larceny at the Old Baily [the London criminal sessions] is ever barred from being a witness?" *Reports*, 105. The Attorney General honestly answered, "I don't know," but the Chief Justice's question appeared to be more argumentative than a genuine search for guidance.

5 · LATER CITATIONS

None. As Samuel Quincy pointed out in *Quincy*, 104–105, S. Quincy n. 2, conviction for even small larcenies excluded witnesses, until all exclusion for convictions was abolished by statute in 1851. See St. (Mass) 1851, c. 233, § 97; St. 1852, c. 312 § 60.

6 · NOTES

Samuel Quincy thought this case was clearly wrong. "[T]he decision appears unaccountable, in view of the well-known rules of the common law on this subject, at that time unaltered by statute." *Reports*, 105, S. Quincy n. 3.

Another way of looking at it was that the Court was clearly right, and anticipated legal reforms still eighty years in the future. As the Chief Justice forcefully pointed out, the issue is not a technical one (i.e., "grand larceny" or "petit larceny"), but a practical question of whether "it is to be supposed that the Person guilty has lost all Sense of Truth, and would not hesitate at violating his Oath." *Reports*, 105. "[I]f the Crime is not of such a Nature as the least to invalidate the Credit of the Witness's Oath, (as in the Case . . . of the Witness now offered), no Doubt [it] may be admitted." *Reports*, 105.

Despite Samuel Quincy's protestations, this decision led to the acquittal of an innocent Defendant. It was a reasonable, balanced application of a rule of evidence.

the Witneſs to be ſworn, directing the Jury to give what Weight they pleaſed to her Evidence.

This Evidence alone cleared Pourkſdorff, by ſwearing ſhe ſtole the Goods herſelf.

ſtroyed the competency of a witneſs. Co. Lit. 6 b. And petit larceny was felony, although it did not produce a forfeiture of land. See 1 Hawk. (ed. of 1795) c. 36, § 6. But the puniſhment for grand larceny (burning in the hand) reſtored the competency of the witneſs (Com. Dig. Teſtmoigne — Witneſs A 3), while that for petit larceny had no ſuch effect, for which reaſon it was ſubſequently provided in England by 31 Geo. 3, c. 35, "That no perſon ſhall be an incompetent witneſs by reaſon of a conviction of petit larceny."

Whether the diſtinction between grand and petit larceny was ever adopted or recognized in Maſſachuſetts — *quære*. In *Commonwealth* v. *Keith*, 8 Met. 531, it was held that a conviction of larceny to the value of forty cents, before a juſtice of the peace, was ſufficient to exclude the witneſs. And there can be no doubt that any conviction of larceny had this effect until all incompetency from crime was finally aboliſhed by Sts. 1851, c. 233, § 97, & 1852, c. 312, § 60. *Commonwealth* v. *Green*, 17 Maſs. 515, 537. *Commonwealth* v. *Keith*, *ub. ſup.*

ILLUSTRATION 28: The "Old Bailey," London, showing a testifying witness. See the reference in *Dom. Rex* v. *Pourksdorff* (1764), *Reports*, 105 (Case 38). From Rudolf Ackerman, *The Microcosm of London* (1808–1811?). The engraving is done by the famous Thomas Rowlandson (1756–1827). Courtesy, Coquillette Rare Books Room, Boston College.

CASE 39

Prefent:

Ch. Juftice, Judge Lynde, Cufhing & Oliver.

BALLARD *v.* MCLEAN.

Rec. 1764. Fol. 111.

Miftake in the Addition of Place will abate a Writ of Review.

Ballard *verf.* McLean.

THIS was a Writ of Review. McLean was called, of Milton, but it was fully proved that he did not belong to Milton. The Queftion was, whether, this being a Writ of *Review*, which iffues out of the *Clerk's Office*, it fhould abate.

Mr.

[P. 106]

Ballard v. *McLean* (1764)
4 George III (Aug.) in the
Superior Court of Judicature

1 · BRIEF DESCRIPTION

The Defendant was wrongly said to be "of Milton" in a writ of review. Even though the error was that of the Clerk's office and the three-year limit for review would expire before another writ could be brought, the writ was abated, by a split court.

2 · COURT RECORDS

Available at Rec. 1764, Fol. 111.

3 · PROFESSIONALS INVOLVED

Richard Dana (1700–1772) argued in support of the writ. Oxenbridge Thacher, Quincy's pupil master, (1719–1765) argued for abatement. See brief biographies in *Appendix 6*.

The Court split. Four Justices sat. Justices Lynde, Cushing, and Oliver voted to abate the writ, and the Chief Justice dissented, stating, "[a]bstracted from the Custom I see no Reason why it [the writ] should abate." *Reports*, 107. The Chief Justice led his colleagues in dissents. See *Appendix 1* and the brief biographies of the Justices in *Appendix 7*.

4 · AUTHORITY

Dana cited *Strange's Reports*, a very popular English reporter in the colonies. See Quincy's *Law Commonplace*, [21], n. 12. It was first published in London in 1755 in two volumes, and covered cases from 1716–1749. The case cited was *Cortisos* v. *Munoz*, 2 *Strange's Reports* 924 (1732), which held that if a Defendant was described *nuper* ("lately") *of London merchant*, the writ was good, even if the Defendant was "commorant in Middlesex." Thacher quite rightly distinguished the case by observing that "had he [the Defendant] been named *nuper* it might have done, but the Plaintiff has declared with Certainty." *Reports*, 107.

Mr. Dana, in Support of the Writ, urged that the three Years (the Time limited by Law for bringing a Writ of Review) would expire before they could bring another Writ; and ſaid further that the Defendant was *late* of Milton, and was called in the original Writ, of Milton, which cauſed the Miſtake; and ſaid it would be a great Hardſhip upon the Plaintiff, when it was no Fault of his, for the Writ iſſued out of the Clerk's Office, that he ſhould be precluded from bringing his Review. Cited 2 Strange, 924, *Cortiſos* vs. *Munoz.*

Mr. Thacher, *contra.* Had he been named *nuper*, it might have done, but the Plaintiff has declared with Certainty. As to Writs of Review, they always have been and are ſubject to the ſame Rules with other Writs; and the Cuſtom has ever been in this Court to ſhow Writs of Review no more Favour than to other Writs.

Juſtices Lynde, *Cuſhing* & *Oliver* for abating it. (1)

Ch. Juſtice. Abſtracted from the Cuſtom, I ſee no Reaſon why it ſhould abate.

---

(1) Where a writ of review was improvidently iſſued, without notice to the oppoſite party, the Court ordered a hearing, but refuſed to quaſh the writ, becauſe, the three years having elapſed, the plaintiff would thereby loſe his right to bring another petition. *Clap* v. *Joſlyn*, 1 Maſs. 133. And in *Brewer* v. *Sibley*, 13 Met. 177, it is intimated that in caſe of review "it would be reaſonable to reſtrict the defence to the merits."

[P. 107]

5 · LATER CITATIONS

None. Later Massachusetts cases were more lenient when quashing a writ would cost a Plaintiff a right to appeal. See *Clap* v. *Joslyn*, 1 Mass. 129, 133 (1804); *Reports*, 107, S. Quincy n. 1. Samuel Quincy also cites *Brewer* v. *Sibley*, 54 Mass. (13 Met.) 175, 177 (1847); *Commonwealth* v. *Green*, 17 Mass. 515, 537 (1822); and *Commonwealth* v. *Keith*, 49 Mass. (8 Met.) 531 (1844).

6 · NOTES

This was a harsh pleading case, where a Clerk Office error of no real consequence cost a Plaintiff a writ of review. Attention to such technicalities of pleading, when real consequences were involved, astonishes modern lawyers. The Chief Justice, at least, would have allowed the writ.

CASE 40

Prefent:

Ch. Juftice, Juftice Cufhing & Juftice Oliver.

BROMFIELD *v.* LITTLE.

Rec. 1764. Fol. 98.

It feems, that there is no Cuftom of Merchants in this Country, of charging Intereft after a Year on the Price of Goods fold, which will raife an implied Contract to pay the fame.

Bromfield *verf.* Little.

IN this Action was a general *Indebitatus Affumpfit* on Account annexed. One Article was a Charge of Intereft.

The Council for the Plaintiff urged, that it was a Cuftom of Merchants here to charge Intereft after a Year: (Several Merchants were fworn on this Head, but they did not agree about the Time, neither whether they did or did not firft inform the Debtor.) The Juftnefs of the Charge was argued from the Charge of Intereft after a Year, *at Home.*

In Behalf of Defendant, 'twas faid, there was no fuch Cuftom here at all; yet if it could be faid there was a Cuftom here to charge after Notice either at or after Sale, certainly not before Notice.

Juft. Oliver. Whether this is a reafonable Cuftom muft firft be confidered. I think it is. I think, too, it appears to be a Cuftom.

Juft. Cufhing. This Cafe is very different from what it is at Home; 'tis there the univerfal Ufage, which makes it the Suppofition of every Party at firft; and, as a Perfon purchafing Goods without any fpecial Promife is fuppofed to promife the Payment

Bromfield v. *Little* (1764)
4 George III (Aug.) in the
Superior Court of Judicature

1 · BRIEF DESCRIPTION

The sole issue in this case is whether the Defendant debtor should pay a customary interest on an outstanding debt after one year. This was the custom "*at Home*" i.e., in England. A split Court held that this custom "however reasonable it may be" had not yet been adopted "here" nor "is it implied in the Contract." So instructed, the Jury did not allow the Plaintiff creditor interest.

2 · COURT RECORDS

Available at Rec. 1764, Fol. 98.

3 · PROFESSIONALS INVOLVED

There was no indication of counsel.

Three judges heard the case. Justice Oliver thought that the custom was "reasonable" and in effect. Justice Cushing held that the custom, "however reasonable" was not in effect "here," and Chief Justice Hutchinson, himself a wealthy merchant and shipowner, agreed with Cushing. The Chief Justice was "glad it is growing into a Custom" but doubted "whether it is so general as it can be supposed in this Case." *Reports*, 109.

4 · AUTHORITY

Except for reference generally to the custom "*at Home*," none cited.

5 · LATER CITATIONS

None.

6 · NOTES

For such a short case, this was highly significant jurisprudentially. The Chief Justice noted that, "This case is of much importance to the Community." *Reports*, 109. All three Justices made it clear that they would look to mercantile custom as a source of law. They even allowed merchant testimony to assist them. "Several Merchants were sworn on this Head, but they did not agree about the Time, neither whether they did or did not first inform the Debtor." *Reports*, 108. The only disagreement between the Justices was whether the custom had sufficiently evolved to be "supposed in this Case." *Id.*, 109.

ment of the Cuſtomary Price, ſo he is ſuppoſed to engage to pay the cuſtomary Allowance for Forbearance; but here, however reaſonable it may be, it is yet otherwiſe, nor is it implied in the Contract.

Ch. Juſtice. This Caſe is of much Importance to the Community. 'Tis agreeable to natural Equity that Intereſt ſhould be allowed; and I am glad it is growing into a Cuſtom; but the Rule is that both Parties ought at the Time of contracting to underſtand it ſo, and I doubt whether it is ſo general as that it can be ſuppoſed in this Caſe.

The Jury did not allow Intereſt.

N. B. The Superiour Court now altered, and the Sitting, inſtead of being the third Tueſday of February and third Tueſday of Auguſt, is the ſecond Tueſday in March and laſt Tueſday in Auguſt. March 12, A. D. 1765. (1)

---

(1) Prov. St. 5 G. 3, c. 6, Maſs. Perpet. Laws, 481.

In addition, all three Justices state explicitly, or imply, that incorporating mercantile custom into the common law was a two-step process. First, "[w]hether this is a reasonable Custom must first be considered." Second, if found "reasonable," is the custom a "universal Usage, which makes it the Supposition of every Party at first. . . ." *Reports*, 108.

Finally, all three Justices ignored the argument of counsel for the creditor that the "Justness of the Charge" was to be established by reference to the custom "*at Home,*" in England. Colonial mercantile custom, in the view of at least Justice Cushing and the Chief Justice, should be determined solely by the custom in the colony, not England.

"Incorporation" of mercantile custom into the common law was an important development in the eighteenth century, best symbolized by William Murray, Lord Mansfield, the great English Chief Justice. See Daniel R. Coquillette, "Legal Ideology and Incorporation IV: The Nature of Civilian Influence on Modern Anglo-American Commercial Law," 67 *Boston University Review*, 877, 934–970. After the Revolution, "custom" became even more important in American jurisprudence, and was emphasized by jurists such as Jesse Root (1736–1822) in his "Preface" to his *Connecticut Reports* (1798), covering the period 1789–1798. American customs, in Root's mind, helped solve the problem of how to have enough law for the new Republic without adopting English law wholesale, something he found distasteful.

As Root observed:

> [A]nother branch of common law is derived from certain usages and customs, universally assented to and adopted in practice by citizens at large, or by particular classes of men, as the farmer merchants, etc., as applicable to their particular business, and to all others of the same description, which are reasonable and beneficial.
>
> These customs or regulations, when thus assented to and adopted in practice, have an influence upon the course of trade and business, and are necessary to be understood and applied in the constructions of transactions had and contracts entered into with reference to theory. To this end courts of justice take notice of them as rules of right, and as having the force of laws formed and adopted under the authority of the people. *Id.*

See the discussion at Daniel R. Coquillette, *The Anglo-American Legal Heritage*, *supra*, 428–433.

This short case illustrated Root's important ideas in actual practice.

CHARGE NO. I

March Term

V Geo. Ter. in Sup. Cur. &c.

Preſent:

The Honourable Ch. Juſt., Lynde, & Cuſhing.

1765. CHARGE TO THE GRAND JURY.

The Charge to the Grand Jury by Ch. Juſtice.

TO relieve the Oppreſſed, to guard the Innocent, to preſerve the Order of Society, and the Dignity of Government is a noble Principle of the Mind. This is the Duty of every Individual of the Community, but is more particularly incumbent, Gentlemen, upon you, as the Grand Inqueſt for this County.

Our Buſineſs, Gentlemen, at this Time, is to diſtribute Juſtice, and to puniſh all Crimes and Offences. It is this latter Part of our Duty that you, Gentlemen, are to aſſiſt us in; to point out and bring forward all Crimes and Offences againſt the Tranquillity and Order of Society which ſhall by any Means come to your Knowledge.

But before I enter upon the particular Branch of your Duty, I ſhall obſerve, that it is a very common

Charge to The Suffolk Grand Jury by Chief Justice Hutchinson 1765—March Term

NOTES: PAGE 110

The "Grand Jury" was a "jury of presentment." As such, it did not decide the ultimate guilt or innocence of a suspect, but merely whether there was adequate reason to bring the suspect to trial, a standard that later became "probable cause." "Grand juries" got their name from the Law French "big" because they were larger than the "petit," or "petty" trial juries. At English law, the number was usually 23, as opposed to a trial jury of twelve. See D. R. Coquillette, *The Anglo-American Legal Heritage*, *supra*, 160–62.

"The presenting body at the assizes or quarter sessions acquired the name 'grand jury,' to distinguish it from trial juries. The grand jury was charged to make presentments from its own knowledge, but the regular practice from at least the 1360s was for draft written accusations (known as bills of indictment) to be prepared in advance of the session. The grand jurors scrutinized these bills, if necessary hearing *ex parte* evidence from accusers; if they considered that there was a case to answer they found the bill 'true,' and it was endorsed *billa vera* ('a true bill'), but if they did not it was endorsed *ignoramus* ('we do not know') and proceedings on the bill ended. The finding of a true bill by the grand jury was not a conviction, or a finding of guilt, and it required only a majority vote of twelve; it was written accusation upon oath, the effect of which was to initiate proceedings between the king and the accused person to try the issue of guilt." J. H. Baker, *An Introduction to English Legal History* (3d ed., London, 1990), 576–577 (notes excluded). See also D. R. Coquillette, *The Anglo-American Legal Heritage*, *supra*, 160–62; J. H. Baker, "Criminal Courts and Procedure at Common Law" in *Crimes in England 1500–1800* (J. S. Cockburn, ed., 1977, pp. 15–48).

The Massachusetts Grand Jury also consisted of 23 and could act by a bare majority of twelve. As the Chief Justice noted "In the Petty Jury, Gentlemen, you are sensible that all must agree in the Verdict; but to every Indictment the Agreement of twelve only is sufficient." See *Reports*, *infra*, 116.

Grand juries evolved in England partly to assist "justices in eyre," often called "assize justices." These were royal high court judges who "rode circuit" from

mon Thing in England to preſent Offences, when there is no Offender known, for wherever there is the one, there is always the other. Whenever there are any notorious Offences, as I obſerved before, in England, they always preſent them. I remember in particular (if it may be called an Offence) that at Middleſex, the Jury preſented, that there was unneceſſary Multiplication of licenſed Houſes, which tended greatly to the Deſtruction of the Health and Morals of the People. I do not mention this as the Caſe here, but only by Way of Example, to ſhow, that wherever you find any notable Things done that are detrimental, or any Things neglected which ought eſpecially to be done that are beneficial to Society, you have, Gentlemen, a diſcretionary Power to preſent them.

I would have you, Gentlemen, to enquire into the State of our Goal, for it has been repreſented, and I believe it but too true, that it is a moſt ſhocking, loathſome Place. For my own Part, when I have been obliged by the Nature of my Office to commit any of my Fellow Creatures, I could not help feeling for them, when I thought where I was ſending them — a dark, damp, and peſtilential Room — to ſuch a Place to ſend our Fellow Creatures muſt cauſe the moſt tender and exquiſite Senſations to Men of the leaſt Senſibility or Humanity. I do not think there is ſuch a Place for the Reception of Priſoners anywhere in the King's Dominions. I do not ſay this by Way of Reflection on the Gentlemen who have the proper Care of our Goal, nor upon the Sheriff* of this County, the Keeper

* Mr. Greenleaf.

county town to county town at regular intervals, hearing cases that should be tried by the common law of the realm, as opposed to local courts and Magistrates. Serious crimes, termed "felonies" from the law French, were so included, as opposed to "misdemeanors," lesser offences of little interest to the central authorities. One simple reason for the distinction was that "felonies" could result in "escheat," or forfeiture, of the Defendant's land to the feudal lord or Crown, matters of keen interest to the central tax collectors.

Grand juries were expected to use any information available to them to discharge their duty. They also had the function under the assize Judge's Commission of Gaol Delivery to inspect the local gaols and dungeons and to be sure those held were either indicted and tried, or released. See J. H. Baker, *An Introduction to English Legal History* (3d ed., London, 1990), 20–25.

In Massachusetts, the Superior Court of Judicature stood in place of English high court judges of the common law, and the Grand Jury served a very similar function, even centuries later. Thus, the Chief Justice emphasized that the Grand Jury could use information that "by any Means come to your knowledge," *Reports*, 110, and that it had a special responsibility to inspect the gaol where accused were held. *Reports*, 111–112. This responsibility, in Massachusetts, had developed to include inspecting conditions in the gaol, rather than just being sure those held were properly tried or released. *Reports*, 111–112. The Grand Jury was also to focus on serious felonies, and could "omit taking Notice of such Misdemeanors, (i.e., 'lesser offences') unless you should think there has been any gross Neglect in the courts of "Inferior Jurisdiction." *Reports*, *supra*, 116.

Was a Grand Jury a tool of the state, or a defender of the innocent and a check on state power? This controversy persists to this day in America. In 1765, it was clear that the Chief Justice saw the Grand Jury as a tool of the prosecution, and that the Grand Jury received "Directions" from the Attorney General. *Reports*, 112. The Chief Justice's instruction on secrecy also showed that the colonial administration would not hesitate to use secret informers, i.e., spies. *Reports*, *supra*, 116. There was, and is, another good reason for Grand Jury secrecy, and notably overlooked by the Chief Justice. Information given to a Grand Jury is not subject to challenge, as it would be in a trial. Secret information of this sort is notoriously unreliable, and that is the primary reason for Grand Jury secrecy today. See Federal Rules of Criminal Procedure, Rule 6, and *Moore's Federal Practice*, § 606.06.

Keeper of our Prifon, who I know to be a Man of great Tendernefs: But from whatever Caufe, Gentlemen, it arifes, whether from Neglect or a Mifunderftanding among the Gentlemen whofe Province it is to look after it, or any Caufe whatever, 'tis your Duty to give your particular Attention to it. I remember, Gentlemen, a Cafe in fome late Reports, of a Sheriff committing a Man to a new plaiftered, wet and unwholefome Room, by which he was put into violent Fever and died; the Sheriff on this was committed, tried and hanged. (1) Our Goal is not intended as a Punifhment, it is only to keep Offenders for Trial, or after Trial till Sentence is fulfilled. Every Man in the Eye of the Law is prefumed innocent till proved guilty. How prepofterous then, Gentlemen, is it to commit a Man to a Place, who whether innocent or not muft run the Hazard of his Life—a Place which will bring a Man of the beft Conftitution in Danger of his Life; how long then will a Perfon of a weakly Conftitution furvive? I muft, Gentlemen, repeat it again, this demands your peculiar Attention, and the Attorney General will give any Directions you may want.

A Government always thinks itfelf happy when the Grand Jury can find no Offenders to prefent. This

(1) *Quære*, whether the Chief Juftice had not in his mind the cafe *Rex* v. *Huggins*, 2 Stra. 882; Ld. Raym. 1574, where the warden of the Fleet Prifon was indicted for the murder of a prifoner by confining him in a "new-built room, the walls being damp and unwholefome." The offence was held to be murder, but the prifoner was acquitted on the ground that it was the act of a deputy. A feries of fimilar cafes is reported in 9 Howell's State Trials, 146–234, but neither of them refulted in a conviction.

The Chief Justice also focused on certain areas where he believed the jurors would be tempted to excuse felonious conduct, contrary to their "Duty." The first was reporting offenses where "no Offender is known," i.e., no identified Defendant. The example given was "multiplication of licensed Houses." *Reports*, 111. The second was "Riots, Routs and unlawful Assemblies," with particular attention to the "Pope Day," the anniversary of the Gun Powder Plot, which featured contests between the street mobs of the North and South End. *Reports*, 113. The Chief Justice glossed over highway robbery, "very rare in this Country," but emphasized forgery, particularly "Forgery of Notes of Hand." *Reports*, 115. The first two offenses, too many bars and charges of riot against individuals who were engaged in a publicly popular-if rough-celebration, were obvious examples of where jurors would be reluctant to act. The third, forgery of notes of hand, was described as a "wicked" crime, "how destructive its Consequences[!]." A lay juror might well fail to understand that negotiable notes were like "Public Bills of Credit," i.e., like cash, and that their forgery was the economic equivalent of highway robbery, albeit with a pen. *Reports*, 115.

One is left wondering if the Chief Justice had a political agenda in March of 1765. Certainly the following "Pope's Day" took on political overtones, following the Stamp Act, as Samuel Quincy observed, *Reports*, 113–114, S. Quincy n. 3, and Grand Jury secrecy for informers could also become important for cases of treason. But there were politically neutral explanations for his exhortations as well, as discussed above.

NOTES: PAGE 111

Chief Justice Hutchinson's concern for prisoners in the Gaol, "our Fellow Creatures," was remarkable, in his day and ours. The Gaol was only used to house those awaiting trial. "Every Man in the Eye of the Law is presumed innocent till proved guilty. How preposterous then, Gentlemen, is it to commit a Man to a Place, who whether innocent or not must run the Hazard for his Life. . . ." *Reports*, 112. The Massachusetts county jails, still used in part for the same purpose, long presented such problems, and judges and counsel today still express similar concerns, ranging from conditions in local jails to extraordinary detention at Guantanamo Bay. See, for example, *Inmates of the Suffolk County Jail* v. *Eisenstadt*, 360 F. Supp. 676 (1973) (U.S.D.C., Mass., Garrity J.) holding that conditions at the former Charles Street Jail were so bad as to

This is not our Cafe. There has been a moft fcandalous and notorious Riot, not only againft Common Law, Natural Law, that is, the Law which every Man has implanted in him, but directly againft a Law of this Province;(2) nay the Offenders had Notice of the very Law, and warned againft a Violation of it; and I queftion whether there is any Law of this Province more univerfally known than this. For your Direction, Gentlemen—Riots, Routs, and unlawful Affemblies are where there are any Number not lefs than three, where they come with an Intent to commit fome unlawful Act—if they take not one Step they ought to be punifhed for this Intent; if they move forward, it is a Rout; if they commit any one Act, it is a Riot; every Man ought to ufe his utmoft Endeavour for the Suppreffion of fuch fcandalous Breaches of the Public Peace; and I am informed that the Magiftrates and others of this Town did their utmoft to prevent that Infult upon Government in this notorious Riot, but it feems all proved ineffectual—You cannot be infenfible that I have Reference to that lawlefs Mob who affembled on the 5th of laft November, (3) moft atrocioufly broke the Peace, put every

---

(2) Anc. Chart. 595. This ftatute was for the fuppreffion of diforders caufed by "tumultuous companies carrying about with them pageants and other fhews through the ftreets and lanes of the town of Bofton." See note (3) infra.

(3) The anniverfary of the Gunpowder Plot, known as "Pope Day," had been for many years the occafion of an annual riot between the "north-enders" and "fouth-enders" in the town of Bofton. Each of thefe rival factions celebrated the day by a proceffion carrying the effigies of the Pope, the Devil and the Pretender upon a platform, under which fmall boys, by means of rods connected with the figures, caufed them to rife up and look into chamber windows as they paffed. The

violate the inmates' rights under the Eighth and Fourteenth Amendments. *Id.*, 690–691. See also *Marion County Jail Inmates* v. *Anderson*, 270 F. Supp. 2d 1034 (U.S.D.C., S. D. Indiana, Barker, J.). As to Guantanamo Bay, see *El-Banna, et al.* v. *Bush*, 394 F. Supp. 2d 76 (2005) (U.S.D.C., D.C., Oberdorfer, J.), finding that petitioners there failed to demonstrate "an imminent threat to their health." *Id.*, 78. Many thanks to Charles Riordan.

NOTES: PAGE 113

The Chief Justice's appeal to "Natural Law, that is the Law which every Man has implanted in him," as well as to the Common Law (i.e., non-statutory law) and the "Law of the Province" (i.e., statutory law) showed juristic sophistication. *Reports*, 113. Note, however, that he especially relied on the statutory law, particularly where the offenders have direct notice of the statute.

every Member of this Town in Confuſion, and many in the utmoſt Hazard of their Lives; and I would mention for the Benefit of all preſent, as they are a pretty large Concourſe of People, that Perſons in general do not know what a Danger they run, in mixing in ſuch a Mob; if there had been any Perſon killed, every Man there would have been liable to be tried for his Life, and by a rigorous Conſtruction of the Law, might have loſt it: It would have lain upon every Perſon to have proved how he came there and what was his Buſineſs; and every Perſon who could have been proved to have been aiding before the Fact, encouraging and aſſiſting after it was begun, and actually doing, or protecting and ſcreening after it was committed, muſt have come to his Trial, and for aught I ſee muſt have been convicted; for there are no Acceſſories in Murder; all are Principals.

There is another Offence — you have ſeen it in the public Prints — of Robbery on the Highway — Money

---

The houſeholders were called upon for contributions for the celebration under the penalty of broken windows; and the two proceſſions, after parading the town, met in Union Street, where they fought for the figures, which were afterwards burnt, either on Copps' Hill or the Common, according as victory remained with the north or ſouth end. See Drake's Hiſtory of Boſton, p. 661.

Before the next anniverſary in 1765, the general indignation occaſioned by the Stamp Act had cauſed a reconciliation to be effected, and both parties joined in the eſcort of a "Union Pope," together with ſeveral additional figures repreſenting Tyranny, Oppreſſion, Slavery, &c. Maſs. Gazette, Nov. 7, 1765; Boſton Evening Poſt, Nov. 11, 1765. The deſcription of this celebration which appeared in both the above papers, concludes as follows: — "This Union and one other more extenſive may be looked upon as the (perhaps the only) happy effects ariſing from the S——p A——t."

[P. 114]

Money demanded and actually taken; an Offence very heinous in its Nature, and very rare in this Country, and I hope it will be univerſally diſcouraged; and I queſtion whether it is univerſally known, that by a late Law of this Province, it is Death to commit a Robbery on the Highway.

Another Offence — I take Notice of it with Pleaſure — that was formerly very common, but has not of late been heard of among us — I mean the Forgery and Counterfeiting our Public Bills of Credit: The Rigour of the Law, the Severity with which this Court has adjudged in ſeveral ſignal Inſtances, their full Determination to perſevere with the ſame Rigour in all ſimilar Caſes has happily been the Cauſe of its Suppreſſion.

Yet there is another Kind of Forgery, very pernicious to the Commonwealth, which will come before you; the Forgery of Notes of Hand: You perceive, Gentlemen, what Confuſion ſuch a Practice muſt introduce, how wicked a Crime this is in its Nature, and how deſtructive its Conſequences; on this Head I need ſay no more.

I will take up no more of your Time, Gentlemen. I will ſpare you, the Court and the Audience; only obſerving further that all Offences, from Murder, the higheſt of all Felonies, down to ſimple Felony, are ſubject to your Inquiry; yet though you ſhould be ſatisfied that there have been a Number of theſe leſſer Offences committed, as theſe come more immediately under the Cognizance of the lower Courts, you may omit taking Notice of ſuch Miſdemeanors,

[P. 115]

Miſdemeanors, unleſs you ſhould think there has been any groſs Neglect in the Courts of Inferiour Juriſdiction.

But before I leave you, Gentlemen, I would obſerve one Word more relative to your Duty. In the Petty Jury, Gentlemen, you are ſenſible that all muſt agree in the Verdict; but to every Indictment the Agreement of twelve only is ſufficient. One other Point there remains, Gentlemen, for you to obſerve, and that is, you are to keep your own and the King's Council; this, Juries in general, diſregarding their Oaths, do not, ſtrictly enough, obſerve — nay, I myſelf have often heard that the Jury had found a Bill, long before it was publiſhed in Court. But, Gentlemen, even after that, you are not liberated from your Oaths — you are to keep the Names of the Informers, and Everything elſe that comes before you in your preſent Capacity, ſecret; and unleſs this is done how will Offenders ever be brought to Juſtice? An Informer comes, purely for the public Good, to reveal ſome groſs Abuſe of the Laws, and hoping he may do ſome Good, yet unwilling that he ſhould be known to be the Perſon. Soon after it is blazed abroad that he was the *Informer*, and every Circumſtance aggravated to make him odious; will he ever again hazard his Reputation — nay, even his Property? will not this deter many good Men from doing eminent Services to the Public? In Conſequence of which many heinous Crimes will go unpuniſhed, many wholeſome Laws will be broken with Impunity. (4)

And

(4) See John Adams's Diary, under the date of the following December.

[P. 116]

And finally, Gentlemen, I would obſerve, that though it may give you great Uneaſineſs to bring Offenders to Puniſhment, yet this, Gentlemen, ſhould not prevent the Performance of what is incumbent on you as the Grand Inqueſt. 'Tis the Good of the Whole demands it; and that Self-Approbation which always attends a Conſciouſneſs of having diſcharged our Duty will ever be an ample Recompenſe.

I ſhall add no more; but only pray that Infinite Wiſdom may direct you, and that the Supreme Fountain of all Goodneſs may aſſiſt you in the Proſecution.

---

cember.—"Who has made it his conſtant endeavour to diſcountenance the odium in which informers are held? Who has taken occaſion in fine-ſpun, ſpick and ſpan, ſpruce, nice, pretty, eaſy, warbling declamations to Grand Inqueſts, to render the characters of informers honourable and reſpectable?" 2 John Adams's Works, 169.

CASE 41

Present:

A full Court.

WHITNEY *v.* WHITNEY.

Rec. 1765. Fol. 136.

Whitney *verſ.* Whitney.

In a Declaration on a Note by the Payee, the Omiſſion of "Order" is an immaterial Variance. *Aliter*, in a Declaration by an Indorſee.

ASSUMPSIT on a Note. Note offered in Evidence to the Jury.

Mr. Adams (objected.) The Word *Order* is omitted; we take it to be an eſſential Variance. There is not a greater Difference between a Bond and

[P. 117]

Whitney v. *Whitney* (1765)
5 George III (Aug.) in the
Superior Court of Judicature

1 · BRIEF DESCRIPTION

This is a general contractual ("assumpsit") action on a Note. The Note apparently was to pay "Plaintiff" instead of the usual "Plaintiff *or* Order." (Defense counsel stated "Order" was omitted, Plaintiff's counsel said only the "or" was left out.) Since the action was brought by the payee, rather than a third party holding the Note by endorsement, the omission made no difference. But the Note apparently went to the Jury on another point, whether it was properly made at all by the payor.

2 · COURT RECORDS

Available at Rec. 1763. Fol. 136.

3 · PROFESSIONALS INVOLVED

John Adams (1735–1826) appeared for the Defendant. Robert Auchmuty (1723–1788) appeared for the Plaintiff. See *Appendix 6* for short biographies.

It was unclear why the Chief Justice did not give his opinion in such a simple case, unless it was because of some conflict of interest.

4 · AUTHORITY

Adams cited *Baynham's Case* (1730), *Fitz-Gibbons Reports* (covering 1727–1732), 130, 131, published in London in 1732, and W. Nelson's *Law of Evidence*, published in London in 1717, 1735, 1739, and 1744. See *Sweet & Maxwell*, *supra*, vol. 1, 300:55 and 379:7, respectively. These authorities were cited for the rather weak and obvious point that some variances in negotiable instruments "are fatal." *Reports*, 118. But this was where the Plaintiff was a third party taking by endorsement, and the date was wrong. Auchmuty also cited an English source, G. Duncombe's *Trials per Pais: a Law concerning Juris Nisi Prius* etc., 399, first published in 1665 and republished eight times by 1739, see *Sweet & Maxwell*, vol. 1, 375:8, observing that Adams's cases were inappropriate.

and a Note, than between a Note negotiable, and not. Such kind of Variances are fatal. Vid. Fitzgib. 131, *Baynham's Caſe;* Law of Evid. 191.

Mr. Auchmuty. The Note is, to pay Plaintiff *Order:* The *or* is left out. Where a Note is nonſenſical we are not obliged to follow it. There can be no Doubt but whether this is Evidence to a Jury or not. In Favour of Juſtice doubtleſs it is. As to the Authorities the Gentleman cites—"a Note of a different Date," is a much ſtronger Caſe, for that is a totally different Note. Cites Trials per Pais. 399.

The Court ruled, that the Note ſhould go in as Evidence, on another Point.* That, as the Note *had not been indorſed*, the Omiſſion of *Order* was immaterial—*otherwiſe* had it been indorſed. (1)

Ch. Juſt. did not give his Opinion.

* Vid. the Caſe, *Ruſſell & Oakes.* (2)

---

(1) S. P. *Fay* v. *Goulding*, 10 Pick. 122—"*Per Curiam.* As the action is brought by the payee this is not a material variance. If the plaintiff were an indorſee it would have been neceſſary to allege that the note was payable to the payee or his order."

(2) *Ante*, p. 50, where it is ſaid by *Ruſſell J.* that there is no difference between notes negotiable and not, until the indorſement.

5 · LATER CITATIONS

As Samuel Quincy noted, *Fay* v. *Golding*, 27 Mass. (10 *Pick.*) 122 (1830) decided the same point of law, where the action was brought by the payee, omission of "or his order" was not a "material variance." *Reports*, 118, S. Quincy n. 1.

6 · NOTES

This was an apparently "open and shut" case where the Note was made to the Plaintiff payee, and had not been endorsed to a third party. Why a lawyer as skilled as John Adams would defend such a case as an "essential variance" is the only mystery.

The Court did say the "Note should go in as Evidence, on another Point," and Josiah Quincy cross referenced Case 21, *Russel* v. *Oakes* (1763), *Reports*, 48. In the *Russel* case the note had been endorsed to the Plaintiff, but had been already paid by the payee, a much more difficult problem—see the discussion at Case 21, Note 6.

CASE 42

Banifter *verf.* Henderfon.

Meffrs. Dana & Gridley, for Banifter.
Meffrs. Auchmuty & Otis, (1) *for Henderfon.*

Special Verdict.

BANISTER *v.* HENDERSON.
Rec. 1766.
Fol. 80.

Cohabitation and univerfal Report are fufficient Evidence of a Marriage to eftablish the Legitimacy of the Demandant in a Real Action.

Devife as follows : " I give all my Houfes, Warehoufes, Lands, Mortgages, Money, Merchandife," &c. &c. " and all that of Right any Ways belongs and appertains to me," " to my three Sons, T., S., and J., to be equally divided among them in three equal Shares or Proportions, after my Debts, Legacies, and Funeral Expenfes are paid ; and if either of my three Sons die without Heirs lawfully begotten

THOMAS BANISTER, Grandfather of the prefent Demandant, made his Will the 25 January, Anno 1708–9, and after divers Legacies follows :

" *Item*, after my juft Debts and Funeral Charges " are paid, I give all my Houfes, Warehoufes, " Lands, Mortgages, Bills, Bonds, Money, Plate, " Debts, Wares, Merchandizes, both at Sea and " Land, as alfo all Books, Bedding, Houfehold " Stuff, Horfes, Cattle, and all that of Right any " Ways belongs and appertains to me, whether " named or not named, to my three Sons, Thomas, " Samuel and John, to be equally divided among " them in three equal Shares or Proportions, after " my

---

(1) James Otis's will, made many years after, during the unfortunate condition of mental derangement in which his life ended, commences as follows : " In the name of God, Amen. — I, James Otis, being in no manner of fear of Death, though called by fome the King of Terrors, and by old Bannifter in his will, a fergeant — " Tudor's Life of Otis, p. 483. And in the will of Thomas Banifter, the teftator in this cafe, of which a copy is on file, appears the following : — " When Thou Jehovah fhall fend Thy inexorable ferjeant Death to arreft this body, and carry it to that dark prifon of the grave," &c.

—— " Had I but time, (as this fell fergeant, Death
Is ftrict in his arreft,)"
HAMLET, Act V., Sc. 2.

[P. 119]

Banister v. *Henderson* (1765)
5 George III (Aug.) in the
Superior Court of Judicature

1 · BRIEF DESCRIPTION

This is another very important case, described by Auchmuty as "a Case of great Expectations and great Importance," *Reports*, 128. Like *Dudley* v. *Dudley* (1762), *Reports*, 12, Case 9, and *Elwell* v. *Pierson* (1763), *Reports*, 42, Case 20, it involved a poorly drafted will. (The will, made on January 25, 1709, raises important questions as to the general competency of the colonial bar at that time, or whether the testator, an obviously rich man, even had legal advice, Otis asking which use of words "is likeliest to get into the Head of a mere Layman. . . ." *Reports*, 136.) There was also a threshold issue as to whether the testator was lawfully married.

The ancestor, Thomas Banister, left his estate to be "equally divided" between his three sons, John, Thomas, and Samuel, "and if either of my three Sons die without Heirs lawfully begotten in Wedlock, I will their Share or Proportion to the surviving Sons or Son of their Heirs forever." *Reports*, 120. The sons died in this order: John (without issue), Thomas (with issue), and Samuel (without issue). Samuel, the last surviving son, "supposing he had a Fee, conveys away this Estate." *Reports*, 124. The Demandant, Banister, heir of Thomas, now sues "the Tenant," to whom Samuel alienated the estate, on the grounds that the land was entailed, with cross-remainders and thus Samuel was only a tenant entail, with no interest to sell that would survive his death. The proper title would, thus, be in the surviving heir of Thomas, as tenant entail. (Note: under the holding in *Baker* v. *Mattocks* (1763), *Reports*, 69, Case 29, that would be the eldest male—as entails were ruled to be not partible in Massachusetts.)

The argument for the Defendant Tenant was four fold: 1) that the testator was not legally married so that the Demandant was not a legal heir; 2) that the words of the will established three equal tenancies in common, with executory devises over, not an entail—thus Samuel, as surviving son, had a legal fee to sell; and 3) that even if an entail was established by the words of the will, it would have been subject to three cross-remainders, and the law allowed only two; and 4) that collateral warranties between the brothers would bind their issue, including the Demandant.

in Wedlock, I will their Share or Proportion to the furviving Sons or Son and their Heirs forever." Alfo a Legacy of £500 previoufly given to a Daughter was in a certain Event "to be paid to my three Sons or their Heirs, to be equally divided among them as I have willed the reft of my Eftate to be divided among them or the Survivors of them." *Held*, that the Brothers took an equal Tenancy in Common in Fee in the Real Eftate, determinable on either's dying without Iffue in the Life of fome other Son, and an executory Devife over of fuch Deceafed's Share to the Survivor or

"my Debts, Legacies and Funeral Charges are paid, "*and if either of my three Sons die without Heirs* "*lawfully begotten in Wedlock, I will their Share or* "*Proportion to the surviving Sons or Son and their* "*Heirs forever.* And the Reafon why I make my "eldeft Son Thomas but *equal* with his Brothers "Samuel and John, is for thefe Reafons; firft, he "hath had a confiderable Share already, Secondly, "I have given his Son £500 if the Lord fpare his "Life — I need add no more Reafons, but this — "they are all equally dear to me."

Afterwards: "I will to my beloved Wife Sarah "Banifter, said Pew for her Life, to order who fhall "fit with her in it, and untill my Grandfon Thomas "Banifter is of Age of twenty-one Years, if he liv-"eth to have *Male Heirs*, I give it to him and *to* "*his Male Heirs lawfully begotten in Wedlock forever*, "both Proprietorfhip and Pew, but if he dieth "without *Male Heirs*, I give it *to the next Male* "*Heirs, and to defcend to the next Male Heirs, with-*"*out any Alienation forever.*" (2)

In

---

(2) The fpecial verdict further found that the three brothers entered under the provifions of the will aforefaid, that Samuel and John (who foon after died without iffue) made a letter of attorney to Thomas, who conveyed the premifes to Giles Dyer, who reconveyed to Thomas, who conveyed again to Dyer one moiety of the premifes. Thomas died, leaving the demandant his fon and other children. Dyer then made a deed of the whole of the premifes to Samuel, who afterwards, together with Frances, the widow of Thomas and mother of demandant, conveyed the premifes to Peter Luce, who conveyed to John Henderfon, father of the tenant, after which Samuel died without iffue. If the demandant was entitled to recover, the jury found for him poffeffion of the whole, or one moiety, or any leffer part to which the Court decided that he was entitled. "But if he be intitled to no part thereof," then for

The Court held that the testator was legally married, despite the absence of a marriage certificate. This was due to the evidence of cohabitation and universal report. But by a closely divided decision, three to two, the Court further held that the Tenant should nevertheless prevail, apparently because the words of the will established tenancies in common with executory devises, rather than an entail with cross-remainders. (According to Quincy, the collateral warranty argument was abandoned by Tenant's counsel, although both he and Samuel Quincy noted that it was a good defense.)

There was no reason given for the ultimate judgment, but the arguments of counsel were set out at length by Quincy. The three prevailing Justices were Lynde, Cushing and Russell, and the dissenters were the Chief Justice and Oliver. Among the prevailing arguments were powerful policy appeals by James Otis, Jr., against the institution of entail. "The Common Law and Policy of England have been, this 4 or 500 Years, tired of these intailed Estates . . . Many have been the ill Effects felt both by State and Individuals. . . ." *Reports*, 140. It was also noted that a decision for the Demandant would be against equity, depriving the Tenant of land "—fairly purchased, long possessed, the Purchase Money used to support the [Banister] Family." *Reports*, 147.

2 · COURT RECORDS

Available at Rec. 1766. Fol. 80. Samuel Quincy noted that an opinion was given by John Read (1680–1749) in 1745 on the same will. See *Banister* v. *Cunningham*, Rec. 1754, Fol. 148. See *Reports*, 156–159. Read came to the opposite conclusion from the Court, finding that the words of the will established an "Estate Tail" with "Cross-Remainders." See *Reports*, 157. He also concluded that the Estate Tail would be partible, giving each heir a tenancy entail, exactly opposite from what the Court eventually decided in *Baker* v. *Mattocks*, *Reports*, 69, Case 29, *supra*. Rarely do we have two major legal reviews of the same words in a colonial will, much less two reviews that come to exactly opposite results! This certainly demonstrates the difficulty of the case.

3 · PROFESSIONALS INVOLVED

Richard Dana (1700–1772) and Jeremy Gridley (1701/2–1767) appeared for the Demandant, and Robert Auchmuty (1723–1788) and the patriot James Otis, Jr. (1725–1783) appeared for the Tenant. See short biographies in *Appendix 6*. These arguments may have been among their greatest. Quincy records brilliant, even biting, exchanges. In addition, each side was asked to file a "brief State of the

Survivors. *Hutchinſon*, *C. J.*, & *Oliver*, *J.*, *diſſ.*

If an Eſtate Tail with Croſs Remainders, whether Conveyances by the Brothers with Collateral Warranty would not bind the Iſſue, *quære?*

Under the Province Charter no Appeal lies to the King in Council, in a Real Action.

In ſettling the ſpecial Verdict, there were three Points the Parties could not agree on. One was, whether the preſent Demandant was legitimate; or, in other Words, whether Thomas and Frances Baniſter, Father and Mother of the Demandant, were legally married.

Thomas and Frances Baniſter came over from England, and lived as Man and Wife, both in Old and New England.

Mr. Auchmuty, again the Legitimacy of the Demandant. Had it been perſonal Eſtate, no Doubt common Report might have done to prove the Marriage, but here is a great Real Eſtate to be determined — ſhall common Fame be relied on in this Caſe? (3) No Certificate of the Marriage, the higheſt, the only legal Evidence. Had it been in a new Country where Records are not kept, there might have been ſome faint Colour for not producing a Certificate, but in England theſe Records are moſt ſtrictly kept; for they know it is the only Evidence that will ſerve; the only Proof of the Legality of Marriage.

Mr.

---

for the tenant coſts. That part of the caſe between the ſtatement of the deviſe and Mr. Dana's argument is reported in the MS. as of the previous term, after the caſe, *Rex* v. *Pourkſdorff.* For convenience the caſe is printed as a whole.

(3) See *Means* v. *Welles*, 12 Met. 361, *Hubbard*, J.—"It was argued that mere cohabitation was not a ſpecies of evidence ſufficient to ſuſtain a writ of right. But we are aware of no diſtinction as to the amount of proof neceſſary to eſtabliſh a marriage in any one caſe more than another, where marriage is a fact to be proved in order to ſuſtain an action."

Case" to assist the Court, and these are reproduced at *Reports*, 145–151. This was a highly unusual procedure. Finally, Quincy reproduced "Another State of Banister's Case which I received from Chief Justice Hutchinson," which he also reproduced. See *Reports*, 151–155.

The latter remains a mystery. It stated with brilliant clarity the argument for the Demandant, but it was apparently not written by Demandant's counsel. We know Chief Justice Hutchinson favored the Demandant's case. Did he write this document?

This was one of the most prominent cases to be decided by a closely divided court, 3 v. 2, with Lynde, Cushing & Russell in the majority, Chief Justice Hutchinson and Oliver in dissent. Hutchinson was the most frequent dissenter in *Quincy's Reports*. See *Appendix 1, infra.*

The "tone" of the legal argument in this case was certainly remarkable—far more personal and combative than what Quincy usually records. Gridley referred to one of the opposing arguments as a "terrible Bugbear." *Reports*, 141. The exchange continued:

"The Lawyers who talk of the Abhorrence of the Law, the Confusion, the Awkwardness, and I don't know what all, of Cross Remainders, were asleep, I believe, and had their Heads muffled up in Napkins.

Mr. Auchmuty. I don't understand such Reflections.

Mr. Gridley. I meant no Reflection on you, Sir.

Mr. Otis. Mr. Auchmuty, I did not take Mr. Gridley intended to reflect upon us, but on all the Judges of England.

Mr. Gridley. What mighty Difficulty to former People I can't tell; 'tis very plain now. Cross Remainders may be among 2; why not 3?"

Such an exchange, while civil by today's standards, was not the norm for an active bar of just over a dozen men, who frequently dined together. Gridley, Otis, Thacher, Adams and Auchmuty even formed a little "Law Clubb" . . . "for the study of Law and oratory." See *Diary and Autobiography of John Adams*, L. H. Butterfield, ed., Cambridge, Mass., 1964), 1, 251. (Hereafter, "*Adams Diary*.") See also Daniel R. Coquillette, "Justinian in Braintree," *Law in Colonial Massachusetts*, eds. Coquillette, Brink, Menand (Boston, 1984), 376–382.

4 · AUTHORITY

Of all of Quincy's cases, this remains the most important for what it tells us about colonial use of legal authority. Not only did Quincy record the arguments of counsel in great detail, but he also noted the reaction of the judges—

Mr. Gridley. In Strictneſs of Law they ought to produce a Copy, and not a Certificate, though generally allowed. It has been ſaid that a Certificate is the higheſt Evidence; but I ſay the Perſons preſent at the Marriage is Evidence higher in its Nature—for how will that ever prove the Identity of the Perſons? Cohabitation and univerſal Report have always been deemed ſufficient Evidence, and I never in the Courſe of my Practice heard it denied before.

Ch. Juſt. Have you no Authorities, Gentlemen?

Mr. Gridley. There is no Authority that the Sun ſhines.

Auchmuty. But there is Evidence.

Ch. Juſt. How do Quakers ever prove Marriage except by Report?

Mr. Auchmuty answered, Favour was ſhown them.

Mr. Gridley. There ſhall be no baſtardizing Iſſue after Death, is a Maxim of the Law.

Auchmuty. A Baſtard can't be Heir till Death, and after Death Baſtardy can't be proved.*

Juſt. Ruſſell only inſtanced in Quakers.

Juſt. Lynde. I can't think a Certificate alone is Evidence, or the beſt—that is greater which Mr. Gridley

* *Qu.* if Cases in Time of Holt, 287, would not have been pertinent.

and added his own critique of both the arguments and the judges. Quincy's critiques, added by way of notes, were usually more accurate than what was happening in the courtroom. These notes leave little doubt that Quincy was a particularly talented young lawyer, a thesis confirmed by his *Law Commonplace*. It is also possible that Quincy was being advised by a senior lawyer. If so, it was not one of the participating lawyers, as Quincy's comments cut both ways. Finally, while almost all of the voluminous authority cited was English, this case was also one of the rare examples of citations to earlier colonial cases—in particular, *Dudley* v. *Dudley*, *Reports*, 12, Case 9, *supra*, and *Elwell* v. *Pierson*, *Reports*, 42, Case 20, *supra*. This would surely have encouraged Quincy's reporting "project." Each of these important aspects of *Banister's Case* will be commented upon below.

A. The Marriage Issue

The Demandant had to prove that he was the legitimate heir of his grandfather, as a threshold issue. But there was no wedding certificate. The question was whether their living together for years as man and wife would be sufficient evidence. Gridley, for the Demandant, appealed to his own long experience, "Cohabitation and universal Report have always been deemed sufficient Evidence, and I never in the Course of my Practice heard it denied before." *Reports*, 122.

But the Chief Justice wanted authority. "Have you no Authorities, Gentlemen?" Gridley's response, "There is no Authority that the Sun shines," obviously displeased the Chief Justice, for he noted again, "I am sorry for Want of Authorities." *Reports*, 122–123. He obviously took the matter into his own hands, and appeared the next day with authority from *Burn's Ecclesiastical Law*, first published in London in 1760, and again in 1763. See *Sweet & Maxwell*, *supra*, vol. 1, 166:22. Burn established that "cohabitation of the Parties" and "publick Fame and Report" was evidence of marriage and, more importantly, that "half Proof, ought to be extended in Favour of Marriage, rather than contrary to it." *Reports*, 123–124. The key passage from *Burn* was directly quoted from Thomas Wood's *A New Institute for the Imperial on Civil Law*, first published in London in 1704, and republished in 1712, 1721 and 1730. This authority apparently resolved the issue for the marriage.

It is worth noting that Thomas Wood, D.S.L. (1661–1722), was a leading English civilian jurist, from the famous group of Roman law learned schol-

Gridley mentioned. Perſons preſent at the Marriage can only prove the identical Perſons. (4) Univerſal Report is, in my Opinion, ſufficient Evidence, corroborated with other Circumſtances, of the Marriage.

Ch. Juſt. From Thomas and Frances Baniſter living in Old and New England as Man and Wife, I think it may well be inferred they were ſo. (5) I am ſorry for Want of Authorities, and that this Point was not left to the Court as well as the Reſt; for it is not properly a Matter of Fact.

The ſecond Point (Matter of a Perſon's Death) was proved to Satisfaction.

The third, whether there was an actual Entry into the demanded Premiſes was given (in Effect) up; for a Deviſe veſts the Eſtate immediately in the Donee; it does not mean an actual Seizin in Law, but Right to Seizin.

The Jury found the two Points in Favour of the Demandant.

N. B. The next morning *Ch. Juſt.* produced the following Authority from Burn's Eccleſiaſt. Law, vol. 2d, p. 36. (6) Tit. Marriage: "The Proof "of

---

(4) S. P. *Commonwealth* v. *Norcroſs*, 9 Maſs. 492. *Ellis* v. *Ellis*, 11 Maſs. 92.

(5) S. P. *Newburyport* v. *Boothbay*, 9 Maſs. 414. *Means* v. *Welles*, 12 Met. 361. *Aliter* in criminal proceedings before St. 1841, c. 20. *Commonwealth* v. *Littlejohn*, 15 Maſs. 163.

(6) Burn's Eccl. Law, Marriage, X. 5.

ars and practitioners centered in Doctors' Commons, London. Richard Burn (1709–1785), a clergyman, frequently relied on civilian expertise. *Banister's Case* is thus an example of colonial American cases that relied on English civilian, rather than common law, authority. See the discussion in Daniel R. Coquillette, *The Civilian Writers of Doctors' Commons, London* (Berlin, 1988), 198–215.

B. The Entail Issue

The central argument in the case was whether Banister's poorly drawn will established an entail with cross-remainders—which would give the Demandant title as Banister's senior male heir—or whether it established tenancies in common between Banister's three sons, with executory devises, which would give the Defendant Henderson good title. See the discussion at Note 6, *infra*. Like any botched will, there was unlikely to be any case directly in point, and many cases available to both sides to argue by analogy. So many sixteenth, seventeenth, and eighteenth-century English cases were invoked, that Gridley complained, "I won't produce 20 Authorities where 1 is necessary; here have been numerous Authorities cited, to what Purpose I know not, unless *Show*." *Reports*, 143 (emphasis in the original). Otis answered, with equal sarcasm, "You must allow children a little ostentation." *Reports*, 143.

Despite the range of the English cases cited on both sides, it became clear in the argument that the lawyers were only imperfectly aware of what the cases held, and were also fairly ignorant of the relevant English statutes. As an example, Dana cited to *Chadock* v. *Cowley* (1625), 2 *Croke's Reports*, 695. (*Croke's Reports*, part 2, covering the period 1582–1641, were first published in London in 1657.) See *Law Commonplace*, [21], n. 6. Otis interrupted, rather unprofessionally, stating, "Are you not sensible, Sir, Lord Holt denies that Case to be Law?" Dana, taken aback, replies, "No: But if he does, he is not infallible: But the Authorities mentioned are sufficient." *Reports*, 126.

It was certainly reasonable for Otis to invoke the name of the great English judge, Sir John Holt (1642–1710), who was Chief Justice of the King's Bench for 21 years, 1689–1710. But Holt had not doubted *Chadock* v. *Cowley*, which found a fee tail by implication, but rather *Hearn* v. *Allen* (1627), 3 *Croke's Reports*, 126, which found, three to two, no fee tail. Since Otis was arguing against the fee tail, Lord Holt's doubts about *Hearn*, expressed in *Nottingham* v. *Jennings*, 1 *Lord Raymond's Reports*, 570 (1st ed. London, 1743), cut *against* Otis, not for him! (Holt said of *Hearn*, "If the said case were law." *Id.*, 570.) Quincy quickly

"of Marriage may be by Witneſſes who were preſ-" ent at the Solemnization; by Cohabitation of the " Parties; by publick Fame and Report; by Con-" feſſion of the married Perſons themſelves, although " their Acknowledgment might be only to avoid the " Puniſhment of Fornication, and by divers other " Circumſtances which, if they amount to a half " Proof, ought to be extended in Favour of Marri-" age, rather than contrary to it. Wood, Civ. Law, " 122."

Mr. Dana. The Demandant Baniſter demands by Force of the Will before me; his Pedigree is ſet forth in the ſpecial Verdict. I need not obſerve that the Intent of Teſtator is to be the ſole Director for Conſtruction of the Words, unleſs a new Eſtate is created contrary to Law. Now from the whole Tenor of the Will the Teſtator's ſole Aim appears to be the keeping his Eſtate in his Family; and this Intention of his is the general Key to the Underſtanding the Will, and, if attended to, will ſhow in the cleareſt Manner he deſigned an Eſtate Tail. He gives his Eſtate "*to his three Sons Thomas, Samuel and John, and if either of my three Sons &c., to the ſurviving* SONS OR SON;" Samuel, (I can't imagine how he came to take it in his Head) ſuppoſing he had a Fee, conveys away this Eſtate; but if this is an Eſtate Tail, it wipes away all Conveyances whatſoever; for Eſtates Tail are inalienable, except by Fine and Recovery, and that reduces it to Fee Simple.

I am ſenſible when a Man gives all his Eſtate without any otherwiſe expreſſing his Intent, a Fee paſſes.

[P. 124]

picked this up, noting "*Qu.* If that Doubt of Lord Holt does not make against Mr. Otis" and later "*Qu.* If the Case . . . would not be in Favour of the Demandant." *Reports*, 126. But neither of the advocates, Dana nor Otis, knew enough English law to catch the error. Quincy, however, did!

The same occurred with a key English statute. The Chief Justice asked Auchmuty, "What do you suppose can bar an Estate tail?" He replied, "Conveyances with collateral Warranty." *Reports*, 128. Indeed, the final argument for the Defendants was that such conveyances barred the issue in this case. This time Gridley interrupted, "Abolished long ago by Act of Parliament." *Reports*, 128. Auchmuty has no immediate answer, and later, rather lamely, remarked, "It is true there is a statute about Warranties, but unless they produce, I shall not answer it," a response prohibited by modern professional rules that require a lawyer to disclose to the court adverse authority not disclosed by opposing counsel. *Reports*, 133. See *A.B.A. Model Rules of Professional Conduct* Rule 3.3 (a)(2).

In truth, the statute in question, 4 & 5 Ann, ch. 16 (1706), was not relevant at all, as it only applied to ancestors making collateral warranty that did not have an estate of inheritance in possession, which would not be the case here under either party's theory, a point picked up by Otis, who also denied "the Statute of Ann to extend here." *Reports*, 140. With this view, Quincy himself agreed. "[A]nd *qu.* if ye Act of Parliament extends, or is binding here." See *Reports*, 145.

The point is that, despite all the quantity of English authority argued in this case, the lawyers themselves were not particularly accurate or skillful in its use. Quincy, on the other hand, knew a lot of English law, and caught some of the errors.

It is also very important to note that, in the end, both sides relied on policy arguments, rather than relying narrowly on authority. The Demandant's lawyers emphasized again and again that the testator had intended an entail, even though he used the wrong technical terms. Dana argued, "On the Whole, the Testator's sole Intent plainly appears to intail his Estate; his Words aptly enough express his Intent; and, as it is consistent with the Rules of Law, it is the Business of the Law to fulfill that Intent." *Reports*, 128.

The opposing side argued against entailed land as a matter of policy, urging the judges to find against an entail unless it has been perfectly created. Otis made an impassioned speech:

paſſes.* 1 Salk. 239, *Hopewell* vs. *Ackland.* If the Teſtator had ſaid no more than "I give all my Houſes," &c., they would have had a Fee; but his Intent through the whole Will being not only to take Care of his Sons, but their Poſterity—and though he gives all "*to his three Sons Thomas, Samuel and John, to be equally divided among them, in three equal Shares or Proportions,*" yet he afterwards explains himſelf—"*If either die without Heirs,*" and he then explains *what Heirs,* "*Heirs lawfully begotten in Wedlock,*" then goes on—"*I will their Share or Proportion to the ſurviving Sons or* SON;" and though the Words following, "*their Heirs forever,*" are not aptly expreſſed, yet they ſhall not vitiate, for his Meaning is evident from all the Words taken together, and his Intent ſhall take Effect.† Cites 1 Salk. 226, 227, *Bliſſet* vs. *Cranwell,* and 2 Vent. 285.

As to his willing "all to his three Sons to be equally divided among them," there are numberleſs Authorities where the firſt Words give a Fee, by giving Lands to a Man and his Heirs forever, yet the after Words, explaining what Heirs he meant, make it a Tail. *Nottingham* vs. *Jennings,* 1 Salk. 233, as in our Caſe. *Soulle* vs. *Gerrard,* 1 Cro. 525. The after Expreſſions ſhew he meant Heirs lawfully begotten in Wedlock, and created a Tail: So in the Caſe laſt cited, the firſt Words ſhall be ſet aſide, becauſe contrary to his Intent. But full to

* Vide 3 Mod. 45, *Reeves* v. *Winnington.*

† *Qu.* whether 8 Rep. 95 b, would not have been a good Authority to this Point.

> The Common Law and Policy of England have been, this 4 or 500 Years, tired of these intailed Estates; and therefore every legal Method has been prosecuted for their Suppression. Many have been the ill Effects felt both by State and Individuals, in Conveyance of these Estates; therefore so far from being favoured they have ever been discountenanced; and surely never was such an Estate as is here contended for, favoured—big with the greatest Confusion and Injustice—inconsistent both with Law and Common Sense. I therefore submit it to your Honour's Judgment, not doubting that Judgment will be rendered according to Law. *Reports*, 140.

It should be noted that this case also shows Quincy referring to *Blackstone's Commentaries* (Oxford, vol. 1, 1765, vol. 2, 1766, vol. 3, 1768, vol. 4, 1769), something he did only once in his *Law Commonplace*. See Quincy's querie "*Qu.* If 2 Black. Comment. ch. 20, pp. 302, 303 and ch. 13, pp. 381, 382 would have been impertinent in this Case." *Reports*, 155. See the discussion of Quincy's use of Blackstone in Introduction, *Law Commonplace*, *Quincy Papers*, vol. 2, 19–20 n. 37.

C. American Authority

Banister left a charge upon the estate: "*Funeral Charges, Debts and Legacies*," which, according to Auchmuty, "many of which were very large." *Reports*, 130. Auchmuty argued that these charges would convert, as a matter of law, "the Estate into a Fee," rather than an entail. *Reports*, 131. This was an argument that the Court had heard before, in *Elwell* v. *Pierson* (1763), *Reports*, 42, Case 20, and is in the famous case of *Dudley* v. *Dudley et al.* (1762), *Reports*, 12, Case 9.

The *Dudley* case involved another wealthy colonist with a poorly drafted will, where the key words—although apparently intending a fee tail—did not use the correct formalities. The estate had a charge—providing firewood for the testator's mother, and that was used to argue for a fee simple, rather than a fee tail. The Court, without giving reasons, declined to find a fee tail. *Reports*, 25. The *Elwell* case also involved a poorly drafted will with a charge to the legatee to "maintain Myself and his Mother during our Lives with sufficient and convenient Maintenance." *Reports*, 43. But in this case the Court found that the legatee "Samuel by the Words would have taken a Tail" but the charge, "the Burden and Duty of Maintenance made it a Fee simple." *Reports*, 48.

Both these cases would have strongly supported the arguments against finding an entail in *Banister's Case*, as Auchmuty argued, "This Point (of Charge) had great Weight, and justly, in those Cases." *Reports*, 131. But Quincy questioned "whether the Case of *Elwell* . . . was not adjudged against the

to our Point is the Cafe of *Chadock* vs. *Cowley*, 2 Cro. 695. Here —

Mr. Otis. Are you not fenfible, Sir, Lord Holt denies that Cafe to be Law? *

Mr. Dana. No: But if he does, he is not infallible: But the Authorities mentioned are fufficient. Cites 3 Lev. 70, *Parker* vs. *Thacker*, and 2 Cro. 415, *Webb* vs. *Hearing* — a Cafe in Point. It appears by all thefe Authorities, *una voce*, that Devifors' Intent fhall govern, the Intent fhall be collected from all the Words together; and though the fame Words give a Fee, yet if other Words explain what Heirs he means, viz[t] "Heirs of the Body," or "*Heirs lawfully begotten in Wedlock*," it fhall make a Tail; and in our Cafe it is a Tail with a Limitation over to "*either of the Sons or* Son," which the Law calls Crofs Remainders. The Intent of our Grandfather was fo fixed to keep his Eftate in his Family, and to make a Tail, that he extends it even to Perfonal Eftate, in which he is "againft the Rules of Law," therefore we don't demand it; † but his Intent in this is ftrongly marked. "*To the furviving Sons or* Son." The Iffue take, as much as if their Father had furvived.

Authorities to fupport the Crofs Remainders. T. Jones,

* *Qu.* if Mr. Otis was not miftaken, and that he blended it with the Cafe of *Hearn* v. *Allen*, 3 Croke, 57, which Ld. Holt feems to doubt of in the Cafe of *Nottingham* v. *Jennings*, 1 Ld. Raym. 570? and *qu.* if that Doubt of Lord Holt does not make againft Mr. Otis?

† *Qu.* if the Cafe *Nottingham* vs. *Jennings*, 1 Ld. Raym. 570, would not be in Favour of the Demandant.

[P. 126]

Law." *Reports*, 131. Earlier Quincy noted, "*Qu.* if any Estate but an *Estate for Life* can be enlarged by *any Charge*. For it is Law that 'no Estate shall pass by Implication of Law against the *express Limitation* of the Party . . . ,'" citing 2 *Coke's Reports*, 556, and 1 *Croke's Reports*, 254. *Reports*, 130–131. Quincy's point was valid. His statement was a direct quotation from *Buckler's Case* (1597), 1 *Coke's Reports* 55a, at 55b, which was so applied in *Hogg* v. *Cross, Will*, 1 *Croke's Reports* (1591), 254, at 255. The error of the Court in *Elwell* is that it found that the testator's words established an entail, and thus the charge could not establish a contrary result as an implication of law. In both *Dudley*, *supra*, *Reports*, 12, Case 9, and in this case, *Banister* v. *Henderson*, the Court did not find that the testator's words established an entail. Conceivably, they could have formed that the testator's words did not establish an express limitation, so that the fact of the charge could be persuasive. Of course, in neither the *Dudley* nor the *Banister* cases did the Court give reasons for finding a fee, rather than an entail.

The relevance of the colonial *Elwell* and *Dudley* cases to major cases like *Banister* must have encouraged Quincy in his efforts to create a Massachusetts law report. The memory of the lawyers was also important, but they frequently appeared on opposite sides of the same issues, and could not be expected to recount the precedents reliably. For example, Gridley argued against the entail in *Dudley*, for the entail in *Elwell*, and for the entail in *Banister*. Auchmuty argued for the entail in *Dudley* and against the entail in *Elwell* and *Banister*. Otis was consistent, arguing against the entail in both *Dudley* and *Banister*. With counsel shifting sides on major issues, accurate reports would be valuable to everyone.

5 · LATER CITATIONS

Banister v. *Henderson* was cited in 1959 in *Stamper* v. *Starwood*, 339 Mass. 549, 553 (1959), on the issue of evidence of marriage. The Court held that length of the marriage and number of children could establish the good faith of the wife in determining whether a bigamous second marriage had become valid under an enabling statute that recognized such marriages, if entered into at least one party in good faith.

As Samuel Quincy noted, more than two cross-remainders were allowed by later English and Massachusetts law. *Reports*, 155–156, S. Quincy n. 9. See *Hall* v. *Priest*, 72 Mass. (6 *Gray*) 18 (1856).

T. Jones, 172, *Holmes* vs. *Meynel.* Thomas Raymond, 452. This laſt Caſe is full in Point. "As for Authorities, you cannot expect many in a Will; every Will ſtands upon its own Legs." Pollexfen, 425. (This Caſe enlarged upon, therefore look into it more eſpecially.) Croſs Remainders may be by Implication. Dyer, 303, Tit. Deviſe. T. Jones, 172.

Ch. Juſt. But it muſt be expreſs Implication. Is this ſo?

Dana. Yes. Vid. Dyer, 303. (This Authority much relied on.)

Gridley. Dyer, Saunders, &c.; four of them of the ſame Opinion, that Croſs Remainders may be between three. 1 Vent. 224, *Cole* vs. *Levingſton.* By the whole Current of the Authorities, Croſs Remainders may be between three; our Caſe is much clearer than is common in theſe Caſes "*To the ſurviving Sons or* SON."

Ch. Juſt. "*And their Heirs forever.*"

Dana. I take it ſo: And he has ſhown what Heirs he meant; "*Heirs lawfully begotten in Wedlock.* The Expreſſion "*If either die,*" is an Anſwer to your Honour.

Ch. Juſt. Did the Teſtator intend a Tail to all of his Sons?

Gridley.

[P. 127]

NOTE: PAGE 138
"*Videbatur*"

The issue being discussed here is whether one could have more than two cross-remainders, a theory necessary to the Demandant's case. Otis was claiming that the untitled case set out in Dyer, *Les Reports* . . . (London, 1738 ed.) at 304 was *obiter dictum* ("a saying by the way") as far as this case was concerned. Dyer's *Les Reports*, covering 1513–1582, was one of the oldest published English reports, first published in London in 1585. See *Sweet & Maxwell*, vol. 1, 299–300:47. As the Dyer case only involved two cross-remainders, this is correct. Common law doctrine has traditionally regarded any judicial opinion "not necessary to a judgment" as "not binding as precedent." See *Jowitt*, *supra*, p. 1255. Gridley's reference to the "Roman Judges" of the civilian tradition and "*videbatur*" ("*videbatur*," it "seems") was inappropriate. See *Reports*, 138. On Roman law "precedent," which was not systematic at all, see W. W. Buckland, *A Text-Book of Roman Law* (3d. ed., Peter Stein, 1963) 638 ("Roman law had no system of precedent"); H. F. Jolowicz, *Historical Introduction to the Study of Roman Law* (1954), 569 (Precedent as "*exemplum*"). My thanks to my distinguished colleague, Charles Donahue Jr.

NOTE: PAGE 143
"*reddendo Singula Singulis*"

This phrase means "by giving each to each," and refers to the legal construction rule that "when one of two provisions in one sentence is apportioned to one of two objects in another sentence . . . the other provision is similarly appropriated to the other object." *Jowitt*, *supra*, 1493. This is done through common sense. Hence in the phrase "'If anyone shall draw or load a sword or gun,' the word 'draw' is applied to 'sword' only, and the word 'load' to 'gun' only . . . because it is impossible to load a sword or draw a gun." *Jowitt*, *supra*, 1493.

NOTE: PAGE 145
"Dr. Sullivan's Lect. On the Laws of England."

Francis Stoughton Sullivan, L.L.D., did not publish his lectures until 1770. See Francis S. Sullivan, *Lectures on the Constitution and Laws of England*, London, 1770, *Sweet & Maxwell*, vol. 1, 108:113. But he began giving the lectures much earlier, at the University of Dublin. See Francis S. Sullivan, *A Plan For the Study of Feudal and English Laws in the University of Dublin*, Dublin, 1761. The *Plan*

Gridley. They took Tails with Crofs Remainders over.

Dana. On the Whole, the Teftator's fole Intent plainly appears to intail his Eftate; his Words aptly enough exprefs his Intent; and, as it is confiftent with the Rules of Law, it is the Bufinefs of the Law to fulfill that Intent.

Mr. Auchmuty. This is a Cafe of great Expectation and great Importance. We differ very much and very materially. In order to elucidate any Point in a Will, the other Parts connected with and referred to it muft all be confidered. Mr. Dana fays the Conveyances will not hurt, but will all be "wiped away" if this is an Eftate Tail: I fay not.

Ch. Juft. What do you fuppofe can bar an Eftate Tail?

Auchmuty. Conveyances with collateral Warranty.

Gridley. Abolifhed long ago by Act of Parliament.

Auchmuty. But firft to the Tail. He has expreffly given Money to go over as the other Eftate: "*My Will is that faid Legacy of* £500 *be equally* "*divided among my three Sons, Thomas, Samuel and* "*John, with the Reft of my Eftate as hereafter is men*-"*tioned.*" And afterwards, if certain Things happen, "*then I will the laft mentioned Sum of* £500 "*fhall*

[P. 128]

was only 9 pages long. Did Quincy have a manuscript copy, or did he add this note, citing to 182–183, after 1770?

6 · GENERAL NOTES

As he began his argument, Auchmuty noted that "This is a Case of great Expectation and great Importance." *Reports*, 128. Why was such a case so important for the colonials? It certainly involved a lot of money and pitted the leaders of the colonial bar against each other, but so did a number of Quincy's cases. Auchmuty added, "We differ very much and very materially." *Id.*, 128. But Auchmuty argued for the entail in *Dudley*, *Reports*, 12, Case 9, and against the entail in both *Elwell*, *Reports*, 42, Case 20, and *Banister*, and Gridley switched sides on the entail issue as well. See Note 4, *C.*, *supra*.

I understand Auchmuty as making a different point. The *Banister* case presented the Court and the lawyers with an unusually stark choice of policy goals and, despite the brave and often inaccurate display of English authority, little persuasive, much less binding, precedent. And as emphasized in *Dudley*, *Reports*, 12, Case 9, the place of entail in the colony had social, economic, and gender importance. See *id.*, Note 6. Finally, as Samuel Quincy noted, there was no Appeal allowed to the King in Council in London in a real action such as this. *Id.*, 25, S. Quincy n.9. See The Charter of the Province of Massachusetts Bay . . . 1691 [Second Charter], *Charters and General Laws*, *supra*, 32. The Second Charter allowed appeals to the King in privy council "in any *personal* action, wherein the matter in difference doth exceed the value of three hundred pounds . . ." (emphasis added). This limitation on real action appeals was not always observed. In *Dudley* v. *Dudley* (1762), *Reports*, 12, Case 9, the Privy Council entered an order for a hearing in May 1765. See discussion at *id.*, Note 6. In a case related to this one, *Banister* v. *Cunningham* (1754), described in Samuel Quincy's note 9, *Reports*, 156, an attempt was made to appeal to the Privy Council, despite the fact it was a real action. According to Joseph Smith, the appeal was allowed at the Council Board, "although denied below." See Joseph H. Smith, *Appeals to the Privy Council from the American Plantations* (New York, 1950), 248, n. 176. See also Privy Council Register, PC 2/104/323, 439, 455. The Privy Council also took a controversial real action case on appeal from the Superior Court of Judicature in 1767 and reversed the judgement below in 1771. See *Jeffries* v. *Donnell*, Privy Council Register, PC 2/112/520, PC

"*ſhall at her Death be paid back again to my* 3 *Sons* "*or their Heirs, to be equally divided among them, as I* "*have willed the Reſt of my Eſtate to be divided among* "*them or the Survivors of them.*" Can his Intent* be ſuppoſed a Tail, when he deviſes Monies to go as his other Eſtate? He very expreſſly intails his Pew, very trifling in its Nature, in the ſtrongeſt Terms, which ſhews he was not ignorant of apt Words to make a Tail.

But to the Doctrine of Implication which the Gentlemen inſiſt on. The Expreſſions to make a Tail muſt be ſtrong and coercive. 2 Bac. 66. "No "Words ſhall be conſtrued to make a Tail without "*plain* Implication." The Courts will never extend Implications, againſt Eſtates Fee, the nobleſt Eſtates, to Fee Tail, Eſtates of a much baſer Nature. *Wild's Caſe*, 6 Coke, 16 b. To make Eſtates Tail "the "Intent ought to be manifeſt and certain, not ob-"ſcure and doubtfull." In the ſame Caſe: "The In-"tent, and not the Words only of the Deviſor, ought "to make it an Eſtate Tail, then this Intent ought "to be manifeſt and certain, and ſo expreſſed in the "Will;" and in our Caſe, as in *Wild's*, no ſuch Intent appears. They have cited no Authorities, but where the Implication has been ſo ſtrong that there was no avoiding the Conſtruction. Cro. Car. 368, *Spirt* vs. *Bence*. In this Caſe, where the Intent is not very clear, the Court will not conſtrue againſt the Common Law. I remember in Croke, Walmſley ſaid, Implication muſt be very ſtrong to diſinherit other

* *Qu.* Might not this be Evidence of his ſtrong Intent, as Mr. Dana hinted?

17

2/113/16/76, 88, 98, discussed by Smith, *supra*, at 163–165. Again, my thanks to Sharon H. O'Connor, my esteemed colleague. Most interestingly, no record has been found of effective local relief in any of these cases, despite Privy Council review. In real actions, as a practical matter, the Court seems to have been on its own.

Here are the legal issues in a nutshell. As observed before, Banister had poor legal advice in drafting his will, despite his great wealth—surely a comment on the colonial profession in 1709! (He may have had no professional help! Otis asks twice about what ideas are "likeliest to get into the Head of a mere Layman." See *Reports*, 136, 137.) Banister's goal was simple, to divide his property equally among his three sons, unless any of the sons died without "Heirs lawfully begotten in Wedlock." If so, the share of the dead son without heirs should go to "the surviving Sons or Son and their Heirs forever." Normally, a bequest that does not vest unless there are legitimate heirs was an entail, but Banister used the wrong words. He should have said, "To Thomas, Samuel and John and the Heirs of their Body (in Tail General) and if Thomas dies without Issue, the Remainder of his Share to Samuel and John in tail; and if Samuel dies without Issue, the Remainder of his Share to Thomas and John in tail; and if John dies without Issue, the Remainder of his Share to Thomas and Samuel in Tail (the cross remainders)." (But this is not what the will said! See the actual terms set out at *Reports*, 119–120.) If Banister had used the right words, it would have been clear that he did not intend to leave either John or Samuel, who died without issue, a vested estate. Tom's eldest son, the Demandant, would have the tenancy in possession, and Samuel's sale to Henderson would be void. (Assuming that you could create more than three cross-remainders. See *Blackstone's Commentaries* (1766), vol. 2, 381.) The "State of Banister's Case," that Quincy "received from Chief Justice Hutchinson," set it all out plainly. (Did Hutchinson himself write this to convince his brethren?) See *Reports*, 151, 154–155.

One technical problem with this "solution" was that it created three cross-remainders. At the time, it was doubtful that more than two could be valid at English common law. As Blackstone said, "[T]o avoid confusion, no cross remainders are allowed between more than two devises. . . ." W. Blackstone, *Commentaries*, vol. 2 (London, 1766), 321. But there was no logical reason why more than two cross remainders could not exist. As Grid-

other Children, and to carry the Intent againſt the Rules of Deſcent. It is ſaid alſo in 3d Mod., the Court will not puzzle themſelves about the Intent of a Man who was perhaps ſick and confuſed in his Senſes at the Time of making the Will, but let it deſcend according to Law. 3 Mod. 104, *Hanchet* vs. *Thelwal.*—"No Reaſon can be given why this Court "ſhould not conſtrue Wills according to the Rules "of the Common Law, where an Eſtate by Implica- "tion is ſo uncertain; for when Men are ſick, yet "have a diſpoſing Power left, they uſually write "Nonſenſe, and the Judges muſt rack their Brains "to find out what is intended."

You are ſenſible when there are pecuniary Legacies to pay, *prima facie* a Fee. What an Eſtate ſoever they took, they had it charged with "*Funeral Charges, Debts and Legacies*," &c., many of which were very large. Theſe and many other Things to be paid, no Perſonal Eſtate appears to be left wherewith to diſcharge them—none found in the Verdict; thus by Reaſon of theſe Charges, it converts the Eſtate into a Fee. 1 Lilly, 451, 2. To the ſame Point is 3 Rep. 21, *Boraſton's Caſe.*

Ch. Juſtice. The Books vary in that Point.

Auchmuty. Where there is a Sum in Groſs, that creates a Fee, but where a Sum is to be paid out of the Annual Profits, that don't alter; that I take to be the Rule.* Your Honours remember the Caſe

* *Qu.* if any Eſtate but an *Eſtate for Life* can be enlarged by *any Charge.* For it is Law that "no Eſtate ſhall paſs by Implication of Law

[P. 130]

ley argued, "Cross remainders may be among 2; why not 3?," *Reports*, 142, and, indeed, as Samuel Quincy noted, later common law held any number valid. *Reports*, 156, S. Quincy n.9.

But not only did Banister use mostly the wrong words to establish an entail for his lands, he actually used mostly the right words to convey an entail male in his church pew! "[T]o my Grandson Thomas . . . if he liveth to have Male Heirs . . . and to his Male Heir's lawfully begotten in Wedlock forever . . . but if he dieth without Male Hiers, I give it to the next Male Heirs, and to descend to the next Male Heirs, without any Alienation forever." *Reports*, 120. As Auchmuty observed, "He very expressly intails his Pew, very trifling in Nature, in the strongest Terms, which shows he is not ignorant of apt words to make a Tail." *Reports*, 129.

One solution, favored by the Demandant, was to figure out Banister's intention, and then implement it, despite the incorrect wording. As Dana argued, "Meaning is evident from all the words taken together, and his Intent shall take Effect." *Reports*, 125. Since the testator clearly intended the land to descend to his sons' issue, if any, and not remain vested in a son without issue, the intent would seem to require a legal entail.

Another solution, favored by the Tenant in Possession who bought the land from Samuel, would be to disfavor entails unless precisely established by the correct terms. In default of correct wording, all three sons would take equal fee simples—subject to executory devises. Even Dana, for the Demandant, admitted that "when a Man gives all his Estate without any otherwise expressing his Intent, a Fee passes." *Reports*, 124. Otis argued, with characteristic eloquence, "The Common Law and Policy for England have been, this 4 or 500 Years, tired of these intailed Estates; and therefore every legal Method has been prosecuted for their Suppression." *Reports*, 140. Not only do they often disinherit women, given the common use of male entails, but they tie up land and are "big with the greatest Confusion and Injustice—inconsistent both with Law and Common Sense." *Reports*, 140. Finally, in this case there was a purchaser who thought he had bought good title. As Auchmuty observed, "[I]t will cause the utmost Confusion thus to eject People out of Lands they have for so many years quietly enjoyed; and . . . to turn them out upon so strained a Construction of Words . . . would be as much against Justice and Equity, as Law and Common Sense." *Reports*, 133. (Often colonial entails were barred by prescription in such cases—perhaps the time here fell just short.)

Cafe *Elwell & Pierfon*, (7) and the Cafe of *Dudley* vs. *Dudley*. (8) This Point (of Charge) had great Weight, and juftly, in thofe Cafes.

The Words on which the Crofs Remainders are founded are Fee Simple; for it is, in Cafe of Death and no Iffue, to the Survivor and "their Heirs forever." Had Banifter the Grandfather intended a Tail, would he have ufed thefe Words,—efpecially when he fo well knew the Words of Tail, as in the Cafe of the Pew?

Ch. Juft. "Heirs lawfully begotten in Wedlock"— is that Tail or Fee?

Auchmuty. A Fee; for if a Man will depart from the Rules of Law, his Eftate fhall go according to the Rules of Defcent. But if there is any Doubt in this Cafe, it is at End: It is clearly then with us, both by the Principles of Law and Equity. 1 Lilly, 454. No Intent fhall go againft the exprefs Words of the Devifor; at this Rate from a Paffage or two inadvertently written, fhall go againft the general Tenor and plain Words of a Will. 2 Bac. 68. To conftrue the Intent againft the Words is directly againft all the Books. The Courts have always detefted Crofs Remainders among more than two;
I

Law againft the *exprefs Limitation* of the Party, altho' the Limitation is void." 2 Rep. 55 b, and fo adjudged in the Cafe of *Hog* vs. *Croffe*, Cro. Eliz. 254. *Ideo* —

Qu. whether the Cafe of *Elwell* (cited above) was not adjudged againft Law.

---

(7) *Ante*, p. 42. (8) *Ante*, p. 12.

Then there was the question about whether the sale to Henderson involved collateral warranties that would bar the Demandant and other issues. As Quincy observed, the Statute 4 & 5 Ann, ch. 16 (1706) did *not* bar collateral warranties from tenants in possession, such as Samuel. Further, Quincy questioned "if ye Act of Parliament extends, or is binding here," probably because the colony had quite a different land law from England. See *Reports*, 145. But see *Baker* v. *Mattocks*, *Reports*, 69, Case 29, a closely divided judgment holding entails not to be partible under colonial law, despite the provincial statute that made fee simple estates partible.

All in all, these were naked policy choices with very little "fig leaf" of genuinely binding legal precedent to hide the Court's preference. And the Court, as in *Baker* v. *Mattocks* (1763), *Reports*, 69, Case 29, was narrowly divided, three to two.

Of all recorded colonial cases, this reveals most graphically the dynamics between the opposing lawyers, and between the bench and bar. As discussed in Note 4, above, the lawyers were at the edge of their competence and made a series of technical errors in using English precedent—most caught by Quincy himself. While they certainly cited to English authority, they also made naked policy arguments to the Court, on both sides. Frequently, their appeals to authority were also "bluff," with both sides ignorant of actual English doctrine. *Banister's Case* was so difficult as to give the leaders of the colonial bar a real test of their expertise. If you assume that an isolated bar of little more than a dozen practitioners was inherently incapable of sophisticated argument, *Banister's Case* will set you straight. But it also demonstrated that Boston was not London.

Banister's Case also was extraordinary in that the Court requested written arguments from the lawyers, the "State of the Case" set out at *Reports*, 146–155. The two "States of the Case" prepared by opposing counsel repeat—in a very concise way—their oral argument. Very different was the third "State of Banister's Case," "which I [Quincy] received from Chief Justice Hutchinson, together with the foregoing State of that Case, by the Demandant's Council." *Reports*, 151. Was this third document prepared by an *amicus curiae* (a "friend of the court")? Was it written by Hutchinson himself? (It supported Hutchinson's dissenting view in favor of the Demandant, but appears to have been quite separate from the "State of the Case" prepared by the Demandant's

I would obſerve upon Raym'd that the Caſes are different. In order to induce the Court to theſe Croſs Remainders, Mr. Dana has obſerved that the Deviſor's whole Intention was to keep his Eſtate in the Family. This is Implication upon Implication which no Lawyer ever heard of. This Intent is got by Implication, and Croſs Remainders are built on that Implication: But the moſt natural Implication is, that he never intended a Tail at all. According to theſe Gentlemen's Way, you may add Implication on Implication *in Infinitum*, and we ſhall have no ſettled Rules of Law to go by. In all their Authorities, the Deviſe was only to two, with Croſs Remainders over, but the Caſe they would extend it to, is among three; and the Reaſon is given—it is to avoid Confuſion by ſplitting Eſtates into a thouſand Parts, and to keep Peace among Men, from diſputing about ſo many confuſed Croſs Remainders: Beſides, the Remainders cited in the Books are not founded upon Implication, but upon Certainty. Mr. Dana has ſaid, there may be Words which import a Fee, changed into a Tail by after Words. Agreed; but no ſuch Words here—nay, the after Words are, " their Heirs forever," a plain Fee. They can't produce a ſingle Authority where the firſt Words controul the laſt; here the laſt Words are Fee. If any Parts claſh, I can't help that; if a Teſtator will deviſe in ſuch a Manner that there is no telling what Eſtate paſſes, it muſt paſs according to Law. " Where *a certain Intent* may be collected, it ſhall be " conſtrued according to that Intent, but where it is " uncertain, it is void. The Intent of the Deviſor " muſt be collected upon *plain* Words, and not " upon Words which engender Confuſion." And Walmſley

[P. 132]

counsel.) In all events, the three "States of the Case" in *Banister's Case* remains a remarkable example of written colonial advocacy.

Finally, it is impossible to read this case without admiration for Quincy as a Reporter. Deprived, by custom, of reasoned opinion from the Justices, he nevertheless corrected counsel's arguments with impressive knowledge and logical acuity. He was a young and inexperienced lawyer, but he had a first class legal mind. Cases such as *Banister's Case* must have convinced him that Massachusetts had reached a point in its legal sophistication where good provincial law reports were needed. There was probably no lawyer in the colony better able than Quincy to fill the need.

There is an excellent student paper by my former research assistant, Kevin W. Cox, Harvard Law School Class of 2005, "Entail on the Eve of the Revolution: Cases from the Reports of Josiah Quincy, Jr.," on file with the Editor, which explores in depth the relationship between *Banister's Case* and Quincy's other entail cases. See also the extensive discussion of *Banister* v. *Cunningham* in Richard B. Morris's classic *Study and History of American Law* (1959), 97–98.

The final judgment, for a fee simple and against the Demandant Banister's entail, was by Justice Lynde, Cushing and Russell, with the Chief Justice and Justice Oliver in dissent. In *Dudley, supra*, the Chief Justice had delivered a judgment of a united court for the fee simple and against the entail. *Reports*, 25. In *Baker* v. *Mattocks, supra*, the issue was different, whether the entail was partible. But a negative judgment would strengthen the "effect of entail." There, the Chief Justice and Judge Cushing voted for partibility, but their three other colleagues felt constrained by both custom and law to support the entail unweakened by partibility. *Reports*, 72–74.

These great cases, *Banister's Case*, *Dudley*, and *Baker* v. *Mattocks*, pushed the pragmatic inclinations of the justices against the letter of the English law. They would go quite a ways in favoring fee simple, as in *Dudley* and *Banister's Case*. But *Baker* v. *Mattocks* was a step too far. Only Justice Cushing would steadfastly find for the fee simple. Like Chaucer's Sergeant at the Law, for Justice Cushing, "all was fee simple to his strong digestion." See Daniel R. Coquillette, *Anglo-American Legal Heritage*, *supra*, 289.

Walmſley ſaid, " It is a good Way when the Words " in a Will are ambiguous, ſo as the Intent may not " be collected, to expound the Will according to " the Law." Cro. Eliz. 742, *Taylor & Ux.* vs. *Sayer.* Is not the Intent here, at beſt, uncertain? Are the Deviſor's Words plain? Don't his Words engender Confuſion? Therefore by the laſt and the other Authorities, the Intent void, and the Rules of Deſcent muſt be obſerved.

The laſt Thing I ſhall mention, having already ſaid enough, is the ſeveral Deeds from Samuel, John and Frances, the Warrantys of which are collateral, and therefore bind the Iſſue. Lit. §§ 709, 716, 717, with Coke's Commentary read at large. 1 Inſt. 373 a, 375 b. 376 a. It is true there is a Statute about Warranties, but unleſs they produce, I ſhall not anſwer it.

Upon the Whole, Eſtates Tail are never implied except when the Intent is obvious — never have been, at Home or here. The Courts are very cautious how they give the Conſtruction of Tail to Words in a Will, eſpecially such Words as theſe; and I believe never known to extend them to create Croſs Remainders among three. I ſhall not recapitulate my Arguments, but only obſerve that it will cauſe the utmoſt Confuſion thus to eject People out of Lands they have for ſo many years quietly enjoyed; and now to turn them out upon ſo ſtrained a Conſtruction of Words inadvertently dropped in a Man's laſt Illneſs, would be as much againſt Juſtice and Equity, as Law and Common Senſe.

Mr.

[P. 133]

Mr. Otis. The prefent Queftion arifes on this Claufe of Mr. Banifter's Will: "*After my juft Debts*," &c. In the Courfe of my Argument I fhall examine what Eftate the Brothers took, whether Tail or Fee. 2dly. If a Tail, whether with Crofs Remainders over. 3dly. If Remainders over, whether the Remainders were in Tail or in Fee. 4thly. If a Tail with Crofs Remainders in Tail, whether the Collateral Warranty will not bind the Iffue.

The Terms Fee Simple, Tail, general and fpecial, Crofs Remainders, Executory Devife are well known, but yet as this Cafe depends pretty much on having clear and precife Ideas of them, your Honours will pardon me, if to refrefh our Memories, I juft run over the feveral Definitions.

(Mr. O. then gave the feveral Definitions of the above Terms, chiefly from Black. Anal. q[d] vid.)

Crofs Remainders, as commonly fpoken of, mean implied Remainders. I will for the prefent allow a Tail, their Whole depending on their fhewing implied Crofs Remainders rationally and legally implied. Hobart, 29, 34, *Counden* vs. *Clerke*. Though the Intent of y[e] Devifor is juftly called the Pole-Star of the Will, yet this is not the only Director; for this I cite the laft Cafe. There are a Variety of Opinions on this Point, and that too among the moft eminent Judges; fome paying an unlimited Obedience to the Teftator's Intention, and others as much flighting it. The true Medium, I take it, is laid down in this Cafe; "the "Devife

[P. 134]

"Deviſe muſt be taken according to the Intent of "the Party Deviſor," yet "ſuch Intent muſt be ſo "expreſſ'd in the Will, that it may be *certain* to "the *Court*, and *not againſt Law.*" Hobart, 32. All the Vagaries of a diſeaſed Mind are not to be attended to; yet the rational and legal Intent of a Teſtator ſhould be obſerv'd.

(Relative to the Croſs Remainders, Mr. O. cited the following Authorities:) Viner, Tit. Remainder; the whole of this Chap. Here "Croſs Remainders ſhall not riſe between 3, unleſs the "Words do very plainly expreſs the Intent of "the Deviſor to be ſo;" "between 3 the Law "will not endure Croſs Remainders, by Reaſon of "the Confuſion which will enſue." "Two Croſs "Remainders may well ſtand together, but *three* "*cannot well ſtand together*; for that would make "ſuch Confuſion as the Law abhors, and that was "the Reaſon of the Judgment in the Caſe of *Gilbert* "vs. *Witty*,* which *Pemberton, Ch. Juſt.* ſaid he took "to be ſound Law. 2 Show. 139, *Holmes* vs. *Meynill.*" And per *Holt, Ch. J.*—"a Croſs Remainder is an "awkward Sort of a Thing; the Caſe of *Holmes* vs. "*Meynill*† has prevail'd, and is not fit to be ſtirr'd "now;" "and *Powell, J.* ſaid that the Caſe never "went down with him, though affirmed on a Writ "of Error, and he has heard learned People ſpeak "againſt it"—(And goes on, and finiſhes the Chapter, and reads the whole of the Caſes cited above by Viner and others.) Viner, Tit. Rem. M. p. 1, 2. Ibid. Tit. Deviſe L. p. 1–6. 10 Rep. *Seymour's Caſe*, 1 Inſt. 1 b, (Fee Sim.)

From

* 2 Croke, 655. † 2 Show. 136.

[P. 135]

From all theſe Authorities there may be ſuch a Conſtruction as is conſiſtent with the Rules of Law, if it be conſtrued a Deviſe in Fee with an Executory Deviſe over. Theſe Authorities are againſt them directly: "3 Croſs Remainders cannot well ſtand together." "Between 3 the Law will not endure Croſs Remainders," and why? "'Twould make ſuch Confuſion as the Law abhors:" they are never favour'd in Law — Holt much againſt them; they are never raiſ'd by Implication; "Croſs Remainders will not ariſe to more than 2 by Implication." Viner, Tit. Rem. X. p. 4, Notes, cites 8 Mod.* 260, *Shaw* vs. *Weigh*; T. Raym'd, 455, *Holmes* vs. *Meynill*. Beſides from the plain Words, the whole Contexture and Tenor of this Will, 'tis plain he intended an Executory Deviſe over of the Deceaſed's Share to ye Survivors or Survivor; certain he never intended a Tail with Croſs Remainders over, — yet if there is the leaſt Doubt, the Caſe is with us. But which is likelieſt to get into the Head of a mere Layman — thoſe Croſs Remainders, which theſe Gentlemen contend for, which, after they have got beyond two, have puzzled the wiſeſt Heads in Europe, or that of an Executory Deviſe over, on a Fee determinable on either of his 3 Sons dying without Iſſue?

Mr. Gridley. Do you think the Teſtator had a clearer Idea of an Executory Deviſe than Croſs Remainders?

Mr. Otis. Though there may be ſome Niceties in the Difference between Executory Deviſes and other

* *Alias*, Caſes in Law and Equity.

[P. 136]

other Devises, yet the general Idea is much more likely to enter into a Layman's Head, than that of Crofs Remainders.

'Tis manifeft from the Words of the Will he intended Equality among his Children. "*The Rea-* "*fon why I make my Eldeft Son but* EQUAL *with his* "*other Brothers,*"—"*They are all* EQUALLY *dear to me:*" Would what thefe Gentlemen contend for be confiftent with this intended Equality? Would not ours? An equal Tenancy in Common being, as we fay, devifed in Fee, determinable on either dying without Iffue in the Life of fome other Son, and then an Executory Devife over of fuch deceafed's Share to the Survivor or Survivors.

The Words in the Will do not make an Eftate Tail. *Hanchet* vs. *Thelwal,* 3 Mod. 105, 6.

In Order to make this Will agree with their Scheme, they are obliged to have Recourfe to double Implications; firft an Eftate Tail is to be implied and then Crofs Remainders. "An Eftate "by Implication was never thought of in a Deed, "nor in a Will, but in Cafes of Neceffity." Cafes in the Time of L'd Talbot, 3, *Glenorchy* v. *Bofville.* One would think this Rule would be fufficient to put an End to their Claim. But if they will have Implication, what fo ftrong for a Fee, as Charges of "Debts and Legacies," &c. This Implication of a Fee is confiftent both with Law and Equity— theirs directly againft both. "A. devifes his Brother, "Lands &c., and *all his Perfonal Eftate,* defiring him "to pay his *Debts and Legacies,—a Fee paffes.*" 2 Vernon,

non, 687, *Ackland* vs. *Ackland*. 3 Cro. 58. 2 Strange, 1175, *Barker* vs. *Suretees*. Thus there was not even an implied Tail in the three Brothers; next there were no Crofs Remainders: The Gentlemen can't find I believe, if they examine all the Books from William the Conqueror down to this Time, where there are Crofs Remainders by Implication, without an exprefs Tail. There are no Crofs Remainders between 3 Brothers to be found in any of the Books, not even that of Dyer, 303. That was nothing but *Talk*. (Mr. O. here expatiates on the aforecited Paffages of Viner.) But taking this Cafe of Dyer to have been adjudged (which is far from being certain), "It *feem'd* to the Court," &c.

Mr. Gridley. *Videbatur* was always ufed by the Roman Judges, and is often in the Books.

Mr. Otis. Let it be fo: It is well known there are *obiter* Opinions, which are properly enough expreffed by "*It feems*," yet are not to be relied on as Law. An *obiter* Opinion, I take it, is about a Medium between what the firft Council in England fay *arguendo*, and the folemn Judgments of the Court, after a full Hearing the Council. The Cafe of Dyer, 303, on which they bottom themfelves is totally different from the Cafe at Bar; excepting this Cafe of Dyer it is fettled that Crofs Remainders fhall not be among more than 2, and this Cafe being among 3, it falls to the Ground. 3 Leon. 115, *Brian* vs. *Cawsen*, as cited by Viner, Tit. Rem. X. p. 5. 1 Leon. 166. *Gilbert* vs. *Witty*, Cro. James, 655. Roll. Abr. 835. Viner, Tit. Devife, Let. K. 4 Mod. 282. Cro. Jam. 590, *Pells* vs. *Brown*. (Thefe Authorities

[P. 138]

Authorities cited by Mr. O. to ſhew the Brothers took by Executory Deviſe.)

I ſhall now ſhow, if all the foregoing Points were againſt us, yet the Collateral Warranty binds the Iſſue, and therefore the preſent Demandant muſt fail; but before I enter on this, the Deeds muſt be looked into, and your Honours will there ſee how the ſeveral Warranties deſcend. It is incumbent upon me to ſhew that Collateral Warranty is a Bar, without Aſſetts, notwithſtanding the Statute of Ann. 10 Rep. 95 b, *Edward Seymour's Caſe.* Lineal Warranty bars with Aſſetts, Collateral Warranty without; it may appear hard, but if the Reaſon is attended to, it will be cleared; it is for the Safety of Men's Eſtates, and that People ſhould not be defrauded of what they *bonâ fide* bought, many Years after Purchaſe. And there are other Artificial Reaſons, as no Man is preſumed to diſinherit his own Blood without leaving him greater Advancement, &c. 1 Inſt. 373 a, b, 375 b, 376 a, &c. Viner, Tit. Voucher, U. b. 2, to U. b. 6. *Holt, Ch. J.*, ſaid, "That the true Reaſon of Collateral "Warranty was the Security of Purchaſers, and for "their Encouragement; as alſo for the eſtabliſhing "and ſettling of ſuch as were in by Title or Deſcent "caſt, and this was the only Security ſuch Perſons "could have at Common Law; and becauſe the "Eſtates of ſuch Perſons as are in by Title, are "much favoured in Law, theſe Covenants that were "for ſtrengthening them were favoured likewiſe." Same Tit. U. b. 5. 12 Mod. 512. The Collateral Warranties which are made void againſt the Heir are thoſe made by any Anceſtor who has *no Eſtate*

Eſtate of Inheritance in Poſſeſſion of the Lands. 4 & 5 Ann, ch. 16. Now, according to their own Suppoſition and the Special Verdict, the Anceſtor making this Collateral Warranty had an Eſtate of Inheritance in Poſſeſſion, and therefore does not come within this Statute; but I deny the Statute of Ann to extend here.

The Common Law and Policy of England have been, this 4 or 500 Years, tired of theſe intailed Eſtates; and therefore every legal Method has been proſecuted for their Suppreſſion. Many have been the ill Effects felt both by State and Individuals, in Conveyance of theſe Eſtates; therefore ſo far from being favoured they have ever been diſcountenanced; and ſurely never was ſuch an Eſtate as is here contended for, favoured — big with the greateſt Confuſion and Injuſtice — inconſiſtent both with Law and Common Senſe. I therefore ſubmit it to your Honours' Judgment, not doubting that Judgment will be rendered according to Law.

Mr. Gridley. "*After my juſt Debts, &c., I give all,*" *&c.* "*If either,*" &c., "*to the ſurviving Sons or Son.*" The Queſtion is, whether there was a Tenancy in Common in Fee, with an Executory Deviſe over, or a Tail with Croſs Remainders: On the other Side they ſay, the firſt Words are Fee, and the after Clauſe, "*If either die without Iſſue,*" makes an Executory Deviſe over: We ſay, if there were no more Words, a Fee, but the after Words make a Tail, and the laſt, Croſs Remainders. When we read a Will, we aim at the Deviſor's Intent; we aim at the general governing Idea of the Teſtator's Mind. If we enter

[P. 140]

enter into the Will, you will find, that the grand and ſole Object of the Deviſor was the Emolument of his Poſterity, and the Perpetuity of his Eſtate in his Family. Let us ſee, if we can't make ſuch a System of Eſtate as will be conſiſtent with the Law, and enforce the Teſtator's Intent; if it is poſſible it ſhall be done: But theſe Croſs Remainders between 3 frighten the Gentlemen; no ſuch Thing in the Books; no ſuch Croſs Remainders by Implication: We will ſee. The firſt Words, "*All, &c.*" a Fee, the Words laſt, a Tail—as for "*Heirs*," the other Words ſhew what he means. "*Heirs lawfully begotten in Wedlock.*" The Gentlemen talk of Implication upon Implication, and Implication upon that again; the Words by which the Tail is made are implied, but a neceſſary Implication. Heirs in general make a Fee, but he ſhews what Heirs he intended; "*If either die, then to the ſurviving Sons or Son,*" this makes the Croſs Remainders. The Sons Thomas, Samuel and John took Tails with Croſs Remainders over, each upon the other: Upon John's Death, Thomas and Samuel were jointly ſeized of John's Part; upon Thomas' dying, Samuel and Thomas' Iſſue were ſeized together; and upon Samuel's Death, the Whole remained to the Father of the preſent Demandant. This was the Intent of the Teſtator, that the Brothers took Tails with Remainders, one upon the other. It is the Buſineſs of the Law to explain the Pregnancy of Expreſſion, and when this Pregnancy is drawn out, this is the mighty Confuſion, this is the terrible Bugbear. The Lawyers who talk of the Abhorrence of the Law, the Confuſion, the Awkwardneſs, and I don't know what all, of Croſs Remainders, were

were aſleep, I believe, and had their Heads muffled up in Napkins.

Mr. Auchmuty. I don't underſtand ſuch Reflections.

Mr. Gridley. I meant no Reflection on you, Sir.

Mr. Otis. Mr. Auchmuty, I did not take Mr. Gridley intended to reflect upon us, but on all the Judges of England.

Mr. Gridley. What mighty Difficulty to former People I can't tell; 'tis very plain now. Croſs Remainders may be among 2; why not 3? If John dies, then to Thomas and Samuel; if Thomas dies, then to Samuel; each have a Tail with a Remainder expectant upon the Death of the others dying without Iſſue. A Fee can't be limited upon a Fee — they ſtrived hard for it in the Caſe of Deviſes, but then it was only for Years. "All the Candles burning at once," as one of the Judges * expreſſed it. *Chadock* vs. *Cowley*, Cro. Jam. 695. Dyer, 303. Here is one Acre to A. and the Heirs Male of his Body, another to B. and another to C. in like Manner. "And if they all die without Iſſue of their or "any of their Bodies or either of them," Remainder over; here are Croſs Remainders among all the 3 Sons. Dyer, 303. The Darkneſs is here diſſipated from Croſs Remainders, the Words, dying "without

* *Twiſden.*

[P. 142]

without Iſſue" are directly againſt Executory Deviſes.*

Mr. Auchmuty has endeavour'd from ſeveral Charges to prove it a Fee. The Manner of Conſtruction in Law is, *reddendo Singula Singulis*; every Thing muſt be rendered according to its Nature. An ample perſonal Eſtate was left — real ſhall never be taken in ſuch Caſe. The Charge was perſonal, and not upon the Land: Beſides, it does not appear that there was no perſonal Eſtate left; the Special Verdict ought to have ſet forth, there was no perſonal Eſtate left; this is not done, ſo that's at an End.†

It has been ſaid, Deviſor deſigned Equality — he did do Equality — all had Tails; the Event as to the Remainders was left to Chance.

I won't produce 20 Authorities where 1 is neceſſary; here have been numerous Authorities cited, to what Purpoſe I know not, unleſs *Show*.

Mr. Otis. You muſt allow Children a little Oſtentation.

Mr. Gridley. I won't ſay the Caſe of *Gilbert & Witty* is not Law, but I will produce Jones to ſhow wherein

* It is ſaid (in Carth. 310) that "It is a certain Rule that a Will shall never operate by Way of Executory Deviſe, if it may take Effect by Way of Remainder." *Qu.* if this Authority would have been impertinent.

† *Qu.* if perſonal Eſtate is not found in the Verdict, whether it is to be preſumed. Vid. 3 Mod. 45, 46.

[P. 143]

wherein it is wrong; Dodridge was certainly wrong, when he ſaid, no Croſs Remainders among 3. 7 Edward 6 (Year Book). Dodridge ought to have read this before he pronounced. It appears by this Book* that Dodridge was wrong, on whom the Gentlemen ſo much rely: 'Tis true I have not produced the Year Book, but I have produced Hobart, whom I can truſt, for he was an Oracle of the Law. 2 Jones, 172, *Holmes* vs. *Meynill.* Pemberton too is with us, one of the Miracles of Mankind; he was not afraid of the Reveries of Sick Men; was not afraid of plaguing his Mind in finding out the Meaning of diſeaſed Minds: He uſed the Aſſiduity becoming a Judge to get the Deviſor's Intent, and when he had found it, he had it fulfilled. 'Tis not the Part of Judges to ſtifle, but to enforce the Deviſor's Intent; you had Croſs Remainders among 3 at the Common Law, and Dyer, 303, has carried them as far as 4. Mr. Otis ſays there was no Judgment in this Caſe. Dyer ſeldom uſes more than "*it ſeems;*" this Mr. Otis knew: It is very ſtrange Dodridge ſhould ſay, no Croſs Remainders between 3, when here is 4, and I have ſhewn the Year Book; Dyer full with us, the greateſt Judge that ever ſat in the King's Bench, — as great in Law as Sir Iſaac Newton in Mathematicks and Philoſophy. Pollexfen, 413. So, taking theſe Authorities, we have 5 Judges againſt 3, Dodridge and other obſcure Names.† Skinner Rep. 17. Ld. Raym'd, *Meynill's Caſe.* I have looked over all their Authorities,

* Hob. Rep. 34. "A Deviſe to 3 Brothers in Tail, and that one shall be Heir to the other, this makes Croſs Remainders." Hob. 34.

† Holt and Powell.

ities, and thefe few I have felected as to the Point, and have obferved on them what is neceffary.

The Intent of the Teftator is the *only* Rule, the *only* Director, whether that Intent is got by Implication or otherwife: His Intent can't be fulfilled without Crofs Remainders, and if Crofs Remainders are good among 2, certainly among 3; they have been carried to 3, and even to 4 according to the Authorities cited; therefore as his Intent is with us, and the Law is with us, your Honours will give Judgment accordingly.

N. B. Mr. Gridley made an Excufe for not fpeaking to the Collateral Warranty, as it was a Point he did not think would be ftarted, and therefore begged time to look into the Books. This Requeft was granted.

Afterwards Mr. Gridley fpoke to this Point, of Collateral Warranty, and, as I heard, fo conclufively that the Council for the Tenants waived the Matter.*

The Court defiring that a brief State of the Cafe, *Banifter* vs. *Henderfon* might be given in by the Council on both Sides, the following States were delivered to the Court.

The

* *Sed quære*, and fee Dr. Sullivan's Lect. on the Laws of England, 182, 3, and *qu.* if ye Act of Parliament extends, or is binding here.

Qu. If 2 Strange, 969, 996, might not with Propriety have been produced in Favour of the Tenants. Vid. *Stephen* v. *Stephen*, Chan. Cafes, 168, 169, &c.; 1 Ld. Raym'd, 208. Vid. 2 Wilfon's Rep. 88 b. *Driver* v. *Standring*.

The State of the Cafe by the Council for the Tenant.

Banifter's Cafe.

Whatever Eftate the Devifees took, was by Implication — not by exprefs Devife.

Implication muft be neceffary, and not barely poffible. 2 Bac. 66 (G). 6 Co. 17. Cro. Car. 368.

Intent to be collected from the whole Will — therefore the Devifes to the Grandfon and the Daughter, as well as joining real and perfonal Eftate muft be confidered. Alfo the Words in Remainder in the Claufe now in Difpute.

From all which it appears, the Teftator never meant to Entail; the Diftinction between the Devife of the Pew and the Reft of the Eftate proves the fame Point.

The Remainder being an Exprefs Eftate in Fee, argues that the firft Eftate was alfo intended in Fee.

The Teftator meant to convey an equal Tenancy in Common, in Fee, determinable on either's dying without Iffue in the Life of fome other Son, and an Executory Devife over, of fuch Deceafed's Share to the Survivor or Survivors.

The Eftate being fubjected to the Payment of Debts and Legacies, is equal to being fubject to Payment

[P. 146]

Payment of certain Sums; and the Eſtate being implied makes a Fee Simple. 2 Vern. 687. 1 Lill. 451, 452. 3 Co. 19, *Boraſton's Caſe*. 1 Cas. Abr. Equ. 176, 9, 10, 12.

But if doubtfull, then Judgment muſt be for us, in Law and Equity; Law, that the Demandant clearly prove his Writ, and Cro. Eliz. 743—what Walmſley ſaid; Equity—fairly purchaſed, long poſſeſſed, the Purchaſe Money uſed to ſupport the Family.

To prove it no Tail, 3 Mod. 104; 3 Cro. 57; 2 Strange, 1172.

Granting for Argument Sake, that the firſt Words create an Eſtate Tail by Implication, yet the Remainders not croſs. Hob. 34. Vin. Tit. Deviſe, X. pl. 1, and Notes. Vin. Remainder, *per tot*; 2 Cro. 655. 2 Show. 139. 8 Mod. 260.

When John died, Tom. and Sam., expreſſly by the Deviſe over, became Jointenants in Fee of his Part; and on Tom.'s Death, all his Part of John's Third that was undiſpoſed went to Sam., by Survivorſhip, and never can go back as a Remainder to the Heirs of Tom.

If Jointenants in Fee, there cannot be Croſs Remainders of that joint Eſtate, for that would be limiting a Fee on a Fee at Large.

The Collateral Warranty binds. 1 Inſt. §§ 709, 716. 1 Co. 63. 10 Co. 97. Vin. Tit. Voucher, U.

[P. 147]

U. b. pl. 5, U. b. 6, pl. 1 & 2, & Notes. W. b. pl. 5. W. b. 4. Notes on pl. 2. U. b. 3, pl. 25, & Notes. Voucher, X. a. 2, pl. 5, U. b. 3, pl. 3. C. b. pl. 3, & Notes.

What is the Diftinction between a Collateral and Lineal Warranty is proved by 1 Inft. §§ 704, 705, & 717.

By the Council for the Demandant.

Cafe of Banifter vs. *Henderfon.*

Mr. Thomas Banifter by his laft Will devifed (among other Things) £500 to his Daughter Mary Banifter; but if fhe did not live to have Iffue, then to be paid to his three Sons to be equally divided amongft them, as he had willed the Reft of his Eftate to be divided among them, or the Survivors of them.

Item. He gave all his Houfes, Lands, Mortgages, Bills, Bonds, Money, Plate, Debts, Merchandizes, both at Sea and Land; as alfo all Books, Bedding, Houfehold Stuff, Horfes, Cattle, *and all that of Right any ways belonged or appertained to him whether named or not named* to his three Sons Thomas, Samuel, and John; to be equally divided amongft them; and if either of his three Sons die without Heirs lawfully begotten in Wedlock, he willed their Share to the furviving Sons or Son, and their Heirs forever.

By this Devife the three Sons took an Eftate in Common

[P. 148]

Common in Tail general in the Lands &c. devifed, with Crofs Remainders in Tail among them of each other's Shares.

Firft. By the Devife of all his Houfes and Lands &c., and all that of Right anyways belonged to him, whether named or not named, a Fee would have paffed to his three Sons by Force of the Words taken by themfelves. Vid. 1 Salk. 239, *Hopewell* vs. *Ackland*, where Alleyn, 28, *Wheeler's Cafe*, and 2 Vent. 285, *Willow's Cafe*, are rely'd on; for the Words are as ftrong and comprehenfive as thofe made Ufe of in thofe Cafes, and muft comprehend all his Eftate, which alone would pafs a Fee; and as by Devife of all his Lands an Eftate for Life paffed, the following Words, unlefs they comprehend his Eftate in thofe Lands, muft be ufelefs.

Secondly. The following Words, "equally to be divided among them," make them Tenants in Common of the Whole. Vid. 1 Salk. 226, *Bliffet* vs. *Cranwell.*

Thirdly. By the fubfequent Words — if either of his three Sons die without Heirs lawfully begotten in Wedlock, he wills their Share to the furviving Sons or Son, and to their Heirs forever — an Eftate Tail general is created of their feveral Shares; for this fhews the Intent of the Teftator to be Heirs of their Bodies, by neceffary Implication; fo that Heirs here fignifies the fame as Iffue; for they could not die without Heirs, living their Brother. Vid. Cro. James, 415, 416, *Webb* vs. *Hearing.*

[P. 149]

Hearing. Same, 448, *King* vs. *Rumball*.* 3 Lev. 70, *Parker* vs. *Thacker*. 1 Salk. 233, *Nottingham* vs. *Jennings*. Cro. James, 695, *Chadock* vs. *Cowley*.

Fourthly. By theſe Words — if either of his three Sons die without Heirs lawfully begotten in Wedlock, he willed their Share to ſurviving Sons or Son, and their Heirs forever — Croſs Remainders in Tail are created among them of their ſeveral Shares; for the Words "if either of them," &c. make Croſs Remainders, expreſs, and differs the Caſe from that of *Gilbert & Witty*. In 1 Vent. 224, *Cole* vs. *Levingſton*, *per Hale, C. J.* Vid. alſo Dyer, 303. Croſs Remainders expreſs among four, exactly agreeing with the preſent Caſe. 2 Jones, 172, *Holmes* vs. *Meynill*, a Croſs Remainder by Implication — whereas this expreſs, and conſequently a much ſtronger Caſe.

In both the ſaid Caſes the Croſs Remainders veſted in Tail, as well as the firſt Eſtate of each in their ſeveral Shares; and by the ſame Reaſon and Law, they ſhall veſt in Tail in the preſent Caſe; ſo that the Eſtate ſhall not revert till all the Sons are dead without Iſſue, and the whole Eſtate Tail entirely ſpent. And this is corroborated by the Limitation to the ſurviving *Son* as well as Sons, which plainly ſhows the Intent of the Teſtator was, that all theſe Remainders to each of the Sons, of the other's Shares, ſhould veſt in Tail immediately by the Deviſe; and this is perfectly agreeable to the Reſolution in

* By the firſt and laſt Caſes in Cro. James, it appears it was not a Contingent Eſtate, but took Place immediately by the Deviſe.

[P. 150]

in the above Cafes, particularly that in Dyer, which correfponds exactly to it, and is full in Point; and this Conftruction renders the whole Devife in every Part of it perfectly confiftent and agreeable to the evident Defign and Intention of the Teftator.

Upon the Whole, the Devife then as was obferved at firft will ftand thus: To Thomas, Samuel and John, in Common in Tail general, with Crofs Remainders in Tail to each of the others' Shares; fo that when John died firft without Iffue, his Eftate was entirely fpent, and the Remainder of his Share came equally to Thomas and Samuel in Tail; when Thomas died leaving Iffue, his Moiety defcended to the Heirs of his Body in Tail, and alfo the Remainder in Tail of John's Moiety, which was vefted in Thomas, defcended upon the Death of Thomas to the Heirs of his Body in Tail; fo that when Samuel died without Iffue, his Moiety alfo came to the Iffue of Thomas in Tail; and no Part of the faid Eftate so devifed can revert to the Heirs of the Devifor till all the Iffue of the Body of Thomas is entirely fpent.

(*Another State of Banifter's Cafe which I received from Chief Juftice Hutchinfon, together with the foregoing State of that Cafe, by the Demandant's Council.*)

Cafe of Banifter vs. *Henderfon.*

The Teftator devifes all his Houfes, Lands, &c., *and all that of Right anyways belonged or appertained to him, whether named or not named*, to his three Sons Thomas,

Thomas, Samuel and John, to be equally divided among them; and if either of his three Sons die without Heirs lawfully begotten in Wedlock, he willed their Share to the ſurviving Sons *or Son*, and their Heirs forever.

It was argued for the Defendant, that this was an Executory Deviſe, &c.

In Anſwer to which, it was urged for the Plaintiff, that it is a ſettled and certain Rule of Law, that a Will ſhall never operate by Way of Executory Deviſe, if it might take Effect by Way of Remainder, viz., if there is a particular Eſtate ſufficient to ſupport it. Vid. Carthew, 310, in the Caſe of *Reeve* vs. *Long;* 2 Saund. 380, *Purefoy* vs. *Rogers*, at the latter End of the Caſe; 2 Bacon, 72, where theſe and ſeveral other Caſes are cited.

By this Deviſe (as we ſhall ſhew clearly) an Eſtate Tail was created in the three Sons, of their ſeveral Shares; which is a particular Eſtate ſufficient to ſupport a Remainder; and therefore by the Rule, the Limitation ſhall take Effect by Way of Remainder, and cannot be conſtrued an Executory Deviſe.

It is inſiſted for the Plaintiff, that, by this Deviſe, the three Sons took an Eſtate in Common in Tail general in the Lands deviſed, with Croſs Remainders in Tail among them of each other's Shares.

To ſhew this, they obſerve —

Firſt. By Deviſe of all his Land, and all that of Right

Right anyways belonged to him, &c., a Fee would have paſſed to the three Sons, by Force of theſe Words taken by themſelves; for this they rely on the Caſe of *Hopewell* vs. *Ackland*, 1 Salk. 239, where Alleyn, 28, *Wheeler's Caſe*, and 2 Vent. 235, *Willow's Caſe*, are rely'd on; for theſe Words are as full and ſtrong as thoſe made Uſe of in theſe Caſes, and muſt comprehend all his Eſtate.

Secondly. The following Words, "equally to be divided among them," make them Tenants in Common; for which Vid. 1 Salk. 226, *Bliſſet* vs. *Cranwell.*

Thirdly. By the ſubſequent Words — if either of his three Sons die without Heirs lawfully begotten in Wedlock, he wills their Share to the ſurviving Sons *or Son*, and their Heirs for ever. By the firſt Part of them, an Eſtate in Tail general is created of their ſeveral Shares: For this ſhows the Intent of the Teſtator to be, Heirs of their Bodies; ſo that Heirs here ſignifies the ſame as Iſſue, for neither could die without Heirs in the general Senſe of the Word, living his Brothers. For this they rely on Cro. James, 415, 416, *Webb* vs. *Hearing;* Same, 448, *King* vs. *Rumball;* Same, 695, *Chaddock* vs. *Cowley*; 3 Lev. 70, *Parker* vs. *Thacker;* 1 Salk. 233, *Nottingham's Caſe.*

N. B. By the above Caſes of *Webb & Hearing*, and *Chaddock & Cowley*, and their Analogy to the preſent, it appears that this was not a contingent Eſtate, but took Place and veſted immediately by the Deviſe.

Fourthly. By the ſame Words, alſo (the latter Part of them), Croſs Remainders are created among the three Sons, of their ſeveral Shares. Theſe Words, "if either of them," &c., make Croſs Remainders expreſs, (1 Vent. 224, *Cole* vs. *Livingſton*) and is not by Implication, but as determinate as if Croſs Remainders had been drawn out at Length. And this differs the Caſe from that of *Gilbert & Witty*, produced on the other Side. Vid. also, Dyer 303, Croſs Remainders in Tail among 4, a Caſe in Point. Alſo 2 Jones, 172, *Holmes & Meynill*, where the Caſe of *Gilbert & Witty* is queſtioned. Vid. Hobart, 34, which Caſe, and that in Dyer, muſt have been overlooked by Juſtice Dodridge. He ſaid, in *Gilbert & Witty*, that it would not be found in any Book that Croſs Remainders could be between three.

It appears, alſo, by the Limitation being to the ſurviving *Son* as well as Sons, that it was the Intent of the Teſtator that the laſt ſurviving Son, the other two dying without Iſſue, ſhould take the Whole. This could not take Effect by any Conſtruction, but the above of Croſs Remainders in Tail executed; but upon this Conſtruction, no Part of the Eſtate could revert to the right Heirs of the Deviſor, until all the Sons were dead without Iſſue, and the whole Eſtate Tail in each ſpent, according to the above Caſe in Dyer.

Upon the Whole, therefore, the Deviſe ſtands thus: To Thomas, Samuel and John in Common, in Tail general; and if Thomas die without Iſſue, the Remainder of his Share to Samuel and John in Tail; and if Samuel dies without Iſſue, the Remainder

mainder of his Share to Thomas and John in Tail; and if John dies without Iſſue, the Remainder of his Share to Thomas and Samuel in Tail.

So that when John died without Iſſue, his Share came to Thomas and Samuel in equal Moieties in Tail, with Croſs Remainders in Tail between them of each other's Shares; and when Thomas died leaving Iſſue, his Share, and his Moiety of John's Share, came to his Iſſue in Tail; and when Samuel died without Iſſue, his Share, and his Moiety of John's Share, came to the Iſſue of Thomas in Tail.

The laſt Words, "*then to the ſurviving Sons or Son, and their Heirs for ever*," could not poſſibly make a Jointenancy in Fee, in Caſe of Death without Iſſue. The Survivor was to have the Whole, which might have been prevented by ſevering the Jointenancy; so that, to anſwer the Teſtator's Intent, a Remainder in Tail veſted in Thomas upon Samuel's Eſtate in Tail in this Moiety; and so *vice versa*, and upon Samuel's Death, this Remainder came veſted in Poſſeſſion.

Judgment was afterwards rendered at Worceſter Court for the Tenants: By the Opinion of *Lynde, Cuſhing & Ruſſell: Chief Juſtice & Oliver* full in Favour of the Demandant.* (9)

* *Qu.* if 2 Black. Comment. ch. 20, pp. 302, 303, and ch. 23, pp. 381, 382, would have been impertinent in this Caſe.

(9) It is to be regretted that we have no means of aſcertaining concluſively on what grounds this deciſion was given. The three points raiſed are briefly as follows: 1. Whether the words of the will created an

an eſtate tail, or a fee with executory deviſes; 2. If an eſtate tail, whether croſs remainders can be created by implication among more than two; 3. Whether collateral warranty will not bind the iſſue. Quincy ſtates that the laſt point was given up by the tenant's counſel; and although it was inſerted in his "ſtate of the caſe," yet its not being mentioned in the others, would ſeem to ſhow that it was, in effect, abandoned. As to the ſecond point, it is true that moſt of the authorities at that day leaned ſtrongly againſt the eſtabliſhment of croſs remainders among more than two. See 3 Bl. Com. 381, 2, cited by Quincy *ſupra*. But upon this ground alone, it is difficult to ſee why the demandant ſhould not have had judgment for one third of the premiſes. And it was ſoon after eſtabliſhed that croſs remainders might ariſe among any number. Cowp. 780. 2 East, 36. *Hall* v. *Prieſt*, 6 Gray, 18, in which laſt caſe they were eſtabliſhed among eight. From theſe conſiderations, it ſeems to us more probable that the deciſion was given upon the firſt point; and we have, accordingly, ſo ſtated it in the marginal note.

But whether the point of collateral warranty was not well taken, *quære*. That the reporter ſo conſidered it, appears from his note, *ante*, 145, and his citation, *ſupra*, of 3 Bl. Com. 303, where it is laid down that collateral warranty is ſtill a bar, "notwithſtanding the ſtatute of Queen Anne, if made by tenant in tail in poſſeſſion."

Among the law papers of John Adams, for acceſs to which we are indebted to the kindneſs of Hon. Charles Francis Adams, we find a copy of an opinion given in 1745, by the diſtinguiſhed lawyer, John Read, upon a caſe which had ariſen upon the ſame clauſe in the will, and in which ſome of the ſame queſtions were involved. That opinion is printed below. The caſe reſulted in favor of the tenants; but it will be ſeen that Mr. Read's opinion coincided with that of the minority of the Court in *Baniſter* v. *Henderſon*, viz., that the deviſe created an eſtate tail with croſs remainders. It appears, alſo, that the point was raiſed which was afterwards decided in *Baker* v. *Mattocks* (*ante*, p. 69), viz., the partibility of eſtates tail; and that the opinion of Mr. Read, and alſo, it would ſeem, of Mr. Pratt (afterwards Chief Juſtice of New York), was in favor of the partibility, coinciding with that of the minority of the Court in *Baker* v. *Mattocks*, and with that of Judge Trowbridge. See *ante*, p. 74, note.

" *Mr. Baniſter's Caſe* v. *Nat. Cunningham.*

1692. The Province Law, p. 3, enacteth that any Man Seized in Fee Simple of Land in this Province may diſpoſe of it at Pleaſure by Deed or Will; or it ſhall be Subject to a Diviſion with his Perſonal Eſtate, viz[t], a double Portion to his eldeſt Son, and equal Shares to the Reſt of his Children.

1708. Mr. Thomas Baniſter deviſed, among other Things, £500 to his Daughter, Mary Baniſter, but if ſhe did not live to have Iſſue, then

then to be paid to his 3 Sons, to be equally divided among them, as he had willed the Reſt of his Eſtate to be divided among them or the Survivor of them."

Item. He gave all his Houſes, Ware-houſes, Lands, Mortgages, Bills, Bonds, Money, Plate, Debts, Wares, Merchandizes, both at Sea and Land, as alſo all Books, Bedding, Houſehold Stuff, Horſes, Cattle, *and all that of Right any ways belonged or appertained to him, whether named or not named, to his Three Sons, Thomas, Samuel and John, to be equally divided among them; and if Either of his Three Sons dye without Heirs lawfully begotten in Wedlock, he willed their Share to the Surviving Sons or Son, and their Heirs for ever.*

The Teſtator died; then his Son John died without Iſſue; then Thomas leaving Iſſue, whereof the Eldeſt Son is ſince deceaſed without Iſſue; but there are now living John, Samuel Anneſley, and Frances Wife of Wm. Bowen. The Teſtator's Son Samuel, ſurviving his two Brothers, mortgaged 7 Acres of Paſture in Boston, Part of the Eſtate deviſed them, to Nathaniel Cunningham, and his Heirs, by Force whereof he entered and held it, and then the Mortgagor died without Iſſue.

Q. Is Nath'l Cunningham's Eſtate in this Paſture good, or not?

A. His Eſtate is void, for the Mortgagor had but one Half, and that in Tail, by the Deviſe above. —

For the Deviſe above, giving all that of Right any ways belonged to the Teſtator, gave every Parcell of his Eſtate, and all the Right he had therein, and is as large as the Expreſſion in the Caſe of *Hopewell* vs. *Ackland*, 1 Salk. 239, viz[t]., "and whatſoever elſe I have not before diſpoſed of;" and therefore would by itſelf pass a Fee Simple to the Three Sons.

And theſe Words added, "to be equally divided among them," would make them Tenants in Common of the Whole. 1 Salk. 226, *Bliſſet* vs. *Cranwell.* But by farther deviſing the Remainder to the Survivor, if either of his Three Sons dye without Heirs lawfully begotten in Wedlock, the Teſtator createth an Entail of their ſeveral Shares. 1 Salk. 233, *Nottingham* vs. *Jennings.* Deviſe to his ſecond Son to hold to him and his Heirs for ever, and for Want of ſuch Heirs, then to his own Right Heirs — adjudged an Eſtate Tail; and the Word Heirs can import nothing more than Iſſue, for he could not die without Heirs, living Heirs of the Father.

Laſtly, by deviſing the Share of ſuch as dye without Heirs lawfully begotten in Wedlock, to the ſurviving Sons or Son, and their Heirs for ever, makes Croſs Remainders among them. So that when John died firſt without Iſſue, the Remainder of his Share came equally to Thomas and Samuel in Tail; when Thomas died leaving Iſſue, his Moiety deſcended to the Heirs of his Body in Tail; and when Samuel died without

[P. 157]

without Iſſue, his Moiety came to the Heirs of the Body of Thomas in Tail. 2 Jones, 172, Holmes vs. Meynell, on Croſs Remainders by Implication, where Croke, James, 655, *Gilbert & Witty*, is queſtioned. See Dyer, 303, Deviſe. Croſs Remainders expreſs among 3, as this Caſe is. And Mr. Samuel Baniſter's ſurviving both his Brethren doth not change his Eſtate, which was an Entail immediate by the Will, Remainder to Thomas and John, and the Heirs of their Bodies. Cro. James, 695, *Chadock* vs. *Cowley*. Therefore by Samuel's Death without Iſſue, his Eſtate is determined; by the Death of John without Iſſue, and of Thomas leaving Iſſue, the Right to this Remainder, by Force of the Gift veſteth in Thomas's Iſſue in Tail, the Reverſion to the Right Heirs of the Donor.

Wherefore the Heirs of ye Body of Thomas ſhall demand and recover the Paſture of Mr. Cunningham by Force ofthe Deviſe aforeſaid.

Q. 2. To whom doth this Paſture fall, — to John the eldeſt Son ſurviving, or to the four Children of Thomas equally?

A. This Paſture deſcends to all his Children equally as Coparceners by the Prov. Law, and they muſt join in Suit.

The Teſtator was Seized of this Paſture as of an Inheritance deſcendible to all his Children as Coparceners as above, and therefore by giving it in Tail to his Sons and the Heirs of their Bodies, he could not alter ye Deſcent, and make that deſcendible to the Eldeſt Son only, which was by Law deſcendible to all ye Children ; for —

1. The fulleſt Words of Limitation to make an Intail, as in a Gift to A. and his Heirs of his Body begotten, have no Tendency to alter the Courſe of Deſcent, but only to limit whoſe Iſſue ſhall inherit, and so how long the Inheritance ſhall endure ; and when that Iſſue is ſpent, the Eſtate reverts to the Donor. Lit. Ten. § 18, 19.

2. The Stat. of Weſt. 2, c. 1, makes no Intail but of ſuch Eſtates as were Fee Simple Conditional at Common Law, and confirms them according to the Will of the Donor, but makes no Alteration of the Courſe of Deſcent. Co. Lit. 18, 19. Therefore Lands of Inheritance, whether intailed or not, always deſcended to the ſame Heirs. So Lands in Burrough Engliſh to the youngeſt Son. Co. Lit. 110, b. Lands in Gavelkind to all the Sons. Co. Lit. 175, &c.

3. If the Donor, intending by expreſs Words to alter the Courſe of Deſcents, gives Lands to a Man and his eldeſt Heirs females of his Body, or Lands holden in Gavelkind, to a Man and his eldeſt Heirs, he cannot thereby alter the Law ; the Word Eldeſt ſhall be rejected, and all the Parceners ſhall inherit. Co. Lit. 27, § 31.

By y^e ſame Reaſon and Law, this Paſture, deſcendible to all his Children as Parceners in Fee Simple by the Prov. Law, now intailed deſcends to all the Children, and they muſt bring the Action.

Boſton, December 19, 1745. *John Read.*

Or

[P. 158]

Or say, —

1. The Nature of an Intail confifts in limiting what Iffue fhall inherit, and how long the Inheritance shall endure, before the Donor or his Heirs may enter as in their Reverfion. Lit. Ten. § 18.

2. The Stat. of *Donis conditionalibus* creates no Eftate Tail but of fuch an Eftate as was Fee Simple at the Common Law, and is defcendible in fuch Form as it was at the Common Law. Co. Lit. 19, *Devant le dit Statute*, &c. — the penultimate Sentence of the fecond Paragraph. Therefore Lands of Inheritance, whether intailed or not, always defcend to y[e] Same Heirs in Either Cafe, Lands in Burrough Englifh to the youngeft Son. Co. Lit. § 165. *Toutes les Terres ou Tenements.* Lands in Gavelkind to all the Sons. Co. Lit. § 265.

N. B. This laft was, I think, in Mr. Pratt's Handwriting.

[P. 159]

ILLUSTRATION 29: Robert Auchmuty (1723–1788). Portrait by Robert Feke (circa 1707–circa 1752), dated 1748. Auchmuty was a leading member of the colonial bar, and became judge of the Massachusetts Vice Admiralty Court (1767–1776). He was proscribed in 1778. Courtesy, Amherst College Museum.

CASE 43

Rochefter Proprietors *verf.* Hammond.

ROCHESTER PROPRIETORS *v.* HAMMOND.

(From Plymouth.)

Pleas in Abatement.

Rec. 1764. Fol. 238.

THE Writ: Attach Nathan Hammond to anfwer the Proprietors of the common and undivided Land belonging to the Old Townfhip of Rochefter, in our County of Plymouth, in a Plea of Ejectment, wherein they demand againft the faid Nathan Hammond Poffeffion of 120 Acres of Common Land that lieth in a Tract of Land containing 210 Acres in Rochefter aforefaid; the whole Tract being bounded as follows, &c.; and fay that on the 20th of December, 1739, in a Time of Peace, in the Reign of our late royal Grandfather, George the 2d, that they, among other Common Lands in the faid Old Townfhip of Rochefter, were seized of faid 120 Acres of Land in their Demesne as of Fee,

In Ejectment, a Defcription of the Land as "120 Acres of Common Land that lieth in a Tract containing 210 Acres," and giving the Bounds of the whole Tract, is bad for Uncertainty.

[P. 159]

Rochester Proprietors v. *Hammond* (1765)
5 George III (Aug.) in the
Superior Court of Judicature

1 · BRIEF DESCRIPTION

This was a writ in abatement to a Plea of Ejectment because the land was not described with certainty. Held, claiming ejectment from 120 acres in a tract of 210 acres, giving only the bounds of the larger tract, is too uncertain.

2 · COURT RECORDS

Available at Rec. 1764, fol. 238.

3 · PROFESSIONALS INVOLVED

Robert Treat Paine (1731–1814), signer of the Declaration of Independence, brought the writ of abatement on behalf of the Defendant. James Otis, Jr. (1725–1783), fellow patriot, represented the Plaintiff Proprietors. See brief biographies in *Appendix 6*.

Justice Russell and the Chief Justice exchanged comments, both expressing doubt as to whether the Sheriff could accurately lay out the claimed land based on the information given.

4 · AUTHORITY

Paine cited *Edward Savel's Case* (1615), 11 *Coke's Reports*, 55a (1st ed., London, 1600). This case held that an *ejectione firmae* does not lie where it is not clear "of what nature the acres are, as land, meadow, pasture, wood etc." *Id.*, 55a. It remained the law in Massachusetts that, in an action for land, all the information the sheriff needs must be given within the writ itself. See Samuel Quincy's note, *Reports*, 162, S. Quincy n. 1, and *Atwood* v. *Atwood*, 39 Mass. (22 *Pick.*) 283, 287 (1839).

5 · LATER CITATIONS

This case was cited in *Pratt* v. *Bates*, 161 Mass. 315, 318 (1844) for the proposition that description of land to interested parties—where the land was being sold subject to contingent remainders—must be certain.

Fee, taking the Profits thereof to the Amount of £5 by the Year; and they ought to hold the ſame quietly; yet nevertheleſs the ſaid Nathan Hammond has, within 20 Years laſt paſt, entered into the ſaid Tract of Land, and now unjuſtly holds the Plaintiffs out of ſaid 120 Acres of Common as aforeſaid; and, tho' requeſted, refuſes to deliver up the Poſſeſſion thereof; to the Damage of the ſaid Proprietors, &c.

Pleas: And the ſaid Nathan Hammond comes and defends, &c., and ſaith the Plaintiffs' Writ and Declaration aforeſaid is bad and ought to abate, for that the Proprietors therein demand againſt the ſaid Defendant Poſſeſſion of 120 Acres of Land, but have not therein ſet forth the Bounds of ſaid Land, nor deſcribed the ſame with ſufficient Certainty, as by Law they ought to have done; 2d, for that the Plaintiffs have not therein ſet forth that the Defendant ever ejected them from ſaid Land, as they ought to have done; 3rd, for that the Plaintiffs have not ſet forth that they were ſeiſed of Land at the Time when the Defendant in ſaid Declaration is ſaid to enter into the ſame, as they ought to have done; and theſe Pleas the Defendant is ready to verify, and thereof prays Judgment.

R. T. Paine.

And the ſaid Nathan comes and ſaith that he holds 98 Acres of Land within the Bounds ſet forth in the Plaintiffs' Declaration, by Virtue of a Deed of Bargain and Sale from his Father, N. Hammond, dated the 26th of March, 1734, who is ſince deceaſed, which Deed includeth a Covenant of

[P. 160]

6 · NOTES

The Rochester Proprietors were trying to protect common land that lay within a larger tract. Otis, their lawyer, argued that "this Land is clearly described; and we have set forth that we demand the southerly Part of the 210–Acre Lot," quoting the Latin maxim "*Id Certum est, quod . . .*" ["*certum est quod certum reddi potest*"] or ["That is certain which is able to be made certain"]. See E. H. Jackson, *Latin for Lawyers*, 132 (1913). This is from *The Earl of Shrewsbury's Case*, 9 *Coke's Reports* 46b at 47a (1611), which is not otherwise in point. Otis's second argument, "But let the Sheriff give us Possession of the whole 'twill certainly be good for our Part recovered," was immediately contradicted by Justice Russell, who rightly pointed out that "if the Sheriff should lay but wrong, would not Hammond remain possest of the whole?"

Protecting common lands, which could easily be based on more than a century's casual usage, must have been difficult, and the specificity required by common law pleading increased that difficulty.

of Warranty againſt all Perſons, and that his ſaid Father held the ſame by Deed of Bargain and Sale, dated January 30, 1699, of John Hammond, who is ſince deceaſed, and which laſt Deed contains a Covenant of Warranty general; and the ſaid Nathan alſo ſaith, that he holds twenty-two Acres of Land within the ſaid Bounds, of Joſeph Jenkins of Edgartown, in the County of Dukes County, by a Deed of Bargain and Sale from him, with a Covenant of Warranty general, dated March 3rd, 1763, and therefore prays Proceſs of this Honourable Court may iſſue to vouch in the Heirs of the ſaid John Hammond and the ſaid Joſeph, to defend his Title to ſaid Land.

R. T. Paine.

Mr. Paine. Your Honours will obſerve that there is not the leaſt Certainty in their Declaration. No Bounds are ſet to the Land demanded, but only the Bounds are given of a certain Tract from whence they are demanded. Now in England you muſt ſet forth not only the Bounds, but alſo the particular Sort of Land, whether Paſture, Meadow Land or not. As in *Savel's Caſe*, 11 Rep. 55. In this Caſe they have gone infinitely wide of the Mark. They have not told us whereabouts the Land they would eject us from lies; their Writ muſt of Conſequence fail.

Mr. Otis. Your Honours will preſume in Favour of the Writ, if not expreſs. The Lot from whence we demand this Land is clearly deſcribed; and we have ſet forth that we demand the ſoutherly Part of a 210-Acre Lot. The Sheriff, when he

21 gives

[P. 161]

gives us Poſſeſſion, may aſſign to us the ſouthernmoſt Part of the Lot, and *Id Certum eſt*, *quod*, &c. But let the Sheriff give us Poſſeſſion of the Whole, 'twill certainly be good for our Part recovered.

Mr. Gridley. They have failed in a material Point. No legal Judgment can ever be grounded on this Proceſs. No Execution, which is the Fruit of Judgment, can ever be levied, ſhould they recover; for a Sheriff ſhall not make that certain which his Precept has not made ſo.

Juſt. Ruſſell. If the Sheriff ſhould lay out wrong, would not Hammond remain poſſeſt of the Whole?

Ch. Juſtice. 'Tis impoſſible for the Sheriff to lay out at all.

Unanimously abated. (1)

---

(1) See *Atwood* v. *Atwood*, 22 Pick. 287, *Wilde*, J. — "When lands are demanded, the deſcription of them muſt be ſo certain that ſeiſin may be delivered by the ſheriff without reference to any deſcription dehors the writ."

[P. 162]

CASE 44

Dom. Rex *verſ.* Mangent.

Life & Death.

Dom. Rex v. Mangent.

Rec. 1765. Fol. 151.

A Certificate from a Miniſter in another Province is admiſſible in Proof of a Marriage,

THIS Cauſe held from 10 in the Morning to 8 at Night, during which Time neither Judges or

---

[P. 162]

Dom. Rex v. *Mangent* (1765)
5 George III (Aug.) in the
Superior Court of Judicature

1 · BRIEF DESCRIPTION

Captioned "Life & Death," this dramatic case did, indeed, involve the possible execution of a woman for "murther of a bastard child" pursuant to Province Laws 8 William III, Chap. 38 (1696), "An act to Prevent the Destroying and Murdering of Bastard Children," which presumed a stillborn bastard to be murdered unless the unfortunate mother had a witness or made no effort to conceal the birth. The defense was that the mother was, in fact married, and the issue was whether a wedding certificate from a minister in another Province "without any Authentication from any Magistrate" could be admitted to prove the marriage. Held, it could be admitted, because the Court had no power to compel the minister or others from another Province to give evidence.

2 · COURT RECORDS

Available at Rec. 1765, fol. 151. It indicated that the woman was acquitted. See Samuel Quincy's note, *Reports*, 163, S. Quincy n. 1.

3 · PROFESSIONALS INVOLVED

The accused was clearly represented by a lawyer, as many sophisticated authorities were invoked on her behalf. The Attorney General was in court for the King, an important precedent. See *Reports*, 163, S. Quincy n. 1. See also *Rex* v. *Doaks* (1763), *Reports*, 90, Case 34. The Attorney General was Edmund Trowbridge (1709–1793), who served as Attorney General from 1749–1767, when he became an Associate Justice for the Superiour Court. Representation of criminal Defendants was originally not a usual English common law practice, but was an important professional tradition in Massachusetts. See the discussion at *Petition of the Jurors in the Trial of Captain Preston and the British Soldiers* (1771), *Reports*, 382, Case 77, *infra*.

4 · AUTHORITY

None were cited for the King, not even the Provincial Law of 1696! A string of English citations were provided for the defense—all on proof or disproof of

or Jury departed. It turned chiefly on Matters of Fact; and the Arguments too prolix to give even a Summary. The Indictment was for MURTHER of a baftard Child. (1)

The Authorities on Behalf of the Prifoner were as follows: 2 H. P. C. p. 438, ch. 46, § 43, Tit. Evid. 1 & 2 Wm. & Mary, 2 H. P. C. 15 ch. p. 104, 105, § 61, p. 118. H. P. C. 428, Evid. § 5, 431. 1 Inft. 373. 1 Salk. 123. 1 Bac. 310, Baftardy. Kelyng, 32, an Authority much enlarged and infifted on.

No Authorities produced on behalf of the King.

N. B. It was ruled in this Caufe, that a Certificate from a Minifter in another Government, of the Marriage of two Perfons, might be admitted to prove the Marriage, though the Certificate was without any Authentication from any Magiftrate. The Reafon for this Admiffion was, that this Court had no Power to compell any one in another Province to give Evidence in a Caufe pending before this Court. In England it is otherwife, for a Latitat iffues in fimilar Cafes from the King's Bench. However, the Ch. Juftice *feemed* to doubt.

Vid. Voltaire's Com. on ye Effays on Crimes, &c. p. 1st.

---

(1) It appears by the record that the prisoner was acquitted, the attorney general having agreed that fhe might give marriage in evidence, "tho' fhe answers to an indictment wherein fhe has the addition of spinfter given her."

bastardy. Most notable were "H.P.C." or William Hawkins, *A Treatise on the Pleas of the Crown*, first published in two books in London in 1716–1721, and in subsequent editions in 1724–1726, 1739 and 1762. See *Sweet & Maxwell*, *supra*, vol. 1, 362–363:27. Hawkins was widely relied on for criminal law issues in the colonies. See *Law Commonplace*, [81], n. 3. Also cited was *Coke on Littleton* ("1 Inst.") originally published in London in 1628. See *Law Commonplace*, [2], n. 1. This concerned a different context, real property inheritance, "[s]o if a man bee within the four Seas [King's Dominions], and his wife hath a child, the Law presumpeth that it is the child of the husband, and against this presumption the Law will admit no proof." Edward Coke, *First Part of the Institutes of the Lawes of England: on Commentarie on Littleton* (London, 1628), 373a. The argument being, of course, if the woman were married, the child would be presumed to be legitimate, and not a bastard. A citation to *Salkeld's Reports* (covering 1689–1712) was also included. The case was *Parishes of St. George* v. *St. Margaret Westminster* (1706), *Salkeld's Reports* 123. See *Law Commonplace,* [19], n. 4 and [32], n. 7. Also cited was Mathew Bacon's *New Abridgement of the Law*, first published in London in 1736 and another favorite of the colonists. The section "Who are Bastards" explained the "four Seas" or "King's Dominions" rule. "This was settled when the King's Dominions extended to the four Seas only; for to pass and repass in the King's Dominions was possible, without any knowledge or proof; but to pass out of another's Dominions into the King's, without some knowledge or Proof . . . was supposed by the Law not possible." *Id.*, vol. 1, 310. See *Law Commonplace*, [37], n. 5. Quincy indicated that particular emphasis was given to *Kelynge's Report of divers Case in Pleas of the Crown* (covering 1662–1669), first published in London in 1708, and then in 1739. The cited page describes an indictment for the "murder of a male bastard child." See *Sweet & Maxwell*, *supra*, vol. 1, 302:73.

5 · LATER CITATIONS

None. But this case showed the Attorney General in his role as chief prosecuting officer. A similar case, *Rex* v. *Doaks* (1763), *Reports*, 90, Case 34, was cited in *Commonwealth* v. *Kozlowsky*, 238 Mass. 379 (1921), for the proposition that the Attorney General could be present in his official capacity during grand jury deliberations. *Id.*, at 386.

6 · NOTES

Quincy said that this "Life & Death" case lasted for ten hours straight, "during which Time neither Judges or Jury departed." Unfortunately, he regarded the "arguments too prolix to give even a summary." But we can largely recreate this most important gender case from the authorities given and the record. At the heart of the case was Provincal Law 8 William III (1696), chap. 38 which reads:

> AN ACT TO PREVENT THE DESTROYING AND MURDERING OF BASTARD CHILDREN.
>
> WHEREAS many lewd women that have been delivered of bastard children, to avoid their shame, and to escape punishment, do secretly bury or conceal the death of their children, and after, if the child be found dead, the said women do allege that the said child was born dead, whereas it falleth out sometimes (although hardly it is to be proved) that the said child or children were murdered by the said women their lewd mothers, or by their assent or procurement,
>
> Be it therefore enacted by the lieutenant governor, council and representatives, convened in general assembly, and it is hereby enacted by the authority of the same, that is any women be delivered of any issue of her body, male or female, which, if it were born alive, should by law be a bastard, and that she endeavour privately, either by drowning, or secret burying thereof, or any other way, either by herself, or the procuring of others, so to conceal the death thereof, that if may not come to light, whether it were born alive or not, but be concealed, in every such case the mother so offending shall suffer death, as in case of murder, except such mother can make proof by one witness at the least, that the child whose death was by her so intended to be concealed was born dead.

Note that the unwed mother of a stillborn baby, with no proof that she intended it any harm, could still be condemned to death if she concealed the baby's death in anyway, unless she had a witness that the baby was born dead. On the other hand, if she were married, there was a legal presumption (if the father were in the Dominion) that the baby was legitimate, and this not "by law be a bastard," in the terms of the statute. See Note 4, above.

We can imagine a panic-stricken girl—perhaps unaware of the law—concealing a stillbirth. All would depend, then, on whether she were legally married to a man who could have conceived the child—or who was at least in the country.

Thus the seemingly dry, technical issue of whether a marriage certificate from an out-of-province clergyman, without any authentication from a magistrate, was admissible in court becomes, literally, a life and death matter.

Josiah Quincy's note asserted that in England the clergyman could be compelled to appear by a Latitat. This writ, named from the Latin, *latitat et discurrit*, "lurks and roams about," would issue to Defendants to answer to personal actions in the King's Bench, in conjunction with the fictitious Bill of Middlesex, even though they were "lurking" in counties other than Middlesex. See J. Baker, *An Introduction to English Legal History*, *supra*, 42. But Chief Justice Hutchinson "seemed to doubt" this, and it is indeed doubtful that even in England such a writ would lie to produce a witness, rather than the Defendant. See *Earl Jowitt*, *supra*, 241, 1062. In practice, the certificate probably would be the best available evidence. Also, the decision saved a woman's life.

CASE 45

Draper (1) *verſ.* Bicknell.

(From Taunton.)

Special Verdict.

DRAPER *v.* BICKNELL.

Rec. 1765. Fol. 304.

A Perſon returned as a Soldier upon the Alarm-Liſt of a Military Company, and who receives a Notice from a Sergeant to appear at Muſter, is thereby rendered liable to the Penalty of the Law for Non-Attendance.

THE Queſtion in this Caſe was, whether a Man, having been only on the Alarm-Liſt for a Number of Years paſt, could be from thence ſo transferred by a general Warning from a Sergeant, or Notification, as to make him liable to the Penalty of the Law for Non-Attendance. (2)

Mr. Otis. Every man is preſumed, *prima Facie*, to be on the Train-Band-Liſt. 'Tis for him to ſhow himſelf exempted; the ſpecial Verdict does not find any ſuch Exemption. The Caſe is too plain to bear Argument.

Mr.

---

(1) In the MS. this caſe is entitled "*Clark* v. *Bicknall.*" Draper was "Clerk" of the company.

(2) The ſpecial verdict found as follows: —

"That in the year 1754, Japheth Bicknell, the plaintiff in review, was "returned to the Governour as a ſoldier upon the Alarm-Liſt of the Third "Military Company in the town of Attleborough. That afterwards, in "the year 1757, the ſaid Japheth was duly warned to appear as a trained "band ſoldier at what was called a little training, which preceded the "General Muſter of said Company, and alſo to appear at ſaid General "Muſter; and that his name was called among the trained band ſol-"diers at both training and General Muſter, and that he did not appear "at either. They further find, that ſome time before ſaid little training, "the Captain of ſaid Company declared that the ſaid Japheth ſhould be "upon the trained band liſt; but whether ſuch declaration was made "before ſaid warning or not, doth not appear. And if, upon the "whole," &c.

The

[P. 164]

Draper v. *Bicknell* (1765)
5 George III (Aug.) in the
Superior Court of Judicature

1 · BRIEF DESCRIPTION

This is, in a sense, an early conscription case. The Defendant, Bicknell, was summoned by a sergeant to appear on March 22, 1757, "at the Meeting House . . . at nine o'clock in the Morning, on the second Beat of the Drum, with Arms compleat, according to law," with a penalty "of twenty Pounds for Non-Appearance." The purpose was to "enlist or impress" men for Lord Loudoun's expeditions against the French. Bicknell, believing himself to be on the secondary "Alarm-List," rather than the primary "Train-Band-List," did not show up. (Apparently he was blind in one eye.) *Reports*, 165, S. Quincy n. 2. Held, he must pay the penalty.

2 · COURT RECORDS

Available at 1765, fol. 304. It includes, as Samuel Quincy notes, the special verdict and, in the files, the notice from Sergeant John Puller to Bicknell.

3 · PROFESSIONALS INVOLVED

James Otis, Jr. (1725–1783), the Patriot, appeared for the company (Draper was the clerk). Edmund Trowbridge (1709–1793), the Attorney General from 1749–1767, appeared for Bicknell. See the short biographies in *Appendix 6*. As Samuel Quincy pointed out, there was a long history of litigation in this case dating back nearly eight years. *Reports*, 166–167, S. Quincy n. 3. Why could Trowbridge appear for Bicknell? Perhaps because the fines went directly to the company, rather than the colonial government. See Note 6, below.

4 · AUTHORITY

None given.

5 · LATER CITATIONS

None.

Mr. Trowbridge. 'Tis found in the Verdict that Bicknell had been on the Alarm-Lift. Now, will fuch general Warning at once bring him into the Train-Band-Lift? This, I take it, would be extending the Power of Officers beyond all Bounds. In fuch Cafe no Man is fafe; for when a Man is on the Alarm-Lift, he is prefumed exempted from Training. Now, after this, how unjuft is it, by fuch a general Warning, to clap him on the Train-Lift and make him liable to fo heavy a Fine! It is putting it in the Power of every Officer to diftrefs his Neighbours, who from long legal Exemption have thought themfelves not liable to be transferred without *fpecial Notice;* and never was it till now pretended fuch Transfer could be made by fuch general

---

The notification to appear, of which a copy is on file, is as follows: —

" Mr. Japheth Bicknell, —

" You, being a Training Soldier in the Company of Militia, under " the Command of Capt. John Stearns, are hereby required in his " Majefty's Name to appear at your Colours upon Tuefday the 22d of " March next, at the Meeting Houfe in the firft Precinct, at nine " o'clock in the Morning, on the fecond Beat of the Drum, with Arms " compleat, according to law; Whereof you are not to fail; it being " according to an Act of the Great and General Court or Affembly of " this Province requiring the fame upon a penalty of paying the Sum " of twenty Pounds for Non-Appearance.

" Attleborough, February 1757. JAMES PULLEN."

The act referred to was that of 1757 by which the Province provided for raifing 1800 men to ferve under Lord Loudoun againft the French; and the mufter, for non-attendance upon which fo heavy a fine was impofed, was held for the purpofe of raifing the above force, " either by inliftment or imprefs." It appears by the papers on file, that the abfent Bicknell was drawn for the expedition, but was afterwards excufed on account of being " blind with the right eye."

[P. 165]

6 · NOTES

Under Province Law of 1675, Chapter 70 of the Colony Laws, "Band Clerks," like Draper, had the power to collect fines for men not appearing and to spend the fines on the needs of the company. See *Anc. Chart.*, *supra*, 160–161, 169. Despite Trowbridge's eloquent argument—"how unjust is it, by such a general warning to clap him on the Train-List and make him liable to heavy a Fine!"—Bicknell had plenty of notice as to the summons and the fine. See *Reports*, 165, S. Quincy n. 2. It was up to him to show up and be exempted. As Otis pointed out, "[t]he Case is too plain to bear Argument." *Reports*, 164. So why did Bicknell fail to show? Even if you were "blind with the right eye" you might still be impressed into service. It was a risk he did not wish to take.

general Warning. Your Honours will therefore be cautious how ſuch an arbitrary and unjuſt Precedent is made.

Mr. Gridley. 'Tis by Martial Law that every Perſon is obliged by ſuch Warning to attend, unleſs exempted. Some Exemptions are only temporary, and they have not ſhewn whether theirs is of this Kind or not. If they abſent themſelves without being legally exempted, they muſt bear the Conſequences.

Judgment for the Plaintiff. (3)

---

(3) The action here reported appears by the record to have been "a plea of review of a plea of review of a plea of debt," — the ſecond review "being authorized by an order of the Great and General Court." The caſe seems to have been obſtinately conteſted through ſeveral years. On the firſt trial in the Inferior Court, the plaintiff had judgment. The defendant appealed and ſucceeded in obtaining a reverſal. The plaintiff then brought his review, and obtained a ſecond judgment. The ſubſequent hiſtory of the caſe is recited as follows, in the defendant's petition for the order abovementioned:

——"Your petitioner manifeſtly made appear to this Honourable "Court, by former petitions, the hardſhip of that judgment; and it "appeared a ſubject worthy the juſtice of this Court to give him a new "trial.

"Accordingly, in the year 1761, the Honourable General Court "gave order for a new trial, and enabled your petitioner to bring a Writ "of Review for that purpoſe.

"This writ being bro't to the Superiour Court in Taunton, A. D. "1761, the defendant Draper pleaded in abatement thereto, that the "pet'r did not name his action, a plea of review of a plea of review, &c. — "for this exception the writ abated and the petitioner had new coſt to "pay to the adverſe party.

"On repreſentation of this matter to this Honourable Court, the "petitioner obtained an order for another Writ of Review, and that "the merits of the cauſe ſhould be conſidered and determined. In this "writ the petitioner took care to amend the fault found with his laſt Writ,

" Writ, and named his plea, a plea of review of a plea of review of a plea " of debt ; and, Alas ! even ſo he could not be right ; for it was objected " by motion that this Honourable Court's order authorized a writ of " review of the action of debt, but not a plea of review of a plea of re- " view, &c. So, on this motion the Court diſmiſſed the writ and " ordered the petitioner to pay coſt.

" Wherefore, the petitioner humbly prays an order may paſs this " Court to enable him to bring forward a new writ of review," " and " that the merits of his cauſe may be at laſt determined."

The prayer of the petition was granted, and an order paſſed, by virtue of which was iſſued the preſent writ, to which the defendant again pleaded in abatement, " that if any order of the Great and General Court of this Province authorizes the plaintiff to bring this writ, a profert of ye copy of ſuch order in Court is not ſufficient, as in this writ, but ſuch order and ye ſeſſion wherein it paſſed ought to have been particularly ſet forth above, and that such order appears by record of ye ſame Court." This plea, however, was overruled, and the caſe at laſt went to trial, and reſulted in the ſpecial verdict and deciſion above reported.

[P. 167]

THIS VOLUME HAS BEEN TYPESET IN CASLON TYPES, PRINTED AT REYNOLDS DEWALT, NEW BEDFORD, MASSACHUSETTS, AND BOUND AT ACME BOOKBINDING, CHARLESTOWN, MASSACHUSETTS

DESIGN BY PAUL HOFFMANN